Deepfakes and Their Impact on Business

Gaurav Gupta
Amity University, Noida, India

Sailaja Bohara
Amity University, Noida, India

Raj K. Kovid
University of Petroleum and Energy Studies, India

Kapil Pandla
PML SD Business School, India

Vice President of Editorial	Melissa Wagner
Managing Editor of Acquisitions	Mikaela Felty
Managing Editor of Book Development	Jocelynn Hessler
Production Manager	Mike Brehm
Cover Design	Phillip Shickler

Published in the United States of America by
IGI Global Scientific Publishing
701 East Chocolate Avenue
Hershey, PA, 17033, USA
Tel: 717-533-8845
Fax: 717-533-8661
E-mail: cust@igi-global.com
Website: https://www.igi-global.com

Copyright © 2025 by IGI Global Scientific Publishing. All rights reserved. No part of this publication may be reproduced, stored or distributed in any form or by any means, electronic or mechanical, including photocopying, without written permission from the publisher.
Product or company names used in this set are for identification purposes only. Inclusion of the names of the products or companies does not indicate a claim of ownership by IGI Global Scientific Publishing of the trademark or registered trademark.

Library of Congress Cataloging-in-Publication Data

ISBN13: 9798369368909
EISBN13: 9798369368923

British Cataloguing in Publication Data
A Cataloguing in Publication record for this book is available from the British Library.

All work contributed to this book is new, previously-unpublished material.
The views expressed in this book are those of the authors, but not necessarily of the publisher.
This book contains information sourced from authentic and highly regarded references, with reasonable efforts made to ensure the reliability of the data and information presented. The authors, editors, and publisher believe the information in this book to be accurate and true as of the date of publication. Every effort has been made to trace and credit the copyright holders of all materials included. However, the authors, editors, and publisher cannot assume responsibility for the validity of all materials or the consequences of their use. Should any copyright material be found unacknowledged, please inform the publisher so that corrections may be made in future reprints.

Table of Contents

Foreword xiv

Preface xvi

Chapter 1
Introduction to Deepfake Technology and Its Early Foundations 1
    Robin Chataut, Texas Christian University, USA
    Aadesh Upadhyay, University of North Texas, USA

Chapter 2
The Impact of Deep Fakes in Markets and Economies 19
    Iris-Panagiota Efthymiou, University of Greenwich, UK
    Theocharis Efthymiou Egleton, London School of Economics, UK

Chapter 3
Assessing the Believability of Deepfake Ads in the Indian Market 51
    Vishnu Achutha Menon, Institute for Educational and Developmental
        Studies, India
    Anish Gupta, University of Delhi, India

Chapter 4
Deepfakes in Action: Exploring Use Cases Across Industries 71
    Shatabdi Chandramani Nannaware, Pune Institute of Business
        Management, India
    Rajasshrie Pillai, Pune Institute of Business Management, India
    Nilesh Kate, Pune Institute of Business Management, India

Chapter 5
The Impact of Deepfakes on Trust and Security in Islamic Banking:
Emerging Threats and Mitigation Strategies 99
    Early Ridho Kismawadi, IAIN Langsa, Indonesia

Chapter 6
Shaping Consumer Perception Through Deepfake Marketing: Ethics and
Implications... 123
    Sonam Rani, Amity University, Noida, India
    Sailaja Bohara, Amity University, Noida, India
    Gaurav Gupta, Amity University, Greater Noida Campus, India
    Mandakini Paruthi, IBS Hyderabad, India
    Shiv Ranjan, Amity University, Noida, India

Chapter 7
Collaboration and Collective Action: Addressing the Deepfake Challenge as
a Community.. 143
    Satya Subrahmanyam, Holy Spirit University of Kaslik, Lebanon

Chapter 8
Financial Fraud and Manipulation: The Malicious Use of Deepfakes in
Business 173
    Pooja Kaushik, Galgotias College of Engineering and Technology, India
    Vikas Garg, Christ University, India
    Anu Priya, G.L. Bajaj Institute of Technology and Management, India
    Shashi Kant, College of Business and Economics, Bule Hora University,
        Ethiopia

Chapter 9
Deepfake Prospects, Mitigating Factors, and Deceptions 197
    Uttam Kaur, Chandigarh University, India
    Prashant Kumar Siddhey, ITM University, Gwalior, India

Chapter 10
The Dark Side of Deepfakes: Fraud and Cybercrime 221
    Svetlana Volkova, Vologda State University, Russia

Chapter 11
The Future of Deepfakes: Emerging Trends and Potential Applications........... 243
    T. Venkat Narayana Rao, Sreenidhi Institute of Science and Technology,
        India
    Maithri Koppula, Sreenidhi Institute of Science and Technology, India
    Goboori Harsh Vardhan, Sreenidhi Institute of Science and Technology,
        India
    Sangers Bhavana, Sreenidhi Institute of Science and Technology, India
    Bolla Sujith Kumar, Sreenidhi Institute of Science and Technology, India

Chapter 12
Preventing Deepfakes From Being Used for Impersonation and Defamation .. 267
Ashu M. G. Solo, Maverick Trailblazers Inc., USA

Chapter 13
Building Resilience: Strategies for Business to Mitigate Deepfake Risks......... 285
Manjeet Singh, Amity University, Noida, India
Deepshikha Bhargava, Amity University, Noida, India
Amitabh Bhargava, Amity University, Noida, India
Kirti Singh, Amity University, Noida, India

Chapter 14
Demystifying Deepfakes: Understanding, Implications, and Safeguards.......... 299
Manjeet Singh, Amity University, Noida, India
Deepshikha Bhargava, Amity University, Noida, India
Amitabh Bhargava, Amity University, Noida, India
Kirti Singh, Amity University, Noida, India

Compilation of References 319

About the Contributors 367

Index... 375

Detailed Table of Contents

Foreword xiv

Preface xvi

Chapter 1
Introduction to Deepfake Technology and Its Early Foundations 1
    Robin Chataut, Texas Christian University, USA
    Aadesh Upadhyay, University of North Texas, USA

The advent of deepfakes has revolutionized the digital landscape, presenting both innovative applications and significant challenges. This chapter will provide a comprehensive overview of deepfake technology, focusing on its creation, detection, and mitigation strategies. By examining the evolution, current state, and future prospects of deepfakes, the chapter aims to provide a thorough understanding of this rapidly advancing field. We will explore the origins and development of deepfake technology, tracing its journey from AI research labs to widespread use on social media and beyond. Additionally, we will delve into the technical foundations and early applications of deepfakes, with a focus on Generative Adversarial Networks (GANs), which are pivotal in synthesizing hyper-realistic audio and video content. The chapter will clarify the complex processes behind deepfakes, detailing how these technologies operate, the data they require, and the ethical dilemmas they raise. The rise of deepfakes has led to concerns about misinformation, privacy violations, and security threats.

Chapter 2
The Impact of Deep Fakes in Markets and Economies 19
Iris-Panagiota Efthymiou, University of Greenwich, UK
Theocharis Efthymiou Egleton, London School of Economics, UK

The advent of deepfake technology has introduced significant challenges and opportunities in markets and economies globally. This paper examines the multifaceted impact of deepfakes on financial markets, corporate reputations, consumer behaviour, and economic stability. By synthesizing recent case studies and academic research, we explore how deepfakes can manipulate stock prices, erode trust in brands, and influence market decisions, leading to potential economic disruptions. We also discuss the role of regulatory frameworks, technological countermeasures, and the ethical considerations in mitigating the risks posed by deepfakes. Our analysis highlights the urgent need for enhanced vigilance, cross-sector collaboration, and innovative solutions to safeguard market integrity and economic stability in the face of this emerging threat.

Chapter 3
Assessing the Believability of Deepfake Ads in the Indian Market 51
Vishnu Achutha Menon, Institute for Educational and Developmental
Studies, India
Anish Gupta, University of Delhi, India

Deepfake technology, utilizing artificial intelligence and machine learning, has revolutionized digital content creation by producing hyper-realistic media that can deceive viewers into believing fabricated scenarios. In the realm of advertising, deepfakes enable marketers to leverage familiar faces—be they celebrities, influencers, or ordinary individuals—to endorse products convincingly. This chapter explores the impact of deepfake advertisements on young adults in India, a digitally engaged demographic susceptible to such technological influences. Despite their potential to captivate and persuade, these advertisements raise ethical concerns regarding trust and authenticity. This study investigates the relationship between deepfake believability and cognitive responses, confusion levels, and persuasiveness among young adults, highlighting the implications for consumer behavior and regulatory frameworks.

Chapter 4

Deepfakes in Action: Exploring Use Cases Across Industries 71

    Shatabdi Chandramani Nannaware, Pune Institute of Business
       Management, India
    Rajasshrie Pillai, Pune Institute of Business Management, India
    Nilesh Kate, Pune Institute of Business Management, India

chapter on deepfakes offers comprehensive insights into how this cutting-edge technology is being applied across diverse industries. Its applications are broad, impacting various sectors by enhancing capabilities, fostering innovation, and prompting critical discussions about ethical use. "The importance of this chapter lies in its ability to inform and prepare stakeholders for the future of deepfake technology, balancing its benefits with the need for responsible and ethical practices." Deep fakes, an unprecedented but controversial development in digital media, are artificially synthesized media using advanced artificial intelligence (AI) and deep learning They are mixed or manipulated in the elements of a work of art, and make a very true but false interpretation. This technology has found utility in a variety of industries, each with its own advantages and challenges.

Chapter 5

The Impact of Deepfakes on Trust and Security in Islamic Banking:
Emerging Threats and Mitigation Strategies 99

    Early Ridho Kismawadi, IAIN Langsa, Indonesia

This research presents an important contribution to the development of digital security policies in the Islamic finance sector, with a particular focus on modern technological threats such as deepfakes. Through an in-depth threat analysis, this study identifies potential risks faced by the Islamic banking industry, especially in terms of security and customer trust. The proposed recommendations include strict regulation of the creation and distribution of synthetic media, the development of more advanced detection technologies, and effective regulatory enforcement. Collaboration between governments, research institutions, and industry is also emphasized as key in designing and implementing policies that are able to respond to technological threats in an adaptive manner. With this approach, the study assists policymakers and regulators in designing strategies that can protect integrity and trust in Islamic banking, as well as ensure sustainability and security in the ever-evolving digital era.

Chapter 6
Shaping Consumer Perception Through Deepfake Marketing: Ethics and
Implications... 123
Sonam Rani, Amity University, Noida, India
Sailaja Bohara, Amity University, Noida, India
Gaurav Gupta, Amity University, Greater Noida Campus, India
Mandakini Paruthi, IBS Hyderabad, India
Shiv Ranjan, Amity University, Noida, India

The advent of deepfake technology has introduced transformative possibilities
in marketing, reshaping consumer perceptions and engagement through hyper-
realistic digital content. This book chapter examines the ethical dimensions and
potential implications of deepfake applications in marketing, specifically focusing
on their power to shape consumer perception. With the ability to create synthetic
yet believable visual and audio representations, deepfakes have provided brands
with innovative tools to captivate audiences and personalize experiences. However,
this comes with ethical concerns, including risks of deception, manipulation, and
consumer mistrust. This chapter explores both the opportunities and challenges
posed by deepfake marketing, emphasizing the need for responsible practices to
maintain transparency, authenticity, and consumer trust. It also discusses regulatory
and policy considerations, proposing ethical frameworks to guide marketers in the
responsible use of deepfake technology.

Chapter 7
Collaboration and Collective Action: Addressing the Deepfake Challenge as
a Community.. 143
Satya Subrahmanyam, Holy Spirit University of Kaslik, Lebanon

This chapter explores the critical role of collaboration and collective action in
addressing the deepfake challenge. As deepfake technology advances, it presents
unprecedented risks to businesses, individuals, and society. This chapter examines
cross-sector partnerships among governments, tech companies, businesses, academia,
and nonprofits to combat deepfakes effectively. It emphasizes the need for legal
frameworks, innovative detection technologies, public education, and digital literacy
to build resilience. Through case studies, the chapter highlights successful strategies
and identifies gaps in current approaches, advocating for proactive solutions to
anticipate future technological developments. Ultimately, it calls for continuous,
unified efforts to create a safer, more trustworthy digital ecosystem.

Chapter 8
Financial Fraud and Manipulation: The Malicious Use of Deepfakes in
Business 173
    Pooja Kaushik, Galgotias College of Engineering and Technology, India
    Vikas Garg, Christ University, India
    Anu Priya, G.L. Bajaj Institute of Technology and Management, India
    Shashi Kant, College of Business and Economics, Bule Hora University,
       Ethiopia

Advanced technologies like Deepfakes are dispatched more frequently in the financial fraud and manipulation to manipulate the stakeholders and markets. Deepfake is synthetic media created using artificial intelligence techniques; the deep fake can impersonate the person's voice, picture, and videos. As a result posing severe risks to the privacy of financial transactions and corporate communications. This chapter focuses on the emerging area of financial fraud with focus on the use of deepfake for stock manipulation and impersonation and spreading fake information. Last, the author offers a complex approach, which deals with both the regulation and the technology, and instruction levels to prevent the financial industry from this sophisticated fraud. It is our belief that carrying out this analysis will help expand the dialogue on financial fraud prevention during the age of artificial intelligence.

Chapter 9
Deepfake Prospects, Mitigating Factors, and Deceptions 197
    Uttam Kaur, Chandigarh University, India
    Prashant Kumar Siddhey, ITM University, Gwalior, India

Deepfakes, which are synthetic yet incredibly lifelike images, sounds, and video produced by computers, are among the most recent advancements in artificial intelligence technology. Due to the speed and breadth of social media, they can swiftly spread to millions of individuals and lead to a variety of deceptive practices in the marketplace. Nevertheless, current knowledge about the effects of deep fakes on the market is incomplete and dispersed. According to our research, the primary dangers facing businesses are the quick obsolescence of current technologies and harm to their reputation, image, and credibility. On the other hand, customers could also experience identity theft, intimidation, extortion, harassment, slander, and revenge porn. Next, we gather and disseminate information about the tactics and defenses against deep fake-based market manipulation. Additionally, we identify and document the several valid prospects provided by this novel technique. We conclude by outlining a research plan for this rapidly developing and crucial field.

Chapter 10
The Dark Side of Deepfakes: Fraud and Cybercrime 221
Svetlana Volkova, Vologda State University, Russia

Even though deepfakes have numerous positive and beneficial applications, such as replacing the faces of deceased actors to complete the movies, creating realistic special effects, visualizing historical events with real figures, or creating personalized advertising materials, deepfakes remain and rightfully associated with fraud and abuse. Since deepfakes are often used unethically and illegitimately, there are a vast number of security threats that they can pose, ranging from invasion of privacy to manipulation of public opinion. The chapter provides a comprehensive overview of the potential targets, domains, and areas where malicious actors might illegitimately utilize deepfake technologies to conduct fraudulent activities and other illegal operations. This chapter thoroughly examines the various ways in which deepfake technology can be abused, co-called its "dark side." Specifically, it delves into the use of deepfakes for committing fraud and financial crimes, corporate espionage, compromising biometric identity, manipulating public opinion, as well as extortion and blackmail.

Chapter 11
The Future of Deepfakes: Emerging Trends and Potential Applications 243
T. Venkat Narayana Rao, Sreenidhi Institute of Science and Technology, India
Maithri Koppula, Sreenidhi Institute of Science and Technology, India
Goboori Harsh Vardhan, Sreenidhi Institute of Science and Technology, India
Sangers Bhavana, Sreenidhi Institute of Science and Technology, India
Bolla Sujith Kumar, Sreenidhi Institute of Science and Technology, India

Deepfakes is a new generation of machine learning algorithms, which has demonstrated the possibility of creating audacious synthetic media and raised serious concerns. Firstly, we discuss the evolution of deep fake technology in terms of algorithmic development, the size of the dataset and the way the technology is trained – which has led to a generation of even more convincing fake videos or fake images. It explores the creation of deepfake tools and the emergence of deepfake platform platforms in making synthetic media more accessible and democratic. Deepfakes use including misinformation, identity theft, and privacy infringements and efforts to contain regulation violations given the fluidity of this digital world are also discussed. This study focus on the technology of deepfakes can be applied including both entertainment and advertising and also education and medicine. This chapter offers a general insight into deepfakes, future developments, and trends in deepfake usage, as well as precautionary measures for the future.

Chapter 12
Preventing Deepfakes From Being Used for Impersonation and Defamation .. 267
Ashu M. G. Solo, Maverick Trailblazers Inc., USA

As technology advances, deepfakes have become a problem. Deepfakes can be used for impersonation and defamation, two of the major problems of the information age. Deepfakes for impersonation have been used to create fake intimate images. This research paper makes 9 recommendations for website policies, 17 recommendations for public policies, and 7 recommendations for public education to combat the use of deepfakes for impersonation and defamation. The author of this research paper previously proposed a field called misinformation identification engineering involving the development of algorithms and software to find, flag, or remove misinformation and disinformation on websites and in other documents.

Chapter 13
Building Resilience: Strategies for Business to Mitigate Deepfake Risks......... 285
Manjeet Singh, Amity University, Noida, India
Deepshikha Bhargava, Amity University, Noida, India
Amitabh Bhargava, Amity University, Noida, India
Kirti Singh, Amity University, Noida, India

This chapter discusses deepfake and delves into its potential benefits and inherent risks. Contrary to the negative perception generally created about deepfake technology, the authors have given evidence to highlight its positive applications and advantages. This chapter also gives equal discussion to the associated dangers in its use, particularly violations which may arise from criminal activities. With that in view, a review of the networks and applications both utilized in the creation of deepfakes, while assessing state-of-the-art open-source tools presently available, has been performed. The chapter goes further to detail the actual process for creating a deepfake video; hence, this provides some first-hand overview of the technology. The main task of this work is to contribute to enhanced resilience against deepfake-related threats by critically reflecting on various factors, such as: relevant rules and regulations within the EU and North Macedonia; an overview of the regulatory landscape.

Chapter 14
Demystifying Deepfakes: Understanding, Implications, and Safeguards.......... 299
Manjeet Singh, Amity University, Noida, India
Deepshikha Bhargava, Amity University, Noida, India
Amitabh Bhargava, Amity University, Noida, India
Kirti Singh, Amity University, Noida, India

Deepfakes are a new generation of AI-manufactured, hyper-realistic synthetic media that is rapidly evolving into a disruptive technology with novel ways of harming others. From its initial use in entertainment and advertising, the misuse of deepfake technology will result in revenge porn, cyberstalking, dissemination of disinformation, and political manipulation, especially during elections, causing huge concern about the erosion of trust in social institutions. While deepfake methods are getting improved and more accessible, the urge for measures to be taken against their negative impacts is getting more pressing. This paper presents the dual nature of deepfakes, both potential benefits and risks. While the deepfake technology can protect intellectual property positively, such as enabling the protection system FORGE, it's dangerous applications create outstanding threats. This becomes all the more ominous with tools available that allow people to create fake identities.

Compilation of References 319

About the Contributors 367

Index 375

Foreword

In the rapidly evolving digital age, deepfakes have emerged as a formidable technological innovation with vast potential and significant risks. What began as a fascinating application of artificial intelligence has rapidly become a topic of global concern, as deepfakes—digitally manipulated media that appears convincingly real—pose challenges across markets, economies, and sectors worldwide. Deepfakes and Their Impact on Business offers a timely, in-depth exploration of these challenges and the broader implications of deepfake technology in today's business landscape.

This volume, meticulously compiled and edited by Gaurav Gupta, Sailaja Bohara, Raj Kovid, and Kapil Pandla, delves into the multi-faceted impacts of deepfakes. Across fourteen well-researched chapters, the book investigates the diverse implications of deepfakes on business environments, from their influence on markets and economies to the threats posed to trust and security. Notably, the authors examine the emerging risks within specific fields, including Islamic banking, where deepfake technology challenges the sector's trust foundations and introduces unique vulnerabilities.

What sets Deepfakes and Their Impact on Business apart is its comprehensive approach. Each chapter presents case studies, empirical analyses, and conceptual explorations that reveal the complex interplay between technology, ethics, and security in the age of deepfakes. From the believability of deepfake ads in the Indian market to collective community action and mitigation strategies, this book addresses how industries can confront and manage the deepfake phenomenon responsibly.

For academics, policymakers, industry practitioners, and even the general reader, this book serves as an invaluable resource, shedding light on the strategic, ethical, and legal frameworks necessary to address the risks posed by deepfakes. It calls for a balanced approach, recognizing deepfakes' potential for both innovation and misuse, and emphasizes the importance of collaboration across sectors to safeguard against its darker applications, including fraud, impersonation, and cybercrime.

I am pleased to introduce readers to Deepfakes and Their Impact on Business, a work that contributes significantly to our understanding of deepfake technology's influence on business practices and societal trust. In its pages, readers will not only find insights but also actionable frameworks for navigating this emerging field with integrity and foresight.

Welcome to a thought-provoking journey through the complex world of deepfakes in business.

Ajay Rana

Amity University, India

Preface

In an era where digital innovation continuously reshapes the business landscape, deepfakes—highly realistic, AI-generated media manipulations—emerge as a potent force with profound implications. This book, *Deepfakes and Their Impact on Business*, reflects our commitment to exploring the crucial intersection between synthetic media and business integrity. Trust has always been a cornerstone of commerce, yet the rise of deepfakes presents an unprecedented challenge to maintaining this trust in a digital world.

As editors, our goal is to bridge the knowledge gap between deepfake research and the practice in business landscape. By demystifying deepfakes' technology, applications, and risks, we present complex concepts in an accessible way, helping businesses to understand both the potential dangers and the strategic responses necessary to address them. Through comprehensive discussions on creation, detection, and mitigation, we offer insights into the multifaceted influence of deepfakes across industries, with a focus on brand integrity, ethical and legal challenges, and regulatory considerations.

This book's content is designed to support a diverse readership, including business leaders, security professionals, and public relations specialists, all of whom play a pivotal role in protecting organizational integrity. By highlighting the current challenges faced by businesses and outlining the urgent need for more advanced detection and mitigation methods, we hope to stimulate further research and foster collaborative solutions. This book's purpose extends beyond information sharing; we seek to foster a proactive approach within businesses to navigate and counter the risks of deepfakes.

Through real-world examples, forward-looking trends, and actionable resilience strategies, *Deepfakes and Their Impact on Business* equips organizations to remain vigilant and resilient. This collection ultimately serves as an indispensable guide for those ready to confront the challenges and harness the opportunities of synthetic media in the business domain.

ORGANIZATION OF THE BOOK

Chapter 1: Introduction to Deepfake Technology and Its Early Foundations

Deepfake technology, powered by advancements in AI, has redefined the digital landscape, offering groundbreaking innovations alongside profound challenges. This chapter explores the origins, evolution, and impact of deepfakes, focusing on their creation, detection, and mitigation strategies. By examining the role of Generative Adversarial Networks (GANs) in synthesizing hyper-realistic content, it highlights the ethical dilemmas and societal risks posed by deepfakes, including misinformation and privacy breaches. This analysis provides valuable insights into navigating the complexities of this transformative yet contentious technology

Chapter 2: The Impact of Deepfakes in Markets and Economies

This chapter explores the profound and varied influence that deepfake technology is exerting on global markets and economies. Through an analysis of financial markets, corporate reputations, consumer behavior, and economic stability, the chapter uncovers how deepfakes can disrupt business and economic ecosystems. Case studies and research illustrate how synthetic media can manipulate stock prices, weaken brand trust, and impact market decisions, potentially leading to economic instability. Furthermore, the chapter discusses the roles of regulatory frameworks, countermeasures, and ethical considerations in addressing these risks, advocating for cross-sector collaboration and innovative strategies to maintain market integrity and economic resilience.

Chapter 3: Assessing the Believability of Deepfake Ads in the Indian Market

Exploring deepfake technology in advertising, this chapter delves into its psychological effects on young adults in India, a demographic particularly susceptible to this innovation. By using AI-generated media to simulate endorsements by popular figures, deepfake ads can both attract consumers and challenge notions of authenticity and trust. The chapter examines how deepfake advertisements impact cognitive responses, create confusion, and influence consumer behavior, ultimately prompting discussions about the regulatory frameworks required to govern this novel approach to digital marketing.

Chapter 4: Deepfakes in Action: Exploring Use Cases Across Industries

This chapter provides a comprehensive look at how deepfake technology is impacting a range of industries, offering both new capabilities and unique challenges. The discussion extends to applications in various sectors, from enhancing creative content to raising ethical questions regarding responsible use. By presenting deepfake's transformative potential, this chapter informs stakeholders about its implications for the future, emphasizing the need for ethical standards alongside technological advancement.

Chapter 5: The Impact of Deepfakes on Trust and Security in Islamic Banking: Emerging Threats and Mitigation Strategies

Focusing on Islamic finance, this chapter examines the vulnerabilities of the sector to deepfake-related security threats, with an emphasis on preserving trust in the industry. A detailed threat analysis addresses the risks that deepfakes pose to the Islamic banking industry's reputation and client relationships, proposing a range of strategies from stricter regulations on synthetic media to more advanced detection technologies. By recommending collaborations among governments, research institutions, and industry players, the chapter underscores the importance of adaptive digital security policies to safeguard integrity and trust within Islamic banking.

Chapter 6: Shaping Consumer Perception through Deepfake Marketing Ethics and Implications

Deepfake technology is revolutionizing marketing, offering innovative ways to engage consumers through hyper-realistic digital content. This chapter explores the dual nature of deepfakes in marketing—unveiling their potential to enhance personalization and captivate audiences while addressing ethical concerns, including deception and consumer mistrust. By examining regulatory frameworks and proposing responsible practices, this chapter highlights the importance of transparency and authenticity, ensuring marketers harness the transformative power of deepfakes ethically and effectively.

Chapter 7: Collaboration and Collective Action: Addressing the Deepfake Challenge as a Community

Recognizing the societal risks posed by deepfake technology, this chapter emphasizes the importance of cross-sector collaboration to combat these threats. By examining partnerships among governments, tech companies, businesses, academia, and nonprofits, the chapter highlights successful strategies and advocates for proactive approaches. Legal frameworks, advanced detection technology, public education, and digital literacy are all presented as essential tools for building a resilient response to deepfakes, ensuring a more secure digital environment for all.

Chapter 8: Financial Fraud and Manipulation: The Malicious Use of Deepfakes in Business

This chapter focuses on the increasing use of deepfake technology for financial fraud, manipulation, and misinformation in the business realm. By exploring cases of stock manipulation, identity theft, and corporate impersonation, it examines the significant security challenges posed by synthetic media. The chapter offers a dual approach—encompassing regulatory and technological solutions—to prevent the financial industry from falling victim to sophisticated deepfake fraud, contributing to broader discussions on fraud prevention in an AI-driven age.

Chapter 9: Deepfakes Prospects, Mitigating Factors, and Deceptions

Exploring both the risks and potential opportunities of deepfakes, this chapter offers a balanced perspective on the technology's impact. It addresses how deepfakes can rapidly spread misinformation and damage brand credibility, while also presenting countermeasures to combat market deception. Additionally, it identifies valid uses for deepfakes and concludes with a research agenda aimed at enhancing our understanding of this evolving technology, laying the groundwork for future studies.

Chapter 10: The Dark Side of Deepfakes: Fraud and Cybercrime

This chapter delves into the ethical and criminal implications of deepfake technology, examining its potential for misuse in fraud, corporate espionage, identity theft, and public opinion manipulation. A comprehensive overview of malicious applications highlights the "dark side" of deepfakes, illustrating the various security threats they pose. Through discussions of specific cases, the chapter provides an in-depth look at how deepfakes are weaponized in cybercrime, calling for heightened security measures and ethical guidelines.

Chapter 11: The Future of Deepfakes: Emerging Trends and Potential Applications

Concluding the book, this chapter explores the future trajectory of deepfake technology, from advancements in algorithmic complexity to its democratization through accessible platforms. By examining both beneficial applications—such as in entertainment, advertising, education, and medicine—and the ongoing challenges in regulating this fluid digital landscape, it offers a forward-looking perspective. The chapter underscores the importance of ethical considerations and precautionary measures to ensure that deepfakes contribute positively to society, providing insights into the future directions and implications of synthetic media.

Chapter 12: Preventing Deepfakes from Being Used for Impersonation and Defamation

With the misuse of deepfakes for impersonation and defamation on the rise, this chapter addresses the technological and policy measures needed to curb these abuses. From website and public policy recommendations to public education initiatives, the chapter presents a multipronged approach to countering malicious deepfakes. The concept of "misinformation identification engineering" is introduced as a framework for developing algorithms and tools to detect and manage misinformation, highlighting the need for proactive measures to maintain online safety and integrity.

Chapter 13: Building Resilience: Strategies for Business to Mitigate Deepfake Risks

This chapter explores deepfake technology, emphasizing its benefits alongside its risks, including potential misuse in criminal activities. It examines networks and tools for creating deepfakes, providing a step-by-step overview of the process. The chapter also evaluates regulatory frameworks in the EU and North Macedonia, contributing to resilience against deepfake-related threats.

Chapter 14: Demystifying Deepfakes: Understanding, Implications and Safeguards

Deepfakes represent a revolutionary yet disruptive AI-driven technology, offering both innovative applications and serious risks. Initially used in entertainment and advertising, their misuse raises concerns about disinformation, cybercrime, and political manipulation, threatening trust in social institutions. This chapter explores the dual nature of deepfakes, highlighting their potential benefits, such as intellectual property protection, alongside the urgent need for measures to counter their harmful impacts.

CONCLUSION

In conclusion, this edited reference book offers a multifaceted exploration of the transformative and disruptive potential of deepfake technology across sectors. Each chapter highlights the duality of deepfakes—their power to innovate as well as to disrupt. Through examining financial markets, advertising, digital security in Islamic banking, and more, our contributors provide a comprehensive view of how deepfakes impact trust, authenticity, and economic stability. Importantly, this book underscores the critical need for collective vigilance, regulatory foresight, and ethical frameworks. As the technology advances, so too must our strategies for detection, prevention, and collaboration to maintain security, foster public awareness, and enhance resilience in the digital age. It is our hope that this work will serve as a valuable resource for researchers, policymakers, industry professionals, and all stakeholders committed to navigating the complex landscape of synthetic media responsibly.

Gaurav Gupta
Amity University, Noida, India

Sailaja Bohara
Amity University, Noida, India

Raj K. Kovid
University of Petroleum and Energy Studies, India

Kapil Pandla
PML SD Business School, India

Chapter 1
Introduction to Deepfake Technology and Its Early Foundations

Robin Chataut
https://orcid.org/0000-0002-2763-9598
Texas Christian University, USA

Aadesh Upadhyay
https://orcid.org/0009-0000-1276-353X
University of North Texas, USA

ABSTRACT

The advent of deepfakes has revolutionized the digital landscape, presenting both innovative applications and significant challenges. This chapter will provide a comprehensive overview of deepfake technology, focusing on its creation, detection, and mitigation strategies. By examining the evolution, current state, and future prospects of deepfakes, the chapter aims to provide a thorough understanding of this rapidly advancing field. We will explore the origins and development of deepfake technology, tracing its journey from AI research labs to widespread use on social media and beyond. Additionally, we will delve into the technical foundations and early applications of deepfakes, with a focus on Generative Adversarial Networks (GANs), which are pivotal in synthesizing hyper-realistic audio and video content. The chapter will clarify the complex processes behind deepfakes, detailing how these technologies operate, the data they require, and the ethical dilemmas they raise. The rise of deepfakes has led to concerns about misinformation, privacy violations, and security threats.

DOI: 10.4018/979-8-3693-6890-9.ch001

Copyright © 2025, IGI Global Scientific Publishing. Copying or distributing in print or electronic forms without written permission of IGI Global Scientific Publishing is prohibited.

INTRODUCTION

Deepfake technology, a term coined in 2017, represents a significant advancement in synthetic media creation. This technology allows for the manipulation and generation of realistic audio-visual content, often replacing one person's likeness with another's using artificial intelligence techniques (Chesney & Citron, 2019). While the term "deepfake" is relatively new, the technological foundations that enabled its development stretch back several decades, encompassing advancements in computer vision, machine learning, and digital image processing. The ability to create convincing deepfakes relies on sophisticated AI algorithms that can analyze vast amounts of visual and audio data to learn how to replicate human appearances, voices, and movements (Westerlund, 2019). These algorithms then use this learned information to generate or manipulate media in ways that can be remarkably lifelike. The development of deepfake technology has been driven by advancements in several key areas, including video manipulation techniques, computer vision algorithms, machine learning, and facial recognition technology.

Early Foundations(1990s-2000s)

Video Manipulation Techniques

The 1990s saw significant advancements in video editing software, making complex video manipulation more accessible. Programs like Adobe Premiere (released in 1991) and After Effects (released in 1993) allowed for increasingly sophisticated video editing. These tools laid the groundwork for more advanced video manipulation techniques, including motion tracking and chroma keying, which became crucial for early attempts at face replacement in videos.

Machine Learning Advancements

The 1990s and early 2000s saw significant progress in machine learning, particularly in the areas of neural networks and statistical learning methods. Support Vector Machines (SVMs), introduced in 1995, became popular for classification and regression analysis, including face recognition tasks (Cortes & Vapnik, 1995). Neural networks, while not new, saw renewed interest and development during this period, laying important groundwork for future deep learning applications.

Facial Recognition Technology

Facial recognition technology, a key component of modern deepfakes, saw significant advancements during this period. The Eigenface approach, developed by Turk and Pentland in 1991, used principal component analysis to efficiently represent faces and became a standard in face recognition for many years (Turk & Pentland, 1991). Later developments, such as Fisherfaces in 1997 and Local Binary Patterns in 1996, further improved the ability of computers to analyze and categorize facial features (Belhumeur et al., 1997), (Ojala et al., 1996).

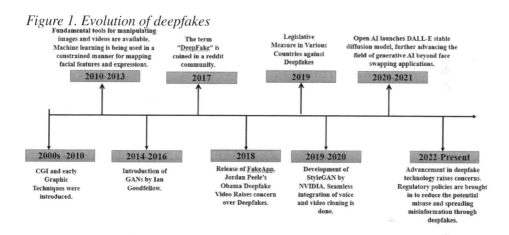

Figure 1. Evolution of deepfakes

Early 2000s: Laying the Ground Work

The early 2000s saw significant advancements in video manipulation and 3D face modeling. In 1997, Bregler.et al developed a video rewrite system that could manipulate video to make it appear as if a person was saying words they hadn't actually spoken Bregler et al., 1997. This technology was an early precursor to the lip-syncing capabilities used in modern deepfakes.In 2003, Blanz and Vetter introduced methods to create 3D face models from a single image, which became crucial for later face-swapping applications(Blanz & Vetter, 2003).

Mid 2010s: Emergence of Face Swapping

The mid-2010s saw significant advancements in face-swapping technology. In 2016, Thies et al. introduced Face2Face, a method for real-time face capture and reenactment (Thies et al., 2016). This technology allowed for the manipulation of facial expressions in video and was a significant step towards realistic face swapping.

Late 2010s: Birth of "Deepfakes"

The term "deepfake" was coined in 2017 by a Reddit user who began sharing face-swapped videos created using deep learning techniques (Kietzmann et al., 2020). This marked the beginning of widespread public awareness of deepfake technology. In 2018, the release of FakeApp, a user-friendly deepfake creation tool, made the technology accessible to a wider audience (Westerlund, 2019). This sparked concerns about the potential misuse of deepfake technology.

THE EVOLUTION OF DEEPFAKE TECHNOLOGY: GANS, DNNS, AND LLMS

Recent advancements in artificial intelligence have significantly enhanced the capabilities of deepfake technology. Three key technologies—Generative Adversarial Networks (GANs), Deep Neural Networks (DNNs), and Large Language Models (LLMs)—have been instrumental in creating more sophisticated and realistic deepfakes.

Generative Adversarial Networks (GANs)

GANs, introduced by (Goodfellow et al., 2014), have become a cornerstone of modern deepfake creation. These networks have two competing neural networks: a generator and a discriminator. Recent advancements in GAN architecture have led to significant improvements in deepfake quality: StyleGAN and its variants: (Karras et al., 2019)introduced StyleGAN, allowing unprecedented control over generated images' style and features. Subsequent versions, StyleGAN2 and StyleGAN3, have further improved image quality and reduced artifacts (Karras et al., 2020). Cycle-GAN: (Zhu et al., 2017) developed CycleGAN, enabling unpaired image-to-image translation, which has been particularly useful for face-swapping applications in deepfakes. Progressive Growing of GANs: This technique, proposed by (Karras et al., 2019), allows for generating high-resolution images by gradually increasing the resolution during training.

Deep Neural Networks (DNNs)

DNNs have been instrumental in various aspects of deepfake creation, from facial recognition to video synthesis: Face Recognition and Analysis: DNNs like DeepFace (Taigman et al., 2014) and FaceNet (Schroff et al., 2015) have significantly improved face recognition capabilities, crucial for accurate face swapping in deepfakes. Video Synthesis: Techniques like DeepVideo (Chan et al., 2019) use DNNs to generate realistic video sequences from a single image, creating moving deepfakes from still images. Audio Synthesis: WaveNet (Van Den Oord et al., 2016) and its successors have dramatically improved the quality of synthetic speech, enabling more convincing audio deepfakes.

Large Language Models (LLMs)

While primarily associated with text generation, LLMs have begun to play a role in deepfake creation, particularly in multimodal applications: Text-to-Speech Synthesis: Models like GPT-3 (Brown, 2020) have been used to generate realistic speech scripts, which can be synthesized into audio using voice cloning technology. Video Description and Generation: Recent advancements in text-to-video models, such as Make-A-Video (Singer et al., 2022), utilize LLMs to generate video content from text descriptions.

Multimodal Deepfakes

Models like DALL-E 2 (Ramesh et al., 2022) (and Stable Diffusion (Rombach et al., 2021) combine language understanding with image generation, opening up new possibilities for creating deepfakes based on textual descriptions.

GENERATION OF DEEPFAKE ATTACKS

Deepfake attacks are sophisticated forms of digital manipulation that leverage artificial intelligence (AI) and machine learning techniques to create highly convincing fake audio, video, or image content. These attacks are primarily generated using deep learning algorithms, particularly generative adversarial networks (GANs) and autoencoders (Guarnera et al., 2024).

The process of generating deepfakes typically involves the following steps:
- **Data Collection:** Attackers gather a large dataset of images or videos of the target individual from various sources.

- **Training:** The collected data is used to train deep learning models, which learn to recreate the target's facial features, expressions, and movements.
- **Face Swapping or Synthesis:** The trained model is then used to generate new content by either swapping faces in existing videos or synthesizing entirely new footage.
- **Refinement:** Post-processing techniques are applied to enhance the realism of the generated content, addressing issues like lighting, skin texture, and seamless blending.

Figure 2. Process in creating deepfakes

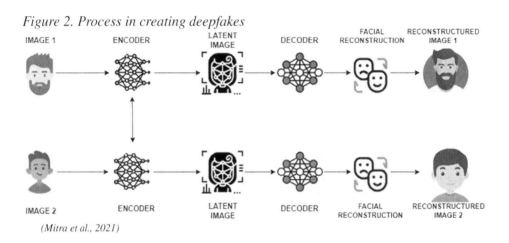

(Mitra et al., 2021)

Recent advancements in AI have significantly improved the quality and efficiency of deepfake generation. Some models can now create convincing deepfakes using only a few images or seconds of audio, making the technology more accessible and potentially more dangerous (Mitra et al., 2021).

Creation of Deepfake in Generative Adversarial Network

Generative Adversarial Networks (GANs) have revolutionized the creation of deepfakes, enabling the production of highly convincing synthetic media. This process involves sophisticated neural network architectures and complex mathematical principles.

GAN Architecture for Deepfake Creation

GANs are a popular architecture for image and video deepfakes. They consist of two competing neural networks:

1. Generator (G): Creates synthetic images
2. Discriminator (D): Distinguishes between real and synthetic images The GAN optimization process is expressed as a minimax game (Goodfellow et al., 2014):
   Where:
   - $p_{\text{data}}(x)$ is the distribution of real data
   - $p_z(z)$ is the prior distribution of input noise
   - $G(z)$ is the generator function
   - $D(x)$ is the discriminator function
   - $V(D, G)$ is the value function of the game

Advanced GAN architectures like StyleGAN and CycleGAN have further improved deepfake quality by introducing style-based generation and unpaired image-to-image translation (Goodfellow et al., 2014; Karras et al., 2019; Zhu et al., 2017).

Large Language Models (LLMs)

LLMs, such as GPT-3 and its successors, are primarily used for text-based deepfakes but can also contribute to multimodal deepfakes. These models are based on the Transformer architecture and use self-attention mechanisms to process and generate text sequences.

The core of an LLM is the self-attention mechanism, which can be expressed as(Vaswani, 2017):

Where Q, K, and V are query, key, and value matrices, respectively, and d_k is the dimension of the key vectors. LLMs are trained on massive datasets using techniques like unsupervised pretraining and fine-tuning. They can generate highly coherent and contextually appropriate text, making them powerful tools for creating textual deepfakes (Brown, 2020).

METHODS USED IN DEEPFAKE DETECTION

Deepfake detection techniques have evolved significantly to counter the increasing sophistication of deepfake generation. Various methods are employed, each with its own strengths and weaknesses. Here's a comparison of some common deepfake detection techniques based on factors such as accuracy, computational requirements, and application scenarios.

Usage of Deepfake Technology

Deepfake technology offers a wide array of beneficial applications across various sectors. In the entertainment industry, deepfakes have revolutionized film production by enabling the de-aging of actors and even the recreation of deceased performers. This technology allows filmmakers to expand their creative possibilities, bringing historical figures to life or extending the careers of beloved actors. In video game development, deep fakes contribute to creating more realistic characters and facial animations, enhancing the immersive experience for players (Westerlund, 2019). The educational sector has also begun to harness the potential of deepfake technology.

Table 1. Comparison of deepfake detecting techniques

Technique	Accuracy	Computationa Require-ments	lApplication Sce-narios	Strength	Weakness
AI-Based Detection (CNNs)	High	High	Real-time applications requiring high accuracy	High accuracy in de-tecting manipulated im-ages and videos.(Taeb & Chi, 2022)	Requires signifi-cant computational resources and can overfit on training data. (Rafique et al., 2023)
Hybrid Models (CNN + LSTM)	High	Moderate to High	Scenarios needing temporal consistency checks.	Combines spatial and temporal anal-ysis for improved detection of video inconsistencies.(El-gayar et al., 2024)	Computationally intensive and may require specialized hardware.(El-gayar et al., 2024)
Graph Neural Networks	Moderate	Moderate	Applications involving complex relational data.	Effective in capturing relationships between different parts of the media content.(El-gayar et al., 2024)	May struggle with generalization across diverse datasets.(El-gayar et al., 2024)
Forensic Analysis	Moderate	Low	Legal and investigative scenarios requiring detailed analysis.	Can provide detailed insights into manipula-tion techniques.	Time-consuming and less effective for real-time detection.(El-gayar et al., 2024)

Historical reenactments can now be made more engaging and interactive, with deepfakes bringing historical figures to life in a way that was previously impossible (Diakopoulos & Johnson, 2019). Language learning applications have incorporated deepfake technology to create immersive environments for practicing conversations, allowing learners to interact with lifelike representations of native speakers. In medical training, deepfakes are being used to simulate patient interactions, providing healthcare professionals with more realistic and diverse training scenarios. In the business world, deepfake technology is transforming communication and marketing strategies. Companies are using deepfakes for multilingual communication, translating and lip-syncing speeches for global audiences (Kietzmann et al., 2020). This application breaks down language barriers and enables more effective international communication. Virtual spokespersons created using deepfake technology offer businesses a novel way to engage with their audience, providing consistent brand representation across various platforms (Vaccari & Chadwick, 2020). The advent of widespread remote work has also benefited from deepfake technology. Enhanced video conferencing applications use deepfake-like technology to improve avatars, making virtual meetings more engaging and personal (Mirsky & Lee, 2021). This application helps to bridge the gap between in-person and virtual interactions, potentially improving collaboration and communication in remote work settings. Artists and creative professionals are exploring deepfakes as a new medium for expression. Digital artists use this technology to create surreal or impossible scenes and characters, pushing the boundaries of visual art (Wagner & Blewer, 2019). Interactive installations incorporating deepfake technology offer audiences personalized and immersive experiences, opening up new possibilities in the world of art and entertainment (Wagner & Blewer, 2019). In the field of accessibility, deepfake technology shows promise in creating more inclusive media. For instance, it can be used to generate sign language interpretations of spoken content or to create audio descriptions for visual media, making content more accessible to individuals with hearing or visual impairments (Ceolin, 2023).

While it's crucial to acknowledge and address the ethical concerns surrounding deepfake technology, its potential benefits are significant and far-reaching. From enhancing entertainment and education to improving communication and accessibility, deepfakes offer innovative solutions to various challenges across different sectors. As the technology continues to evolve, it's likely that we will discover even more positive applications, further underscoring the importance of responsible development and use of this powerful tool.

MISUSES OF DEEPFAKE

Misuse in Political Spheres

One of the most concerning areas of deepfake misuse is in the political arena. The ability to create convincing fake videos of political figures has the potential to significantly influence public opinion and election outcomes.

Disinformation Campaigns

Deepfakes have become a powerful tool in disinformation campaigns. (Chesney & Citron, 2019) highlight how deepfakes can be used to create false narratives about political candidates or events. For example, a deepfake video could show a politician making inflammatory statements they never actually made, potentially swaying voter opinions or inciting unrest. The 2020 U.S. presidential election saw several instances of deepfakes being used to spread misinformation. While many of these were clearly labeled as parodies, the potential for more sophisticated and malicious use remains a significant concern (Paris & Donovan, 2019).

Undermining Democratic Processes

The mere existence of deepfake technology can undermine democratic processes by eroding public trust in media and institutions. (Vaccari & Chadwick, 2020) found that exposure to deepfakes increased feelings of uncertainty and decreased trust in news media among study participants. The "liar's dividend" phenomenon allows individuals to cast doubt on genuine video evidence by claiming it's fabricated, thus adding another layer of complexity to the already challenging information environment (Westerlund, 2019).

International Relations and Diplomacy

In the realm of international relations, deepfakes pose a unique threat. ("The Epistemic Threat of Deepfakes," 2020) discusses how deepfakes could be used to fabricate evidence of international crimes or to create false intelligence. Such misuse could escalate tensions between nations or justify military actions based on pretenses.

Misuse in Personal and Social Contexts

While political misuse of deepfakes garners significant attention, the technology's impact on individuals and social relationships is equally concerning.

Non-Consensual Pornography

One of the earliest and most prevalent misuses of deepfakes has been in the creation of non-consensual pornography. (Citron & Franks, 2014) describe how deepfake technology has been used to superimpose victims' faces onto pornographic content without their consent. This form of sexual exploitation can cause severe psychological harm to victims and damage their personal and professional lives.

A study by Sensity AI found that 96% of deepfake videos online were non-consensual porn, with the vast majority targeting women (Ajder et al., 2019). The ease of creating these videos and the difficulty in having them removed from the internet compound the harm to victims.

Cyberbullying and Harassment

Deepfakes have become a new tool in cyberbullying and online harassment. Malicious actors can create embarrassing or compromising fake videos of their targets, leading to emotional distress, reputational damage, and, in some cases, real-world consequences such as job loss or social ostracism (Kietzmann et al., 2020).

Identity Theft and Fraud

The ability to create convincing fake videos and audio of individuals opens up new avenues for identity theft and fraud. (Ajder et al., 2019) discuss how deepfakes could be used to impersonate individuals in video calls or voice conversations, potentially leading to financial fraud or unauthorized access to sensitive information.

Market Manipulation

Deepfakes could be used to manipulate financial markets by creating false videos of company executives making statements about financial performance or major business decisions. Even a short-lived deepfake could cause significant market movements before being debunked (Westerlund, 2019).

Corporate Espionage

In the realm of corporate espionage, deepfakes present a new threat. Malicious actors could use deepfake technology to impersonate executives or employees to gain access to sensitive information or influence business decisions (Ajder et al., 2019).

Fake News Proliferation

Deepfakes represent a new frontier in the spread of fake news. The ability to create convincing video evidence to support false narratives makes it increasingly difficult for journalists and fact-checkers to combat misinformation (Vaccari & Chadwick, 2020).

Erosion of Trust in Media

As deepfakes become more prevalent, there is a risk of growing public skepticism towards all media content, even authentic footage. This erosion of trust in media institutions could have far-reaching consequences for public discourse and democracy (Ajder et al., 2019).

Challenges in Verification

Newsrooms and media organizations face significant challenges in verifying the authenticity of video content in the age of deepfakes. The time pressure of breaking news stories combined with the sophistication of deepfake technology makes it increasingly difficult to ensure the veracity of content before publication (Westerlund, 2019).

Legal Gray Areas

Current laws in many jurisdictions are ill-equipped to deal with the unique challenges posed by deepfakes. While some countries have introduced legislation specifically targeting deepfakes, many legal systems are still catching up to the technology (Chesney & Citron, 2019)

Issues of consent, copyright, and defamation become particularly complex when dealing with synthetic media. For instance, who owns the rights to a deepfake video – the creator of the algorithm, the person who used the algorithm, or the individuals whose likenesses are used in the video?

Ethical Considerations

The ethical implications of deepfakes extend beyond legal considerations. Questions arise about the nature of truth and authenticity in the digital age. There are also ethical concerns about the use of deepfakes in areas such as entertainment and education. While there may be benefits to using deepfakes to recreate historical figures or enhance film productions, these uses also raise questions about authenticity and the potential for misrepresentation.

Psychological and Societal Impact

The proliferation of deepfakes has significant psychological and societal implications.

Trust and Reality Skepticism

Exposure to deepfakes can lead to increased skepticism about the authenticity of all digital content. This "reality apathy" could result in a society where people are less likely to believe even authentic content, potentially leading to increased conspiracy theories and social division (Vaccari & Chadwick, 2020).

Psychological Harm to Individuals

Individuals targeted by malicious deepfakes can experience severe psychological harm. The fear of being targeted can lead to self-censorship and reduced participation in public discourse. Victims of deepfake pornography, in particular, often experience trauma, anxiety, and depression (Citron & Franks, 2014).

Societal Polarization

The use of deepfakes in political disinformation campaigns can exacerbate existing societal divisions. By presenting false "evidence" that confirms pre-existing biases, deepfakes can further entrench people in their ideological positions and make cross-partisan dialogue more difficult (Diakopoulos & Johnson, 2019).

Combating Deepfake Misuse

While the challenges posed by deepfake misuse are significant, efforts are underway to combat this threat.

Technological Solutions

Researchers are developing increasingly sophisticated methods for detecting deepfakes. These include analyzing visual artifacts, inconsistencies in facial movements, and even the unique "fingerprints" left by different GAN models (Mirsky & Lee, 2021). However, as detection methods improve, so too does the technology for creating deepfakes, resulting in an ongoing arms race between creation and detection technologies.

Legal and Policy Responses

Governments and international bodies are beginning to develop legal frameworks to address deepfake misuse. For example, China has implemented regulations requiring deepfakes to be labeled and prohibiting their use to spread false information. In the United States, several states have passed laws specifically addressing deepfakes, particularly in the context of elections and non-consensual pornography (Citron & Franks, 2014).

Media Literacy Education

Enhancing public media literacy is crucial in combating the negative effects of deepfakes. Education initiatives that teach critical thinking skills and raise awareness about the existence and potential misuse of deepfakes can help individuals better navigate the complex information landscape.

CONCLUSION

The misuse of deepfakes presents a complex and multifaceted challenge to society. From political disinformation to personal harassment, the potential for harm is significant and wide-ranging. As deepfake technology continues to evolve and become more accessible, it is crucial that technological, legal, and educational responses keep pace. Addressing the misuse of deepfakes will require a coordinated effort from technologists, policymakers, educators, and the public. By fostering critical thinking, developing robust detection methods, and creating appropriate legal frameworks, we can work towards mitigating the harms of deepfake misuse while still harnessing the potential benefits of this powerful technology. As we navigate this new digital landscape, it is essential to remain vigilant and adaptable. The challenges posed by deepfakes are likely to evolve, and our responses must evolve with them. By staying informed and proactive, we can work towards a future where the benefits of synthetic media can be realized without compromising truth, privacy, and social trust.

REFERENCES

Ajder, H., Patrini, G., Cavalli, F., & Cullen, L. (2019). The state of deepfakes: Landscape, threats, and impact. *Amsterdam: Deeptrace, 27.*

Belhumeur, P., Hespanha, J., & Kriegman, D. (1997). Eigenfaces vs. fisherfaces: Recognition using class specific linear projection. *IEEE Transactions on Pattern Analysis and Machine Intelligence*, 19(7), 711–720. DOI: 10.1109/34.598228

Blanz, V., & Vetter, T. (2003). Face recognition based on fitting a 3d morphable model. *IEEE Transactions on Pattern Analysis and Machine Intelligence*, 25(9), 1063–1074. DOI: 10.1109/TPAMI.2003.1227983

Bregler, C., Covell, M., & Slaney, M. (1997). Video rewrite: Driving visual speech with audio. *Seminal Graphics Papers: Pushing the Boundaries, Volume 2.* https://api.semanticscholar.org/CorpusID:2341707

Brown, T. B. (2020). Language models are few-shot learners. *arXiv preprint arXiv:2005.14165.*

Ceolin, F. (2023). Beyond deepfakes: The positive applications of ai-enhanced video synthesis [Accessed: 2024-10-02].

Chan, C., Ginosar, S., Zhou, T., & Efros, A. A. (2019). Everybody dance now. *Proceedings of the IEEE/CVF international conference on computer vision*, 5933–5942.

Chesney, R., & Citron, D. K. (2019). Deep fakes: A looming challenge for privacy, democracy, and national security. *California Law Review*, 107, 1753–1820.

Citron, D. K., & Franks, M. A. (2014). Criminalizing revenge porn. *Wake Forest Law Review*, 49, 345. https://api.semanticscholar.org/CorpusID:153729297

Cortes, C., & Vapnik, V. N. (1995). Support-vector networks. *Machine Learning*, 20(3), 273–297. https://api.semanticscholar.org/CorpusID:52874011. DOI: 10.1007/BF00994018

Diakopoulos, N., & Johnson, D. (2019). Anticipating and addressing the ethical implications of deepfakes in the context of elections. SSRN *Electronic Journal.* DOI: 10.2139/ssrn.3474183

El-gayar, M., Abouhawwash, M., Askar, S., & Sweidan, S. (2024). A novel approach for detecting deep fake videos using graph neural network. *Journal of Big Data*, 11(1), 22. Advance online publication. DOI: 10.1186/s40537-024-00884-y

Goodfellow, I., Pouget-Abadie, J., Mirza, M., Xu, B., Warde-Farley, D., Ozair, S., Courville, A., & Bengio, Y. (2014). Generative adversarial nets. *Advances in Neural Information Processing Systems*, ●●●, 27.

Guarnera, L., Giudice, O., & Battiato, S. (2024). Mastering deepfake detection: A cutting-edge approach to distinguish gan and diffusion-model images. *ACM Transactions on Multimedia Computing Communications and Applications*, 20(11), 1–24. Advance online publication. DOI: 10.1145/3652027

Karras, T., Laine, S., & Aila, T. (2019). A style-based generator architecture for generative adversarial networks. *Proceedings of the IEEE/CVF conference on computer vision and pattern recognition*, 4401–4410. DOI: 10.1109/CVPR.2019.00453

Karras, T., Laine, S., Aittala, M., Hellsten, J., Lehtinen, J., & Aila, T. (2020). Analyzing and improving the image quality of stylegan. *Proceedings of the IEEE/CVF conference on computer vision and pattern recognition*, 8110–8119. DOI: 10.1109/CVPR42600.2020.00813

Kietzmann, J., Lee, L. W., McCarthy, I. P., & Kietzmann, T. C. (2020). Deepfakes: Trick or treat? *Business Horizons*, 63(2), 135–146. DOI: 10.1016/j.bushor.2019.11.006

Mirsky, Y., & Lee, W. (2021). The creation and detection of deepfakes: A survey. *ACM Computing Surveys*, 54(1), 1–41. DOI: 10.1145/3425780

Mitra, A., Mohanty, S. P., Corcoran, P., & Kougianos, E. (2021). A machine learning based approach for deepfake detection in social media through key video frame extraction. *SN Computer Science*, 2(2), 98. DOI: 10.1007/s42979-021-00495-x

Ojala, T., Pietikäinen, M., & Harwood, D. (1996). A comparative study of texture measures with classification based on featured distributions. *Pattern Recognition*, 29(1), 51–59. https://doi.org/https://doi.org/10.1016/0031-3203(95)00067-4. DOI: 10.1016/0031-3203(95)00067-4

Paris, B., & Donovan, J. (2019). Deepfakes and cheap fakes. data & society.

Rafique, R., Gantassi, R., Amin, R., Frnda, J., Mustapha, A., & Alshehri, A. (2023). Deep fake detection and classification using error-level analysis and deep learning. *Scientific Reports*, 13(1), 7422. Advance online publication. DOI: 10.1038/s41598-023-34629-3 PMID: 37156887

Ramesh, A., Dhariwal, P., Nichol, A., Chu, C., & Chen, M. (2022). Hierarchical text-conditional image generation with clip latents. *ArXiv, abs/2204.06125*. https://api.semanticscholar.org/CorpusID:248097655

Rombach, R., Blattmann, A., Lorenz, D., Esser, P., & Ommer, B. (2021). High-resolution image synthesis with latent diffusion models. *2022 IEEE/CVF Conference on Computer Vision and Pattern Recognition (CVPR)*, 10674–10685. https://api.semanticscholar.org/CorpusID:245335280

Schroff, F., Kalenichenko, D., & Philbin, J. (2015). Facenet: A unified embedding for face recognition and clustering. *Proceedings of the IEEE conference on computer vision and pattern recognition*, 815–823. DOI: 10.1109/CVPR.2015.7298682

Singer, U., Polyak, A., Hayes, T., Yin, X., An, J., Zhang, S., Hu, Q., Yang, H., Ashual, O., Gafni, O., Parikh, D., Gupta, S., & Taigman, Y. (2022). Make-a-video: Text-to-video generation without text-video data. *ArXiv, abs/2209.14792*. https://api.semanticscholar.org/CorpusID:252595919

Taeb, M., & Chi, H. (2022). Comparison of deepfake detection techniques through deep learning. *Journal of Cybersecurity and Privacy, 2*(1), 89–106. Taigman, Y., Yang, M., Ranzato, M., & Wolf, L. (2014). Deepface: Closing the gap to human-level performance in face verification. *Proceedings of the IEEE conference on computer vision and pattern recognition*, 1701–1708.DOI: 10.3390/jcp2010007

The epistemic threat of deepfakes. (2020). *Philosophy & Technology*. https://pubmed.ncbi.nlm.nih.gov/32837868/

Thies, J., Zollhofer, M., Stamminger, M., Theobalt, C., & Nießner, M. (2016). Face2face: Real-time face capture and reenactment of rgb videos. *Proceedings of the IEEE conference on computer vision and pattern recognition*, 2387–2395. DOI: 10.1145/2929464.2929475

Turk, M., & Pentland, A. (1991). Eigenfaces for Recognition. *Journal of Cognitive Neuroscience*, 3(1), 71–86. DOI: 10.1162/jocn.1991.3.1.71 PMID: 23964806

Vaccari, C., & Chadwick, A. (2020). Deepfakes and disinformation: Exploring the impact of synthetic political video on deception, uncertainty, and trust in news. *Social Media + Society*, 6(1), 205630512090340. DOI: 10.1177/2056305120903408

Van Den Oord, A., Dieleman, S., Zen, H., Simonyan, K., Vinyals, O., Graves, A., Kalchbrenner, N., Senior, A., Kavukcuoglu, K., ... (2016). Wavenet: A generative model for raw audio. *arXiv preprint arXiv:1609.03499, 12*.

Vaswani, A. (2017). Attention is all you need. *Advances in Neural Information Processing Systems*.

Wagner, T., & Blewer, A. (2019). "the word real is no longer real": Deepfakes, gender, and the challenges of ai-altered video. *Open Information Science*, 3(1), 32–46. DOI: 10.1515/opis-2019-0003

Westerlund, M. (2019). The emergence of deepfake technology: A review. *Technology Innovation Management Review*, 9(11), 39–52. DOI: 10.22215/timreview/1282

Zhu, J.-Y., Park, T., Isola, P., & Efros, A. A. (2017). Unpaired image-to-image translation using cycle-consistent adversarial networks. *Proceedings of the IEEE international conference on computer vision*, 2223–2232. DOI: 10.1109/ICCV.2017.244

Chapter 2
The Impact of Deep Fakes in Markets and Economies

Iris-Panagiota Efthymiou
https://orcid.org/0000-0001-9656-8378
University of Greenwich, UK

Theocharis Efthymiou Egleton
London School of Economics, UK

ABSTRACT

The advent of deepfake technology has introduced significant challenges and opportunities in markets and economies globally. This paper examines the multifaceted impact of deepfakes on financial markets, corporate reputations, consumer behaviour, and economic stability. By synthesizing recent case studies and academic research, we explore how deepfakes can manipulate stock prices, erode trust in brands, and influence market decisions, leading to potential economic disruptions. We also discuss the role of regulatory frameworks, technological countermeasures, and the ethical considerations in mitigating the risks posed by deepfakes. Our analysis highlights the urgent need for enhanced vigilance, cross-sector collaboration, and innovative solutions to safeguard market integrity and economic stability in the face of this emerging threat.

DOI: 10.4018/979-8-3693-6890-9.ch002

Copyright © 2025, IGI Global Scientific Publishing. Copying or distributing in print or electronic forms without written permission of IGI Global Scientific Publishing is prohibited.

INTRODUCTION AND BACKGROUND

Deepfakes are computer-generated media where the face and body movements in images and videos are swapped or replaced. The earliest versions of deepfakes were created by users fusing images from high-quality coverage of the person to be impersonated with images of adult film actors. In the original application of the technology, deep learning algorithms were used to replace the faces in pornographic videos, overlaying the features of people, including celebrities and politicians, with those of film actors. Since then, deepfake technology has been widely used in many applications, including pornography, hoaxes, disinformation, and fake news. Initially, detecting the deep nature of deepfakes was relatively easy due to the high levels of noise in the images they produced, but their quality continued to improve as the technologies used to develop and train the deep learning algorithms grew and advanced.

Deepfake technologies also substantially reduce the cost of creating fake content. To be convincing, a deepfake often still requires access to an extensive dataset of images and videos of the person to be impersonated. However, large numbers of images and videos of politicians, celebrities, and other well-known figures are already publicly available. In October 2019, a widely shared and very convincing deepfake video portrayed Mark Zuckerberg giving a speech about Facebook's influence and control. The video was created from real footage of Zuckerberg at a 2017 conference and a sophisticated machine-learning model that transposed his face onto the original speaker's body. (Veerasamy and Pieterse2022) This supports the point made by scholars about the Future of Life Institute that deepfake materials spread much faster than other types of disinformation or fake news, achieving an estimated seventy-one per cent higher sharing rate than alternative content sources. Part of the allure of deepfake technologies is their customizable nature. A user attempting to defeat image or video recognition technology can tailor the attack to achieve a high level of success. When success breeds confidence, deepfake images and videos can perform significantly more effectively and evade content moderation algorithms with ease.

By now, you may have come across deepfake videos. Essentially, deepfake is a portmanteau of 'deep learning' and 'fake' and usually entails using machine learning and neural networks to learn the features of a face and then plot one face onto another. This was primarily achieved using a Generative Adversarial Network (GAN) made of a generator and a discriminator that plays a min-max two-player game. Often, generative models (such as a GAN) are used to take a random input and 'generate' a new sample in the feature space, typically closely mimicking the real data distribution.

However, deep learning technology is becoming less and less of a novelty, and now anyone with a powerful enough computer, and the know-how, can generate these deepfakes. This has broad-reaching implications for personal privacy, democratic processes, media manipulation, nation-state and corporate espionage, and cyber warfare among other things. (Masood et al.2023) Training requires a lot of computing power and the correct software packages, or alternatively connecting to moving AI's cloud service.

Generative AI is simplifying and reducing the cost of committing fraud. Nonetheless, using gen AI enables malicious individuals to commit large-scale fraud by simultaneously targeting numerous victims with minimal resources. In just 2022, the FBI reported 21,832 cases of business email fraud, resulting in around $2.7 billion in losses. The Deloitte Center for Financial Services predicts that in a scenario of "aggressive" adoption, losses from generative AI email fraud could reach approximately US$11.5 billion by 2027.

According to the U.S. Département of the Treasury (March 2024), "highlights the finance industry's vulnerabilities when it comes to social engineering — particularly the utilization of deepfakes and LLMs for targeted phishing and business email compromise, and synthetic identity fraud". The financial implications of deepfake technology, in the United States of America, for example for voice deepfakes and some other synthetic identity attacks, as reported by business was around of 33% of fraud events (2023) and it could cost to the taxpayers more than a $1 trillion over the course of 2024.

The number of incidents similar to this one is expected to increase in the coming years as malicious individuals utilize more advanced and accessible generative AI technology to commit fraud against banks and their clients. Deloitte's Center for Financial Services forecasts that fraud losses in the US could rise to US$40 billion by 2027, up from US$12.3 billion in 2023, with a 32% annual growth rate.

1. DEFINITION AND TECHNOLOGY BEHIND DEEPFAKES

There is no agreed-upon definition of deepfakes, although as the word implies, it is derived from the combination of the terms "deep learning" and "fake" (the English word for false or fake). However, a deepfake is commonly described as a piece of media content (most often, but not exclusively, a video) that is synthetically created by artificial intelligence. It has also been defined as a technique for human image synthesis based on artificial intelligence, usually used to generate images or videos that are manipulated or custom-made to show something that didn't happen. The speech or body language of the protagonists in the video has been modified to create an illusion that is real. The process of creating a deepfake is similar to that of developing an artificial neural network to solve a problem using data, except in this case, the problem is modelled in such a way that the system creates false output. (Khoo et al.2022)

The technology used in deepfakes primarily employs variations of established deep learning methods such as Convolutional Neural Networks and Generative Adversarial Networks. The former is utilized to produce fabricated content, while the latter is employed to enhance the capabilities of a model known as a "discriminator" that becomes increasingly adept at identifying the content as fake, as the former improves at generating fabricated content. Case studies demonstrating the potential of this technology have showcased substantial technical advancement in the realm of computer imagery, a field that was initially introduced by a research project published in 2014 by Ian Goodfellow and his team (Xu et al.2021) Many of these innovations pertain to generative models, able to synthesize high-quality images that appear nearly identical to authentic ones, particularly in the case of faces. (Atone and Bhalchandra, 2023) The visually impressive outcomes yielded by these methods signify a notable advancement when compared to prior techniques.

Deepfakes are hyper-realistic video or audio forgeries that employ human image synthesis to produce false depictions of events. They have garnered widespread public, political, and academic attention in recent years. The use of sophisticated technology to create fake videos for various purposes is on the ascendant. Developed for political and entertainment objectives, deepfakes signify a new means of assessing the reliability of information, a matter of paramount importance in numerous industries, particularly in financial markets. (Hancock and Bailenson, 2021) False information can destabilize such markets, potentially causing them to malfunction (Fletcher, 2020). In this chapter, we examine financial deepfakes, used to manipulate stock prices to generate artificial profits and discuss their potential impact on the actual economy, and will examine some examples of deepfakes. In March 2019, the initial deepfake attack was uncovered by Euler Hermes, an insurance company that ultimately covered the expenses incurred by the incident. The scheme commenced with a phone call to the CEO of a U.K. energy company from someone purporting to be the head of the company's German parent organization, mimicking the boss's voice flawlessly, including tone, inflexion, and subtle German accent. The imposter requested that the CEO transfer $243,000 to what was believed to be a Hungarian supplier's account.

Additionally, in July 2020, Motherboard reported on an unsuccessful deepfake phishing effort targeted at a technology company. Even more disconcerting, a report from Recorded Future in April 2021 presented evidence that malicious individuals are increasingly exploring the use of deepfake technology for cybercrime. The report demonstrates how members of specific dark web forums, as well as communities on platforms like Discord and Telegram, are deliberating on the use of deepfakes for social engineering, fraud, and blackmail. Furthermore, Consultancy Technologent has cautioned that new trends in remote work are exposing employees to a heightened risk of falling victim to deepfake phishing and reported three such cases among its clients in 2020.

Healthcare is a challenging sector for deepfake technology. Deepfakes can be damaging to the reputation of doctors and health professionals, potentially hazardous to the health and welfare of certain recipients, or have implications for the broader provision of medical services. (Qureshi & Khan, 2024) (Hoek et al., 2024) For instance, an audio deepfake could be used in a competing doctor's surgery or a general practitioner's practice to imply that a specialist had given ill judgment or advice. As a result, care provision would be guided by inaccurate health information, hampering the process of ensuring that sick patients receive the appropriate care and medication, which has consequences for public health and the care provision process. The relaxation of trust between a patient and a general practitioner or consultant jeopardizes the ability to implement appropriate care recommendations.

Then, the transformational power of some deepfake applications is at its most acutely critical in highly ethical medical settings, including cosmetic operations where doctors must inform patients when exploring beauty adjustments and recovery care. (Duong et al., 2024) (Navarro et al., 2024) (Malik et al., 2024) In such scenarios, the patient's pre-existing image could be used as a basis for the deepfake face replacement approach, by feeding social extensions into the deepfake prediction and creating inappropriate images. If such deepfake consequences go ahead using normal imaging technologies, such objectives could be directed without directly consulting the people who are the subject of the fabricated material. This may also derive from a damaged self-image, create tenderness, and adjust overall perceptions of what changed concerning the existing image. With technologies like deepfakes that will be able to satisfy a deep fascination to create buzz and social capital, it will be difficult to predict where ownership of celebrities and other high-value users over their own image turns into commercial opportunities.

Deepfakes in politics have garnered significant attention because manipulated political content can be particularly harmful. (Battista, 2024) (Sharma et al., 2023) Few specific examples of deepfakes that defame politicians or candidates remain in the literature. All made explicit visual and face-swap fakes misattributing what politicians did not say. There is no evidence that these deepfakes have had a significant impact on recent elections. While no direct evidence that deepfakes have had a significant impact on an election has emerged, scholars have discussed at length the potential damage of these videos released in the midst of an election campaign.

Access to future realistic political deepfakes could seriously harm the reputation and credibility of candidates if the public does not react with scepticism to deepfakes revealed as "fake." (Momeni, 2024) (Schiff et al., 2023) Ultimately, the "agenda-setting power," or at least the attention that a deepfake receives, could still demonstrate great "power" as that particular deepfake goes viral on social media platforms. There may also be compelling evidence to suggest that election video propaganda manipulation is intricately connected to the deep learning AI facial fakes made with a politician's face. In witness testimony on this topic of deepfakes, it was emphatically noted that deepfake policy should consider existing legislative proposals and regimes targeting election manipulation from foreign adversaries, including best practices for data handling, proactive disinformation monitoring and removal, individualized truth in advertising requirements, and mandatory deepfake identification and warning labels as a comprehensive package for the Federal Election Commission and the government to enforce upon platforms

Deepfakes have the potential to really cause chaos in society by messing with how democracy and free will function, and also by putting the public in danger with fake revenge porn and false information. (Battista, 2024) (Kopecky, 2024) As technological and scientific innovation becomes increasingly complex, laws and lawmakers grapple with the problems associated with trying to regulate such actions. Criminalizing deepfakes in and of itself is a flawed approach given the importance of the preservation of individual rights to freedom of expression. (Malik et al., 2024) (Gupta, 2023) However, the legal and regulatory landscape involved with deepfakes remains in a nascent stage. This examination begins by examining the prevailing laws surrounding deepfakes in different countries, followed by the consequential question of who should be legally responsible for them. The conclusion will compare the law to technological development before discussing relevant remedies.

2. THE BUSINESS IMPLICATIONS OF DEEPFAKES

A deepfake could be published of a mass murderer who just happens to wear a jacket featuring a well-known firm. Should the firm's brand suffer from the association with a killer, stock prices could respond negatively. In extreme cases, or when the connection to the firm is very concrete, an impression has been positioned in the mind of a firm's stakeholders, then the potential damage to the firm's reputation is not shelved. Such a possibility might not just be the result of an intentionally generated deepfake. As cyber criminals become more capable of committing sophisticated acts of digital impersonation, they could surreptitiously embroil a firm in this type of crisis or scam. (Emami, 2022)

As technology advances, executive management in organizations typically remains, on average, unaware of advances in fields of knowledge seemingly disparate from their primary domain. Thus, the survey found that 77% of executives in 1,500 companies around the globe were largely unprepared to defend themselves against deepfake technology. This is a critical blind spot for organizations if they are unprepared to handle the fallout of deepfakes being designed featuring key members of an organization and the necessary advertisements to dispel the false to protect the integrity of the business and the reputation of the leader. (Kopecky, 2024) Such a situation could not only negatively influence the value of the firm but also potentially move share prices.

Impact on Business Sectors

To counter the growing risks posed by the increasing use of synthetic images, sounds, or videos for nefarious or criminal purposes, business sectors must become aware of the capabilities and implications of this technology on their business sectors, improve protective workforce, risk management, and technical deepfake validation competencies. (Jones, 2020) To ensure the detection of high-quality and low-cost (free) deepfakes shared and hosted on social media platforms and other high-risk applications, new technologies for remote detection of deepfake manipulation will need to be developed to prove that powerful artificial intelligence and deep learning technology will not carve a hole in the extensive list of objectives only months or a few years after installation. Extraction solutions must not fail, and detection solutions must constantly strive for faster, trustworthy, and reliably non-invasive detection while ensuring compliance with data privacy and security regulations, and minimizing false expenses, complaints, and harassment. (Juefei-Xu et al.2022)

The recent emergence of deepfake and other synthetic media technologies means businesses need to be aware of the major and consistent business and security risks these capabilities threaten on the selling and buying sides. (Sareen, 2022) The rapid growth in of deepfake capabilities, applications, and availability of off-the-shelf software will stay pulse with innovations in stopping or downplaying deepfake solutions. The evolution of more authentic and undetectable deepfake solutions will increase the business risks due to the loss of trust, corporate brand and reputation damage, employee work disruption, economic losses, or human and physical damages. (Lyu, 2024) At the same time, the increasing supply and use of deepfakes for malicious intent will continue to elevate the risks and demands and expense for reliable deepfake detection and validation solutions by growing the business demand for regular and continuous deepfake validation of sensitive multimedia content along the supply chain.

The potential of deepfake technology to transform many spheres – from influencing a nation's subjective reality to shaping an individual's career – is immense (Fusiek, D.A. et al., 2022). From a business perspective, some immediate use cases are evident. While human image synthesis is not new, its technological add-on, speech synthesis, is what distinguishes deepfakes (Gambín et al.2024). Indeed, human image synthesis has been applied for decades in computer graphics and remains a challenging endeavour. Its success was initially seen as a negative application (that is, turning no-name actresses into adult film stars impersonating well-known figures). Yet, deepfake technology has evolved. First, it has advanced speech synthesis to the degree that one does not need a text with extensive audio samples to simulate one speaking in another place and at another time. Second, and more importantly, the technological means of deepfakes now exist and are user-friendly.

Deepfake technology has business implications that are specific to the corporate domain. These business implications place the power of synthesized realistic images and videos squarely in the hands of consumers and employees who create user-generated deepfakes either for entertainment or other purposes. Furthermore, business uses are primarily the targets or subjects of either intended or unintended deepfake exposure. In this research, we shed light on these business implications and explore their strategic and ethical dimensions. For businesses, this research provides timely insights to develop proactive approaches that will enable them to effectively navigate the challenges of deepfakes and harness the opportunities for strategic influence.

Economic Sectors at Risk

For Bateman, any individual or a group of individuals could themselves, or some of their assets, be the target of deepfakes. (Bateman, J. 2022). The first asset is the stakes. For example, the individual could be a political or business leader, a celebrity, a fraud victim, a troubled public figure, family and friends, and politicians could be diagnosed with various health issues that would ruin their reputation. Sometimes, the chief-level employees of a business could be targeted: with the help of fake audio and deepfake videos, fraudsters or activists could manipulate the true intentions of some directors to gain the financial benefit of stock market manipulation. At other times, prominent individuals could be attacked as well. The individuals warned are people with a high level of access or influence such as the spouse, family, or friends of a military, political, or business leader who could be targeted as a weak link to gather essential intelligence.

There are certain sectors which are at a higher risk. Digital experts think that financial markets are one of the sectors that are more susceptible to deepfake attacks. According to Professor Bronk, misinformation can lead to a severe situation in financial markets, so these markets must adapt rapidly. (Bronk, C. 2018) One of the key roles of the financial system is to invest resources effectively and allocate capital to ensure the greater well-being of present and future societies. Also, written media, digital communications, and the AV industry are considered to be highly vulnerable to being faked effectively with deepfake technology. Attacks can also pose a risk to free speech in its widest sense. Free, fair, and transparent elections, as well as the proper functioning and exercise of the democratic process, a functioning society, and free media, are considered important for political purposes. (Chesney, B., & Citron, D. 2019) Chambers, S. (2021)

Case Study 1: Stock Price Manipulation

In 2019, the monetary markets experienced a critical illustration of the potential affect of deepfakes. An uncommonly persuading deepfake sound clip risen, evidently highlighting the CEO of a major freely exchanged company declaring their unexpected acquiescence. In spite of being totally created, this declaration caused a sudden and considerable drop within the company's stock cost as speculators responded to the apparently definitive source. The deepfake at first showed up true blue sufficient to cause far reaching freeze among shareholders and showcase members, coming about in quick sell-offs and a significant, albeit transitory, diminish within the company's showcase valuation. The company's communication group and outside investigators had to quickly intercede to refute the sound clip, affirming it to be a advanced fraud. After the deepfake was uncovered, the stock cost slowly recouped, but not without clearing out a enduring affect on the advertise. This occurrence highlighted the vulnerability of monetary markets to deepfake innovation, illustrating how quickly and viably deepfakes can be utilized to control stock costs and financial specialist conduct. (Vâlsan et al., 2022)

Case Study 2: Corporate Espionage

A noteworthy occurrence of corporate secret activities illustrated the progressed utilize of deepfake innovation in arrange to commit money related extortion. In this case, a deepfake sound recording was utilized to imitate the CEO of a huge multinational organization. The sound was fantastically persuading, precisely reproducing the CEO's voice and discourse designs. This deepfake sound was at that point utilized to coordinate a senior back officer inside the company to exchange a expansive entirety of cash to a false account. Due to the realness of the voice, the fund officer complied without prompt doubt, effectively exchanging stores to the fraudsters. The extortion was as it were found after the exchange had been completed and schedule checks revealed the unauthorized exchange. By that time, the stores had as of now been moved through a arrangement of worldwide accounts, making recuperation troublesome and eventually causing critical money related misfortune for the company.

This situation brought attention to several important issues:

- The sophistication of deepfake technology: The details and precision in the deepfake audio were enough to fool experienced corporate personnel.
- Vulnerability of internal controls: The usual verification processes were not enough to catch the fraudulent deepfake, showing the need for stronger security measures.
- Impact on corporate trust: The breach damaged trust within the company, highlighting the importance of verifying sensitive communications through multiple channels.

The incident showed the need for companies to use advanced technological solutions and protocols to detect and reduce the risks of deepfake-enabled fraud (Kalpokas & Kalpokiene, 2022). Better employee training, multi-factor authentication, and use of AI-based detection tools are essential steps in protecting against such advanced threats.

Misuse of Deepfakes

To indicate the costs, the Federal Bureau of Investigation (FBI) has already warned against the occurrence of deepfake crimes in the not-so-distant future. The special agency review made it explicit that their use would not be suitable only for criminals but also for nation-states to carry out politically motivated disinformation campaigns or corporate competitors to gain an unfair advantage. As incumbent methods for recognizing the authenticity of digital content are useless when it comes to distinguishing fakes, a new cat-and-mouse game starts. (Breen, D. C., 2021). Hence, all suggested regulatory approaches, no matter how suitable and beneficial they are, must encompass some form of inaccessibility for better implementation.

Advancements in deep learning technology have introduced some of the most disruptive tools, broadening our abilities. (Efthymiou, I. P., & Egleton, T. E., 2023). We can now generate fake ultra-photorealistic content, and some of its applications create new economic efficiencies by streamlining traditional human tasks like content production and distribution, design, and software creation.(Sinnreich, A., & Gilbert, J., 2024). Nonetheless, deepfakes can, to no lesser extent, contribute to reducing existing economic asymmetries by providing blackmailers, spies, impostors, analysts, or fraudsters with a range of extremely enhanced coercive powers. (Ienca, 2023) (Barber, 2023) Consequently, they challenge various aspects and levels of business wellness, such as shareholder value, operating costs, bigger questions of intellectual property or technology theft, and most disturbingly, core operations or the very existence of some types of organizations.

3. STRATEGIES FOR DETECTION AND MITIGATION

Given the rapid expansion of the deepfake arsenal, it is important to introduce technical measures to defend against them as quickly as possible. These mitigation efforts represent an opportunity for policymakers; several of the suggestions contained in this section are structured around the development of advanced technologies. In addition to the concrete suggestions in subsequent sections, it will be important to gather as much data and as many capabilities as are available, in order to precisely gauge the potential of deepfakes to affect financial markets or economic stimuli measures designed to counter deepfakes. (Whittaker et al.2021) Only with these understandings can society develop appropriate tools to respond. Since the underlying technologies of deepfake production will still be fairly simple to use, developing rapid communication chains and procedures to uncover the truth of fake news is vastly important, such as those undertaken with fake news and elections. (Efthymiou I. P., 2020)

To address the growing concern over deepfakes, several policymakers have made formal proposals. While addressing the theoretical implications of deepfakes is important, active efforts are critical to address the security and operational concerns relating to deepfakes. This work introduces a range of potential policy solutions to enable society to enjoy the promise of progressing AI and increased speech synthesis capabilities while creating the trust and security necessary to safeguard against the harms of deepfakes. Mitigation is the most practical step that can be taken (Mekhail Mustak et al., 2022)

To possibly nullify the use of deepfake content for adversarial purposes, companies can signal the originality of the media they publish, use DRM technologies to securely carve up, watermark, and distribute content, and adopt sophisticated machine learning technology in production, operations, and publishing/management. (Sharma, D. et al., 2023) By adopting appropriate technologies and tools, they can create and safely manage a secured parallel universe to swiftly provide the public with a response to the release of such reference-proof fabricated content. First and foremost, companies can discourage the widespread dissemination of widely popular deepfake content on their platforms by not engaging in speculative posting without due authentication. The burden is also on big technology corporations and social media platforms to detect and handle deepfake content in the same manner as other harmful content. (Westerlund, M. 2019). As global coordination does not currently exist, standard threats must be exploited in both the organized and unaffiliated sectors to deal with implementations of malicious deepfake practices, terrorist use, or political interests. In some areas, vulnerability poses a significant threat and yet can appear particularly severe for those who cannot afford to procure advanced technologies or prioritize citizen training in the detection of deepfake evidence.

An increasing number of initiatives focus on mitigating the risks present by the technology, such as the AI Foundation's Reality Defender Program, the research contest held by Facebook and Microsoft seeking to create deepfake detection tools, and the SFIAD (Shared Task on Deepfakes and Image Splicing Detection). These initiatives finance the development of methods, identify the ways in which deepfake content is distributed across multiple platforms, and test the capacity of detection tools.

Among the approaches finalists have adopted are tampering model architectures and trusting image regions. In particular, tampering with model architectures is done by closely examining the deepfake generation technique and implementing dedicated detection strategies. Instead of training discriminators that look at the entire image, the selected teams chopped the source video into 1s segments and computed a confidence score for each. Using this iterative process, they combined the outputs into a timeline to identify indicators that the video might be a deepfake. On the other hand, trusting image regions permitted the minimizing of pre-processing and labelled data requirements, lowering the computational inference time, and developing a method suitable for deployment in a live camera setting. Their decision was to trust parts of the image estimated using the Jasp model. With a fuse/projection layer, they enhanced their output signal with the local information of the frames.

The most promising strategies for detecting deepfakes are those that aim to disentangle intrinsic visual cues from fine-grained signal characteristics, as intrinsic anomalies depend on strict formal constraints that they have to preserve. One crucial limiting factor, however, is that establishing the authenticity of an image as evidence in legal proceedings requires the original image to be available and the authenticity to be independently established by forensic tools - when a deepfake originates from an entirely synthetic identity, the lack of pre-existing images makes criminal activities easier and prosecution much more challenging.

Technological Solutions

Concerning audio, methods have been proposed for detecting deepfakes based on irregular breathing, video-detected artefacts merged onto the audio or the nonsmooth nature of doctored speech. Some of these behavioral and technical artefacts that can be detected in doctored audio are related to the pitch and power of the speech signal, as well as inconsistencies between the spoken and sung voice, the prevalence of inserted glitches, and tone shifts as a result.

Some researchers have taken a different approach to detecting deepfakes and quantifying the uncertainty associated with their detection. These researchers draw upon many of the same reasons why deepfakes fool people in detecting their existence – these involve technical artefacts, as well as involved facial expressions, blinking, and gaze following. However, most of these techniques are not truly open-

rights and involve the licensing of proprietary software. There are also many similar technological solutions to detecting deepfakes being proposed, especially based on artificial intelligence, computer science, and digital signal processing. (Demir, I., & Ciftci, U. A., 2021) For example, one method uses a software agent to "look" at the eyes of fake images and distinguish between real reflections coming from a human's eyes (e.g. a reflection of eyes contacted by light) and reflections that are technically impossible (e.g. the reflection of light coming from behind the camera). Similarly, another system was developed to detect deepfakes in videos based on the reflections of light on the human iris, certain statistical features on the human face, as well as occurrences of blinking in the video.

There have been technological methods proposed, especially through advances in computer science and image analysis. These advancements have primarily been designed to determine if an image or video has been altered, and are based on a combination of software, deep learning, and artificial intelligence. A majority of these methods rely on detecting certain artefacts that were created as a result of the generally imperfect methods used to create deepfakes. Manual verification is a commonly employed approach in which trained analysts conduct video verification, and these specialized content screens face various technical and ethical challenges that need to be addressed. For example, the slow reaction time of specialists makes automatic alert scenarios impractical.

Technology alone is unlikely to make all deepfake predictions more widely available to the public. Technologies such as blockchains promise a secure and anonymous environment to bid for and reveal rewards key factors in solving incentive policies. User education and increased dissemination of high-quality, reliable and trustworthy information can help users make informed judgments about the content of their daily lived experiences while diversity and re-engagement secure public confidence in more policy development rules It is also vital to develop policies that enable innovation and effective use of new technologies by society-inspired institutions.

The fast pace of technological development has made it possible for developed algorithms to support the identification and blocking of manipulated content available on various social media platforms in real-time. Some companies, such as Microsoft, have developed these technologies and they are already in use in cooperation with other companies. Deepfake detection hides various machine learning models, but they do not only struggle when very little data is available. (Hao et al., 2022) Over time, deepfake manipulation techniques with poor performance will mature and raise the percentage of undetected deepfake manipulations, resulting in significant false positives and children are not confused by improperly identified content. Although a variety of mathematical solutions can help identify manipulated deepfake files, a multi-system alliance with different methodologies is the recommended approach for coal algebraic dedicated deep belief detection.

Mitigation Strategies and Deepfake

The effects and social implications of deepfake technology have contributed to a growing market for technology aimed at combating it and mitigating its effects (Alanazi et al., 2024). Interestingly, many of the same actors who are sophisticated enough to generate deepfake media are also working on detection and mitigation technologies (Mustak et al.,2023) (Samuel-Okon et al.,2024). In this way, a kind of arms race has emerged, with so-called 'white hat' and 'black hat' actors chasing each other's technological development round and round. As the technology grows increasingly accessible, so also is a growing suite of tools to combat it. However, the early iterations of such technologies have had very low success rates against sophisticated deepfakes and in many cases still do, leading to relatively low adoption rates in real-world use.

A large number of approaches have been suggested to combat deepfake face swap content that wastes time in the video stream input, preserving deep learning-based approaches. A recently published survey considers the evolving nature of tools in the field by examining deepfake generation as an adversarial problem, noting that 'fake' networks that aim to produce false content may soon be thwarted by 'fake detectors' that search out such content. Online tools have recently emerged that use AI to assist in the detection of digitally manipulated faces by looking for specific visual artifacts; these are based on known failings of face swap and other deepfake methods in currently available tools. One of the biggest challenges is the increasing complexity of deepfake video generation and post-hoc manipulation techniques available on open forums, resulting in a rapid expansion of the nature of attack methods, all appearing in rapid succession. This comes with the further challenge of gradually increasing consistency and believability of the visual and audio content, suggesting to the consumer that the video is fake, such that the focus must be on improvements to content preservation techniques as well as delivery tamper resistance. (Pawelec, 2022) (Jin et al., 2023)

4. REGULATORY CHALLENGES AND RESPONSES

Some commentators are calling for regulation of the big digital platforms such as Google, Facebook, and Twitter to compel them to remove identified deepfakes, but it will be difficult to legislate effectively in real time to give governments and watchdogs the wherewithal to fulfil such a role. Neither can the platforms themselves be expected to self-regulate at the expense of their raison d'être. The online business model of the giant platforms is predicated on 'user-generated content' – a business model which derives significant financial advantage from social media's increasing levels of interactivity. Meanwhile, it is incongruous as well as politically unfeasible for governments and regulatory authorities to target individual social media users. (Kalpokas & Kalpokiene, 2022)

The very unique attributes of deepfakes mean that existing or new, targeted legislation is unlikely to be a satisfactory solution to eradicating their adverse effects. Indeed, such legislation could also have unwarranted side effects which could limit its efficacy. Governments and regulatory authorities have limited levers to act on the producers of highly sophisticated deepfakes who operate without concern for the legal consequences. (Shirish & Komal, 2024)

There are only three potential levers by which to attempt to control the online dissemination of malicious content which is presumed to be the main threat posed by deepfakes:

1) the online service providers,
2) the online advertisers who fund and profit from malicious content, and
3) the individuals who receive and authenticate suspect online content.

Current Legal Frameworks

The law cannot reduce, manage, or regulate the risk of deepfakes. Information sharing company agreements or education identifying fraudulent text use cases to increase public or citizens' awareness can minimize risk. For instance, because the requisite technology exists and continues to evolve exponentially, laws aimed at criminalizing the use of deepfake technology are not a way forward. As risk increases when parties value the false reality, the maxim "caveat emptor" applies—let the buyer or custodian beware. ActionTypes of transactions with anonymous parties and types of transactions that intend for explicit performance-based values, such as self-executable smart contracts, or those confirmed by the tamper-evident, publicly verifiable agreement on the chain can reduce deepfake risks.

The industry's response has been to develop technology that can effectively identify and categorize deepfakes. What measures are various countries taking to control the use of this technology? Let's examine the approaches of a few countries.

China

In 2019, the Chinese government implemented legislation requiring individuals and entities to publicly disclose their use of deepfake technology in videos and other media. The rules also forbid the dissemination of deepfakes without a clear indication that the content has been artificially produced. Additionally, China has established regulations for deepfake providers, effective as of January 10, 2023, under the oversight of the Cyberspace Administration of China (CAC). (Portrait, A., 2023) These regulations impact providers and users of deepfake technology and outline processes for the entire lifecycle of the technology, from creation to distribution. The provisions mandate that companies and individuals using deep synthesis must obtain consent, verify identities, register records with the government, report illegal deepfakes, provide recourse mechanisms, include watermark disclaimers, and more. (Routledge. John, L. E. E. 2022).

Canada

Canada's approach to regulating deep counterfeiting involves a comprehensive three-pronged strategy focused on prevention, detection and response. The government aims to prevent the emergence and spread of deep counterfeiting by increasing public awareness and developing preventive technology. Canada invests in research and development of detection technologies to detect deep counterfeits. In response, the government is considering new legislation that would make it illegal to create or distribute deep fakes with malicious intent. In addition, current Canadian law already prohibits sharing intimate images without consent, and the language of the Canada Elections Act may also apply to the creation of deep fakes. Canada has taken preliminary steps to address the negative impact of deep rigging, including securing a 2019 election and creating a public registry of critical election incidents to investigate deep rigging. (Judge, E. F., & Korhani, A. M. 2021) (*Holly Ann et al.,* 2021)

EU

The European Union has taken a proactive stance in regulating deep counterfeiting and calls for more research to detect and prevent them, as well as legislation requiring clear labeling of artificially produced content. Artificial Intelligence Regulatory Framework, General Data Protection Regulation, Copyright System, E-Commerce Directive, Digital Services Act, Audiovisual Media Directive, Disinformation Code of Practice, Disinformation Action Plan and Democracy Action Plan. important European political guidelines. regulatory frameworks relating to counterfeiting. The EU has proposed legislation to force social media companies to remove deep fakes and other misinformation from their platforms. The EU code of conduct on disinformation, updated in June 2022, included penalties for offenders of up to 6 percent of global revenue. Originally introduced as a voluntary self-regulatory tool in 2018, the Code now supports the Digital Services Act. The Law on Digital Services, which entered into force in November 2022, improves the monitoring of digital platforms in case of various abuses. According to the proposed EU AI law, providers of deep fakes would have to comply with transparency and disclosure rules. (Gevaert, C. M. 2022). (Laux, J., et al., 2024)

South Korea

With its significant technological progress, South Korea was among the pioneers in investing in AI research and regulatory exploration. In January 2016, the South Korean government declared its intention to allocate 1 trillion won (approximately USD 750 million) to AI research over 5 years. In December 2019, South Korea unveiled its National Strategy for AI. In 2020, the country enacted a law criminalizing the dissemination of deepfakes that could potentially "cause harm to public interest," with violators facing penalties of up to five years in prison or fines reaching 50 million won (equivalent to around 43,000 USD). Advocates are pushing for South Korea to address digital pornography and sex crimes by implementing additional measures, such as education, civil remedies, and recourse. (Wang, S., & Kim, S., 2022)

United Kingdom

The British government has taken different measures to handle the danger of deepfakes. These incorporate giving reserves for inquire about on deepfake location innovations and collaborating with industry and scholarly teach to create viable strategies for distinguishing and tending to deepfakes. The UK has too apportioned assets to back inquire about and mindfulness campaigns, such as the Sufficient campaign, which points to address the destructive impacts of exact retribution or deepfake explicit entertainment. Whereas comprehensive enactment disallowing the creation or dispersion of malevolent deepfakes has not however been ordered, the government declared in November of final year that deepfake control would be included within the exceedingly expected Online Security Charge. This choice was made in reaction to police information uncovering that roughly 1 in 14 grown-ups in Britain and Ridges have been undermined with the dispersal of hint pictures. (2024)

United States

Although there are currently no federal regulations regarding deepfakes, a number of states have enacted legislation addressing their use, particularly with regard to deepfake pornography. California and Texas were the first states to pass such laws in 2019. California criminalized the distribution of deepfakes of political candidates within 60 days of an election through AB 730, which expired on 1 January 2023. Additionally, California passed AB 602, which prohibits the creation and distribution of pornographic deepfakes without consent. New York also enacted a deepfake law, S5959D, in 2021, imposing potential fines, jail time, and civil penalties for the unauthorized dissemination or publication of sexually explicit depictions of individuals. In 2019, Virginia passed § 18.2-386.2, which makes it illegal to create and distribute sexually explicit deepfakes, with certain exceptions for parodies and political commentary, as well as requiring the Attorney General to form a working group to further study deepfakes. (Helmus, T. C., 2022) (Patz, J., 2024)

At the government level, the DEEP FAKES Accountability Act introduced in 2019, points to compel deepfake makers to reveal their utilize, avoid the dissemination of deepfakes planning to misdirect watchers amid an decision or hurt an individual's notoriety, and force potential fines and detainment for violators. (Łabuz, 2023) The charge too calls for the foundation of a errand constrain inside the Office of Country Security to analyze and moderate the affect of deepfakes on national security, as well as expanded financing for investigate into identifying and relieving the hurt caused by deepfakes.

5. ETHICAL AND LEGAL CONSIDERATIONS

It is difficult to make a case for deepfakes given the level of ethical and societal concerns they have aroused. The more pressing question, however, is whether, and to what extent, legislatures can regulate this technology. (Esezoobo and Braimoh, 2024) (Patz, 2024) (Farouk and Fahmi, 2024) The rapid pace at which new technologies develop results in legislatures struggling to regulate societies. (Brown & Marsden, 2023) (Wyszomirska, 2023) (Vijayagopal et al., 2024) Given the complexity and constant change in digital technologies, predicting the development of all different aspects and enacting complete and comprehensive legislation to address the different risks and threats in the context of technology will be a significant challenge.

There are many existing laws that deal with digital media, impersonation, identity fraud, and consumer protection. These regulations, however, are fragmented and far from being enough to provide a comprehensive response to deepfakes or are simply not effectively enforced or are noted as maintaining limitations in practice. An overview of these is helpful, but these laws are limited in their clarity about the prohibitability and enforceability in cases of using one's own digital likeness as well as being unable to regulate to what extent people can be depicted using their likeness. In addition, such laws do not provide a comprehensive response to the violation of privacy (Wang et al., 2024) (Solove, 2024) The absence of such efficient laws means that those seeking to regulate or respond to the threat of deepfakes will need to consider alternative approaches to legal frameworks.

A proposed solution discusses framing deepfakes within private and public law, which invokes liability for harm as well as data protection. (Gupta, 2023) (Apolo and Michael, 2024) Placing liability on the technology companies would give litigation incentives to devise technology that will not cause substantial damage to individuals. The guidance, however, is fairly limited by being incapable of regulating, preventing, or trying to manage illicit products on small platforms other than using some unclear mandatory executive action promises. There is some debate about the enforceability of proposed pieces of regulation in combating deepfakes, with some suggesting that they would be exceedingly difficult to enforce. Regulating speech according to its relationship to the truth envisions a misuse of power leading to a culture of surveillance, self-censorship, and limiting freedom of expression, as well as various alternatives that can be used to address disinformation short of content bans. It is important to evaluate and discuss the feasibility of any potential solutions. (Vese, 2022) (Kozyreva et al.2023) As a result, it is recommended that more comprehensive solutions involving legal liability and enforcement should be considered.

Ethical Implications of Deepfake Technology

Deepfake technologies raise numerous ethical questions about what is real, whom we can trust, and how we define and experience reality. (Pawelec, 2024) (Mullen, 2022) An opaque market for counterfeit information that opportunists can exploit adds to the urgency of debating our societal norms. As synthetic media presents a person's face, body, or voice as representative of that person, a question of authenticity begins to emerge (Cardenuto et al., 2023). With synthetic media becoming as convincing in representation as a human, it is necessary to turn to the question of responsibility. (Riemer & Peter, 2024) (Al-kfairy et al., 2024)

The first case is the potential harm and reputational damage that may arise surrounding people's privacy. (Wong et al., 2023) (Roemmich et al., 2023) Discussions in these areas often turn to actions whereby activists seek to undermine the reputation of those who seek to undermine their privacy. Yet, while care must be taken in these technologies and their representation of individuals, it ought to be noted that demonstrating a leader or high-profile character acting in an explicit way is of societal and political importance (Arato & Cohen, 2022). However, the question turns to the ethics of the creators and distributors of deepfake content. In this, what we can see from research around non-consensual materials are the ethical responsibilities of those who create, distribute, and benefit from such content. Often these responsibilities are part of the legal process. In videos, generating consent is nuanced. So too with celebrity lookalikes as warped figures of parody, to develop opportunities for harmful misuse. It is a mockery of the face recognition system, but perhaps there is something more, something more dangerous about the political distortions of the self-image that society places upon the face. (Rothbart and Bere, 2024) (Coeckelbergh, 2024) (Hutson and Smith, 2024). Representation becomes reality and the debasement of the person.

Fundamental to our exploration of the ethical domain also centers around society's understanding of what a deepfake is. We have considered the legislation through consent and the protection of personal data, but so too are we entering territory where we also mislead and manipulate society. (Tuysuz and Kılıç, 2023) (Abdul Hussein & Bogren, 2023) (Li & Wan, 2023) (Alanazi et al., 2024) Thus, as we move forward, deepfakes must be aligned with public opinion. Yet as the line becomes blurred, we submit a profound ethical question: is truth always a moral default? Further, as a society, we must determine our tolerance for parody and satire, free speech, and political dissidence when merged in the digital age. (Feldman, 2024) (Assagaf, 2023) (Matamoros et al., 2023) None of what we have considered should violate current legislation as it stands. So the course of action is much as we have suggested. A multi-level regulatory body should come together to safeguard individual reputations but raises important questions about true consent and where law can or should lie in regulating content. It also raises important ethical questions such as those around the perceived morality of using celebrity images, data privacy, free speech, and lines regulating when humour becomes harmful. This in uncertain technological territory demands a broader ethical and social debate beyond compliance with existing regulations. An ethical and moral basis for content belongs at the core of any debate about safeguarding society.

These technologies seem to offer significant potential for doing societal harm as well, primarily by manipulating public audiences. Deepfakes have the capability of misleading their audience and significantly altering perceptions of that audience's reality. (Hancock and Bailenson, 2021) There is significant concern about the ability of deepfakes to be used to advance the "fake news" agenda. (Ahmed, 2023) The potential for a misinformed citizenry to impact democratic society is such that deepfakes of public officials can seriously upset the established systems that societies rely on for governance (Kamarck & West, 2024). An example shows the applicability of deepfakes and their threat to societal institutions: multiple incidents in the news where either video or audio content was manipulated deceptively, including an altered video clip of a public figure.

The ability of average computer users to be taken in by AI-based trickery that has been produced for nothing more than entertainment has implications for the current state of information and communication. Educators and technologists who think that fostering individual elites who are an exception to mass manipulation is the solution must reconsider. As manipulated video and audio content becomes ever more realistic and deeply available, more people may begin to see reality as composed of subjective truths. The danger of deepfakes is that if everyone can lose photo-skeptical inhibition, soon no one will have the discernment to figure out whether video content is authentic or not. (Verma, 2023) The move to embrace personalized responsibility approaches, similar to those typified by media that stubbornly insist that they already rigorously evaluate the quality of the news they report, would be an abandonment of everyday people who have inherently limited time and cognitive resources. Given that advancements in technology drive future discourse, a more suitable approach would be the maintenance and development of infrastructural protections to both improve distinction and slow the spread of misleading information.

A person's sense perception is assumed to offer a reasonable explanation for what is or isn't really occurring. Even a media-literate population that is vigilant about deepfake misinformation would not have a guarantee of true, as-it-happens news. (Shin, 2024) (Kumar, 2024) Though better-distributed awareness of deepfakes may assist in limiting harm, protection from deepfake content will also require more than improved public awareness and media literacy. The trustworthiness of the very sources that produce and report the news is a key element of the trustworthiness of a visual medium, and restoration of that will require individual intentions to change as well as more structural disincentives, particularly in the production and dissemination of deepfakes and deepfake information.

In addition to their hard legal implications, deepfakes can have soft emotional implications on their victims, invoking a sense of powerlessness, anxiety, and long-term trauma, and exacerbating a lack of trust in close relationships within the family or among colleagues, especially if the videos are damaging, indecent, or degrading. (Laas, 2023) To further complicate matters, it may not be legal to take down harmful deepfakes if the victim is subjected to humiliation or defamation, especially if they are considered public figures. More ubiquitously, the availability of deepfakes may further contribute to the promulgation of fake news and alter "evidence" in crimes. Similar anxieties about media credibility and the reliability of evidence could harken back to the "death of trust," eroding the public's confidence in media and their ability to recognize credible sources. Although current deepfake technology may more readily fool audiences than technical experts, viewers remain susceptible to manipulation by deepfakes, particularly if they are effectively "laundered" by special interests before being disseminated.

Advancements in deepfake technology raise several bioethical and legal concerns. The creation and distribution of deepfakes are not only unethical in themselves, but they can also have deep-reaching implications on people's real lives. Deepfakes can be used to create fake nude images or videos of celebrities or public figures, potentially damaging their reputations. It may make it hard to verify genuine videos or images that show them engaging in similar behaviors because it will be easier to believe that they are simply other deepfakes. Criminals can also use deepfake technology to create videos that show people committing crimes that they did not commit, leaving them vulnerable to legal action or prosecutions. (Mekkawi, 2023) Deepfakes are spreading dangerous conspiracy theories and harmful misinformation, which is a public health issue.

CONCLUSION AND FUTURE OUTLOOK

Deepfake technology is a small part of AI (complex data-driven, combinatorial, and iterative scientific computing); AI from recent decades has been part of a disruptive economy. The stakes and the time axis for deepfakes are remarkably longer than for examples like the first-generation 'internet bubbles' and it takes years until deepfakes could become a targeted threat. For this year and next year, an acceleration of public reviews of the existing art or key dependencies is most likely stimulated by ethical and economic aspects. These encourage investors to stay tuned to identify and exploit commercial opportunities in competitively remunerative industries.

The public and private sectors must be proactive, united, and agile to respond to the deepfake challenge, with an understanding that doing so is in the best interest of society and democracy. To legitimize the deepfakes defense effort, all organizations – whether they are technology, commercial, or government entities – can start by promoting this critical public awareness.

Deepfakes present complex and multifaceted challenges to the business community across a wide range of industries, demanding a comprehensive approach. Stakeholders must possess a crystal-clear understanding of the extent and implications of the deepfake threat, as it has the potential to wreak havoc on various aspects of the industry. They must develop a robust response strategy that can effectively mitigate the potential negative impacts associated with deepfakes. Additionally, in this unpredictably associated world, following the broadly shifted strategies for making and disseminating deepfakes is of most extreme significance. The consistent advancement of this field requires a proactive approach wherein makers, stage administrators, and person watchers all have common duties. By recognizing and grasping these obligations, and by remaining ahead of the potential dangers, organizations can way better secure themselves and their partners.

In addition to strong authentication, organizations should prioritize the deployment of advanced monitoring systems. These systems should be equipped with cutting-edge artificial intelligence (AI) algorithms that can analyze and detect deepfakes in real time. By continuously monitoring digital and physical spaces, these systems can swiftly identify any signs of deepfake presence and take immediate action to prevent further damage. By investing in AI-powered monitoring systems, organizations can effectively safeguard their environments from the harmful effects of deepfakes.

Collaboration and data sharing are vital in combating the deepfake danger. Organizations ought to effectively lock in with industry peers, specialists, and law requirement organizations to trade information, best hones, and bits of knowledge into rising patterns. By cultivating solid systems of bolster and collaboration, organizations can collectively create techniques to identify, anticipate, and moderate the dangers related with deepfakes. By sharing data and working together, partners can set up a joined together front against this common risk, businesses can build up a more flexible protection pose. In conclusion, deepfakes posture genuine dangers to organizations over different businesses.

To successfully address this risk, organizations ought to execute a comprehensive approach that incorporates progressed confirmation strategies, AI-powered observing frameworks, versatile security systems, and collaboration with industry peers. By doing so, organizations can explore the complex scene of deepfakes with strength and certainty, moderating the potential dangers and securing their computerized and physical spaces from hurt.

REFERENCES

Abdul Hussein, M. & Bogren, W. (2023). Social Media's Take on Deepfakes: Ethical Concerns in the Public Discourse. diva-portal.org

Ahmed, S. (2023). Navigating the maze: Deepfakes, cognitive ability, and social media news skepticism. New Media & Society. researchgate.net

Al-kfairy, M., Mustafa, D., Kshetri, N., Insiew, M., & Alfandi, O. (2024). Ethical Challenges and Solutions of Generative AI: An Interdisciplinary Perspective. Informatics. mdpi.com

Alanazi, S., Asif, S., & Moulitsas, I. (2024). Examining the societal impact and legislative requirements of deepfake technology: a comprehensive study. researchgate.net

Apolo, Y., & Michael, K. (2024). Beyond A Reasonable Doubt? Audiovisual Evidence, AI Manipulation, Deepfakes, and the Law. [HTML]. *IEEE Transactions on Technology and Society*, 5(2), 156–168. DOI: 10.1109/TTS.2024.3427816

Arato, A. & Cohen, J. L. (2022). Populism and civil society: The challenge to constitutional democracy. [HTML]

Assagaf, A. S. A. (2023). Legal analysis of freedom of expression and online humour in Indonesia. The European Journal of Humour Research. europeanjournalofhumour.org

Barber, A. (2023). Freedom of expression meets deepfakes. Synthese. springer.com

Battista, D. (2024). Political communication in the age of artificial intelligence: an overview of deepfakes and their implications. Society Register. amu.edu.pl

Breen, D. C. (2021). Silent no more: How deepfakes will force courts to reconsider video admission standards. *J. High Tech. L.*, 21, 122.

Bronk, C. (2018). Blown to Bits. *Understanding Cybersecurity: Emerging Governance and Strategy*, 109.

Brown, I. & Marsden, C. T. (2023). Regulating code: Good governance and better regulation in the information age. [HTML]

Cardenuto, J. P., Yang, J., Padilha, R., Wan, R., Moreira, D., Li, H., ... & Rocha, A. (2023). The age of synthetic realities: Challenges and opportunities. APSIPA Transactions on Signal and Information Processing, 12(1). nowpublishers.com

Chambers, S. (2021). Truth, deliberative democracy, and the virtues of accuracy: Is fake news destroying the public sphere? *Political Studies*, 69(1), 147–163. DOI: 10.1177/0032321719890811

Coeckelbergh, M. (2024). Why AI Undermines Democracy and what to Do about it. [HTML]

Demir, I., & Ciftci, U. A. (2021, May). Where do deep fakes look? synthetic face detection via gaze tracking. In ACM symposium on eye tracking research and applications (pp. 1-11).

Duong, T. V., Vy, V. P. T., & Hung, T. N. K. (2024). Artificial intelligence in plastic surgery: advancements, applications, and future. Cosmetics. mdpi.com

Efthymiou, I. P., & Egleton, T. E. (2023). Artificial intelligence for sustainable smart cities. In *Handbook of research on applications of AI, Digital Twin, and Internet of Things for sustainable development* (pp. 1–11). IGI Global. DOI: 10.4018/978-1-6684-6821-0.ch001

Efthymiou-Egleton, I. P., Egleton, T. W. E., & Sidiropoulos, S. (2020). Artificial Intelligence (AI) in Politics: Should Political AI be Controlled? *International Journal of Innovative Science and Research Technology*, 5(2).

Emami, J. (2022). Social Media Victimization: Theories and Impacts of Cyberpunishment. [HTML]

Esezoobo, S. O., & Braimoh, J. J. (2024). Integrating Legal, Ethical, and Technological Strategies to Mitigate AI Deepfake Risks through Strategic Communication. Valley International Journal Digital Library, 914-928. vipublisher.com

Farouk, M. A., & Fahmi, B. M. (2024). Deepfakes and Media Integrity: Navigating the New Reality of Synthetic Content. Journal of Media and Interdisciplinary Studies, 3(9). ekb.eg

Feldman, O. (2024). Communicating political humor in the media: How culture influences satire and irony. [HTML]

Filimowicz, M. (2022). Deep fakes: algorithms and Society. [HTML]

Fletcher, G. G. S. (2020). Macroeconomic consequences of market manipulation. Law & Contemp. Probs.. duke.edu

Gambín, Á. F., Yazidi, A., Vasilakos, A., Haugerud, H., & Djenouri, Y. (2024). Deepfakes: Current and future trends. [springer.com]. *Artificial Intelligence Review*, 57(3), 64. DOI: 10.1007/s10462-023-10679-x

Gevaert, C. M. (2022). Explainable AI for earth observation: A review including societal and regulatory perspectives. *International Journal of Applied Earth Observation and Geoinformation*, 112, 102869. DOI: 10.1016/j.jag.2022.102869

Gioti, A. (2024). Advancements in Open Source Intelligence (OSINT) Techniques and the role of artificial intelligence in Cyber Threat Intelligence (CTI). unipi.gr

Gupta, K. (2023). *The Future of Deepfakes: Need for Regulation*. Nat'l LU Delhi Stud. LJ. [HTML]

Hao, H., Bartusiak, E. R., Güera, D., Mas Montserrat, D., Baireddy, S., Xiang, Z., . . . Delp, E. J. (2022). Deepfake detection using multiple data modalities. In Handbook of digital face manipulation and Detection: From DeepFakes to morphing attacks (pp. 235-254). Cham: Springer International Publishing. oapen.org DOI: 10.1007/978-3-030-87664-7_11

Helmus, T. C. (2022). Artificial intelligence, deepfakes, and disinformation. *RAND Corporation*, 1-24.

Hight, C. (2022). Deepfakes and documentary practice in an age of misinformation. [HTML]. *Continuum (Perth)*, 36(3), 393–410. DOI: 10.1080/10304312.2021.2003756

Hoek, S., Metselaar, S., Ploem, C., & Bak, M. (2024). Promising for patients or deeply disturbing? The ethical and legal aspects of deepfake therapy. Journal of Medical Ethics. bmj.com

Holly Ann Garnett and Michael Pal. Judge, E. F., & Korhani, A. M. (2021).

Hutson, J., & Smith, A. (2024). AI Satire and Digital Dystopia: The Dor Brothers Crafting Imperfection and Political Commentary in Contemporary Video Art. ISRG Journal of Arts, Humanities and Social Sciences, 2(5). lindenwood.edu

Ienca, M. (2023). On Artificial Intelligence and Manipulation. Topoi. springer.com

Jin, X., Zhang, Z., Gao, B., Gao, S., Zhou, W., Yu, N., & Wang, G. (2023). Assessing the perceived credibility of deepfakes: The impact of system-generated cues and video characteristics. [HTML]. *New Media & Society*, ●●●, 14614448231199664. DOI: 10.1177/14614448231199664

Judge, E. F., & Korhani, A. M. (2021). *A Moderate Proposal for a Digital Right of Reply for Election-Related Digital Replicas: Deepfakes*. Disinformation, and Elections.

Juefei-Xu, F., Wang, R., Huang, Y., Guo, Q., Ma, L., & Liu, Y. (2022). Countering malicious deepfakes: Survey, battleground, and horizon. [springer.com]. *International Journal of Computer Vision*, 130(7), 1678–1734. DOI: 10.1007/s11263-022-01606-8 PMID: 35528632

Kamarck, E. & West, D. M. (2024). Lies that Kill: A Citizen's Guide to Disinformation. [HTML]

Khoo, B., Phan, R. C. W., & Lim, C. H. (2022). Deepfake attribution: On the source identification of artificially generated images. [HTML]. *Wiley Interdisciplinary Reviews. Data Mining and Knowledge Discovery*, 12(3), e1438. DOI: 10.1002/widm.1438

Kopecky, S. (2024). Challenges of Deepfakes. *Science and Information Conference*. [HTML]

Kozyreva, A., Herzog, S. M., Lewandowsky, S., Hertwig, R., Lorenz-Spreen, P., Leiser, M., & Reifler, J. (2023). Resolving content moderation dilemmas between free speech and harmful misinformation. [pnas.org]. *Proceedings of the National Academy of Sciences of the United States of America*, 120(7), e2210666120. DOI: 10.1073/pnas.2210666120 PMID: 36749721

Kumar, A. (2024). Submission of Written Evidence to the House of Lords Communications and Digital Committee Inquiry on The Future of News: Impartiality, Trust, and Technology. gold.ac.uk

Laas, O. (2023). Deepfakes and trust in technology. [HTML]. *Synthese*, 202(5), 132. DOI: 10.1007/s11229-023-04363-4

Łabuz, M. (2023). Regulating deep fakes in the artificial intelligence act. Applied Cybersecurity & Internet Governance. acigjournal.com

Langmia, K. (2023). Black Communication in the Age of Disinformation: DeepFakes and Synthetic Media. [HTML]

Lankes, R. (2023). Corrosive AI: Emerging Effects of the Use of Generative AI on Political Trust. corrosiveai.com

Laux, J., Wachter, S., & Mittelstadt, B. (2024). Trustworthy artificial intelligence and the European Union AI act: On the conflation of trustworthiness and acceptability of risk. *Regulation & Governance*, 18(1), 3–32. DOI: 10.1111/rego.12512 PMID: 38435808

Li, M., & Wan, Y. (2023). Norms or fun? The influence of ethical concerns and perceived enjoyment on the regulation of deepfake information. [HTML]. *Internet Research*, 33(5), 1750–1773. DOI: 10.1108/INTR-07-2022-0561

Lyu, S. (2024). DeepFake the menace: mitigating the negative impacts of AI-generated content. Organizational Cybersecurity Journal: Practice, Process and People. emerald.com

Malik, S., Surbhi, A., & Roy, D. (2024). *Blurring boundaries between truth and illusion: Analysis of human rights and regulatory concerns arising from abuse of deepfake technology*. AIP Conference Proceedings. [HTML]

Masood, M., Nawaz, M., Malik, K. M., Javed, A., Irtaza, A., & Malik, H. (2023). Deepfakes generation and detection: State-of-the-art, open challenges, counter-measures, and way forward. [PDF]. *Applied Intelligence*, 53(4), 3974–4026. DOI: 10.1007/s10489-022-03766-z

Matamoros Fernandez, A., Bartolo, L., & Troynar, L. (2023). Humour as an on-line safety issue: Exploring solutions to help platforms better address this form of expression. *Internet Policy Review*, 12(1). Advance online publication. qut.edu.au. DOI: 10.14763/2023.1.1677

Mekkawi, M. H. (2023). The challenges of Digital Evidence usage in Deepfake Crimes Era. Journal of Law and Emerging Technologies. jolets.org

Momeni, M. (2024). Artificial Intelligence and Political Deepfakes: Shaping Citizen Perceptions Through Misinformation. Journal of Creative Communications. sagepub.com

Mullen, M. (2022). A new reality: deepfake technology and the world around us. Mitchell Hamline L. Rev.. mitchellhamline.edu

Mustak, M., Salminen, J., Mäntymäki, M., Rahman, A., & Dwivedi, Y. K. (2023). Deepfakes: Deceptions, mitigations, and opportunities. [sciencedirect.com]. *Journal of Business Research*, 154, 113368. DOI: 10.1016/j.jbusres.2022.113368

Navarro Martínez, O., Fernández-García, D., Cuartero Monteagudo, N., & Forero-Rincón, O. (2024). Possible Health Benefits and Risks of DeepFake Videos: A Qualitative Study in Nursing Students. [mdpi.com]. *Nursing Reports*, 14(4), 2746–2757. DOI: 10.3390/nursrep14040203 PMID: 39449440

Pastor Galindo, J. (2023). Opportunities, risks and applications of open source Intelligence in cybersecurity and cyberdefence. Proyecto de investigación. um.es

Patz, J. (2024). The Dual Nature of Deepfakes: An Analysis of the Deepfake Discourse in the USA: Benefits, Threats, Challenges, and Solutions. utwente.nl

Pawelec, M. (2022). Deepfakes and democracy (theory): How synthetic audio-visual media for disinformation and hate speech threaten core democratic functions. Digital society. springer.com

Portrait, A. (2023). The Cyberspace Administration of China. *The Emergence of China's Smart State*, 9.

Qureshi, J., & Khan, S. (2024). Artificial Intelligence (AI) Deepfakes in Healthcare Systems: A Double-Edged Sword? Balancing Opportunities and Navigating Risks. *preprints*.org

Riemer, K. & Peter, S. (2024). Conceptualizing generative AI as style engines: Application archetypes and implications. International Journal of Information Management. sciencedirect.com

Roemmich, K., Schaub, F., & Andalibi, N. (2023, April). Emotion AI at work: Implications for workplace surveillance, emotional labor, and emotional privacy. In Proceedings of the 2023 CHI Conference on Human Factors in Computing Systems (pp. 1-20). acm.org DOI: 10.1145/3544548.3580950

Rothbart, D., & Bere, M. (2024). Political narcissism of right-wing extremists: Understanding aggression of the proud boys. [HTML]. *Peace and Conflict*. Advance online publication. DOI: 10.1037/pac0000759

Routledge John, L. E. E. (2022). Cyberspace Governance in China.

Samuel-Okon, A. D., Akinola, O. I., Olaniyi, O. O., Olateju, O. O., & Ajayi, S. A. (2024). Assessing the Effectiveness of Network Security Tools in Mitigating the Impact of Deepfakes AI on Public Trust in Media. Archives of Current Research International, 24(6), 355-375. manu2sent.com

Sareen, M. (2022). *Threats and challenges by DeepFake technology*. DeepFakes. [HTML] DOI: 10.1201/9781003231493-8

Schiff, K. J., Schiff, D. S., & Bueno, N. (2023). The Liar's Dividend: The Impact of Deepfakes and Fake News on Trust in Political Discourse. osf.io

Sharma, D. K., Singh, B., Agarwal, S., Garg, L., Kim, C., & Jung, K. H. (2023). A survey of detection and mitigation for fake images on social media platforms. *Applied Sciences (Basel, Switzerland)*, 13(19), 10980. DOI: 10.3390/app131910980

Shin, D. (2024). Conclusion: Misinformation and AI—How Algorithms Generate and Manipulate Misinformation. In Artificial Misinformation: Exploring Human-Algorithm Interaction Online (pp. 259-277). Cham: Springer Nature Switzerland. [HTML]

Shirish, A. & Komal, S. (2024). A socio-legal enquiry on deepfakes. California Western International Law Journal. hal.science

Sinnreich, A., & Gilbert, J. (2024). *The Secret Life of Data: Navigating Hype and Uncertainty in the Age of Algorithmic Surveillance*. MIT Press. DOI: 10.7551/mitpress/14040.001.0001

Sippy, T., Enock, F., Bright, J., & Margetts, H. Z. (2024). Behind the Deepfake: 8% Create; 90% Concerned. Surveying public exposure to and perceptions of deepfakes in the UK. *arXiv preprint arXiv:2407.05529.*

Solove, D. J. (2024). Murky consent: an approach to the fictions of consent in privacy law. BUL Rev.. bu.edu

Tuysuz, M. K., & Kılıç, A. (2023). Analyzing the Legal and Ethical Considerations of Deepfake Technology. [journalisslp.com]. *Interdisciplinary Studies in Society, Law, and Politics*, 2(2), 4–10. DOI: 10.61838/kman.isslp.2.2.2

Vâlsan, C., Druică, E., & Eisenstat, E. (2022). On Deep-Fake Stock Prices and Why Investor Behavior Might Not Matter. Algorithms. mdpi.com

Veerasamy, N., & Pieterse, H. (2022, March). Rising above misinformation and deepfakes. In International Conference on Cyber Warfare and Security (Vol. 17, No. 1, pp. 340-348). academic-conferences.org DOI: 10.34190/iccws.17.1.25

Verma, N. (2023). Deepfake technology and the future of public trust in video. utexas.edu

Vese, D. (2022). Governing fake news: the regulation of social media and the right to freedom of expression in the era of emergency. European Journal of Risk Regulation. researchgate.net

Vijayagopal, P., Jain, B., & Ayinippully Viswanathan, S. (2024). Regulations and Fintech: A Comparative Study of the Developed and Developing Countries. [HTML]. *Journal of Risk and Financial Management*, 17(8), 324. DOI: 10.3390/jrfm17080324

Wang, S., & Kim, S. (2022). How do people feel about deepfake videos of K-pop idols?.   , *47*(2), 375-386.

Wang, S., & Kim, S. (2022). Users' emotional and behavioral responses to deepfake videos of K-pop idols. *Computers in Human Behavior*, 134, 107305. DOI: 10.1016/j. chb.2022.107305

Wang, X., Wu, Y. C., Zhou, M., & Fu, H. (2024). Beyond surveillance: privacy, ethics, and regulations in face recognition technology. Frontiers in big data. frontiersin.org

Westerlund, M. (2019). The emergence of deepfake technology: A review. *Technology Innovation Management Review*, 9(11), 39–52. DOI: 10.22215/timreview/1282

Whittaker, L., Letheren, K., & Mulcahy, R. (2021). The rise of deepfakes: A conceptual framework and research agenda for marketing. *Australasian Marketing Journal*, 29(3), 204–214. qut.edu.au. DOI: 10.1177/1839334921999479

Wong, R. Y., Chong, A., & Aspegren, R. C. (2023). Privacy Legislation as Business Risks: How GDPR and CCPA are Represented in Technology Companies' Investment Risk Disclosures. Proceedings of the ACM on Human-Computer Interaction, 7(CSCW1), 1-26. acm.org

Wyszomirska, M. (2023). Technological Developments as a New Challenge for Modern Legislation. Safety & Fire Technology. cyberleninka.ru

Xu, S., Wang, J., Shou, W., Ngo, T., Sadick, A. M., & Wang, X. (2021). Computer vision techniques in construction: A critical review. [HTML]. *Archives of Computational Methods in Engineering*, 28(5), 3383–3397. DOI: 10.1007/s11831-020-09504-3

Chapter 3
Assessing the Believability of Deepfake Ads in the Indian Market

Vishnu Achutha Menon
https://orcid.org/0000-0003-4028-3685
Institute for Educational and Developmental Studies, India

Anish Gupta
University of Delhi, India

ABSTRACT

Deepfake technology, utilizing artificial intelligence and machine learning, has revolutionized digital content creation by producing hyper-realistic media that can deceive viewers into believing fabricated scenarios. In the realm of advertising, deepfakes enable marketers to leverage familiar faces—be they celebrities, influencers, or ordinary individuals—to endorse products convincingly. This chapter explores the impact of deepfake advertisements on young adults in India, a digitally engaged demographic susceptible to such technological influences. Despite their potential to captivate and persuade, these advertisements raise ethical concerns regarding trust and authenticity. This study investigates the relationship between deepfake believability and cognitive responses, confusion levels, and persuasiveness among young adults, highlighting the implications for consumer behavior and regulatory frameworks.

DOI: 10.4018/979-8-3693-6890-9.ch003

INTRODUCTION

Deepfake advertisements use artificial intelligence and machine learning techniques to create highly realistic and convincing digital content that mimics real people. These technologies can manipulate images, videos, and audio to make it appear as though someone is saying or doing something they never did. In the context of advertising, deepfakes can feature celebrities, influencers, or even ordinary individuals endorsing products or services in ways that seem authentic but are entirely fabricated. The technology behind deepfakes leverages deep learning algorithms, particularly Generative Adversarial Networks (GANs), to produce synthetic media that is nearly indistinguishable from real footage. This can be used to create compelling advertisements that capture attention, generate buzz, and potentially manipulate consumer behavior. In India, the young adult population is particularly susceptible to the influence of deepfake advertisements due to their high levels of digital engagement and social media use. Young adults, who are typically more tech-savvy and spend a significant amount of time online, are prime targets for marketers employing deepfake technology. These advertisements can be more persuasive and engaging, leveraging popular celebrities or influencers to enhance their appeal. However, the use of deepfakes in advertising raises ethical concerns, especially regarding trust and authenticity. In a market like India, where digital literacy is rapidly growing but still varies widely, the ability to discern deepfake content from real media can be challenging for many. This vulnerability can lead to misinformation, manipulation, and potential harm, as consumers might make purchasing decisions based on misleading endorsements. Addressing these issues requires increased awareness, regulation, and the development of technologies to detect and mitigate the impact of deepfakes in the advertising industry. The objective of this book chapter is to explore the believability of the deepfakes in advertisements, focusing on cognitive, confusion and persuasiveness of the advertisements among young adult population.

REVIEW OF LITERATURE

Deepfakes, sophisticated AI-generated fake media, have become a significant concern due to their potential to deceive and manipulate public perception. This manipulation has a direct correlation with social media news skepticism, where individuals become increasingly wary of the information presented to them (Ahmed, 2023b). The intricate nature of deepfakes challenges human cognitive abilities, resulting in a complex interplay between deception, skepticism, and trust. The relationship between deepfakes exposure and social media news skepticism is well-documented. As individuals encounter more deepfakes, their trust in social media news diminishes. This skepticism is fueled by the frequent exposure to manipulated content, leading to a heightened awareness and critical attitude toward online news sources. During the 2020 U.S. Presidential Election, deepfake videos of political figures circulated widely, causing viewers to question the authenticity of all political content on social media platforms. This skepticism is not limited to one domain; it extends to various news topics, making it challenging for genuine information to be accepted without doubt. Craig et al. (2012) found that the human brain exhibits disproportionately greater activity when processing moderately deceptive claims compared to those that are either highly believable or highly deceptive. This suggests that moderate deception requires more cognitive resources to discern, likely because it falls within a grey area where the brain must engage in more detailed analysis to determine authenticity. A deepfake video that subtly alters a public figure's speech to include slightly misleading information can be more cognitively taxing for viewers to evaluate than a blatantly obvious fake or an entirely believable clip.

Individuals are more inclined to share video deepfakes than other forms, such as cheapfakes or audio deepfakes (Ahmed & Chua, 2023). Video deepfakes, which combine both visual and auditory elements, are often more engaging and convincing, leading to higher shareability. An example of this can be seen in the viral spread of a deepfake video featuring a celebrity endorsing a product. The visual and auditory coherence of such videos makes them more compelling and thus more likely to be shared compared to an audio-only deepfake or a poorly edited video (cheapfake). Karpinska-Krakowiak and Eisend (2024) argue that simple disclosures, such as a brief statement indicating the content is a deepfake, do not significantly reduce the perceived realism of the portrayal. This ineffectiveness can be attributed to the cognitive biases and heuristics that viewers rely on. Even if a deepfake video of a CEO making a controversial statement comes with a disclaimer, viewers may still perceive the video as somewhat real due to the lifelike depiction and their pre-existing beliefs about the CEO's character. Human cognition and perception are often insufficient to detect synthetic media, especially for those untrained or inexperienced in identifying such content (Preu et al., 2022). This insufficiency means that even with growing awareness about deepfakes, many people cannot distinguish between real and fake media. A deepfake of a well-known newscaster delivering false information can be indistinguishable from the real person for most viewers, leading to the spread of misinformation. The critical issues surrounding deepfakes, from their impact on social media news skepticism to the challenges in human cognitive detection, highlight the need for advanced detection technologies and better public awareness. As deepfakes become more sophisticated, so must the strategies to combat their deceptive influence on society.

Deepfakes, AI-generated synthetic media that convincingly mimic real individuals, have become a powerful tool for media manipulation, raising numerous concerns about their impact on perception, trust, and media literacy. Individuals tend to believe that deepfakes have a greater influence on others than on themselves (Ahmed, 2023a). This phenomenon, known as the third-person effect, suggests that people perceive themselves as less susceptible to media manipulation while viewing others as more vulnerable. In a study where participants were shown a deepfake video of a politician making false statements, many believed that others would be more likely to be deceived by the video than they themselves would be. This perception can lead to underestimating personal vulnerability to deepfakes, making individuals less critical of the content they consume. The effectiveness of deepfakes in media manipulation lies in their realism (Nieweglowska et al., 2023). High-quality deepfakes can mimic facial expressions, voice, and mannerisms with remarkable accuracy, making it difficult for viewers to distinguish between real and fake. A deepfake video of a celebrity endorsing a product can appear so authentic that even fans familiar with the celebrity's appearance and voice may be unable to detect the deception. This realism enhances the persuasive power of deepfakes, making them a potent tool for spreading misinformation.

People have a cognitive bias towards mistaking deepfakes for authentic videos (Köbis et al., 2021). This bias is partly due to the trust humans generally place in visual and auditory information. Viewers might accept a deepfake video of a well-known news anchor delivering false news as genuine because it conforms to their expectations of how the anchor appears and speaks. This bias underscores the challenge of combating deepfake-induced misinformation, as individuals are predisposed to believe what they see and hear. Non-traditional advertising practices, such as product placements or branded content, are often embedded within programs or editorial content (Buijzen, 2013). Deepfakes can enhance these practices by seamlessly integrating products or messages into videos featuring popular figures. A deepfake of a fitness influencer subtly promoting a particular brand of sportswear within their workout video can be more persuasive and less intrusive than traditional advertisements, leveraging the influencer's perceived endorsement to boost credibility and engagement.

Deepfakes contribute to a sense of generalized indeterminacy and cynicism (Vaccari & Chadwick, 2020). The widespread awareness of deepfake technology can lead to a pervasive skepticism towards all media, fostering a cynical attitude where people question the authenticity of even genuine content. After several deepfake scandals, viewers might start doubting the authenticity of all political speeches or news reports, leading to an erosion of trust in media institutions and a broader sense of uncertainty about what is real. Media literacy education has been shown to reduce the effects of disinformation messages (Hwang et al., 2021). By teaching individuals how to critically evaluate media content and recognize potential manipulation tactics, media literacy programs can mitigate the influence of deepfakes. Students who receive training in media literacy are better equipped to identify inconsistencies and signs of digital manipulation in videos, reducing their susceptibility to deepfake-induced misinformation. This education is crucial in building a more informed and resilient public capable of navigating the complexities of modern media landscapes. The intricate dynamics of deepfake perception, realism, and bias highlight the profound impact these synthetic media have on public trust and media consumption. As deepfakes become increasingly sophisticated, enhancing media literacy and developing advanced detection technologies are essential steps to mitigate their manipulative potential and preserve the integrity of information in the digital age.

The digital medium often leads to cognitive retreat, where readers may engage in less deep thinking and critical analysis compared to traditional reading (Gaillard et al., 2021). Shallow processing refers to the tendency to process information on a superficial level. When consuming news articles online, readers might skim through the content, focusing on headlines and key points without engaging in thorough analysis. This can make individuals more susceptible to believing deepfakes, as they may not critically evaluate the content. Overconfidence in one's ability to discern real from fake media is another issue associated with digital reading. People often overestimate their ability to detect deepfakes, which can lead to increased vulnerability to misinformation. Individuals might believe they can spot a deepfake video based on obvious visual cues, but modern deepfakes are often so sophisticated that these cues are not easily detectable without specialized knowledge.

The media meta-frame, which encompasses the broader context and narrative surrounding a piece of content, significantly influences audience response (Lee et al., 2021). A deepfake video presented within a sensationalist or conspiratorial meta-frame is likely to evoke stronger emotional reactions and increase its perceived credibility among viewers already inclined towards such narratives. The type of video also plays a crucial role. Informative or educational deepfakes might be scrutinized more critically than entertainment-oriented deepfakes. A deepfake video of a political figure giving a speech is likely to be examined more carefully than a deepfake of a celebrity in a comedic skit. The number of dislikes on a video can impact audience perception. Videos with a high number of dislikes might be perceived as less credible or trustworthy. However, this can also have a counterintuitive effect where some viewers, motivated by contrarian attitudes, might dismiss the dislikes and perceive the content as being unfairly targeted, thereby reinforcing their belief in the deepfake. Contrary to what might be expected, deepfakes are not necessarily more persuasive than textual disinformation (Hameleers et al., 2022). This can be attributed to the fact that textual information allows for more elaborate argumentation and can be more easily tailored to the reader's existing beliefs and biases. A well-crafted fake news article that aligns with the reader's political views might be more persuasive than a deepfake video that could be dismissed as visually manipulated. Simple priming, which involves providing users with basic information about deepfakes before exposure, significantly increases their ability to recognize such media (Iacobucci et al., 2021). If viewers are informed about common deepfake techniques and told to look for specific inconsistencies in facial movements or audio synchronization, they are more likely to identify deepfakes. This suggests that awareness and education can play a crucial role in mitigating the impact of deepfake technology. The complex interplay of cognitive processing, media dynamics, and user education underscores the challenge of addressing deepfake-induced misinformation. While digital media consumption habits can make individuals more susceptible to deepfakes, awareness and education strategies, such as priming, can enhance their ability to recognize and critically evaluate synthetic media. As deepfake technology evolves, ongoing research and adaptive countermeasures will be essential in safeguarding information integrity.

Research by Andreadakis (2020) indicates no significant linear relationship between the believability of deepfake advertisements and the cognitive senses of young adults. This suggests that factors beyond basic cognitive processing influence the believability of deepfake ads for this demographic. Young adults may rely more on social cues, contextual factors, or emotional responses when evaluating deepfake content. This implies that the success of deepfake advertisements in convincing young adults does not straightforwardly depend on how they cognitively process the information. Deepfake video advertisements are beneficial for designers, developers, marketing managers, and other stakeholders in the hotel industry (Sivathanu & Pillai, 2023). These advertisements can create highly personalized and engaging marketing content, showcasing hotel facilities and services in a captivating manner. A deepfake ad could feature a virtual tour of a hotel, presented by a well-known travel influencer, making the advertisement more appealing and credible to potential guests. This innovative approach allows stakeholders to leverage deepfakes to enhance customer engagement and marketing effectiveness. Younger participants are more likely to find deepfakes humorous (Napshin et al., 2024). This perception can influence how young adults interact with and share deepfake content. A deepfake video featuring a popular celebrity in a comedic scenario might be widely shared among younger audiences, not necessarily because they believe it to be real, but because they find it entertaining. This humorous engagement can drive virality and increase the reach of deepfake advertisements, albeit in a different context than originally intended by marketers. Deepfakes and their explanation within VR environments introduce new dimensions of interaction and perception (Kunnumpurath et al., 2024). In VR, deepfakes can be used to create immersive and interactive experiences, where users can engage with highly realistic simulations of people or scenarios.

Research by Ternovski et al. (2021) shows that warnings about deepfakes in political videos increase disbelief among young adults but do not improve their ability to discern real from fake content. For example, when viewers are alerted that a political video might be a deepfake, they become more skeptical of its content. However, this skepticism does not necessarily translate into better discernment or accurate identification of deepfakes. This finding suggests that while warnings can raise awareness, they might not be sufficient to enhance critical evaluation skills, highlighting the need for more comprehensive media literacy education. Adapted ads, which are tailored to specific audiences, are slightly more persuasive and better liked than unadapted ads (Hornikx & O'Keefe, 2009). An advertisement for a smartphone that highlights features particularly appealing to tech-savvy young adults is likely to be more effective than a generic ad. This tailoring can enhance relatability and relevance, making the ad more engaging and persuasive. Participants often feel they have less autonomy in controlling their exposure to newsfeed ads (Youn & Kim, 2019). This perceived lack of control can lead to negative reactions towards advertisements and the platforms displaying them. Young adults scrolling through their social media feeds may feel bombarded by ads they did not choose to see, which can foster resentment and reduce the effectiveness of the advertisements. A single exposure to a commercial with materialistic cues does not significantly increase materialism (Cartwright & Opree, 2016). This indicates that materialistic values are likely shaped by more sustained and repeated exposures rather than one-time interactions. Seeing an ad that promotes luxury goods once is unlikely to alter a person's materialistic values, whereas consistent exposure over time might have a more substantial impact.

The presence of a fake news flag increases cognitive activity and the time users spend considering the headline (Moravec et al., 2018). When users see a fake news flag, they are prompted to think more critically about the content, leading to deeper processing and evaluation. A news article flagged as potentially fake might cause readers to scrutinize the information more closely and seek additional sources to verify its authenticity. The effects of alcohol advertising on the drinking intentions of those aged 15 to 20 years are mediated by their cognitive responses to the advertising messages and the positive expectancies they form (Fleming et al., 2004). An ad portraying alcohol consumption as fun and socially rewarding can shape young viewers' positive expectations about drinking, thereby increasing their intention to drink. This highlights the importance of the cognitive and emotional processes triggered by advertising in shaping behaviors.

Pennycook and Rand (2017) found that the tendency to ascribe profundity to randomly generated sentences correlate positively with perceptions of fake news accuracy. This indicates that individuals who are more likely to find deep meaning in nonsensical statements are also more prone to believe fake news. A person who finds deep significance in a randomly generated philosophical quote may also be more susceptible to believing a fake news story that appears profound or insightful. This cognitive bias suggests that people who are less discerning about the source or content of information are more vulnerable to misinformation. Swartz (1984) found that the presence of one source characteristic does not impact the other source characteristic. This means that the credibility or trustworthiness of a source is not necessarily influenced by other attributes of the source, such as expertise or attractiveness. A news anchor's professional appearance does not necessarily affect their perceived honesty or reliability. This finding underscores the complexity of source evaluation, where different characteristics are independently assessed by the audience.

Smith and Offodile (2019) found no significant linear relationship between the believability of deepfake advertisements and the cognitive senses of the young adult population. This suggests that factors beyond cognitive evaluation influence the perceived believability of deepfake ads. Emotional engagement, prior beliefs, and social context may play more significant roles in determining whether young adults believe a deepfake advertisement. Allen (2023) found that almost two-thirds of study participants were unable to correctly identify a sequence of just four videos as either genuine or deepfake. This high error rate highlights the difficulty individuals face in distinguishing real content from synthetic media, emphasizing the sophisticated nature of deepfake technology. Viewers might struggle to identify a deepfake video of a celebrity due to the high level of detail and realism in the deepfake, leading to widespread misinformation.

The study by Miksa & Hodgson (2021) found that their research refuted the initial hypothesis and other studies conducted in the field of persuasion knowledge. This indicates that the mechanisms and effectiveness of persuasion strategies may not be as straightforward or universally applicable as previously thought. While some studies may suggest that transparency about the persuasive intent of advertisements can reduce their effectiveness, Miksa & Hodgson's findings imply that this might not always hold true, suggesting a need for more nuanced understandings of how persuasion knowledge operates across different contexts and demographics. Sanghvi & Rai (2015) found no significant correlation between internet addiction and emotional intelligence among young adults in Bangalore. This suggests that internet addiction does not necessarily impair or enhance one's ability to perceive, control, and evaluate emotions. A young adult who spends excessive time online might still possess high emotional intelligence, contrary to concerns that internet addiction inherently diminishes emotional capabilities. Spasova (2023) found that persuasive strategies such as scarcity and social proof effectively influence youths. These strategies leverage psychological principles to drive behavior. An advertisement that creates a sense of urgency by highlighting limited availability (scarcity) or showcases testimonials from peers (social proof) can significantly impact young adults' decision-making. This is crucial for marketers aiming to target this demographic with tailored strategies that resonate with their cognitive and emotional responses. Tal-Or (2007) found the absence of third-person perception in children compared to older people unusual. Third-person perception refers to the tendency to believe that others are more affected by media messages than oneself. The absence of this perception in children suggests they might not yet have developed the cognitive bias that makes them think others are more susceptible to influence. Children might believe that a persuasive message affects everyone, including themselves, equally, while older individuals might believe that they are less influenced than others.

Allen et al. (2022) found that almost two-thirds of study participants were unable to correctly identify a sequence of just four videos as either genuine or deepfake. This highlights the sophistication of deepfake technology and the challenge it poses for viewers. The high error rate indicates that deepfakes can easily deceive the average person, underlining the need for better detection tools and educational initiatives to improve media literacy. Participants often overestimate their ability to detect deepfakes at the individual video level (Somoray & Miller, 2023). This overconfidence can lead to a false sense of security, making individuals more susceptible to deepfake content. Someone might confidently share a deepfake video, believing they have correctly identified it as genuine, thereby contributing to the spread of misinformation. Deepfake news is more credible and has higher viral behavioral intention among individuals with congruent issue attitudes (Shin & Lee, 2022). This means that people are more likely to believe and share deepfake news that aligns with their preexisting beliefs and opinions. A politically biased deepfake video is more likely to be accepted and propagated by individuals who already hold similar political views, amplifying echo chambers and misinformation spread. Vaccari & Chadwick (2020) found no significant linear relationship between the believability of deepfake advertisements and the cognitive senses of the young adult population. This suggests that factors other than cognitive evaluation, such as emotional engagement, social influence, and contextual relevance, play a more significant role in how young adults perceive the believability of deepfake advertisements. A deepfake ad that evokes strong emotions or is endorsed by peers might be more convincing than one that relies solely on rational appeal.

Deepfakes present both threats and opportunities for advertisers (Kietzmann et al., 2021). On one hand, deepfakes can enhance creative advertising by producing highly personalized and engaging content. Sports brand could use deepfake technology to place a consumer's face on an athlete's body in an ad, creating a unique and memorable experience. This can significantly boost engagement and brand recall. However, the threats are substantial. Deepfakes can be used to create misleading advertisements, potentially damaging a brand's reputation and consumer trust. A deepfake ad might falsely show a celebrity endorsing a product they have never used, leading to legal and ethical concerns. This misuse can erode public trust not only in the brand but in advertising as a whole, highlighting the need for stringent regulations and ethical guidelines in the use of deepfakes in marketing. Product information, social role/image, being good for the economy, not being materialistic, and truthfulness significantly affect Neoteric-inheritors' attitudes towards advertising (Ting et al., 2015). Neoteric-inheritors, typically younger and more socially conscious consumers, are influenced by ads that provide clear and accurate product information and portray positive social roles or images. They prefer brands that contribute positively to the economy and society and reject materialistic values. For instance, advertisements by companies like Patagonia that emphasize sustainability and social responsibility resonate well with these consumers.

Restricting televised e-cigarette advertising may reduce e-cigarette initiation among youth (Duke et al., 2016). Research indicates that exposure to e-cigarette ads on television can significantly influence young people's perceptions and behaviors, making them more likely to try e-cigarettes. A study found that youth exposed to televised e-cigarette ads were more likely to initiate e-cigarette use compared to those who were not exposed. This underscores the importance of regulating the advertisement of potentially harmful products to protect vulnerable populations like youth from developing unhealthy habits. Deepfakes may have far-reaching societal implications that go beyond deception (Weikmann et al., 2024). While the potential for deception is a primary concern, the broader societal impacts of deepfakes include the erosion of trust in media and information. Deepfakes could be used to create fake news or manipulate political speeches, undermining democratic processes and trust in public institutions. Deepfakes can contribute to the spread of misinformation and cyberbullying, where individuals are targeted with fabricated videos that can harm their personal and professional lives.

Hypothesis

1. There is no significant linear relationship between believability of the deepfake advertisement and cognitive senses of the young adult population.
2. There is no significant linear relationship between believability of the deepfake advertisement and confusion in the young adult population.
3. There is no significant linear relationship between believability of the deepfake advertisement and persuasiveness in the young adult population.

Methodology

The study focuses on the believability of deepfakes in advertisements as the independent variable. The believability scale has been well-validated in previous research, showing high reliability with alphas ranging from .86 to .97 (Beltramini, 1988). To measure the cognitive response, the study utilized a reliable scale with previously reported alphas between .76 and .89, indicating consistent measurement across different studies (Homer, 1995). The confusion induced by the advertisements was assessed using a scale with alphas around .74, ensuring the reliability of the measurement (Lastovicka, 1983). For the persuasiveness of the advertisements, a scale with an alpha of .88 was employed, demonstrating a high level of reliability (Chang, 2003). The survey was conducted in Karnataka from September 2023 to January 2024, involving 515 respondents. Stratified random sampling was used to ensure a representative sample of the young adult population. Data analysis began with correlation analysis to examine the relationships between variables, followed by regression analysis to determine the impact of the believability of deepfake advertisements on cognitive response, confusion, and persuasiveness.

Results

Table 1. Descriptive statistics and correlation matrix

Variable	Mean	SD	(1)	(2)	(3)	(4)
Believability	35.5767	3.46739	1	.843**	.683**	.664**
Cognitive	23.9883	3.33532		1	.801**	.688**
Confusion	13.6835	2.19719			1	.599**
Persuasiveness of the Ad	10.0757	1.89205				1

The descriptive statistics and correlation matrix reveal key insights into the relationships among Believability (BL), Cognitive (CG) responses, Confusion (CF), and Persuasiveness of the Ad (PA) (Table 1). The high mean and relatively low standard deviation of Believability (M=35.5767, SD=3.46739) suggest that participants generally found the advertisements to be believable, with little variation in their responses. Cognitive responses had a moderate mean (M=23.9883, SD=3.33532), indicating moderate cognitive engagement with some variability. Confusion had a lower mean (M=13.6835, SD=2.19719), suggesting participants experienced relatively low confusion, with consistent responses. Persuasiveness of the Ad had a moderate mean (M=10.0757, SD=1.89205), with little variation. The correlation matrix shows significant positive relationships among the variables. Believability strongly correlates with Cognitive (r=.843**), Confusion (r=.683**), and Persuasiveness (r=.664**), indicating that higher believability is associated with stronger cognitive engagement, more confusion, and greater persuasiveness. Cognitive responses also strongly correlate with Confusion (r=.801**) and Persuasiveness (r=.688**), suggesting that as participants engage more cognitively, they also experience more confusion and find the ads more persuasive. Additionally, Confusion moderately correlates with Persuasiveness (r=.599**), indicating that higher confusion is somewhat linked to higher persuasiveness. These findings highlight the crucial role of Believability in shaping cognitive responses, confusion, and the persuasiveness of advertisements, suggesting that while increasing believability enhances engagement and persuasiveness, it may also introduce confusion that needs to be managed in ad design.

Table 2. Linear regression predicting believability from cognitive

Predictor	β	t	R^2	Adj. R^2	F	Sig.
Believability	.843	35.529	.711	.710	1262.334	<0.001

The linear regression analysis predicting Believability from Cognitive responses provides significant insights into their relationship (Table 2). The beta coefficient (β) for Believability is .843, indicating a strong positive relationship between Cognitive responses and Believability. This suggests that as Cognitive engagement increases, Believability also increases substantially. The t-value of 35.529 signifies that this relationship is statistically significant, and the very high F-value of 1262.334, with a significance level (Sig.) of less than 0.001, further confirms the robustness of this model. The R-squared (R^2) value is .711, meaning that approximately 71.1% of the variance in Believability can be explained by Cognitive responses. The adjusted R-squared (Adj. R^2) is very close at .710, indicating minimal shrinkage and reinforcing the model's strong explanatory power. These results underscore that Cognitive engagement is a significant predictor of Believability, explaining a substantial portion of its variance. This strong predictive power highlights the importance of cognitive processes in shaping how believable advertisements are perceived to be.

Table 3. Linear regression predicting believability from confusion

Predictor	β	t	R^2	Adj. R^2	F	Sig.
Believability	.683	21.200	.467	.466	449.455	<0.001

The linear regression analysis predicting Believability from Confusion provides important insights into their relationship (Table 3). The beta coefficient (β) for Believability is .683, indicating a strong positive relationship between Confusion and Believability. This suggests that as Confusion increases, Believability also increases notably. The t-value of 21.200 indicates that this relationship is statistically significant, and the high F-value of 449.455, with a significance level (Sig.) of less than 0.001, further supports the robustness of this model. The R-squared (R^2) value is .467, meaning that approximately 46.7% of the variance in Believability can be explained by Confusion. The adjusted R-squared (Adj. R^2) is very close at .466, indicating minimal shrinkage and reinforcing the model's strong explanatory power. These results show that Confusion is a significant predictor of Believability, explaining a considerable portion of its variance. This strong predictive power highlights the complex nature of how confusion can influence the perceived believability of advertisements.

Table 4. Linear regression predicting believability from persuasiveness of the ad

Predictor	β	t	R^2	Adj. R^2	F	Sig.
Believability	.664	20.120	.441	.440	404.826	<0.001

Table 4 presents the findings from a linear regression analysis aiming to predict Believability based on the Persuasiveness of the Ad. The beta coefficient (β) of .664 indicates a strong positive relationship between these variables, suggesting that higher perceived Persuasiveness of the Ad correlates with increased Believability. The high t-value of 20.120 confirms the statistical significance of this relationship, supported further by a substantial F-value of 404.826 ($p < 0.001$), indicating the robustness of the regression model. The R-squared (R^2) value of .441 indicates that approximately 44.1% of the variance in Believability can be explained by variations in the Persuasiveness of the Ad, a finding reinforced by the Adj. R-squared of .440, indicating minimal model shrinkage. These results underscore the critical role of perceived ad Persuasiveness in shaping Believability perceptions, highlighting its significant influence on how advertisements are perceived and evaluated by audiences.

DISCUSSION

Believability plays a pivotal role in influencing how audiences respond cognitively to advertisements, their levels of confusion, and the overall persuasiveness of the message conveyed. When advertisements are perceived as believable, viewers are more likely to engage deeply with the content, processing information in a way that aligns with their perception of truthfulness. This heightened engagement often enhances the overall persuasiveness of the advertisement, as viewers are more inclined to accept and trust the message being communicated. However, alongside these benefits, increased believability can also introduce complexities. The potential for confusion arises when viewers are presented with information that is perceived as credible but perhaps contradicts their existing beliefs or understanding. This cognitive dissonance can lead to confusion or uncertainty, challenging the effectiveness of the advertisement in delivering a clear and persuasive message. Therefore, while enhancing believability is crucial for capturing audience attention and trust, it becomes imperative for advertisers to manage potential confusion through thoughtful ad design and message alignment.

Effective ad design should strive to strike a balance where believability is maximized without compromising clarity and coherence. This involves meticulous crafting of messages that resonate with the target audience's values and knowledge, minimizing the likelihood of conflicting interpretations or misunderstandings. Strategies such as providing additional context, using clear and transparent communication, and aligning the advertisement's claims with verifiable evidence can help mitigate confusion while maintaining high levels of believability and persuasiveness. While believability serves as a cornerstone for effective advertising, its influence on cognitive responses, confusion levels, and persuasiveness underscores the nuanced challenges faced in ad creation.

The significant linear relationship observed between the believability of deepfake advertisements and cognitive engagement among young adults underscores the profound impact of realistic digital content on viewers' cognitive processes. Deepfake technology, designed to create highly convincing simulations of reality, effectively captures attention and prompts deep cognitive processing. As young adults perceive these advertisements as more believable, they are likely to invest greater mental effort in comprehending and interpreting the content. This heightened cognitive engagement not only influences how individuals process information but also shapes their overall receptiveness to the messages conveyed through deepfake advertisements.

The finding of a significant linear relationship between the believability of deepfake advertisements and confusion levels among young adults highlights a critical concern regarding the potential misinformation and uncertainty introduced by advanced digital manipulation. Deepfakes, by simulating realistic scenarios or individuals, blur the distinction between fact and fiction, leading viewers to experience heightened confusion about the authenticity of what they perceive. As young adults perceive deepfake content as more believable, they may struggle to discern between genuine information and fabricated content, potentially undermining their ability to make informed judgments and decisions based on accurate information.

The observed significant linear relationship between the believability of deepfake advertisements and their persuasiveness among young adults emphasizes the persuasive potential inherent in technologically sophisticated digital content. When deepfake advertisements are perceived as highly believable, they leverage the perceived credibility and authenticity associated with realistic portrayals to effectively persuade viewers. This influence is rooted in the ability of deepfakes to tap into viewers' trust in visual and auditory cues, shaping attitudes and behaviors through compelling narratives and persuasive appeals.

While these findings highlight the nuanced effects of deepfake technology on cognitive engagement, confusion levels, and persuasiveness among young adults, several critical considerations must be addressed. Ethical concerns surrounding the creation and dissemination of deepfakes necessitate careful reflection on the potential for misinformation and the erosion of trust in media and information sources. Regulatory frameworks are needed to govern the responsible use of deepfake technology, balancing innovation with the protection of individuals and societal integrity. Additionally, efforts to enhance media literacy and educate the public about deepfake detection and mitigation strategies are crucial in empowering individuals to navigate the complexities of digitally manipulated content responsibly. By addressing these challenges proactively, stakeholders can harness the potential benefits of deepfake technology while safeguarding against its detrimental impacts on individuals and society.

CONCLUSION

The analysis demonstrates that Believability (BL) has a substantial positive correlation with Cognitive (CG), Confusion (CF), and Persuasiveness of the Ad (PA), with correlation coefficients of 0.843, 0.683, and 0.664, respectively, all significant at the 0.01 level. Descriptive statistics reveal that participants rated Believability highly, Cognitive and Persuasiveness moderately, and Confusion relatively lower. Regression analyses indicate that Believability is a strong predictor of Cognitive, accounting for 71.1% of its variance. It also significantly predicts Confusion and Persuasiveness, explaining 46.7% and 44.1% of their variances, respectively. Among these, Believability exerts the greatest influence on Cognitive, followed by Confusion and Persuasiveness. These findings underscore the critical role of Believability in shaping cognitive responses, confusion, and the persuasiveness of advertisements.

REFERENCES

Ahmed, S. (2023a). Examining public perception and cognitive biases in the presumed influence of deepfakes threat: Empirical evidence of third person perception from three studies. *Asian Journal of Communication*, 33(3), 308–331. DOI: 10.1080/01292986.2023.2194886

Ahmed, S. (2023b). Navigating the maze: Deepfakes, cognitive ability, and social media news skepticism. *New Media & Society*, 25(5), 1108–1129. DOI: 10.1177/14614448211019198

Ahmed, S., & Chua, H. W. (2023). Perception and deception: Exploring individual responses to deepfakes across different modalities. *Heliyon*, 9(10), e20383. DOI: 10.1016/j.heliyon.2023.e20383 PMID: 37810833

Allen, C., Payne, B., Abegaz, T., & Robertson, C. (2022). What You See Is Not What You Know: Deepfake Image Manipulation.

Allen, C., Payne, B., Abegaz, T., & Robertson, C. (2023). What you see is not what you know: Studying deception in deepfake video manipulation. *Journal of Cybersecurity Education Research and Practice*, 2024(1). Advance online publication. DOI: 10.32727/8.2023.25

Andreadakis, Z. (2020). Deep fakes and intelligence in the digital landscape - preliminary systematic review findings. SSRN *Electronic Journal*. DOI: 10.2139/ssrn.3516344

Beltramini, R. F. (1988). Perceived believability of warning label information presented in cigarette advertising. *Journal of Advertising*, 17(2), 26–32. https://www.jstor.org/stable/4188673. DOI: 10.1080/00913367.1988.10673110

Buijzen, M. (2013). Media, advertising, and consumerism: children and adolescents in a commercialized media environment. In Lemish, D. (Ed.), *The Routledge International Handbook of Children, Adolescents and Media* (pp. 297–304). Routledge.

Cartwright, R. F., & Opree, S. J. (2016). All that glitters is not gold: Do materialistic cues in advertising yield resistance? *Young Consumers*, 17(2), 183–196. DOI: 10.1108/YC-12-2015-00573

Chang, C. (2003). Party bias in political-advertising processing—Results from an experiment involving the 1998 Taipei mayoral election. *Journal of Advertising*, 32(2), 55–67. DOI: 10.1080/00913367.2003.10639129

Craig, A. W., Loureiro, Y. K., Wood, S., & Vendemia, J. M. C. (2012). Suspicious minds: Exploring neural processes during exposure to deceptive advertising. *JMR, Journal of Marketing Research*, 49(3), 361–372. DOI: 10.1509/jmr.09.0007

Duke, J. C., Allen, J. A., Eggers, M. E., Nonnemaker, J., & Farrelly, M. C. (2016). Exploring differences in youth perceptions of the effectiveness of electronic cigarette television advertisements. *Nicotine & Tobacco Research: Official Journal of the Society for Research on Nicotine and Tobacco*, 18(5), 1382–1386. DOI: 10.1093/ntr/ntv264 PMID: 26706908

Fleming, K., Thorson, E., & Atkin, C. K. (2004). Alcohol advertising exposure and perceptions: Links with alcohol expectancies and intentions to drink or drinking in underaged youth and young adults[1]. *Journal of Health Communication*, 9(1), 3–29. DOI: 10.1080/10810730490271665 PMID: 14761831

Gaillard, S., Oláh, Z. A., Venmans, S., & Burke, M. (2021). Countering the cognitive, linguistic, and psychological underpinnings behind susceptibility to fake news: A review of current literature with special focus on the role of age and digital literacy. *Frontiers in Communication*, 6, 661801. Advance online publication. DOI: 10.3389/fcomm.2021.661801

Hameleers, M., van der Meer, T. G. L. A., & Dobber, T. (2022). You won't believe what they just said! The effects of political deepfakes embedded as Vox populi on social media. *Social Media + Society*, 8(3), 205630512211163. DOI: 10.1177/20563051221116346

Homer, P. M. (1995). Ad size as an indicator of perceived advertising costs and effort: The effects on memory and perceptions. *Journal of Advertising*, 24(4), 1–12. DOI: 10.1080/00913367.1995.10673485

Hornikx, J., & O'Keefe, D. J. (2009). Adapting consumer advertising appeals to cultural values A meta-analytic review of effects on persuasiveness and ad liking. *Annals of the International Communication Association*, 33(1), 39–71. DOI: 10.1080/23808985.2009.11679084

Hwang, Y., Ryu, J. Y., & Jeong, S.-H. (2021). Effects of disinformation using deepfake: The protective effect of media literacy education. *Cyberpsychology, Behavior, and Social Networking*, 24(3), 188–193. DOI: 10.1089/cyber.2020.0174 PMID: 33646021

Iacobucci, S., De Cicco, R., Michetti, F., Palumbo, R., & Pagliaro, S. (2021). Deepfakes unmasked: The effects of information priming and bullshit receptivity on deepfake recognition and sharing intention. *Cyberpsychology, Behavior, and Social Networking*, 24(3), 194–202. DOI: 10.1089/cyber.2020.0149 PMID: 33646046

Karpinska-Krakowiak, M., & Eisend, M. (2024). Realistic portrayals of untrue information: The effects of deepfaked ads and different types of disclosures. *Journal of Advertising*, ●●●, 1–11. DOI: 10.1080/00913367.2024.2306415

Kietzmann, J., Mills, A. J., & Plangger, K. (2021). Deepfakes: Perspectives on the future "reality" of advertising and branding. *International Journal of Advertising*, 40(3), 473–485. DOI: 10.1080/02650487.2020.1834211

Köbis, N. C., Doležalová, B., & Soraperra, I. (2021). Fooled twice: People cannot detect deepfakes but think they can. *iScience*, 24(11), 103364. DOI: 10.1016/j.isci.2021.103364 PMID: 34820608

Kunnumpurath, B., Menon, V. A., & Paul, A. (2024). ChatGPT and virtual experience: Student engagement in online script writing - an experimental investigation among media students. In *Advances in Computational Intelligence and Robotics* (pp. 32–50). IGI Global.

Lastovicka, J. L. (1983). Convergent and Discriminant Validity of Television Rating Scales. *Journal of Advertising*, 12(2), 14–23. DOI: 10.1080/00913367.1983.10672836

Lee, Y., Huang, K.-T., Blom, R., Schriner, R., & Ciccarelli, C. A. (2021). To believe or not to believe: Framing analysis of content and audience response of top 10 deepfake videos on YouTube. *Cyberpsychology, Behavior, and Social Networking*, 24(3), 153–158. DOI: 10.1089/cyber.2020.0176 PMID: 33600225

Miksa, N., & Hodgson, R. (2021). The Persuasion Knowledge Model within Instagram Advertisements. *Journal of Student Research*, 10(4). Advance online publication. DOI: 10.47611/jsrhs.v10i4.1821

Moravec, P., Minas, R., & Dennis, A. R. (2018). Fake news on social media: People believe what they want to believe when it makes no sense at all. SSRN *Electronic Journal*. DOI: 10.2139/ssrn.3269541

Napshin, S., Paul, J., & Cochran, J. (2024). Individual responsibility around deepfakes: It's no laughing matter. *Cyberpsychology, Behavior, and Social Networking*, 27(2), 105–110. DOI: 10.1089/cyber.2023.0274 PMID: 38265805

Nieweglowska, M., Stellato, C., & Sloman, S. A. (2023). Deepfakes: Vehicles for radicalization, not persuasion. *Current Directions in Psychological Science*, 32(3), 236–241. DOI: 10.1177/09637214231161321

Pennycook, G., & Rand, D. G. (2017). Who falls for fake news? The roles of analytic thinking, motivated reasoning, political ideology, and bullshit receptivity. SSRN *Electronic Journal*. DOI: 10.2139/ssrn.3023545

Preu, E., Jackson, M., & Choudhury, N. (2022). *Perception vs. Reality: Understanding and evaluating the impact of synthetic image deepfakes over college students. 2022 IEEE 13th Annual Ubiquitous Computing, Electronics & Mobile Communication Conference.* UEMCON.

Sanghvi, H., & Rai, D. U. (2015). Internet Addiction and its relationship with Emotional Intelligence and Perceived Stress experienced by Young Adults. *International Journal of Indian Psychology*, 3(1). Advance online publication. DOI: 10.25215/0301.061

Shin, S. Y., & Lee, J. (2022). The effect of deepfake video on news credibility and corrective influence of cost-based knowledge about deepfakes. *Digital Journalism (Abingdon, England)*, 10(3), 412–432. DOI: 10.1080/21670811.2022.2026797

Sivathanu, B., & Pillai, R. (2023). The effect of deepfake video advertisements on the hotel booking intention of tourists. *Journal of Hospitality and Tourism Insights*, 6(5), 1669–1687. DOI: 10.1108/JHTI-03-2022-0094

Smith, A. D., & Offodile, O. F. (2019). Ethical dilemmas associated with social network advertisements. In *Advances in IT Standards and Standardization Research* (pp. 337–369). IGI Global. DOI: 10.4018/978-1-5225-7214-5.ch015

Somoray, K., & Miller, D. J. (2023). Providing detection strategies to improve human detection of deepfakes: An experimental study. *Computers in Human Behavior*, 149(107917), 107917. DOI: 10.1016/j.chb.2023.107917

Spasova, L. (2023). The third-person effects and susceptibility to persuasion principles in advertisement. *Revista Amazonia Investiga*, 12(62), 105–114. DOI: 10.34069/AI/2023.62.02.8

Swartz, T. A. (1984). Relationship between source expertise and source similarity in an advertising context. *Journal of Advertising*, 13(2), 49–54. DOI: 10.1080/00913367.1984.10672887

Tal-Or, N. (2007). Age and third-person perception in response to positive product advertisements. *Mass Communication & Society*, 10(4), 403–422. DOI: 10.1080/15205430701580557

Ternovski, J., Kalla, J., & Aronow, P. M. (2021). *Deepfake warnings for political videos increase disbelief but do not improve discernment: Evidence from two experiments.* DOI: 10.31219/osf.io/dta97

Ting, H., Sarawak, U. M., de Run, E. C., & Sarawak, U. M. (2015). Attitude towards advertising: A young generation cohort's perspective. *Asian Journal of Business Research*. DOI: 10.14707/ajbr.150012

Vaccari, C., & Chadwick, A. (2020). Deepfakes and disinformation: Exploring the impact of synthetic political video on deception, uncertainty, and trust in news. *Social Media + Society*, 6(1), 205630512090340. DOI: 10.1177/2056305120903408

Weikmann, T., Greber, H., & Nikolaou, A. (2024). After deception: How falling for a deepfake affects the way we see, hear, and experience media. [The International Journal of Press]. *The International Journal of Press/Politics*, 19401612241233539. Advance online publication. DOI: 10.1177/19401612241233539

Yeom, S. (2021). Teaching and assessing data literacy for adolescent learners. In *Deep Fakes, Fake News, and Misinformation in Online Teaching and Learning Technologies* (pp. 93–123). IGI Global. DOI: 10.4018/978-1-7998-6474-5.ch005

Youn, S., & Kim, S. (2019). Newsfeed native advertising on Facebook: Young millennials' knowledge, pet peeves, reactance and ad avoidance. *International Journal of Advertising*, 38(5), 651–683. DOI: 10.1080/02650487.2019.1575109

Chapter 4
Deepfakes in Action:
Exploring Use Cases Across Industries

Shatabdi Chandramani Nannaware

https://orcid.org/0009-0008-8510-623X

Pune Institute of Business Management, India

Rajasshrie Pillai

Pune Institute of Business Management, India

Nilesh Kate

Pune Institute of Business Management, India

ABSTRACT

chapter on deepfakes offers comprehensive insights into how this cutting-edge technology is being applied across diverse industries. Its applications are broad, impacting various sectors by enhancing capabilities, fostering innovation, and prompting critical discussions about ethical use. "The importance of this chapter lies in its ability to inform and prepare stakeholders for the future of deepfake technology, balancing its benefits with the need for responsible and ethical practices." Deep fakes, an unprecedented but controversial development in digital media, are artificially synthesized media using advanced artificial intelligence (AI) and deep learning They are mixed or manipulated in the elements of a work of art, and make a very true but false interpretation. This technology has found utility in a variety of industries, each with its own advantages and challenges.

DOI: 10.4018/979-8-3693-6890-9.ch004

Copyright © 2025, IGI Global Scientific Publishing. Copying or distributing in print or electronic forms without written permission of IGI Global Scientific Publishing is prohibited.

1. INTRODUCTION

In the rapidly evolving world of digital media, deepfakes are one of the most thrilling and controversial developments. This high-reality synthetic media is created using advanced artificial intelligence, especially deep learning. Deep Fake is a combination of AI technology and machine learning that combines, combines, replaces, or superimposes components into an artifact, blurring the distinction between real and fake, Deepfake first reached public demand in 2017 and can appear in a variety of digital media—audio, visual, or audiovisual—as noted by (Kietzmann et al., 2020) such as multi-image content or easily interchange with other faces and bodies You can either mix and match(Maras & Alexandrou, 2018) (Whittaker et al., 2021) The term "deep fake" combines "deep learning" and "falsehood," highlighting the critical role of deep nerves in making this persuasive connection. Deepfakes take advantage of video, audio, or photographs to create unrealistic but more convincing representations of reality, by portraying that someone said or did something they did not do. Powered by artificial intelligence, deepfake technology has grown rapidly and influenced many industries. Using deep learning algorithms to create hyper-realistic video and audio, deep algorithms can realistically alter a person's appearance, voice, or behavior especially the infamous deep fakes in the entertainment industry that used to resurrect dead or alive actors in films Designed to create example brand new scenes, using deepfake technology to recreate the likeness of the dead Peter Cushing in Rogue One: "*A Star Wars Story*, deepfake technology was used to recreate the likeness of the late Peter Cushing". Although deepfakes have the ability to be used in a negative way in the entertainment and creative industries though, they're also mainstream horror. Malicious applications include misinformation, fraud, and explicit non-consent, which raise ethical, legal, and security concerns. In the business sector, deepfakes are increasingly being utilized for virtual presentations and training, allowing executives or trainers to appear in multiple places simultaneously or even in different languages. However, the technology also poses significant risks, particularly in cybersecurity and political arenas. Deepfake videos have been used to spread misinformation or create fraudulent communications, leading to high-profile incidents like a CEO scam in the UK, where a deepfake voice was used to trick an executive into transferring funds.

While deepfakes hold potential for innovation in areas such as entertainment and education, they also present ethical and security challenges, necessitating robust countermeasures to prevent misuse. The rise of deep webs has generated heated debate among technologists, policymakers, and ethicists. Key challenges include developing reliable identification technologies and establishing legal frameworks to prevent abuse without stifling innovation. This chapter will explore the technological foundations, real-world applications, social implications, and ongoing efforts to mitigate the negative effects of deep impact, resulting in a comprehensive understanding of this complex digital phenomenon in various industries presented with the current review of the literature and case study examples:

Key Areas

Entertainment and Media

Deepfakes use artificial intelligence and machine learning to create extremely lifelike but wholly fake films and audio (Mustak et al., 2023). These edited media might make people appear to say or do things they didn't do. In the entertainment industry, this might range from resurrecting departed performers for new performances to developing totally new content that appears extraordinarily lifelike. However, the negative side of this technology is just as potent. Deepfakes, which range from misinformation campaigns to malicious personal attacks, can do permanent harm to reputation and trust. The impact of AI on the entertainment industry, with a particular focus on Deep Fake and digital humans. AI has revolutionized CGI, VFX, dubbing, aging, voice cloning, and music cloning, creating hyper-realistic digital replicas. These developments raise legal and ethical issues, particularly in relation to copyright and publicity law. Debates and proposed legislation such as the NO FAKES Act and the EU AI Act are ongoing to address these challenges. The future of AI in entertainment remains uncertain as industry players seek to strike a balance between innovation and rights protection (Meeka Bondy, 2023). Deepfakes use various AI's in the Media and Entertainment industry as below:

GANs: "deep learning" and generate "fake" information using generative anti-networks (GANs). In GANs introduced in 2014, a generator generates data, and a discriminator verifies it, and they work together to generate the actual data collection.

Dubbing: A.I. David Beckham's PSA about asthma was dubbed into nine languages using AI, ensuring perfect facial movement.

Aging and De-Aging: AI enables virtual digital couples of individuals of different ages. It enhances de-aging with thousands of images from the actors' previous films as seen in Martin Scorsese's "The Irishman."

Voice Cloning: Tone painting creates artificial voices. Recent advances capture language structure in small samples. Val Kilmer's voice in "Top Gun: Maverick" was well-received, but Anthony Bourdain's posthumous interview in the record sparked mixed reactions.

Music Cloning: Improvisation also includes songs, with voices as deep as those of classical musicians. "Heart on My Sleeve," featuring AI-generated vocals from The Weekend and Drake, went viral to showcase the technology's impact.
Digital: AI poses challenges for artists, especially fans who can use their digital likenesses regularly for free. However, some actors are using AI for new opportunities, such as digitalization.
Face Swapping: Initially, the popular facial transformation in porn excited and frightened audiences. Apps like Zao allow users to put their faces into movies, which makes them more popular.

Marketing and Advertising

Deepfakes are additionally utilized to break down linguistic boundaries, as shown in English soccer legend David Beckham's Malaria (Figure 1) No More campaign. Deepfakes allowed Beckham to deliver his message in nine distinct languages(*Deepfake Technology for Entertainment: The Pros and Cons*, 2022).

Figure 1. How deepfake is used on the face to break down linguistic boundaries

"Deepfakes and Generative Adversarial Networks (GANs) use advanced AI tools to generate authentic and authentic advertising content. As this technology is increasingly adopted in the advertising industry, advertising abuse will present many opportunities and challenges Brand managers, ad planners, strategists, creative team members, producers, models, distributors, and regulators will need to carefully consider the potential impact of these redesigned ads on their businesses, and the ethical threats problems will require careful management". Additionally, regulators will face the challenge of developing policies to ensure transparency and authenticity in advertising, while models and operators may need to rotate for certain industries of which they can be replicated without direct involvement. The rise of deep fakes could also lead to new marketing tactics, such as virtual influencers and hyper-targeted campaigns, and dramatically change the advertising landscape(Campbell, Plangger, Sands, Kietzmann, et al., 2022)

One of such campaign Mondelez India and Ogilvy India won the Creative Excellence Grand Prix at Cannes Lions 2023 for their "Shah Rukh Khan – My Advertisement" campaign. The new campaign used AI to create tailored ads for Shah Rukh Khan, helping local merchants promote their stores (Figure 2). The campaign improved productivity by 35% and supported 200,000 small shops across India. It exemplified the power of AI in marketing, which increased engagement and sustained Cadbury's position as a trusted brand. The campaign also won a Silver Creative Power Lion.

Figure 2. Shah Rukh Khan: My Advertisement" campaign

Advertising manipulation is becoming increasingly common through the use of advanced AI techniques such as Deep Fake and GAN. This technology creates high-reality artificial advertisements that are difficult for consumers to identify. Comprehensive research combines insights from the literature to provide a framework for understanding the impact of advertising changes on consumers(Campbell, Plangger,

Sands, & Kietzmann, 2022) This framework highlights how such changes can affect perceptions of authenticity and creativity, and affect false advertising awareness and advertising persuasion. This becomes especially relevant when crafted advertising is comprehensive and personalized.

Education and Training

Deepfake technology opens up many possibilities in education. Schools and teachers have long used media, audio, and video in the classroom. Deepfake can enable teachers to deliver a far more engaging alternative to traditional visual and media programs. It can create immersive learning experiences. Imagine interactive lessons from historical figures or realistic medical simulations for training purposes. AI-generated synthetic media can bring historical figures to life, creating a more interactive and engaging classroom experience(Roe & Perkins, 2024). A video production featuring the voice and image of a reenactment or historical figure can be highly impactful and engaging, making it an excellent teaching tool. For example, recreating JFK's impromptu closing speech during the Cold War using artificial voice can explicitly educate students on the topic in creative ways. In addition, prosthetic human bodies, advanced industrial devices, and complex industrial tasks can be modeled and simulated in a mixed-reality world to facilitate learning and collaboration You can use Tools such as Microsoft Hololens have been used to enhance these immersive educational experiences(Roe & Perkins, 2024). Exploring in-depth aspects of teachers' and students' perspectives and vulnerabilities in different cultural contexts helps establish knowledge baselines and identify unique risks faced by marginalized groups(Roe & Perkins, 2024)

Health Care

This involves superimposing human characteristics on another person's body, as well as modifying audio, to create a realistic human experience. Actor Val Kilmer lost his distinctive voice to throat cancer in 2015, but Sonantic's deepfake technology has recently been deployed to allow Kilmer to "speak"(The actor's son burst into tears when he heard his father's "voice" again).

Personalized health information: Deepfake technology can be used to create personalized videos that educate patients about their condition and treatment options, enabling them to access complex medical information. AI and deepfake technologies power transformation in healthcare, from improving diagnosis and patient outcomes to improving medical training and patient engagement. However, as this technology continues to evolve, addressing ethical concerns and ensuring that it is used responsibly will become increasingly important for participation in healthcare programs. Medical professionals can use Deepfake technology to simulate advanced training, improving care through realistic practice scenarios. Deepfake simulations are revolutionizing medical education by providing immersive training for operations, rare disease treatment, and culturally sensitive communication skills. Personalized deepfake films can improve patient education by clearly explaining diagnosis, treatment options, and potential adverse effects in an engaging and relatable manner, leading to better knowledge and adherence. AI-powered avatars can improve clinical diagnostics by providing virtual consultations, detecting rare diseases early through tailored risk assessments, and supporting telemedicine consultations. In addition to clinical applications, Deepfake technology is being used to enhance physician empathy. Researchers at Taipei Medical University used a facial recognition system to convert patients' facial expressions into video, helping doctors improve their facial expressions while monitoring patients' privacy detection rate of over 80% in data from around the world, this study highlights the power of a deep pack to transform patient-physician communication(Nagendra Rao, 2024).

Politics and Public Affairs

AI deepfakes are increasingly influencing politics and public affairs worldwide, using sophisticated algorithms to create highly realistic fake videos or images These depths can influence public opinion, political campaigns, and elections greater than. For example, in the 2020 U.S. presidential election, candidates were spreading deep webs to spread misinformation and influence voters' opinions AI-generated content poses new challenges for Indian elections in 2024, such as the misinformation spread through WhatsApp during the 2019 general elections. The image reveals a fabricated message in connection with the Dainik Bhaskar story, refuting the news agency's alleged charges for the distribution of the story(Sahana Venugopal & Saumya Kalia, 2024).Deep fake in Public Affairs uses AI to create real but fake audio, video, or images to spread misinformation to manipulate public opinion. This depth can be used to undermine political opponents, influence elections, and undermine public trust in the media and government institutions. Some of the benefits of deep fake include potentially useful uses in entertainment and education, where they can bring historical figures to life or depict complex situations for educational purposes but the shortcomings are great. Deep factions can undermine public trust, create a false narrative, and manipulate democratic processes. They can maliciously defame individuals, incite violence, or manipulate banks. Efforts to curb the negative impact of deepfake include the development of detection technologies and legal frameworks. For example, the EU's AI Act and the proposed NO FAKES Act in the US is aimed at tackling AI abuse and ensuring accountability. Collaboration between governments, technology companies, and the public is crucial to provide ethical guidelines and technological solutions to mitigate the risk posed by deep groups Harnessing new AI capabilities is a delicate balance between protecting citizens' integrity and requires constant monitoring and adaptation of strategies to combat the evolving challenges of deepfake technology. India has launched the Deep Fake Analysis Unit (DAU) to tackle AI-induced anomalies during elections. DAU allows suspicious audio and video to be uploaded through the WhatsApp tipline for verification purposes. Since its launch in August 2024, DAU has processed hundreds of submissions, exploring AI applications in a variety of ways. The program aims to educate the public on identifying artificial media and partners with several agencies to strengthen fact-checking efforts (Pamposh Raina, 2024)

Sports and Fitness

A study conducted by the REVEAL research center at the University of Bath discovered that employing deepfakes in training films can boost learning efficiency and satisfaction. In two trials involving fitness training and public speaking, people performed better and felt more confident after witnessing deepfake videos of themselves rather than videos of others. The study emphasizes the significance of ethical norms in preventing the misuse of deep fakes while also highlighting potential good applications(University of Bath, 2023).

A study (Li & Cui, 2021) describes a human body posture estimate technique that is integrated into a golf training system using artificial intelligence and big data technology. The technology, which uses data from a Kinect sensor, evaluates trainers' and coaches' swing postures using AI-based target detection and posture assessment techniques. It generates joint angle trajectories and posture similarities for performance comparison. Future ambitions include extending this technique to different sports for more extensive testing and dynamic analysis. Similarly, the human body posture determine algorithm used in the golf training system is adaptable to different sports and fitness activities.

For example:
Basketball: The system might assess shooting form and defensive postures to assist players improve their skills.
Running: Assessing stride and posture can help runners increase efficiency and reduce the risk of injury.
Yoga: It may give real-time feedback on poses to ensure proper alignment and form.
Weightlifting: The device can monitor lifting practices to improve performance and prevent injuries.

IT

Deepfake technology uses machine learning algorithms to change videos, making it appear that someone did or said something they never did. While people use it for enjoyment or learning, there is a big risk that it will disseminate false information and be abused. Videos are widely used for skill development, enhancement, and motivation. Video self-modeling (VSM) improves performance by imparting individual skills to those not yet identified. Traditional VSM is labor-intensive and requires extensive drawing and manual adjustments. Fake Forward solves this by using deepfakes to create videos in which they facsimile themselves from other people's poses, replacing their faces with the user's. This approach rapidly increases performance in the gym and increases confidence in public speaking. Additionally, Fake Forward's approach can be extended to sports and fitness activities, effectively providing personalized training and motivation(Clarke et al., 2023)AI and deepfake technologies have made significant strides in information technology, transforming various applications and raising ethical concerns. For example, AI algorithms are now widely used for cybersecurity, and machine learning models are used to detect and respond to threats in real time. Darktrace, an AI cybersecurity company, uses machine learning to create "immune systems" that automatically detect and mitigate cyber threats and is now using deepfake technology to create realistic virtual environments in games and entertainment. Epic Games has introduced Deep Fake technology to enhance character animation in its virtual engine, making characters look lifelike and respond to player interactions, but this same technology has risks, since it can be misused to create a misleading video, which affects trust in digital products. In 2020, University of California Berkeley researchers highlighted deepfake's ability to manipulate information and influence public opinion, emphasizing the importance of robust analytical tools (Mirsky & Lee, 2021) As organizations increasingly adopt AI and deep fake technologies, balancing innovation with ethical considerations to protect the integrity of information and public trust is Important.

Finance and Capital Management

Artificial Intelligence (AI) and deep fake technologies have a profound impact on finance and capital deployment, creating opportunities and challenges for AI, with the ability to analyze large data sets, predict market trends, and provide investment strategies a good deal is changing how financial institutions operate but deep fake technologies, the Use of AI for hyper-realistic but false audio videos, or images, pose additional risks, especially in terms of securities market fluctuations. AI is enhancing decision-making in finance through predictive analytics, which can accurately forecast market dynamics and financial risks. The algorithm analyses historical data to identify trends and trends, enabling investors to make more informed decisions. For example, hedge funds and trading firms are using AI to develop sophisticated trading strategies that can execute trades at optimal times, maximizing returns Furthermore, AI greatly improves fraud detection. Machine learning algorithms can analyze transaction data in real time, identifying anomalies that could indicate fraudulent activities. This proactive approach helps financial institutions minimize losses and increase safety. For example, JPMorgan Chase uses AI to monitor transactions and identify suspicious activity to reduce the incidence of fraud (Tom Lydon, 2023). Productivity is another area where AI excels. Routine tasks such as data entry, compliance checks, and automated customer service not only reduce costs but also reduce human error. AI-powered chatbots, like those used by Bank of America's Erica, provide 24/7 customer support and handle questions and transactions with ease. Despite its benefits, deepfake technologies pose significant risks to the economy and capital. Deepfakes can be used to create fake authentic communications, such as voice or video messages from adults, allowing for fraud. In 2019, the CEO of a UK energy company was approved for fraudulently remitting $243,000 by impersonating a deep voice(Catherine Stupp, 2019). The financial industry must balance the new capabilities of AI with the security risks posed by deep packs. Continuous monitoring and advanced detection systems are required. Companies like Deeptrace are developing AI-powered solutions to identify and reduce widespread deepfakes (Robert Chesney & Danielle Citron, 2018) Additionally, collaboration between the government, the technology industry, and the public is critical to establish ethical guidelines and technical solutions to protect public trust In conclusion, while AI offers transformational benefits for finance and capital management, the emergence of deepfakes requires careful oversight and strict regulation. Balancing innovation and security is essential to harness the power of AI to mitigate the risks of deepfake technologies.

Public Perception and Awareness of Deepfakes

Research and studies on public understanding public understanding of deep fakes varies greatly and is influenced by factors such as media exposure, educational attainment, and technology in general. Studies and surveys reveal a mixed knowledge and understanding of what deepfake is, and its potential impact. A Pew Research Center study found that only half of American adults have heard of Deep Fake, and many have little understanding of the technology and its implications. Similarly, a DeepTrace Laboratory study revealed that although public awareness about DeepTrace is growing A large part is still unaware of the technical issues and potential risks associated with the technology (Henry Ajder et al., 2019). Furthermore, research shows that there is a generational divide in awareness. Younger individuals, who are active on social media and aware of digital content, have a better understanding of deepfake compared to older generations (Harris Poll, 2021). These differences suggest the need for efforts in targeted instruction to bridge the gap in public understanding among different age groups.

Media Representation of Deepfake

Media representatives play an important role in shaping public perceptions of deepfake technologies. The media's portrayal of in-depth stories is often sophisticated, focusing on the potential for abuse in cases of high-profile news, fake news, political incorrectness, and celebrity scandals they are in it The mainstream media has increasingly emphasized the negative aspects of the deep movements, such as the potential for political manipulation, identity theft, and objection to pornography (Vincent et al., 2019) For example; significant media coverage of infamous in-depth videos about politicians such as Barack was done by Obama and Donald Trump. There has been attention, highlighting the potential of this technology to spread misinformation and undermine media credibility (Sample et al., 2019). However, they are also trying to highlight the effective use of deep taxes in the media. Some studios have reported on other uses in the film industry, such as the use of deep fakes to reduce the age of actors or to resurrect dead actors for new roles (NickBryantNY, 2020) This balanced definition helps them gain a more nuanced understanding of deep fake technology, both the risks and benefits Disclosed.

2. IMPLICATIONS OF DEEPFAKE AI

This chapter on "Deepfakes in Action: Exploring Use Cases Across Industries" effectively engages a wide range of stakeholders including practitioners, academics, policymakers, and the general public, and Its applications span multiple scales:

Implications for Stakeholders

Industry Professionals and Innovators

Entertainment and Media: Filmmakers and producers can use deep technology to enhance storytelling, create more engaging content, and reduce production costs. Eg: Multinational conglomerate ITC recently collaborated with AI creative company Akool to produce a #HarDilKiFantasy ad (Figure 3) campaign for its biscuit brand Sunfest Dark Fantasy, in which participants could share the screen with Shah Rukh Khan. It enabled anyone to produce an ad for their local store and use

Shah Rukh Khan's face and voice to promote their company without having to pay for endorsements. Mondelez, Cadbury's parent company, received several awards at the Cannes Lions Festival of Creativity, including India's first Titanium Lion for an innovative AI-created Ad (Sharmita Kar, 2023).

Figure 3. Har dil fantasy ad

Marketing and Advertising: Retailers can use personalized advertising campaigns to better target specific demographics and increase engagement and conversion rates.

Academics and Researchers

Content Creation in Education: Deepfakes can be used to create truly instructive videos with historical figures or experts not available for live lectures. For example, students can watch an in-depth video of Albert Einstein explaining his theories, making learning engaging and accessible.

Language and Cultural Studies (Pronunciation): The deepfake video features a native speaker demonstrating very complicated pronunciation and words. For example, a native speaker might say "pero" (dog) and "pero".

Cultural Context: The video contains cultural context, such as ordering food at a Spanish restaurant or asking for directions in a Spanish-speaking country. In the deepfake video, the narrator provides context-specific language, helping Alex understand not only the words but cultural nuances as well.

This chapter provides a comprehensive analysis of the current state of deepfake technology as a valuable resource for further research and academic discourse. It can stimulate further research on ethical implications, technological developments, and regulatory frameworks needed to responsibly manage deep technologies.

Policymakers and Regulators

Deepfake's technology, which uses AI to create automated media, presents both opportunities and challenges for policymakers and regulators. On the one hand, Deepfake can be used for creative and educational purposes, such as filmmaking, historical recreation, and training simulations. On the other hand, they pose serious risks such as misinformation, identity theft, and privacy violations. Policymakers should navigate these two dimensions to implement laws that encourage innovation while protecting the public interest. This includes developing policies to identify and record deepfake content, ensure accountability for content creators, and impose penalties for misuse (Westerlund, 2019). Also, collaborating with tech companies to develop detection tools resources, and public information campaigns for risk mitigation are needed. Regulators face the challenge of balancing freedom of expression with the need to prevent harm. This requires clear guidelines that distinguish permissible uses of profound falsehoods from those that are harmful or deceptive. Given the global nature of digital media, international collaboration is also important. Addressing these issues will enable policymakers and regulators to leverage the benefits of deepfake technologies while protecting individuals and the public from potential risks(Danielle K. Citron & Robert Chesney, 2024)

> **Predictive Analytics:** AI can analyze big data to predict social trends, economic changes, and potential regulatory impacts, helping policymakers make informed decisions Understanding the capabilities and risks of deepfake is essential to develop policies that protect against abuse while encouraging beneficial use.
> **Training Tools:** Deepfake technology can be used to create realistic simulations for training purposes, helping policymakers and regulators better understand complex issues and human behaviour.
> **Improved Communication:** Deepfake technology can be used to create engaging public service reports, making it easier for policymakers to communicate complex ideas effectively.

General Public

Increased public awareness of the potential and risks of deepfakes can help individuals become more users of digital information.

However, the prevalence of deepfake technology raises serious misinformation and credibility concerns. In 2020, in-depth videos were used in political campaigns, causing confusion and violence. The potential for negative use highlights the importance of developing effective screening tools.

Researchers have been working on AI algorithms to detect deepfake content, which aims to preserve the integrity of information shared on social media platforms (Nakamura et al., 2021). As AI and deepfake technologies continue to evolve, the general public needs to be vigilant about sources of information and the implications of media manipulation on social trust.

Promotes media literacy, and helps people identify and question potentially misleading harmful, or profound information.

AI Deepfakes: Gaming and Virtual Reality

In the realm of gaming and virtual reality (VR), AI Deep Fake is revolutionizing behavioral reality by enabling ultra-realistic avatars and virtual creatures, primarily through Generative Adversarial Networks (GANs). Major Improvements For example, in the game "Cyberpunk 2077," CD Projekt Red used advanced AI-powered techniques to create detailed, dynamic facial expressions that react in real-time to players' actions, and contribute to a more engaging gaming experience. Similarly, in VR, Deep Fake technology is used to create highly realistic avatars that can mimic real-time text and emotions expressed by players. This innovation enhances user interaction in virtual environments, making it more natural and immersive. An example is "Horizon Workrooms" by Meta (formerly Facebook), which uses AI to create lifelike avatars that accurately reflect user gestures and facial expressions, improving communication and productivity in virtual meetings.

Deepfake technology also enhances interactive experiences by facilitating highly functional and flexible virtual worlds. Avatars and NPCs (non-player characters) using AI capabilities can interact with players in a discreet and personalized way. In "The Last of Us Part II," the developers used an in-depth study program to create more realistic human interactions and stronger emotional responses, adding to the depth of the story in the game (Maddy Myers, 2020)This use of Deep Fake technology in gaming and VR is transforming user experiences by making the virtual world more immersive and interactive, and finally bridging the gap between digital and physical realities. Artificial Intelligence (AI) and deepfake technologies are transforming the gaming and streaming industries. AI enables realistic behavioral interactions and dynamic environments, while Deep Fake technology enhances personalization and immersion. In the game, Deepfake allows players to see their faces in avatars and interact with each other as celebrities in real time (Marcus Tsui, 2024). Streamers and esports operators use Deepfake to create interesting content by transforming their faces into familiar characters and adding new elements to their broadcasts. These enhancements enhance the user experience, making digital entertainment more interactive and personalized.

Enhanced Characters: Games like "The Elder Scrolls" and "Cyberpunk 2077" use Deep-fake technology allows players to upload photos of themselves and see their realistic facial expressions on a gaming avatar, providing free immersion fill-in with themselves and grow in real-time.

Avatar Interaction: Apps like Avatarify allow users to put their faces on celebrities in real-time as they play, adding a fun and novel dimension to multiplayer interactions:

Voice-Up of NPCs: Deepfake technology provides more realistic voices for non- playable characters (NPCs), making interactions more dynamic and reducing repetitive dialogue.

History and Famous Cameos: In narrative games, deepfakes recreate famous historical figures or figures for inclusion in game narratives, enhancing the storytelling aspect. Deepfake-enhanced live.

Streams and Esports: Streamers and esports operators use deep fake technology to transform their faces into familiar characters or characters during a live stream, creating interesting effects(Marcus Tsui, 2024)

Music and Live Performances

Virtual concerts and holograms AI deepfakes are having a huge impact on the music industry, especially with virtual concerts and holograms. Artists can now perform in virtual spaces, providing fans with immersive experiences that transcend physical limitations. For example, Avicii's virtual performance at Ultra Music Festival 2019 featured a hologram of the late DJ, which allowed fans to experience a posthumous concert with visual effects and amazing music (Ultra Music Festival, 2019) Such a deep fake this use of technology to celebrate artists' legacies and to engage audiences in new ways and offers a powerful medium. Posthumous release Deepfake technology is also used to release posthumous releases, allowing the voices of deceased musicians to be resurrected for new songs. A notable example is Tupac Shakur's hologram show at Coachella 2012, which demonstrated how deep fake and hologram technology can bring iconic images back to the stage (Chenda Ngak, 2012) This technology allows for innovative effects with shape and tone the nature of artists who are no longer present plays a role alive The musical work bridges the gap between past and present.

E-Commerce

Virtual try-ons In e-commerce, AI and deepfake technologies are transforming the shopping experience with virtual try-ons. This innovation allows customers to visualize the products themselves without physically testing the products, increasing convenience and reducing returns. A prime example is L'Oréal's ModiFace technology, which uses AI to enable users to try on different makeup products in real-time through their smartphones ModiFace's deepfake-powered virtual try-on platform creates a realistic picture of different cosmetics in front of the user as they are perceived, thereby helping consumers make informed purchasing decisions.

3. IMPORTANCE OF DEEPFAKE AI

Technological Advancement

Deepfake technology represents a significant advance in AI and ML capabilities. Understanding its uses and implications is critical to enabling innovation and addressing the associated ethical challenges.

Exposing more comprehensive features across sectors highlights the flexibility of AI capabilities, encouraging investment and growth in this application. Deepfake detection remains a challenge even with the rapid development of multimedia technologies and the increasing number of devices and applications(Rana et al., 2022)

Ethical and Social Implications

By analyzing both positive and negative consumption, the chapter offers a balanced view of the ethical considerations of deep taxation.

Emphasizes the importance of developing and using these technologies responsibly, and recommends policies to mitigate risks such as disinformation and invasion of privacy. E.g.: **Joe Biden Robocall**: In February 2024, an audio deepfake mimicking Joe Biden's voice was used in an automated telephone call targeting Democratic voters in New Hampshire. The message urged people not to vote in the state's primary election, showcasing the potential of deep fakes to interfere with democratic processes (Max Matza, 2024).

Weaponization of Misinformation: The potential for malicious deep fakes to spread propaganda and manipulate public opinion is a serious threat (Whyte, 2020). Imagine fabricated videos of political leaders inciting violence or spreading harmful falsehoods.

Erosion of Trust: As deepfakes blur the lines between reality and fabrication, trust in media and institutions could erode. This could have profound consequences for journalism, democracy, and interpersonal relationships.

Privacy Violations & Harassment: Deepfakes can be weaponized to create non-consensual intimate imagery or to harass and defame individuals

(Mahmud & Sharmin, 2021). This raises serious ethical and legal concerns about consent and online safety.

Economic Impact

The economic impact of AI and deepfake technologies is multifaceted, affecting a variety of industries. AI has the potential to increase productivity, spur innovation, and create new markets. For example, AI's automation capabilities can save costs in manufacturing and logistics by improving optimization and quality control in supply chains AI-driven personalization enhances customer experience in e-commerce, increasing sales and customer loyalty (Bughin et al., 2018)

The financial side is particularly vulnerable, as deepfakes can manipulate banks with false claims from officials. To mitigate these risks, companies are investing in AI-based detection tools, creating an arms race between deepfake developers and detection devices. Policymakers and agencies must work together to balance innovation and security between regulation and security (Chesney & Citron, 2019).

It also addresses potential financial risks, such as redundancies and costs associated with dealing with abusive deep fakes Eg. Hong Kong investment fraud: A Hong Kong investor was tricked into transferring $25 million when he joined a video conference with members of Deep Fake who he believed were the CFO and employees of his company. This example highlights how Deep Fake can be used for financial fraud by impersonating credible individuals (Heather Chen & Kathleen Magramo, 2024)

Future-Proofing Skills and Knowledge

Key areas for future-proofing Understanding Deepfake Technology Definition and Approach: Deepfakes use AI techniques such as Generative Adversarial Networks (GANs) to create more realistic fake images, video, or audio.

Functions: From entertainment to business to misinformation and the potential for abuse in cyber threats. Skills development Technologies: Know the basics of AI, machine learning, and deep learning. Familiarize yourself with the tools and programs used to create deepfakes.

Detection Techniques: Develop proficiency in detecting and combating deep birds using forensic tools and AI detection techniques.

Ethical considerations: Understanding ethical implications and developing policies for the responsible use of AI.

Continuous learning and adaptation Stay Updated: Keep up to date with the latest developments in AI and deepfake technology. Follow relevant research papers, blogs, and industry news.

Training and certification: Take courses and certifications in AI, cybersecurity, and digital forensics.

> It is important for staff and students to understand Deep Fake to stay relevant in a rapidly evolving technological environment.
>
> This chapter attempts to provide insights of the causes of deepfakes as well as how to adapt to future trends by ensuring they remain competitive in respective industries. Providing readers with knowledge that can help them adapt to future trends, ensuring they remain competitive in their respective industries. A common belief is that negative feedback about a brand negatively affects all aspects of the brand. However, this study shows that branding errors and complexity have different effects on consumer evaluations. Specifically, branding errors negatively affect attitudes and purchase intentions but do not affect brand image. In contrast, strong words negatively affect brand image but not behaviour or purchase intention. Moreover, the relationship between brand image and consumer behavior and attitudes varies depending on the complexity of the issues. At low intensity, brand image positively influences attitudes and intentions, whereas at high intensity it does not (Yu et al., 2018)

Detection Techniques

> **Signature-Based Detection:** Uses known malicious data patterns to identify threats. Effective against known threats but never zero attacks.
>
> **Anomaly-Based Detection:** Refers to deviations from normal behaviour to detect unknown threats. Useful for zero-day attacks but prone to false positives.
>
> **Inference-Based Search:** Uses algorithms to identify suspicious behavior. The balance between signature and anomaly-based methods.
>
> **Behavior Detection:** Monitors user behaviour to detect malicious activity. Effective for insider threat detection.

Strategies for Raising Awareness: Strategies for public awareness and educating the public about deep falsehoods require a multi-pronged approach that includes collaboration between academics, media organizations, policymakers, and technology companies. Here are some effective ways:

Education Campaign: The implementation of comprehensive educational campaigns can significantly increase public understanding of deep birds. These campaigns can be carried out through schools, universities, and community organizations, focusing on the technical aspects of deepfakes, their potential uses, and associated risks.

Media Literacy Programs: Integrating media literacy programs into the educational curriculum can provide individuals with the skills to effectively evaluate digital content. These policies should emphasize the importance of verifying information and identifying media victims, to reduce the chances of deep insider deception.

Public Performance Statements (PSAs): Governments and NGOs can use PSAs to spread the word about Deep Fake. These ads can be placed on television, radio, and social media to reach a wider audience and raise awareness of the existence and implications of deepfake technology.

Working with Tech Companies: Technology companies, especially social media platforms, play an important role in curbing the spread of deepfakes. Partnering with these companies to develop and implement deep detection tools could help identify and label piracy, thereby enabling users to identify and prevent the spread of misinformation.

Deepfake Future in Industry: Deepfake technology, powered by AI, has a wide range of potential applications in various industries. However, it also presents significant challenges and ethical concerns.

Potential Applications

Entertainment: Deepfakes can be used to create realistic visual effects in movies and TV shows, potentially reducing the cost and time required for traditional special effects. They can also be used to digitally resurrect actors or create synthetic performances.

Advertising and Marketing: Imagine creating personalized advertising campaigns where a brand spokesperson delivers a message tailored to individual viewers. Deepfakes could make this a reality.

Education and Training: Deepfakes can create engaging and interactive learning experiences. Imagine historical figures giving lectures or simulations for training purposes in fields like medicine or aviation.

Virtual Reality and Gaming: Deepfakes can enhance realism and immersion in virtual environments, creating lifelike characters and experiences.

Challenges and Concerns

Misinformation and Disinformation: The potential for deepfakes to spread false information is a major concern. Malicious actors could use deepfakes to manipulate public opinion, damage reputations, or incite violence.

Privacy Violations: Deepfakes can be used to create non-consensual intimate imagery or to impersonate individuals without their consent, raising serious privacy concerns.

Job Displacement: As deepfake technology advances, it could potentially automate jobs in fields like acting, voice acting, and even news reporting.

Ethical Considerations

Transparency and Consent: It's crucial to establish clear guidelines and regulations regarding the creation and distribution of deepfakes, ensuring transparency and obtaining consent from the individuals being depicted.

Detection and Verification: Developing robust methods for detecting deepfakes and verifying the authenticity of digital content is essential to combat misinformation.

Accountability and Responsibility: Establishing mechanisms for holding individuals accountable for creating or spreading harmful deepfakes is crucial.

The future of deepfakes in industry depends on addressing these challenges and ethical concerns. Striking a balance between innovation and responsibility will be key to harnessing the potential benefits of this technology while mitigating its risks.

Figure 4. Academic research from 2022 -2024

Year ↓	Documents ↑
2024	50
2023	57
2022	41

The figures show the annual distribution of papers listed in Scopus for 2022, 2023, and 2024. The data showed an increasing number of papers, with 41 in 2022, 57 in 2023, and 50 in 2024, respectively, This indicates an increase in academic activity, especially an increase in 2023. A slight decline in 2024 could indicate a trend in literature or a temporary decline in production.

Figure 5. Distribution of papers

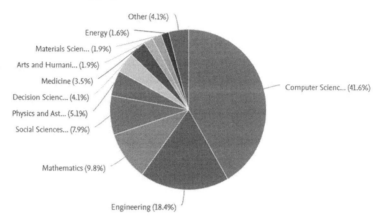

The rapidly growing field of artificial intelligence (AI) has been reflected in academic research aimed at understanding and mitigating potential risks and using deepfake technologies has been conducted by three individuals, they have contributed to a growing awareness It happens to address the technical challenges and ethical concerns associated with deepfakes One of the main focus areas in recent research is complex AI models that can lead to very deep processing and discovery. For example, Sharma, Kumar, and Sharma (2024) present a GAN-based CNN model designed to enhance the capabilities of generative AI applications, especially in the case of Deep Fake, and their work published in EAI Endorsed Transactions on Internet of Things Events highlights the importance, of a common challenge in AI-analyzed media this analysis highlights the ongoing efforts to enhance the creative potential of deepfake technologies and the need for security and authenticity in digital content the emphasis of the. Another significant contribution is from (Dogoulis et al.2023), who explored methods for improving the detection of synthetically generated images, a key aspect of combating deepfakes. Their research, presented at the ACM International Conference, highlights the advancements in detection algorithms that leverage machine learning techniques to distinguish between real and fake images. The study is particularly relevant as deepfake technology becomes more sophisticated, making it increasingly difficult to identify manipulated content using traditional detection methods. The authors' focus on enhancing detection capabilities is critical in the fight against misinformation and the misuse of deepfake technology.

In addition to image-based deepfakes, the dataset also includes research on audio deepfakes, which pose unique challenges and threats.(Liu et al. 2023) introduced a novel approach to detecting audio deepfakes in their paper published in the *Proceedings of the Annual Conference of the International Speech Communication Association*. Their work demonstrates the importance of addressing the vulnerabilities in voice authentication systems, which are increasingly being targeted by deepfake audio technologies. The paper presents a method that not only improves detection accuracy but also offers insights into the broader implications of audio deepfakes in cybersecurity and personal privacy.

The ethical implications of deepfake technology are also a recurring theme in the dataset. As deepfakes become more prevalent, concerns about their potential misuse for malicious purposes, such as political manipulation, cyberbullying, and the spread of false information, have grown. This is reflected in the various studies that emphasize the need for regulatory frameworks and ethical guidelines to govern the use of deepfake technology. For example, Sohan, Solaiman, and Hasan (2023) conducted a comprehensive survey on deepfake video detection datasets, published in the *Indonesian Journal of Electrical Engineering and Computer Science*. Their work provides a critical review of existing datasets and offers recommendations for future research that can better address the ethical challenges posed by deepfakes. Moreover, the dataset reveals a trend towards interdisciplinary collaboration, with researchers from computer science, ethics, law, and media studies working together to tackle the multifaceted challenges of deepfake technology. This collaborative approach is essential for developing comprehensive solutions that not only advance the technical aspects of deepfake detection and generation but also consider the societal and ethical dimensions. The academic research on AI and deepfake technology, as captured in this dataset, reflects a broad and deep engagement with the challenges and opportunities presented by this emerging field. From improving detection algorithms to addressing ethical concerns, researchers are making significant strides in understanding and managing the impact of deepfakes on society. As the technology continues to evolve, ongoing research and collaboration across disciplines will be crucial in ensuring that deepfakes are used responsibly and ethically, minimizing their potential for harm while maximizing their creative and innovative potential.

4. CONCLUSION

The emergence of deepfake technologies has brought innovation and controversy to various industries, offering a mixture of possibilities and challenges. From entertainment and media to information technology, sport, business, education and healthcare, deepfakes have had an incredible impact, causing them to consider the potential benefits and their ethical challenges. In entertainment and media, Deep Fake changed the way content was created and consumed. By enabling the resurrection of dead actors, the adaptation of existing games, or the creation of entirely new characters, Deepfake has expanded the creative possibilities but this also raises questions about authenticity and intellectual property. The ability to create hyperreality can blur the line between fact and fiction, allowing it to be misused as fake news or manipulative media that can influence public opinion influence. The IT industry has also embraced deep technology, especially in virtual assistants and customer service. Companies are looking for ways to use Deepfake to create more personal and engaging interactions, such as AI-generated avatars that can mimic human words and speech This can enhance the user experience, but it also raises concerns in terms of privacy and the possibility of abuse, such as voice-based phishing. The attack in sports and fitness, Deepfake is used to create virtual athletes, simulate training scenarios, and analyze player performance. These activities can provide valuable insights and enhance training strategies, but also carry the risk of data manipulation and unfair advantage Accurate sports information and fair competition must be protected to ensure ethical use of deep technologies. The use of Deepfake to create more personalized and targeted campaigns in marketing and advertising has increased. Brands can now provide real spokespersons, influencers, or customer testimonials that resonate more with audiences. But this also opens the door to deceptive practices, where consumers can be fooled by synthetic props or replicas, undermining brand confidence, in education and training, Deepfakes offers the ability to create immersive and interactive learning experiences. Through realistic simulations and individualized training modules, teachers can increase student engagement and understanding. For example, providing first-person accounts can bring historical figures to life, making historical lessons more vivid and memorable. However, the ethical implications of changing educational content need to be carefully considered, as there are some fine distinctions. Healthcare providers are beginning to demand deeper patient care, medical education, and telemedicine. Deep Fake can map patient conditions for training purposes or create remote physician services, improving access to healthcare services. However, the health risks of deep lock technology are significant, especially in terms of patient privacy and the possibility of fraud. Misuse of Deepfake in medical practice can lead to misdiagnosis or the spread of false medical information, with potentially serious consequences. Despite the widespread use of Deep Fake in industry, this technology presents distinct challenges. The potential for abuse in the form of disseminating misinformation, committing fraud, and violating privacy highlights the need for strict ethical guidelines and legal frameworks As deepfake technology continues to develop, balancing innovation and accountability becomes increasingly important. Looking ahead, the future of Deepfake is likely to include improvements in diagnostic and validation methodologies, and the development of ethical standards to guide their practice among industry leaders, policymakers, and technologists performance will be important in the future where depth can be used for good purposes. With proper management and ethical considerations, deepfake technology can transform industries and enhance the human experience, but it must be handled with care and commitment to protect trust and integrity.

REFERENCES

Henry Ajder, Giorgio Patrini, Francesco Cavalli, & Laurence Cullen. (2019). *THE STATE O F DEEPFAKES LANDSCAPE, THREATS, AND IMPACT.*

Bondy, M. (2023, October 6). https://www.ageofdisruptionblog.com/2023/10/deepfakes-digital-humans-and-the-future-of-entertainment-in-the-age-of-ai/

Bughin, J., Seong, J., Manyika, J., Chui, M., & Joshi, R. (2018). Notes from the AI frontier: Modeling the impact of AI on the world economy. *McKinsey Global Institute, 4*(1).

Campbell, C., Plangger, K., Sands, S., & Kietzmann, J. (2022). Preparing for an Era of Deepfakes and AI-Generated Ads: A Framework for Understanding Responses to Manipulated Advertising. *Journal of Advertising*, 51(1), 22–38. DOI: 10.1080/00913367.2021.1909515

Campbell, C., Plangger, K., Sands, S., Kietzmann, J., & Bates, K. (2022). How Deepfakes and Artificial Intelligence Could Reshape the Advertising Industry The Coming Reality of AI Fakes and Their Potential Impact on Consumer Behavior. *Journal of Advertising Research*, 62(3), 241–251. DOI: 10.2501/JAR-2022-017

Clarke, C., Xu, J., Zhu, Y., Dharamshi, K., McGill, H., Black, S., & Lutteroth, C. (2023). FakeForward: Using Deepfake Technology for Feedforward Learning. *Proceedings of the 2023 CHI Conference on Human Factors in Computing Systems.* DOI: 10.1145/3544548.3581100

Danielle, K. (2022). *Citron, & Robert Chesney*. Deepfakes and the New Disinformation War.

Kar, S. (2023, February 27). *How Advertisements Are Using Deepfake: Is There A Cause For Concern?* Tom Lydon. (2023, November 20). *How AI will make payments more efficient and reduce fraud.*

Kietzmann, J., Lee, L. W., McCarthy, I. P., & Kietzmann, T. C. (2020). Deepfakes: Trick or treat? In *Business Horizons* (Vol. 63, Issue 2, pp. 135–146). Elsevier Ltd. DOI: 10.1016/j.bushor.2019.11.006

Li, C., & Cui, J. (2021). Intelligent Sports Training System Based on Artificial Intelligence and Big Data. *Mobile Information Systems*, 2021, 1–11. DOI: 10.1155/2021/1430512

Mahmud, B. U., & Al Sharmin, A. (2021). Deep Insights of Deepfake Technology : A Review. *ArXiv, abs/2105.00192*. https://api.semanticscholar.org/CorpusID: 233481934

Maras, M.-H., & Alexandrou, A. (2018). Determining authenticity of video evidence in the age of artificial intelligence and in the wake of Deepfake videos. *The International Journal of Evidence & Proof*, 23(3), 255–262. DOI: 10.1177/1365712718807226

Matza, M. (2024, January 23). *Fake Biden robocall tells voters to skip New Hampshire primary election.*

Mirsky, Y., & Lee, W. (2021). The Creation and Detection of Deepfakes: A Survey. *ACM Computing Surveys*, 54(1), 1–41. DOI: 10.1145/3425780

Mustak, M., Salminen, J., Mäntymäki, M., Rahman, A., & Dwivedi, Y. K. (2023). Deepfakes: Deceptions, mitigations, and opportunities. *Journal of Business Research*, 154, 113368. https://doi.org/https://doi.org/10.1016/j.jbusres.2022.113368. DOI: 10.1016/j.jbusres.2022.113368

Myers, M. (2020, June 12). *The Last of Us Part 2 review: We're better than this.*

Nakamura, T., Nagata, Y., Nitta, G., Okata, S., Nagase, M., Mitsui, K., Watanabe, K., Miyazaki, R., Kaneko, M., Nagamine, S., Hara, N., Lee, T., Nozato, T., Ashikaga, T., Goya, M., & Sasano, T. (2021). Prediction of premature ventricular complex origins using artificial intelligence–enabled algorithms. *Cardiovascular Digital Health Journal*, 2(1), 76–83. https://doi.org/https://doi.org/10.1016/j.cvdhj.2020.11.006. DOI: 10.1016/j.cvdhj.2020.11.006 PMID: 35265893

NickBryantNY. (2020, December 19). *The year 2020: A time when everything changed.*

Raina, P. (2024, August 6). *Year of elections: Lessons from India's fight against AI-generated misinformation.*

Rana, M. S., Nobi, M. N., Murali, B., & Sung, A. H. (2022). Deepfake Detection: A Systematic Literature Review. In *IEEE Access* (Vol. 10, pp. 25494–25513). Institute of Electrical and Electronics Engineers Inc. DOI: 10.1109/ACCESS.2022.3154404

Nagendra Rao. (2024, February 29). *Deepfakes: Healthcare's Future is Here, and It's Not What You Expect.*

Roe, J., & Perkins, M. (2024). *Deepfakes and Higher Education: A Research Agenda and Scoping Review of Synthetic Media.* https://doi.org/DOI: 10.13140/RG.2.2.17544.02562

Sample, M., Sattler, S., Blain-Moraes, S., Rodríguez-Arias, D., & Racine, E. (2019). Do Publics Share Experts' Concerns about Brain–Computer Interfaces? A Trinational Survey on the Ethics of Neural Technology. *Science, Technology & Human Values*, 45(6), 1242–1270. DOI: 10.1177/0162243919879220

Tsui, M. (2024, January 10). *14 best deepfake apps and websites in 2024.*

University of Bath. (2023, October 6). *Two experiments make a case for using deepfakes in training videos.*

Vincent, A. T., Schiettekatte, O., Goarant, C., Neela, V. K., Bernet, E., Thibeaux, R., Ismail, N., Khalid, M. K. N. M., Amran, F., Masuzawa, T., Nakao, R., Korba, A. A., Bourhy, P., Veyrier, F. J., & Picardeau, M. (2019). Revisiting the taxonomy and evolution of pathogenicity of the genus Leptospira through the prism of genomics. *PLoS Neglected Tropical Diseases*, 13(5), e0007270. Advance online publication. DOI: 10.1371/journal.pntd.0007270 PMID: 31120895

Westerlund, M. (n.d.). The Emergence of Deepfake Technology. *RE:view.*

Whittaker, L., Letheren, K., & Mulcahy, R. (2021). The Rise of Deepfakes: A Conceptual Framework and Research Agenda for Marketing. *Australasian Marketing Journal*, 29(3), 204–214. DOI: 10.1177/1839334921999479

Whyte, C. (2020). Deepfake news: AI-enabled disinformation as a multi-level public policy challenge. *Journal of Cyber Policy*, 5(2), 199–217. DOI: 10.1080/23738871.2020.1797135

Yu, M., Liu, F., Lee, J., & Soutar, G. (2018). The influence of negative publicity on brand equity: Attribution, image, attitude and purchase intention. *Journal of Product and Brand Management*, 27(4), 440–451. DOI: 10.1108/JPBM-01-2017-1396

Chapter 5

The Impact of Deepfakes on Trust and Security in Islamic Banking:
Emerging Threats and Mitigation Strategies

Early Ridho Kismawadi
https://orcid.org/0000-0002-9420-5212
IAIN Langsa, Indonesia

ABSTRACT

This research presents an important contribution to the development of digital security policies in the Islamic finance sector, with a particular focus on modern technological threats such as deepfakes. Through an in-depth threat analysis, this study identifies potential risks faced by the Islamic banking industry, especially in terms of security and customer trust. The proposed recommendations include strict regulation of the creation and distribution of synthetic media, the development of more advanced detection technologies, and effective regulatory enforcement. Collaboration between governments, research institutions, and industry is also emphasized as key in designing and implementing policies that are able to respond to technological threats in an adaptive manner. With this approach, the study assists policymakers and regulators in designing strategies that can protect integrity and trust in Islamic banking, as well as ensure sustainability and security in the ever-evolving digital era.

DOI: 10.4018/979-8-3693-6890-9.ch005

Copyright © 2025, IGI Global Scientific Publishing. Copying or distributing in print or electronic forms without written permission of IGI Global Scientific Publishing is prohibited.

INTRODUCTION

Sharia Banking is a major player in the wave of Financial Technology that is taking over and championing ethical financing principles that are in line with Sharia law (Ali et al., 2020; Asyiqin & Alfurqon, 2024; Santoso et al., 2023). However, the new era of deepfake technology represents a more serious threat to that trust and security upon which the industry flourishes. Deepfakes, or hyper-realistic digital forgeries generated by artificial intelligence (AI), has sunk in its teeth as the latest frontier fighting back in this misinformation war that poses an existential threat to democracy across America. This kind of manipulation would not only be a security concern to individuals, but also an institutional threat against the legitimacy and credibility in Islamic Banking System.

Deepfakes are artificial intelligence (AI)-based technologies that are capable of creating highly realistic, but completely fake audio, video, or image content. The technology presents serious challenges for many sectors, including banking, due to its ability to deceive and manipulate the public. In the context of Islamic banking, the threat of deepfakes can disrupt the principles of trust, integrity, and transparency that are the basis for the operations of Islamic financial institutions. The use of deepfakes can damage an institution's reputation, create uncertainty, and jeopardize transaction security. This has the potential to damage customer trust in the Islamic financial system, which is highly dependent on ethical values. As such, it is important to understand the profound impact of these technologies and develop mitigation strategies to maintain the stability and integrity of Islamic banking.

For example, a leading Islamic bank experienced a fraud attack using a deepfake video featuring the bank's CEO. In the video, the "CEO" appears to announce changes in investment policies that are contrary to sharia principles, such as allowing investments in gambling and alcohol companies. The fake video spread quickly through social media, causing confusion among customers. As a result, many customers withdraw their funds because they believe that the bank has violated its sharia commitments. Although the bank later succeeded in proving that the video was fake, their reputation was tarnished and customer trust was shaken. In addition, the scammers used deepfake technology to create fake voice recordings of an Islamic bank executive who ordered the branch manager to transfer large amounts of funds to a fake account. Since the voice sounded identical to the executive's original voice, the manager did not realize that it was a scam and immediately transferred the funds. When fraud is exposed, banks face huge financial losses and their reputations are damaged due to a lack of internal security controls. Another example of a deepfake video showing a director of an Islamic bank receiving bribes from businessmen is widely spread on social media. Although proven to be fake after digital forensic analysis, the bank's reputation has been damaged, and customers are starting to doubt the integrity of the institution. These fake videos create a wave of distrust that adversely affects bank operations and lowers public confidence in their commitment to sharia principles.

In this paper, we will investigate how deepfake technology influences trust and security framework in Islamic banks. This brings up to a quick whistle-stop overview of the natural ethical and operational principles upon which Islamic banking is governed — How can trust be anything but very difficult against such a backdrop?? In the third part of this chapter, we start with what do you deepfakes and then cover how minor second-order failures arise from these first principles by permitting deception or fake news or just destroying customer trust. This paper will also discuss the major risks within Islamic Banking security affected by deepfake technologies and international vulnerabilities that can arise. We then look at the present as a source by providing case studies and examples from recent years to give insight into real/immediate threats that are taking root in the industry with deepfakes.

Next, we rolled out a number of mitigation techniques to eliminate these new threats. These involve, among other things, the application of more sophisticated detection methods and regulatory improvements along with an increased awareness on the side of all stakeholders. Islamic banks can insulate themselves from irreparable damages that may happen as a result of the prevalence of deepfake technology by being at the forefront and guiding force, leading an effort to proactively combat these issues; reaffirming their integrity and trust (inshallah).

This research is also important for the field with its novelty of a deep dimension to such threat in Islamic banks and robust detection along-with response policy/plan. This paper explores how deepfakes may not undermine trust in novel manners, also accepting new security hazards from conducting safe transactions or connections with clients. This weighs into the argument about cybersecurity for Islamic financial institutions. Powerful AI-infused image and video analysis solutions trained in detecting deepfake irregularities (as depicted) One of the most significant sides to consider are custom detection codes and playbooks Editor's Note: Our recommendation for Islamic banks is that they need to enforce potent Image/ Videos Analysis with a capacity training into them powerful algorithms serving precisely such matters. The paper underscored the need for regulatory overlap and policy examination. V has so forth concluded that policymakers should resort to strong legal provisions in counteracting the emergence of synthetic media as an instrument that poses a danger for Islamic banks, rather than discard its prompt impact. This input is very critical for policy makers and regulators as well as banking practitioners who can create strategic outlines to mitigate the deepfakes risk that threatens sanctity of Islamic Banking through reliance on trust and integrity.

To the best of our knowledge, this is possibly one of the few studies to focus on deepfakes as a newly neglected threat for Islamic banking. The unique aspect of this space is that it combines ethical standards with the mechanisms of Islamic banking as well digital manipulation techniques to solve for pain points in a non-traditional route. This paper is of theoretical and practical importance, drawing on real-life cases to illustrate how deepfakes compromise trust and integrity in the financial sector given ideals under high-trust. While this study imparts only the defensive mechanisms determined to ensure an Islamic banking tenet, namely implementing modern detection technologies and practical policy recommendations alike. The paper offers a model that provides paramount implications and contributions to stakeholder in Islamic banking industry against rapidly change of technology threat with blending ethical perspectives towards technological solution.

Intersection Between Advanced Technology and Ethical Principles of Sharia Banking

Deepfake technology, which leverages artificial intelligence (AI) to create highly realistic digital representations of individuals or events, has become a topic of great concern in recent years (Guarnera et al., 2020; Raza et al., 2022; Westerlund, 2019). Though it was first created for entertaining and imagination, now people are utilizing it in many unethical ways which create severe issues to security especially when we talk regarding the financial industry. It is a troublesome side for Islamic banking as deepfakes have straightway refuted the trust element Integrity and ethics are few of those paramount principles, on which operations run in this realm. Originally developed to conform with the principles of Sharia law and encourage ethical conduct and social justice, Islamic banking is faced today with a key challenge: how does it remain true in an increasingly digital world?

Integrating advanced artificial intelligence (AI)-based detection technology is the main key in fortifying Islamic banking from deepfake threats. AI technology can serve as the first line of defense by detecting digital manipulation in real-time before the fake content causes reputational damage or financial loss. The AI system supported by visual and sound processing algorithms can recognize patterns that do not match the original characteristics of the video, image, or sound recording, so that banks can immediately take mitigation measures. However, while AI detection is critical, ongoing education for employees and customers should also be a priority. Ensuring that every individual in the banking chain is aware of the threat of deepfakes and the measures to recognize and report anomalies, will strengthen the bank's overall defense system. Customers who are well informed about the risks of this technology will also be more skeptical of suspicious information, thus reducing the likelihood that they will be deceived. The implementation of consistent ethical practices in accordance with sharia principles remains the foundation in maintaining customer trust. Islamic banking, which places integrity as a core value, needs to ensure that every technological innovation adopted not only aims to detect threats but is also aligned with the moral and ethical values on which it operates. The combination of advanced technology with a commitment to education and ethics will create an effective holistic bulwark, ensuring that customer trust is maintained even in the midst of rapid technological advancements.

The ethical principles on which Islamic banking is based include the prohibition of any form of fraud (gharar), manipulation, and uncertainty that can harm other parties (Biduri & Tjahjadi, 2024; Suryanto & Ridwansyah, 2016). Shariah also emphasizes the values of transparency, justice and protection for all stakeholders in a financial transaction. Deepfake — which allows for the creation of deceptive digital content that can be indistinguishable from real life violates each of these core tenets. Engineered means the creation of videos, audio or images are identical at least superficially with a giant body = Authentic. This creates various opportunities for fraud and manipulation which hurt customers, but also erode the credibility of an Islamic banking institution.

One of the biggest threats posed by deepfakes is against trust, which is the main foundation of any financial relationship (Bazarkina & Pashentsev, 2019; Gambín et al., 2024; Mai et al., 2023). While transparency and honesty are in the equation of building trust, some level of confidence also comes from knowing that all operations performed related to Islamic banking are Sharia based. Consider for example deepfake of bank executive posting fake news, such a scenario disrupts financial markets by spreading false claims and creating complex fraud scenarios influence how the public perceives customers leading to confusion -resulting loss consumer's trust. Deepfake scams can soon erode the trust from customers of Islamic financial institutions Eventually, it could lead to more erosion in public confidence on the industry as a whole which will have a larger effect of threatening stability and sustainability for Islamic banking business.

That would be bad enough if it only meant that people might become convinced of lies, but deepfakes represent an existential threat to any kind of public institution. For Islamic banks like other financial institutions, the trust and image of society is very important to attract more customers. In the hands of an irresponsible party, Deepfakes can be used to ruin Islamic banking reputations which will allow them to spread fake news and libel about it. Just imagine the ramifications a single deepfake video could have if made of an Islamic bank executive, breaking one unethical line and this going viral across social media leading to billions in damages as people no longer can trust their money with that bank or even type. When a lot of negative falsehoods come to light, reputational standing is lost forever and even clients and business partners begin to doubt the institution's values which can lead them not only cease using services but also withdraw funds causing more material losses.

In this context, Islamic banking is faced with the unique challenge of maintaining its ethical values amid rapid technological advancements (Alhammadi et al., 2022; Alwi et al., 2021; Kismawadi, 2024b; Musa et al., 2020; Ridho Kismawadi et al., 2023). As these malicious technologies grow stronger at alarming rate, the Islamic banking industry need to reinvent themselves by adopting and incorporating those into their systems without losing focus on what it really stands for. This in part means putting initiative behind technically complex surveillance and detection systems, like those needed to recognize deepfakes; it also includes the formulation of consumer protections that mitigate digital manipulation. Secondly, Islamic banks also have to help their customers understand all risks about deepfakes and how they can be aware of such scam management.

There is nonetheless, one issue that would continue to haunt Islamic banks and they will be how they keep their halo of trust intact in an environment when digital risks are on a significant rise. With artificial intelligence and deepfakes inventing all sorts of new means to erode these values, it is truer than ever for Islamic banks what Ziglar said: "the opposition will treat you just like the way a customer serves". As a result of that Islamic banks must now rely on technology but also need to keep resonating its core principles through providing better transparency, open communication customer level and take one step forward toward adherence the ethical standards.

Besides the technical and regulatory perspectives, ethical considerations surrounding deepfakes in Islamic banking merit a careful discussion. Deepfake technology, on the other hand undermines the fundamental elements of honesty and fairness which are at heart with how Islamic banks function. However, at the same time this technology offers an opportunity for research in how AI and digital technologies could be implemented responsibly respecting Sharia values. The broader conversation to be had opens up the world of how can technology help ethical goals in Islamic finance, and where it gets regulated and watched for incorrect abuse.

Deepfake technology creates profound ethical challenges for Islamic banking, especially in maintaining trust and integrity amid rapid technological advancements (Do et al., 2022; Raza et al., 2022). But more importantly, deepfakes test the ethical principles that underpin the operations of Islamic banking industry equally as much as they do its technical competence in digital security. For addressing these, Islamic banks should have a strategy that involves technology oversight, market education of customers and the reinforcement in regulatory terms but more importantly ethical values behind them. In this way, Islamic Banks can avoid obsolescence in the digital age without sacrificing traditional trust and integrity of Islamic banking.

Threats to Institutional Trust and Security

In the context of Islamic banking, the use of deepfakes can pose a serious threat to customer trust and institutional security (Kaur & Arora, 2021; Salem et al., 2019; Shankar & Jebarajakirthy, 2019). Deepfake, whose only purpose is fraud and the unbearable crime that accompanies it using artificial intelligence. To illustrate, fraudsters could impersonate bank officials and create deepfake videos with voice recordings so that members of the internal team or customers can be manipulated into making an unauthorized transaction by providing their confidential information. It goes beyond issues of financial fraud and extends into fake news that can generate negative reputation and lead to monetary loss for a bank. Rumours of a bank having problems monetarily, or that they have some type internal scandal can cause people to run on the banks and remove their funds as if it is going out style, which plays havoc with liquidity in any business.

These trust losses have significant long-term impacts, including direct financial losses, reputational damage, and impacts on regulation and compliance (Basaran-Brooks, 2022; Jevne et al., 2023; Mohammad et al., 2022). Trust, of course, is paramount in the customer experience with a financial institution – If deepfakes can make things look real when they are really fake then it will undoubtedly break down that trust. The reputational damage from deepfakes could make the bank less competitive in the market and will take a lot of time and resources to get back. In response to the potential of deepfakes, Islamic finance institutions have since stepped up their security and regulatory measures that include adopting detection technology for spotting calculated deceit pack some extra steps through verification process as well as tighter policies. Banks must educate employees and customers, as well as spend on sophisticated detection technology and the implementation of verification procedures to keep risk at bay while maintaining credibility in financial systems.

Deepfakes pose a serious threat to Islamic banking, making it mandatory for strict protocols and procedures which mitigate such concerns. It is critically more imperative that the employees and customers are educated, motivated/trained to identify risks of introducing this technology. Continuous training is there to equip them with the knowledge and expertise needed for identification of valid data against fake one, which will help in lowering down the percentage number that leads toward fraud. Buying up deepfake detection capabilities is a good first step for appropriate recognition and translation of fake media. Such technology must possess a filtering system that is capable of detecting video and audio manipulation, hence to ensure the integrity of communication in financial transactions.

Checks must also be made with great care to verify that the information one receives and on which one acts for executing a transaction is authentic. This can be things such as double authentication methods or verification via other method of communication and that way, the risk of fraud attacks reduces greatly. This way not only will the security of an Islamic banking company get stronger but they also can gain customers trust by giving them a view that how advanced digital threats protection tools these institutions have. Islamic banks need strong policies and regulations that provide deepfake technology-related technical, procedural measures. Developing policies that enforce transparency and accountability when using these technologies can help mitigate negative uses of the technology. Meanwhile, compliance with industry standards and regulatory guidelines by BSPIs will also help the Islamic banking institutions to better fend off digital security threats.

Deepfakes pose a broad and complex set of risks to Islamic banking, institutions will require an entire approach in managing such unprecedented threats. Through education, tech advancement and accurate verification processes or policies implemented Islamic banking institutions can keep the trust to their customer preserving institutional security thus business continuity. There is an obvious need to tackle the challenges if we are not only to safeguard the credibility of Islamic banking but also ensure stability and confidence in financial system at large.

Influence on the Image and Reputation of Sharia Banking

Deepfake, a technology that allows the creation of content that looks authentic but is actually fake using artificial intelligence (AI), has the potential to have a significant impact on the image and reputation of Islamic banking (Hasan & Salah, 2019; Kietzmann et al., 2020; Westerlund, 2019). Image and reputation are valuable assets for any financial institution, and Islamic banking is no exception. In the Islamic banking industry, where trust and integrity are crucial, deepfake attacks can damage a bank's reputation and affect public perception in a substantial way.

The image of Islamic banking is built on sharia principles that involve fairness, transparency, and compliance with Islamic ethics in financial transactions (E R Kismawadi, Irfan, M., Al Muddatstsir, U. D., & Abdulkarim, 2023; Hirsanudin & Martini, 2023; Ishak, 2019; Kismawadi, 2023; Rama, 2020) This image is very important because it affects how customers, investors, and the general public view Islamic financial institutions. Deepfakes can damage this image by creating information or events that appear to come from legitimate sources but are not actually true.

In whatever format deepfakes are expressed, Islamic banking is an image and reputation business. In one example, a deepfake video could be used to depict the CEO of an Islamic bank announcing that it was going to change its investment policy in breach of sharia principles resulting in public confusion and alarm. Those that perceive in the video to be believable may decide to withdraw their fund or diverted them one elsewhere, this puts a bank vying for the institution image of sharia principles efforts at risk. For example, deepfakes can be utilized in spread of a vast number fake news about economic aspects like any scandal placed to bank employees recording how they get bribes. And that even if a video is entirely doctored, the hit to a bank's reputation can be massive there are questions about fraud and transparency related with institutions.

Deepfakes can also spread disinformation regarding financial distress, such as false statements that a bank is suffering from liquidity problems or unable to make payments due. And this seemingly good information may panic the market, made in a hurry to withdraw funds by clients and sell shares of investors which can be painful for banks' financial health and reputation. Deepfakes could potentially be put to use producing forged videos of investment products that run afoul of sharia mores being launched, shocking customers and hurting the bank as a morally Islamic lender. Videos that make it look like government officials or regulators are saying bad things about or threatening banks can also take down B-bucks. Could lead to legal consequences and substantial damage to reputation, despite the fact that the statement may not be accurate.

Deepfakes may further compromise the reputation of banks engaged in social or philanthropic acts with video content that makes it look like they are misappropriating resources from these programs. Considering one of the main challenges that banks face is in relation to their image as friendly and trustworthy companies, this can have far-reaching consequences by reducing public support for other social initiatives. Every one of these examples highlights how deepfakes can attack the image and reputation of Islamic banking, making it necessary to have mitigation strategies that work properly in order to keep more than a star alive. The negative light deepfakes can cast on Islamic banking could also be worse in countries that are not yet fully aware about and accept the concept of Islamic banking. Deepfakes breed uncertainty and confusion, therefore enhancing a sceptical atmosphere regarding the Islamic financial sector in general. The reputation of Islamic banking plays an important role in keeping strong customer& business partner relationships. Having those good reputation shows trust and reliability, quite essential for the financial industry. On a grander scale, the reputation of businesses that rely on realistic media for their services can be compromised by deepfake attacks.

Deepfake attacks on Islamic finance organizations may result in reputation damage in multiple facets. For one, if customers or the public learn that they have been defrauded by deepfakes trust in the bank can be lost to an unassailable degree. Trust is the foundation of a good human relationship and trust cannot be dictated that affects long-term business relationships with consuming customers are one of them, as well as also provides partners who rely heavily on trust in financial transactions such Islamic banking. The second is the impact on Islamic Banks' reputation depends how good they are at managing deepfake attacks. Because if the banks miss these attacks and unable to shut them down effectively, it might be seen as an institution that is not competent: incompetent enough for customers confidence safekeeping their information. A bad response only intensifies the crisis of trust and causes further reputational harm. On order hand, reputational damage from deepfakes could inflict longer-term scars on the Islamic banking brand. Their pride or reputation may be repaired eventually, with time and the same diligence that goes into rebuilding a burnt bridge. And bank in this period will lose some customers, miss out on business and suffer a loss to its brand. In Islamic banking, having a good appearance and reputation is important to make the business sustainable. Deepfakes that tarnish the image and reputation have significant long-term sustainability implications for a bank. Reputation: The simple act of a security breach is bad enough, but for an organization and its brands it can be financially crippling leading to loss customers, lost revenue and additional recovery measures that are costly.

The reduced number of customers might also lead to a drop in revenue, which can have an impact on the financial well-being of the bank. If customers lose confidence and withdraw their deposits, it creates a banking run for consumer banks that they must manage in order to maintain liquidity and efficient operations. If the reputation needs restoring, a bank faces further costs for its rebuilding through marketing campaigns and PR to mitigate any crisis that in turn places an added strain on already tight budgets at individual banks (who may have fewer resources now available) which detracts from their capacity to invest or develop.

Islamic banks need to act proactively in order to minimize the risks of deepfakes against image and reputation. Develop your crisis communications strategy long before a deepfake attacks so that you are prepared to respond immediately when it happens. This plan should address how the bank will respond in a timely, transparent and accurate manner as well as educate customers on what constitutes potential risks and what is being done to maintain the integrity of their funds. Additionally, Islamic banks need to invest in deepfake recognition and prevention capabilities for both their data as well information. This means counterfeit content can be identified and remedied before it has the chance to harm a bank's brand. Furthermore, third has scope for more awareness and training between employees as well as customers on the threats deepfakes pose. Training can go a long way so that they may properly identify potential threats and act accordingly, lessening the possible implications of a deep fake attack. Islamic banking institutions therefore must take appearance seriously, a favourable image requires continuous and transparent communication. This in turn will then support banks to build trust with the public and prevent any negative backlash from potential deepfake attacks which can damage a bank's reputation.

The disruptiveness that deepfakes possess could also have a large impact on the image of Islamic banking. Deepfake attacks can tarnish the good image of a bank who on public perception and tarnishing such goodwill was likely to cause serious reputational damage. The effects of these impacts can lead to a loss of economies, reduced customer numbers and sales drops as well in some cases increased costs for reputation recovery. The results suggest that potential digital frauds can introduce liquidity risks for Islamic banking institutions, so there is a need to implement mitigation strategies among which are forming crisis communication plans, investing in detection technology and training their employees/customers as well build the positive image. This requires a proactive, comprehensive and end-to-end approach enabling fallout in their marketability characterized by digital technology which is determining the sustainability of banks.

Innovative Mitigation Approaches

Deepfake detection technology plays a key role in protecting financial institutions from digital threats (Hu et al., 2022; Mirsky & Lee, 2021; Tolosana et al., 2020; Westerlund, 2019). Islamic banks can use different advanced detection tools and techniques to tackle deepfakes. This includes specialized machine learning algorithms that are meant to identify signs of manipulation in video and audio. The system is able to detect abnormal visual and audio patterns like disparities in facial movements or irrelevant sounds generated during conversation. Studies have shown that deepfake detection methods focus on factors such as eye movements, ensure lip sync and audio quality is consistent in order to conclude if the content has been produced by AI. Methods built on blockchain can used in verifying digital contents as well. Blockchains: This provides the information system with an immutable ledger that can record all updates that have been made to a file, enabling authenticity verification publicly while maintaining security. With this technology, Islamic banks can confirm that any critical information and financial documents they convey or receive are authentic thus lessening the threat of fraud due to deepfakes.

Among the deepfake mitigation strategy, regulatory reform is crucial. There should be a specific legislation with, which all the governments or regulatory agencies around the world try to address these kinds of threats through this deepfake technology. One potential solution is through legislation that would grant penalties to individuals responsible for creating and spreading deepfake content designed with malintent. Some of those rules might have to do with being upfront about their manipulation, informing the public that something is manipulated instead of just hiding it. Data protection and privacy provisions should also be written in the regulatory reforms. This can be problematic when Deepfakes are then used to view and manipulate private data. As a result, legislation that limits access to personal data and obliges institutions to report leakage of such info would reduce some deepfake threats. Given the global nature of their threat, international cooperation with respect to regulation is also crucial. Collaborative international action can help countries address the pervasive, corrosive effects of deepfakes and protect their key financial links.

Part of the solution to deepfakes is raising awareness among industry actors. It is important that Islamic banks inform their employees, clients and partners of these risks and how to detect them. Training should impart on all stakeholders a better understanding of how deepfakes work, the red flags and markers for fake content, as well as ways they now can protect themselves. Train to identify it: Confirming the source of information, verifying the material from numbers /channels you trust and etc. due its identification techniques You should also train your employees on how to report and respond to deepfake threats, such as teaching them what kind of content can be suspect and what steps they need in case that they get scammed by a Deep Nude or any other similar scam. Islamic banks could also raise public awareness concerning the dangers of deepfakes, through training programs and communication campaigns in addition to internal trainings. Banks can also play a part in resisting the spread of fake news and stave-hoarding by giving unambiguous responses to questions from their customers or general public on what is going around in banking sector after that there will be more confidence gain between its citizens about it.

So, to beat the deepfake security, Islamic banks are instantly required to get step forward and adopt new technology which supports their robust safety. For example, the continuous development of artificial intelligence (AI) technology means new ways to detect deepfake exist: enhanced algorithms for recognizing patterns and AI-assisted software which can automatically scan content to determine if there is any manipulation involved. Innovations in the field can also be part of building it up like data analytics. Banks have the ability to detect fraudulent or unusual behaviours in real-time by using big data and predictive analytics to monitor digital activity. This technology gives banks the ability to catch threats early before they escalate into actual problems, so that banks have time to step in and address any damage. However, in the process of developing effective mitigation strategies there also needs to be collaboration with third parties such as cybersecurity firms and research establishments including universities. Islamic banks can do this by collaborating with those who understand deepfake technology well and identify previously un-discovered solutions for improved countermeasures.

It is also important to continue research on deepfake technology, detection methods and countermeasures. To protect themselves and prepare for attacks yet to come, it is important that Islamic banks stay abreast of developments in technology as well as constantly-changing threats. To safeguard the integrity and assurances of full, faith-based compliance in Islamic banking; novel mitigations to deepfakes are essential. Islamic banks can better mitigate deepfake risks by utilizing advanced detection technologies, enforcing regulatory reforms, raising awareness of the risk factors among stakeholders and evolving their technological infrastructure with cutting-edge tech solutions. Working with third-parties and continued research ensures that financial institutions remain ahead of the curve in keeping themselves — and their customers, safe from newly emerging digital threats. These actions not only protect the reputation and safety of Islamic banks, but also strengthen sustainability and confidence in the financial sector as a whole.

The Evolution of Technology Threats and Adaptive Response in Islamic Banking

Traditional security systems have been under assault as technology threats, in particular deepfakes (the use of machine learning to create convincing fakery), evolve at an incredible velocity. Deepfake a product of developments in artificial intelligence (AI) and machine learning technology that makes it possible to create authentic-seeming, but entirely falsified digital content. These threats become more and more advanced, which is harder to catch the actual attacks regarding how challenging enough it may be for countless sectors including Islamic banking. The Islamic banking sector needs an agile response for both technology and regulation to counteract this evolution of the threat. The discussion highlighted that measures for mitigation must continuously evolve with advances in technology.

Since then, the threat posed by deepfakes has evolved. Initially, deepfakes were exclusively used for films that looked too good to be true or as mere amusement. But now, with advancements in technology deepfakes can make realistic content that looks almost no different from the original. This also covers doctored videos and audios of people in settings where they were never there, as well real-sounding yet entirely fake statements made by high-ranking officials.

It has also become increasingly accessible and cheaper, making it possible for a wider range of people and organizations to produce misleading media. It makes the misuse of deepfakes more widespread in different sectors like Islamic banking. These threats can stem from the production of videos or whisper tapes capturing bank executives engaged in illegal acts, wrongdoings and additionally through distorting information for fraudulent completions. While these techniques have been around for a couple of years, the advancements made in AI algorithms make deepfakes even more sophisticated. By developing content that looks and sounds more fluid, idiosyncratic to the English language or similar enough otherwise as to pass by most automated filters. Therefore, deepfake threats are becoming more and more impossible to detect using conventional methods and hence require even newer tactics that need to be adjustable for these advanced videos.

Islamic banking should acquire tech-based solutions to overcome the next-level peril of deepfakes the publication notes several key strategies, with a larger expansion of the deepfake detection strategy being one main avenue. Technologists continue to work on ways that we can detect the signs of subtle manipulation. These include employing more sophisticated machine learning methods and data analytics techniques that can identify suspicious patterns and irregularities in digital content. In addition, Islamic banks could weigh the possibilities of introducing blockchain technology into their infrastructure to maintain a standardised ledger across borders. Especially for digital files, blockchain records can ensure the content has not been altered and hence a more transparent FAT (Fast Appeal Technology) as well. The greater the adoption and integration of blockchain in banks, a higher guarantee that all significant documents or financial communications received by them or their transmission to external entities are authentic; therefore, mitigating risk but without solving it entirely when blocking deepfakes. Technology is not the only solution, as investment in training and education are also crucial. Employees and clients must be trained to detect the signs of deepfake content so that they can instead act upon suspecting such manipulation. Everyone involved is benefitted when an effective training program prepares each of us for the steamroller approach of technological threats and reduces their conversion into successful fraud. Regulations to combat deepfake threats must be adaptive in nature. The regulations cannot be static; they should take into consideration the changing technologies and possible challenges. This would require, among many other things, new laws passed that are tailored to deepfakes and prescribe penalties for any individuals who release the malicious use of deepfake content. These rules should have aspects which make it compulsory for someone in such areas to state that the work they do is manipulation based, there by securing users.

Regulatory reforms should also consider the data protection and privacy. Deepfakes can also be used to gain access and control on personal information which is harmful, for this reason tighter regulations in terms of who has the ability to obtain your data files and if a breach does occur that an institution must disclose would reduce liability with deep fakes. Regulation plays an important part as well, and this is where international cooperation also takes the centre stage. The looming deepfake menace is a global one and requires cooperation from all countries in order to combat fake news. As the world used to deal collective on international standards and strategies, then every country can benefit from them by joining in.

However, the use of deepfake technology will only continue to become more advanced as time goes by; therefore, it is crucial for Islamic banks to closely follow technological advances and revise their mitigation tactics accordingly. This means keeping up to date on the latest trends in technology, studying new ways of detecting and mitigating threats, assessing existing security policies or protocols and updating them as needed. Islamic banks must stay sharp in the face of changing tactics, with continuous review and assessment exercised on current detection and response systems. This involves also regular technology updates and training to guarantee that all stakeholders have the most recent awareness about existing risks as well as available solutions.

Islamic banks must engage and collaborate with third parties like technology companies, research institutions in order to remain innovative. The collaboration could assist banks in keeping up with rapid technological advances to better combat such threats and create stronger solutions. Deepfakes are the scourge of evolving technological threats that require an ever-adapting stance from the Islamic banking industry. As it becomes ever easier to do high-quality deepfakes, Islamic banking must embrace creative strategies of preventing such crime or fraud largely in the form technology innovations and also by regulation. The threat can be countered by the use of more sophisticated detection technologies, changes in regulations and increasing awareness among industry actors. The integrity and trust of Islamic banking through effective mitigation strategies must be monitored continuously for technological development. Islamic Banks can hold onto their security and sustainability with an adaptive approach to remain resilient in the face of such evolutionary technological threats.

Strict and Proactive Regulation

As these abuses take on new forms and advancements in deepfakes suggest further deceptive methods, policymaking must remain stringent and well-informed. Deepfake technology, which makes absurdly legitimate fake digital content possible can be used against the wealth of information about security and trust in Islamic banking sector. As a result, it is important that strong regulations are set in place to define how these synthetic media can be made and distributed. This should include regulations that mandate all deepfake content be watermarked with clear labels and standards for verifying digital media. It seeks to verify that anything presented around does not fail the outlet, so a recipient and affected get together can immediately locate radius on what amount of trade there is or should likely be.

The regulations must have teeth they should include stiff penalties for violators. Sanctions may include monetary penalties, imprisonment or both depending upon the seriousness of any breach committed by you. Deepfakes should trigger a serious response in the law enforcement, which can lead to create special institution or appointment of units to dealing with this phenomenon as well as very accessible reporting methods. To keep pace with the proliferation of deepfake videos in popular culture and hopefully, impede dark money's ability to manufacture disinformation campaigns among citizens worldwide; it can only happen through international cooperation. Foredate calls for countries to cooperate on transnational regulations, helping end legal lacunae in some areas that allow illegal activities.

R&D in more sophisticated deepfake detection technology is equally essential as part of mitigation strategies. More investment in research to create new methods for detection or means of being innovative is one piece to the puzzle that may improve our ability to catch these threats sooner. Policymakers should support coordination of governments, research institutions and technology industry in order to expedite technological assets that can be incorporated within the Islamic banking security system. Educating the public about deepfakes risks is another important. There needs to be an awareness campaign of what deepfakes are and how they can recognize/ deepfake content. When deepfakes do penetrate an environment and history suggests they will, with ever greater sophistication and impact having the entire training infrastructure in place to identify a state-of-the-art threat should not only allow for quicker reporting but also response.

Rules have to be dynamic and adaptive as well, updated or modified in accordance with technological advancements. The law should evolve while the technology advances, with frequent review in partnership with those technologically savvy stakeholders. Lastly, there needs to be importance on transparency and accountability in the creation as well as distribution of digital content creating a more secure and reliable atmosphere. Through this preventive policy, Islamic banking can secure the integrity of trust and security in a more complex digital era. International cooperation in dealing with the threat of deepfakes in Islamic banking can be achieved through practical measures that adapt existing models and frameworks. One of them is the establishment of the Global Alliance for Deepfake Detection, which involves Islamic banks, financial regulators, and technology providers from various countries. This alliance, similar to the Financial Action Task Force (FATF) model, can develop a global standard for deepfake detection technology and share effective detection techniques. Additionally, blockchain technology can be integrated to verify the authenticity of digital content, providing an additional layer of security in ensuring that information published by Islamic banks is genuine (Kismawadi, 2024a). The construction of the International Surveillance Centre, which adopts Interpol's Cyber Crime Directorate model, can also serve to monitor global threats and provide an early warning system for the Islamic banking industry. International financial regulators, such as the Basel Committee on Banking Supervision (BCBS), can develop new regulatory standards that require Islamic banks to use internationally recognized detection technologies. In addition, cross-border education programs can be organized to train bank staff on the use of AI technology and awareness of deepfake threats. Real-time information sharing mechanisms, such as the SWIFT model, can also be applied to provide early warning and share data related to deepfake fraud between Islamic banks around the world. This framework ensures that Islamic banks can face digital threats with better coordination, maintaining customer trust and operational integrity.

An integrated framework that combines technology with cultural and ethical considerations is essential in dealing with the complexity of deepfake threats, particularly in the Islamic banking sector, which bases its operations on Sharia principles. Within this framework, advanced technologies such as artificial intelligence (AI)-based detection are used as the first line of defence to detect and prevent digital manipulation, while still paying attention to Islamic ethical values that emphasize honesty, transparency, and justice.

The AI technology applied in the detection of deepfakes must be carefully selected and adjusted to not only function technically but also support Sharia values. For example, AI detection systems can be developed to identify content that does not comply with ethical norms, preventing the spread of fake videos or audios that could mislead customers or damage the bank's reputation. Here, blockchain verification technology can also be utilized to ensure that the digital information used in transactions or communications is truly trustworthy, thus avoiding gharar (uncertainty) which is prohibited in Islam. However, technology alone is not enough. The culture and ethics that are the foundation of Islamic banking need to be integrated into this strategy. This can be done by educating customers and bank employees about the threat of deepfakes and ethical values that must be maintained. Increased awareness of the importance of trust and honesty in financial relationships can strengthen banks' resilience against such threats. In this case, regular training for staff to recognize digital manipulation, along with the enforcement of higher ethical standards, will add an additional layer of protection that is not only technical but also moral.

The framework should also encourage the application of the principle of transparency, where every official communication from an Islamic bank executive is verified through different official channels, such as websites and direct emails, to reduce the risk of confusion caused by deepfake content. In this regard, transparency is an integral part of the bank's operations that not only protects customers from potential fraud but also ensures that every step taken is in line with Sharia principles that demand clarity and honesty in financial transactions.

CONCLUSION

The Islamic banking community is under pressure from deepfakes with possibly devastating implications for trust and security. Deep fakes are also getting quite possible when it comes to Islamic banking a sector that places a strong emphasis on moral values and integrity. In fact, the so-called Sharia principles are characteristic of two Islamic banks as a distinct form in terms both from certain economic aspects and standards business practice, and they face not least traditional modern challenges to which they must adapt without giving up their core values. Deepfakes being able to generate content that is practically indistinguishable from the original, poses a threat of seemingly real communications making their way for malicious intentions leading potential damage at customer trust and conducting an honest business. Numerous recommendations can be made by Islamic banks to address this challenge. Islamic Banks should deploy state of the art deepfake detecting technology in their platforms at first. One imperative is the need to invest in prices artificial intelligence (AI) based detection solutions that are able to notice and forestall digital manipulation before it compromises the repository. More robust detection will enable Islamic banks to more rapidly spot this type of activity and intercede before it gets out-of-hand.

Islamic banking will need to establish foreign cooperation so as the parties can work together when it comes time for implementing a regulatory framework designed functionally against deepfakes. Since this technology also ignores territorial boundary, frankly it will be efficient only when the countermeasures against legal gaps can be global. Co-operation among countries and around the globe financial institutions will aid in establishing a more robust regulation that shields Islamic banking as well other than protecting overall finance industry. Lastly, we need to educate the public about deepfakes. Continuous information and training campaigns should be run to reach all stakeholders including but not limited the (real or anticipated) customers, front line banking staff as well as regulators know what risks they are up against also can educate them on How would these other products stack up when compared with this particular one that is in focus. This way, through public awareness campaigns they may help to ensure people are better informed about the potential for fraud and scams in their everyday dealings with financial institutions.

In light of these results, one implication that emerges is the responsibility for Islamic banks to not only depend on technology in order to sustain trust and integrity, but also insist upon ethical values via rewarding (the maintenance) by vis-à-vis transparency with clients as well as enforcing their standards. At a time of fast-paced innovation in technology, Islamic banks are required to adhere by the Shariah framework that shapes their businesses. This shows that although technology may come in handy by tracing and protecting from threats, it is ethical values like honesty; integrity etc., which should be the final bedrock at every phase tackled. According to the researchers behind the paper not only do they open a wider discussion for how technology can be utilized in support of ethical objectives and widespread culture but also for how regulations must adapt to channel financial innovation and close pathways that facilitate technological derogation with Islamic finance practice. This, for example may require updating existing regulations to encompass new threats from technologies such as deepfakes and Islamic banks have must be prepared for these changes. This also entails that the regulators need to be more vigilant towards tracking innovation and ensuring their rules are in pace with fresh developments.

Moreover, this research argues an integrated framework can be used to address with the technological threats for Islamic banking industry. That means looking not only to technological answers, but at the people and culture aspects of Islamic banking. Similarly, training Islamic bank staff in ethics and ensuring that they communicate more effectively with customers are components of a grander strategy to uphold integrity as well as trust in an Islamic banking environment. This will not only shield Islamic banking from technological challenges but also help to strengthen their relations with the customers and all other stakeholders.

Deepfake has various impacts to trust and security in Islamic banking therefore it is not only a simple issue. The challenge lies in the Islamic banks that need to remain alert and dynamic towards this phenomenon. Nevertheless, in this process they must not compromise on their core values and every action taken is Shariah based. So, Islamic banking can significantly contribute into the global financial system and surpass its best quality that has become their trademark.

REFERENCES

Alhammadi, S., Alotaibi, K. O., & Hakam, D. F. (2022). Analysing Islamic banking ethical performance from Maqāid al-Sharī'ah perspective: Evidence from Indonesia. *Journal of Sustainable Finance & Investment*, 12(4), 1171–1193. DOI: 10.1080/20430795.2020.1848179

Ali, H., Ahmad, I., & Kamaruddin, B. H. (2020). Efficiency performance of smes firms: A case study of islamic financing guarantee scheme of credit guarantee corporation. *Malaysian Journal of Consumer and Family Economics*, 24(S2), 120–134. https://www.scopus.com/inward/record.uri?eid=2-s2.0-85094199040&partnerID=40&md5=dc630d9fc4ec36051821a66ce6964737

Alwi, Z., Parmitasari, R. D. A., & Syariati, A. (2021). An assessment on Islamic banking ethics through some salient points in the prophetic tradition. *Heliyon*, 7(5), e07103. Advance online publication. DOI: 10.1016/j.heliyon.2021.e07103 PMID: 34124400

Asyiqin, I. Z., & Alfurqon, F. F. (2024). Musyarakah Mutanaqisah: Strengthening Islamic Financing in Indonesia and Addressing Murabahah Vulnerabilities. *Jurnal Media Hukum*, 31(1), 1–18. DOI: 10.18196/jmh.v31i1.20897

Basaran-Brooks, B. (2022). Money laundering and financial stability: Does adverse publicity matter? *Journal of Financial Regulation and Compliance*, 30(2), 196–214. DOI: 10.1108/JFRC-09-2021-0075

Bazarkina, D. Y., & Pashentsev, Y. N. (2019). Artificial intelligence and new threats to international psychological security. *Russia in Global Affairs*, 17(1), 147–170. DOI: 10.31278/1810-6374-2019-17-1-147-170

Biduri, S., & Tjahjadi, B. (2024). Determinants of financial statement fraud: The perspective of pentagon fraud theory (evidence on Islamic banking companies in Indonesia). *Journal of Islamic Accounting and Business Research*. Advance online publication. DOI: 10.1108/JIABR-08-2022-0213

Do, T.-L., Tran, M.-K., Nguyen, H. H., & Tran, M.-T. (2022). Potential Attacks of DeepFake on eKYC Systems and Remedy for eKYC with DeepFake Detection Using Two-Stream Network of Facial Appearance and Motion Features. *SN Computer Science*, 3(6), 464. Advance online publication. DOI: 10.1007/s42979-022-01364-x

Gambín, Á. F., Yazidi, A., Vasilakos, A., Haugerud, H., & Djenouri, Y. (2024). Deepfakes: Current and future trends. *Artificial Intelligence Review*, 57(3), 64. Advance online publication. DOI: 10.1007/s10462-023-10679-x

Guarnera, L., Giudice, O., & Battiato, S. (2020). Fighting deepfake by exposing the convolutional traces on images. *IEEE Access : Practical Innovations, Open Solutions*, 8, 165085–165098. DOI: 10.1109/ACCESS.2020.3023037

Hasan, H. R., & Salah, K. (2019). Combating Deepfake Videos Using Blockchain and Smart Contracts. *IEEE Access : Practical Innovations, Open Solutions*, 7, 41596–41606. DOI: 10.1109/ACCESS.2019.2905689

Hirsanudin, H., & Martini, D. (2023). Good Corporate Governance Principles in Islamic Banking: A Legal Perspective on the Integration of TARIF Values. *Journal of Indonesian Legal Studies*, 8(2), 935–974. DOI: 10.15294/jils.v8i2.70784

Hu, J., Liao, X., Wang, W., & Qin, Z. (2022). Detecting Compressed Deepfake Videos in Social Networks Using Frame-Temporality Two-Stream Convolutional Network. *IEEE Transactions on Circuits and Systems for Video Technology*, 32(3), 1089–1102. DOI: 10.1109/TCSVT.2021.3074259

Ishak, M. S. I. (2019). The principle of ma la ah and its application in Islamic banking operations in Malaysia. *ISRA International Journal of Islamic Finance*, 11(1), 137–146. DOI: 10.1108/IJIF-01-2018-0017

Jevne, F. L., Hauge, Å. L., & Thomassen, M. K. (2023). User evaluation of a national web portal for climate change adaptation – A qualitative case sstudy of the Knowledge Bank. *Climate Services*, 30, 100367. Advance online publication. DOI: 10.1016/j.cliser.2023.100367

Kaur, S., & Arora, S. (2021). Role of perceived risk in online banking and its impact on behavioral intention: Trust as a moderator. *Journal of Asia Business Studies*, 15(1), 1–30. DOI: 10.1108/JABS-08-2019-0252

Kietzmann, J., Lee, L. W., McCarthy, I. P., & Kietzmann, T. C. (2020). Deepfakes: Trick or treat? *Business Horizons*, 63(2), 135–146. DOI: 10.1016/j.bushor.2019.11.006

Kismawadi, E. R. (2023). *Islamic Banking And Economic Growth: A Panel Data Approach*. Iranian Economic Review., DOI: 10.22059/ier.2023.365739.1007815

Kismawadi, E. R. (2024a). Blockchain technology and islamic finance: Empowering small businesses for financial sustainability. In *Technopreneurship in Small Businesses for Sustainability* (pp. 50–77). DOI: 10.4018/979-8-3693-3530-7.ch004

Kismawadi, E. R. (2024b). Contribution of Islamic banks and macroeconomic variables to economic growth in developing countries: Vector error correction model approach (VECM). *Journal of Islamic Accounting and Business Research*, 15(2), 306–326. DOI: 10.1108/JIABR-03-2022-0090

Kismawadi, E. R., Irfan, M., Al Muddatstsir, U. D., & Abdulkarim, F. M. (2023). Fintech innovations: Risk mitigation strategies in Islamic finance. In *Fintech Applications in Islamic Finance* (pp. 35–58). AI, Machine Learning, and Blockchain Techniques., DOI: 10.4018/979-8-3693-1038-0.ch003

Mai, K. T., Bray, S., Davies, T., & Griffin, L. D. (2023). Warning: Humans cannot reliably detect speech deepfakes. *PLoS ONE, 18*(8 August). DOI: 10.1371/journal.pone.0285333

Mirsky, Y., & Lee, W. (2021). The Creation and Detection of Deepfakes. *ACM Computing Surveys*, 54(1), 1–41. Advance online publication. DOI: 10.1145/3425780

Mohammad, S. J., Tahtamouni, A., Aldaas, A. A., & Sumadi, M. A. (2022). Preventing money laundering during the placement stage: The Jordanian commercial banks case. *International Journal of Public Law and Policy*, 8(1), 37–51. DOI: 10.1504/IJPLAP.2022.120663

Musa, M. A., Sukor, M. E. A., Ismail, M. N., & Elias, M. R. F. (2020). Islamic business ethics and practices of Islamic banks: Perceptions of Islamic bank employees in Gulf cooperation countries and Malaysia. *Journal of Islamic Accounting and Business Research*, 11(5), 1009–1031. DOI: 10.1108/JIABR-07-2016-0080

Rama, A. (2020). Strategic pricing by Islamic banks and the impact on customer satisfaction and behavioral intention. *Journal of Islamic Accounting and Business Research*, 11(9), 2017–2033. DOI: 10.1108/JIABR-04-2019-0078

Raza, A., Munir, K., & Almutairi, M. (2022). A Novel Deep Learning Approach for Deepfake Image Detection. *Applied Sciences (Basel, Switzerland)*, 12(19), 9820. Advance online publication. DOI: 10.3390/app12199820

Ridho Kismawadi, E., Irfan, M., & Shah, S. M. A. R. (2023). Revolutionizing islamic finance: Artificial intelligence's role in the future of industry. In *The Impact of AI Innovation on Financial Sectors in the Era of Industry 5.0* (pp. 184–207). DOI: 10.4018/979-8-3693-0082-4.ch011

Salem, M. Z., Baidoun, S., & Walsh, G. (2019). Factors affecting Palestinian customers' use of online banking services. *International Journal of Bank Marketing*, 37(2), 426–451. DOI: 10.1108/IJBM-08-2018-0210

Santoso, A. L., Kamarudin, F., Amin Noordin, B. A., & Wei Theng, L. (2023). Islamic ethics commitment and bank outcomes: Evidence in South East Asia. *Cogent Economics & Finance*, 11(1), 2175458. Advance online publication. DOI: 10.1080/23322039.2023.2175458

Shankar, A., & Jebarajakirthy, C. (2019). The influence of e-banking service quality on customer loyalty: A moderated mediation approach. *International Journal of Bank Marketing*, 37(5), 1119–1142. DOI: 10.1108/IJBM-03-2018-0063

Suryanto, T., & Ridwansyah, R. (2016). The Shariah financial accounting standards: How they prevent fraud in islamic banking. *European Research Studies*, 19(4), 140–157. DOI: 10.35808/ersj/587

Tolosana, R., Vera-Rodriguez, R., Fierrez, J., Morales, A., & Ortega-Garcia, J. (2020). Deepfakes and beyond: A Survey of face manipulation and fake detection. *Information Fusion*, 64, 131–148. DOI: 10.1016/j.inffus.2020.06.014

Westerlund, M. (2019). The emergence of deepfake technology: A review. *Technology Innovation Management Review*, 9(11), 39–52. DOI: 10.22215/timreview/1282

Chapter 6
Shaping Consumer Perception Through Deepfake Marketing:
Ethics and Implications

Sonam Rani
http://orcid.org/0000-0002-2894-0366
Amity University, Noida, India

Sailaja Bohara
Amity University, Noida, India

Gaurav Gupta
https://orcid.org/0000-0003-1507-1357
Amity University, Greater Noida Campus, India

Mandakini Paruthi
http://orcid.org/0000-0002-1081-8282
IBS Hyderabad, India

Shiv Ranjan
Amity University, Noida, India

ABSTRACT

The advent of deepfake technology has introduced transformative possibilities in marketing, reshaping consumer perceptions and engagement through hyper-realistic digital content. This book chapter examines the ethical dimensions and potential implications of deepfake applications in marketing, specifically focusing on their power to shape consumer perception. With the ability to create synthetic

DOI: 10.4018/979-8-3693-6890-9.ch006

yet believable visual and audio representations, deepfakes have provided brands with innovative tools to captivate audiences and personalize experiences. However, this comes with ethical concerns, including risks of deception, manipulation, and consumer mistrust. This chapter explores both the opportunities and challenges posed by deepfake marketing, emphasizing the need for responsible practices to maintain transparency, authenticity, and consumer trust. It also discusses regulatory and policy considerations, proposing ethical frameworks to guide marketers in the responsible use of deepfake technology.

INTRODUCTION

Definition of Deepfake Marketing

Deepfake marketing leverages deepfake technology to create highly immersive and engaging marketing experiences through advanced storytelling techniques (Frank, 2022). Deepfake technology, rooted in deep learning, enables computers to perform tasks independently without explicit programming (Frank, 2022). This technology also incorporates computer vision, which allows machines to recognize and identify objects within images and videos (Frank, 2022). For instance, computer vision can utilize deep learning algorithms to detect whether an image contains a specific object, such as a dog (Frank, 2022). The process of creating deepfakes for marketing involves image synthesis, where one image is combined with another to produce a realistic composite (Frank, 2022). By utilizing these sophisticated technologies, marketers can create content that captivates audiences in novel and compelling ways, though they are still in the early stages of experimentation ((Frank, 2022).

Understanding Deepfakes in Consumer Marketing

Deepfake technology has become a captivating yet controversial force in the world of marketing. As the lines between reality and manipulation blur, the use of deepfakes in marketing raises significant ethical concerns. This technology enables the creation of synthetic media that makes it increasingly difficult to discern fact from fiction, presenting both new risks and opportunities for the advertising industry (Wright, 2023b). One striking example of the impact of deepfakes on consumer marketing occurred in late March 2023, when images of Pope Francis wearing a white Balenciaga puffer jacket went viral on social media. These images, which also showed the pontiff donning stylish sunglasses, gloves, slacks, and sneakers—attire not typically associated with the Catholic Church's highest office—shocked and amused the world. The virality of these deepfake images highlights the powerful influence that synthetic media can wield in shaping public perception and driving engagement. The use of deepfake technology in marketing has also involved high-profile celebrities such as Taylor Swift, Selena Gomez, Elon Musk, and Joe Rogan, who have been deepfaked in various campaigns. These applications of deepfake technology not only capture consumer attention but also bring to the forefront significant ethical dilemmas. Concerns about consent, misinformation, and the potential for manipulation underscore the need for a careful and responsible approach to leveraging deepfakes in marketing strategies.

Deepfake Technology in the Marketing Industry

Deepfake technology is revolutionizing the marketing industry by providing more immersive and personalized experiences through storytelling (Frank, 2022e). This technology, which falls under the umbrella of deep learning—a machine learning method that enables computers to learn tasks independently—leverages computer vision to recognize and synthesize images (Frank, 2022e). For instance, deep learning algorithms in computer vision can identify objects in photos or videos, such as distinguishing a dog in an image (Frank, 2022e). The practical applications of deepfake technology in marketing are vast and transformative. By 2024, deepfakes and AI are expected to redefine marketing strategies, allowing CEOs and other executives to address global audiences in multiple languages with flawless precision, and enhancing customer interactions through hyper-realistic avatars (Sarkhedi, 2024). This convergence of deepfakes and AI not only pushes the boundaries of traditional marketing but also introduces new ethical considerations (Sarkhedi, 2024). Marketers can utilize deepfakes in various innovative ways to boost engagement and drive business growth. These include enhancing ad campaigns, dynamic influencer marketing, revitalizing explainer videos, diversifying product demonstrations, animating cold email outreach, substituting speakers in online conferences, and creating corporate training and educational videos (Foundation Labs, 2024; Restackio, n.d.). The technology's ability to hyper-personalize advertising, such as adapting speech and lip movements without requiring models to learn new languages, exemplifies its potential in delivering highly tailored marketing messages (Schwarz, 2023). However, while the opportunities presented by deepfake technology are considerable, they also come with a set of legal and ethical challenges. Marketers must navigate these carefully to avoid misuse and ensure the responsible application of such powerful tools (Schwarz, 2023).

Technology Advancements

Recent Advancements in GANs for Deepfake Quality Recent advancements in Generative Adversarial Networks (GANs) have significantly enhanced the quality and realism of deepfake media. GANs play a crucial role in the creation of hyper-realistic synthetic images and videos by utilizing a two-component system: the generator and the discriminator. The generator's task is to create synthetic content that closely resembles real images, while the discriminator's role is to differentiate between real and synthetic content. Through this adversarial process, both components continually improve, leading to the production of increasingly convincing media (Restackio, n.d.). The entertainment industry has capitalized on these advancements for visual effects and creative storytelling, allowing filmmakers and content creators to manipulate videos and swap faces in ways that are both imaginative and realistic (Ollie, 2024)
. However, the implications of these hyper realistic deepfakes extend beyond entertainment. They pose significant ethical and security challenges, as they can be used to spread misinformation, manipulate political outcomes, and damage reputations (Abbas, 2024),

HOW GANS IMPROVE REALISM IN DEEPFAKE MEDIA

Generative Adversarial Networks (GANs) have significantly advanced the realism of deepfake media in recent years. These AI algorithms consist of two neural networks: a generator and a discriminator, which compete against each other to create highly realistic media (Ollie, 2024b)
. The generator creates fake content, while the discriminator evaluates its authenticity. This process continues iteratively, with both networks improving over time, leading to highly convincing deepfakes (Ollie, 2024b)
. The quality and realism of deepfakes have been notably enhanced due to recent advancements in GANs. These improvements have made deepfakes more difficult to distinguish from genuine media, allowing them to be used for a variety of purposes, from entertainment to malicious activities (Vyas, 2019). As GAN technology evolves, the generated deepfakes become increasingly sophisticated, posing significant challenges for detection and prevention (*A Framework for Detection in an Era of Rising Deepfakes*, 2024). The demographic analysis of deepfake videos reveals a selective production process influenced by specific attributes like gender, nationality, and profession. This targeted approach reflects the nuanced motivations behind the creation and dissemination of deepfake content, with 99% of deepfake pornographic content comprising female subjects (*2023 State of Deepfakes: Realities, Threats, and Impact*, n.d.). The intersection of technology, creativity, and audience

preferences highlights the intricate dynamics in the development and application of deepfake media (*2023 State of Deepfakes: Realities, Threats, and Impact*, n.d.). As GANs continue to improve, the ethical implications of their use become more pronounced. The technology's capability to generate realistic deepfakes brings with it a responsibility to address potential misuse and develop frameworks to maintain ethical boundaries (Vyas, 2019; Ollie, 2024b).

Applications in Marketing

Deepfake technology has become a captivating yet controversial force in the world of marketing, blurring the lines between reality and manipulation (*The Rise of Deepfake Marketing - What Are the Cons and Pros? | Brand Vision*, n.d.-b). This innovative technology is being used in various creative ways, from ad campaigns to influencer marketing, providing brands with novel approaches to engage with audiences (*The Rise of Deepfake Marketing - What Are the Cons and Pros? | Brand Vision*. (n.d.-b). Some of the key applications of deepfake technology in marketing include enhancing dynamic influencer marketing, reviving explainer videos, animating cold email outreach, and creating corporate training videos *The Rise of Deepfake Marketing - What Are the Cons and Pros? | Brand Vision*. (n.d.-b). One notable campaign was carried out by Deutsche Telekom, which utilized deepfake video technology to warn of the dangers of 'sharenting' through their #ShareWithCare initiative (Webster, 2023). Additionally, in 2018, Zalando launched a campaign featuring model Cara Delevingne across 290,000 localized ads, achieved through deepfake technology to produce various alternative shots and voice fonts. This campaign ran on Facebook across 12 countries, gaining 180 million impressions on social media (Chitrakorn, 2021). Deepfakes have also been employed to create impactful educational and entertaining videos for clients, demonstrating their versatility in various content formats. Despite these innovative uses, the ethical dilemmas and risks associated with deepfakes, such as the potential for misuse and the difficulty in discerning fact from fiction, continue to be a significant concern within the marketing industry (W. Wright, 2023a).

Key Technological Advancements in Deepfakes 2023

The advancements in deepfake technology have seen significant progress in 2023, driven by rapid improvements in artificial intelligence (AI) and machine learning techniques. These developments have greatly enhanced the quality and realism of deepfakes, making them increasingly difficult to detect by both the human eye and existing detection technologies (Christie, 2023). One notable advancement is the use of deep learning algorithms which have refined the ability to generate synthetic media, including videos, audio, and images, that appear remarkably authentic. Researchers have also been working on new detection methods, such as AI models that can identify colour abnormalities and authentication techniques like digital watermarks to determine if a media file has been manipulated. The impact of these technological improvements on consumer marketing is profound. The high quality of deepfakes can be leveraged in creating realistic and engaging marketing content, potentially transforming advertising strategies. For instance, the Republican National Committee's use of AI-generated imagery in a political ad exemplifies how deepfakes can create compelling narratives that captivate audiences (Bond, 2023). However, this also raises concerns about misinformation and the ethical implications of using such technologies in marketing (Christie, 2023).

Improvements in Deepfake Quality in Recent Years

Deepfakes have seen significant technological advancements in recent years, leading to increased quality and realism. These improvements are primarily driven by advancements in artificial intelligence, particularly through the use of deep learning and generative adversarial networks (GANs) (Cruz, 2024). These technologies enable the creation of highly realistic images, videos, and audio recordings that can be difficult to distinguish from genuine media (Cruz, 2024). The enhanced realism of deepfakes has broadened their applications in various fields, including consumer marketing. Businesses can now create realistic synthetic media for advertisements, promotional videos, and virtual brand ambassadors, which can engage consumers in more interactive and personalized ways. However, this same realism has also led to significant challenges, as bad actors exploit these advancements for disinformation, blackmail, harassment, and financial fraud (Cruz, 2024). As a result, it has become increasingly important for individuals and organizations to develop skills in identifying and protecting against harmful deepfakes (Cruz, 2024).

ETHICAL CONSIDERATIONS

Primary Ethical Concerns of Deepfake Technology in Marketing:

Deepfake technology involves the use of artificial intelligence (AI) to create or alter video content, making it appear as though individuals are saying or doing things they never actually did. This technology, while fascinating, introduces complex dynamics into the influencer marketing landscape, which relies heavily on authenticity and trust (A, 2024). Brands looking to leverage deepfakes in their marketing campaigns must navigate the fine line between innovative engagement and ethical responsibility. The marketing and advertising space is rapidly evolving with tools like AI and automation enabling companies to maximize consumer engagement through compelling and personalized campaigns (N. Wright, 2024). However, the potential for misuse is significant. To ensure ethical use of deepfakes, brands must prioritize data privacy and security (N. Wright, 2024). Companies need to adopt robust ethical and regulatory frameworks to mitigate risks related to identity representation, consent, and misrepresentation (Leighton, 2024). The use of deep-fake technology must be transparent to avoid misleading consumers and to maintain their trust (Leighton, 2024). By implementing these measures, brands can harness the creative potential of deepfakes while safeguarding their ethical standards and organizational values (N. Wright, 2024).

Ethical Use in Marketing Campaigns

Deepfake technology involves the use of artificial intelligence (AI) to create or alter video content, making it appear as though individuals are saying or doing things they never actually did. Brands looking to leverage deepfakes in their marketing campaigns must navigate the fine line between innovative engagement and ethical responsibility. The marketing and advertising space is rapidly evolving with tools like AI and automation enabling companies to maximize consumer engagement through compelling and personalized campaigns (N. Wright, 2024). However, the potential for misuse is significant. To ensure ethical use of deepfakes, brands must prioritize data privacy and security (N. Wright, 2024). Companies need to adopt robust ethical and regulatory frameworks to mitigate risks related to identity representation, consent, and misrepresentation (Leighton, 2024). The use of deepfake technology must be transparent to avoid misleading consumers and to maintain their trust (Leighton, 2024). By implementing these measures, brands can harness the creative potential of deepfakes while safeguarding their ethical standards and organizational values.

RISKS AND CHALLENGES

Deepfake technology has rapidly infiltrated the marketing landscape, offering a new level of immersive storytelling and creative freedom for brands (Frank, 2022d; Writer, 2023). However, this innovative tool also brings significant ethical concerns and risks that brands must carefully navigate. One of the primary risks associated with deepfake technology in marketing is the potential for misinformation and disinformation. A single fake video or manipulated image can drastically impact a company's market value in a short amount of time, underscoring the immediacy and potential devastation of such threats (Marr, 2024). Privacy violations represent another significant challenge. The algorithms behind deepfake technology can create convincing imitations of individuals without their consent, potentially leading to severe invasions of privacy and misuse in various contexts (Marr, 2022). Notable incidents include the unauthorized use of celebrities' likenesses, such as those of Taylor Swift, Selena Gomez, Elon Musk, and Joe Rogan, which have sparked debates over ethical boundaries in digital marketing. Furthermore, the potential for financial fraud is a critical concern. Deepfake technology can be employed to create deceptive media that can manipulate stock prices or market perceptions, posing a severe threat to financial stability and investor confidence (Marr, 2024). As businesses increasingly rely on media to make strategic decisions, the integrity of this media becomes paramount to safeguard against manipulative tactics. While deepfake technology holds promise for innovative marketing strategies, it is a double-edged sword that necessitates robust detection methods and regulatory frameworks to mitigate its risks. Companies must be vigilant in addressing these challenges to ensure that the benefits of deepfake marketing do not come at the cost of ethical integrity and consumer trust (Writer, 2023; Bowie & Kajal, 2024; Sahota, 2023).

Technologies for Detecting Deepfakes

Deepfake technology has evolved rapidly, creating hyper-realistic videos and audio clips that are deceptive to the human eye and ear. This evolution has led to a significant increase in deepfake fraud attempts, skyrocketing by an astonishing 3000% since 2023 (Ughade, 2024). The pressing scenario underscores the crucial significance of deception detection instruments. These instruments utilize advanced AI algorithms, machine learning, and other sophisticated techniques to detect fake videos, recordings, audio clips, and images, thereby helping organizations and individuals protect themselves against this growing threat (Ughade, 2024). Various tools and techniques have been developed to combat the rise of deepfakes. One prominent example is Reality Defender, a deepfake detection tool that leverages AI to identify manipulated media. This tool, along with others like Sentinel, helps in analyzing digital content to determine its authenticity (McFarland, 2024; Bellini, 2023). Sentinel, for instance, is an AI-based protection platform used by democratic governments, defence agencies, and enterprises across Europe. Users can upload digital media via the Sentinel website or API, and the system analyzes the content, generating detailed reports that visualize where and how the media has been manipulated (Bellini, 2023). Furthermore, the significance of detecting deepfakes extends beyond technology. It involves holistic changes within organizations to combat deepfake impersonation scams effectively. Businesses need to incorporate identity verification and fraud monitoring as central components of their financial onboarding processes (Goldman-Kalaydin, 2024). The combination of AI detection tools and human discretion enhances the success rates in identifying and mitigating the dangers of deepfake technology (Brooks, 2023)

The use of AI-enabled detection technologies is keeping pace with the advancements in deepfake algorithms by employing diverse techniques and algorithms to identify forgeries. Over 300 articles focused on creating detection tools for deepfakes have been published in the IEEE Xplore digital library within the first six months of 2024 alone, indicating extensive research and development in this area (Bligen, 2024). As AI technology continues to improve, the ability to identify fake content becomes crucial for nullifying disinformation and protecting brand trust and reputation (Goldman-Kalaydin, 2024).

Strategies for Rebuilding Brand Trust

Rebuilding brand trust after a deepfake incident involves a multi-faceted approach to address the immediate damage and prevent future occurrences. The first critical step is to acknowledge the incident publicly and transparently. Companies must quickly communicate with their customers, stakeholders, and the public about the deepfake incident, clarifying that the content is fraudulent and does not represent the brand's values or actions (Frank, 2022e; Clark, 2023c). Deploying robust verification mechanisms is essential. This can include leveraging AI-driven detection platforms that identify and flag potential deepfakes before they can spread widely. Training employees to recognize the signs of deepfake content also helps in early detection and response (Woollcott, 2024; Clark, 2023c). By demonstrating a proactive stance, brands can reassure their audience of their commitment to integrity and security (Frank, 2022e; Woollcott, 2024). Developing a comprehensive incident response plan that includes social listening and monitoring is crucial. This plan should outline the steps for immediate action when a deepfake is identified, such as notifying affected parties, containing the spread of misinformation, and coordinating with legal authorities if necessary (Clark, 2023c). Ensuring that all communication channels provide consistent and accurate information helps in maintaining control over the narrative (Frank, 2022e; Clark, 2023c). Furthermore, brands should engage in continuous education and awareness campaigns. Informing consumers about the nature of deepfakes and how to identify them empowers the audience to discern credible content from manipulated media. This builds a community that is less susceptible to disinformation and more supportive of the brand's efforts to combat such threats (Frank, 2022e; Clark, 2023c). Ultimately, rebuilding trust is an ongoing process that requires vigilance, transparency, and a proactive approach to cybersecurity and public relations. Brands must integrate these strategies into their broader crisis management and communication plans to safeguard their reputation in the evolving digital landscape (Charles et al.,2022)

How Brands Can Avoid Misleading Consumers with Deepfakes

The rapid evolution of deepfake technology has introduced both opportunities and challenges for brands. Deepfakes—AI-generated videos that convincingly depict people doing or saying things they never actually did—have the potential to be used for both benign and malicious purposes (Week, 2024). As this technology becomes more sophisticated and accessible, brands must navigate the ethical implications of using deepfakes in their marketing campaigns. To avoid misleading consumers while leveraging the engaging potential of deepfakes, brands should adopt several key strategies. First, transparency is essential. Brands should disclose when deepfake technology is used in their campaigns to ensure that consumers are not deceived. This transparency builds trust and allows consumers to engage with the content knowingly. Second, brands should use deepfakes in a way that respects the individuals depicted. For example, they should obtain explicit consent from any person whose likeness is being replicated. This is particularly important when using the likenesses of celebrities, such as Taylor Swift, Selena Gomez, Elon Musk, and Joe Rogan, who have all been featured in deepfake marketing campaigns Third, brands should implement robust verification processes to ensure the accuracy and appropriateness of the content before it is released. This includes working with experts in AI and deepfake technology to create high-quality and ethical content (Cooper, 2024). Finally, brands should continuously educate themselves and their consumers about the potential risks and ethical considerations associated with deepfakes. By raising awareness and promoting responsible use, brands can help mitigate the potential for misuse and maintain their reputation (Cooper, 2024).

Proactive Measures Against Deepfake Technology

As deepfake technology continues to evolve, organizations must implement proactive measures to safeguard against potential threats and protect their brand trust and reputation. First, organizations should invest in advanced detection tools that can distinguish between authentic and manipulated content. These tools are critical in identifying deepfakes before they can cause harm (S. L. C. Writer, 2024). Additionally, companies should adopt a multi-layered approach to cybersecurity. This includes training employees to recognize the signs of deepfake attacks and implementing robust verification processes for sensitive communications, such as video calls purportedly from senior executives (Fisher Phillips, 2024). Cybersecurity professionals should also be vigilant about the data and images shared online, as these can be weaponized to create deepfakes (*How to Protect Against Deepfake Attacks and Extortion*, 2023).

Organizations can further mitigate risks by authenticating content provenance. This practice helps maintain public confidence by ensuring that the content shared is genuine and has not been tampered with (Oversight Committee Republicans Verified account, 2023). Furthermore, policymakers and regulatory bodies are encouraged to explore legislative options that address the unique challenges posed by deepfakes, creating a legal framework to deter and punish malicious actors (Engler, 2019). In anticipation of future advancements making deepfakes easier and cheaper to produce, organizations should continuously update their security measures and stay informed about emerging threats. This proactive stance includes preparing for deepfake-related cybercrime and foreign influence operations, which are likely to more prevalent as technology advances (*Deepfakes: What They Are & How Your Business Is at Risk*, n.d.). Lastly, adopting a comprehensive risk management strategy that incorporates the latest research and insights on deep threats will enable organizations to better navigate this evolving landscape (Berzinski, 2024)

LEGAL MEASURES AND FRAMEWORKS

Current Legal Measures Against Deepfake Technology 2023

The National Security Agency (NSA), along with U.S. federal agency partners, has issued new advice on the synthetic media threat known as deepfakes, recognizing it as a significant cybersecurity challenge for National Security Systems (NSS), the Department of Defence (DoD), and Defence Industrial Base (DIB) organizations (NSA, 2023). The joint Cybersecurity Information Sheet (CSI) titled "Contextualizing Deepfake Threats to Organizations" was released to assist organizations in identifying, defending against, and responding to deepfake threats, with contributions from the Federal Bureau of Investigation (FBI) and the Cybersecurity and Infrastructure Security Agency (CISA) (NSA, 2023). Deepfakes are artificially created images or videos that use voice cloning and artificial intelligence (AI) to make it appear as though an individual did or said something they did not (Kite-Powell, 2023)

. The rise of this technology has raised concerns, especially with the upcoming 2024 presidential elections and the discussions held by U.S. Senate Majority Leader Chuck Schumer with tech leaders at the AI forum in September 2023 (Kite-Powell, 2023). Deepfakes often target public figures to discredit them or spread misinformation, posing a significant threat to their character and credibility, as highlighted by Scott Hermann, CEO of IDIQ (Kite-Powell, 2023). From its development in the 1990s to the launch of a widely available app in 2018, deepfake technology has advanced considerably and become more accessible to the general population (Deansr, 2023). While deepfake technology has legitimate uses in education, film, and retail, it has also been misused for political attacks, creating non-consensual pornography, and fraudulent business activities (Deansr, 2023. To mitigate these threats, legal measures and frameworks are being developed to help businesses protect their brand trust and reputation from the potential damage caused by deepfakes. This emerging field is constantly evolving as technology advances and new threats emerge, necessitating ongoing efforts to strengthen and update these legal frameworks (NSA, 2023; Kite-Powell, 2023; Deansr, 2023).

Frameworks to Protect Brand Reputation from Deepfakes

As the threat environment for corporates continues to evolve rapidly, managing cyber risks, particularly those posed by deepfakes, has become increasingly critical for leadership teams (Deansr, 2023). Deepfakes, highly realistic synthetic media created using artificial intelligence, present significant risks to brand trust and business operations. These risks are accentuated by their potential for misuse in targeting high-profile figures, leading to misrepresentation and financial loss. A notable example is the $25 million loss suffered by a Hong Kong company due to a deepfake scam, underscoring the urgent need for robust communication strategies and internal safeguards (Deansr, 2023). Companies increasingly rely on authentic media to shape their brand and make critical business decisions. The infiltration of deepfakes within this media poses substantial risks, with misinformation and disinformation identified as severe near-term global threats in the World Economic Forum's 2024 Global Risks Report (*Deepfakes Pose Businesses Risks—Here's What to Know*, 2024b). Consequently, it is imperative for commercial chief information security officers, executives, and boards to understand and mitigate these risks to protect their brand reputation effectively (*Deepfakes Pose Businesses Risks—Here's What to Know*, 2024b). Implementing comprehensive internal safeguards and communication strategies is essential. Organizations need to adopt advanced detection technologies, invest in continuous staff training, and establish clear protocols for responding to deepfake incidents. Additionally, fostering a culture of vigilance and scepticism towards unverified media can help in mitigating the risks posed by deepfakes. These frameworks collectively serve to protect brand reputation from the potential damage caused by deepfake technology, ensuring business continuity and market stability.

Pre-Emptive Measures for Brand Protection

Brands face significant risks from the proliferation of deepfakes, necessitating proactive measures to protect their reputation and maintain consumer trust. To safeguard against these threats, several strategies can be employed. Firstly, leveraging advanced deepfake detection technologies is crucial. Utilizing AI-driven platforms and sophisticated recognition tools, including blockchain and biometrics, can enhance the credibility of brand content by identifying manipulated media promptly (Academy, 2024b), (Clark, 2023). Regularly updating these tools to keep pace with advancements in deepfake technology is essential. Secondly, brands should establish comprehensive deepfake attack protocols. Despite a recent study revealing that only 13% of companies currently have such protocols in place, developing and implementing detailed response plans can significantly mitigate potential damage (C. Brooks, 2024). These plans should encompass immediate actions for incident response, social listening to monitor online mentions, and guidelines for communicating with the public during a deepfake crisis (Clark, 2023b). Furthermore, education and training are pivotal. Brands must educate their employees, especially those in public-facing roles, on recognizing the signs of deepfake content. Training programs that highlight manual clues and provide insights into the latest detection techniques can empower teams to identify and address deepfakes before they escalate (Clark, 2023). Creating a transparent communication strategy is also vital. In the event of a deepfake incident, maintaining transparency with consumers about the steps being taken to address the issue helps preserve trust. Proactively communicating the measures in place to combat deepfakes can reassure consumers of the brand's commitment to integrity and authenticity (Academy, 2024b; Pal, 2023). Lastly, legal preparedness plays a significant role. Understanding the legal implications and having a robust legal framework to address potential deepfake scenarios can help brands navigate the challenges of liability, financial losses, and erosion of consumer trust (Academy, 2024b). Collaborating with legal experts to draft policies and procedures specific to deepfake incidents ensures a swift and compliant response. By implementing these pre-emptive measures, brands can strengthen their defences against the growing threat of deepfakes, ultimately preserving their reputation and maintaining the trust of their consumers (Academy, 2024b; Clark, 2023; Pal, 2023).

CONCLUSION

The advent of deepfake technology in marketing has brought forth unprecedented possibilities and ethical complexities. It has enabled brands to create realistic content, offering a different manner in which storytelling and consumer engagement can be done. There are always two sides to the coin, these technologies also pose significant ethical challenges, to be specific these are issues regarding consent, authenticity, and potential for misinformation. The use of deepfake technology requires careful consideration to avoid deceptive practices and uphold consumer trust. Responsible application, transparency, and adherence to ethical frameworks are essential for marketers seeking to leverage deepfake technology effectively. As this technology evolves, brands, policymakers, and society must collaborate on establishing robust regulatory measures, advancing detection tools, and promoting ethical standards to harness the benefits of deepfakes while minimizing risks. Ultimately, a balanced approach that combines innovation with ethical integrity will ensure that deepfake marketing contributes positively to the digital landscape.

REFERENCES

Abbas, A. (2024, June 25). *Hyperrealistic Deepfakes: A Growing Threat to Truth and Reality*. Unite.AI. https://www.unite.ai/hyperrealistic-deepfakes-a-growing-threat-to-truth-and-reality/

Academy, E. (2024, May 7). Understanding the Impact of Deepfakes on Brand Trust - Online Business School. *Best Courses in Digital marketing*. https://esoftskills.com/dm/understanding-the-impact-of-deepfakes-on-brand-trust/

Academy, E. (2024b, May 7). Understanding the Impact of Deepfakes on Brand Trust - Online Business School. *Best Courses in Digital marketing*. https://esoftskills.com/dm/understanding-the-impact-of-deepfakes-on-brand-trust/

Bellini, A. (2023b, October 18). Deepfakes Tools for Detection - Abe Bellini - Medium. *Medium*. https://medium.com/@abebellini/deepfakes-tools-for-detection-20c24cde976b

Berzinski, M. (2024, September 27). Three essential steps for organizations to safeguard against deepfakes. *TechRadar*. https://www.techradar.com/pro/three-essential-steps-for-organizations-to-safeguard-against-deepfakes

Bligen, R. (2024, August 8). *Spotting the Deepfake - IEEE Transmitter*. IEEE Transmitter. https://transmitter.ieee.org/spotting-the-deepfake/

Bond, S. (2023, April 27). AI-generated deepfakes are moving fast. Policymakers can't keep up. *NPR*. https://www.npr.org/2023/04/27/1172387911/how-can-people-spot-fake-images-created-by-artificial-intelligence

Bowie, J., & Kajal. (2024, November 6). *Deepfake: Navigating the Future of Innovation and Privacy Risks*. Pickl.AI. https://www.pickl.ai/blog/deepfake-facing-the-future-with-intrusion-and-innovation/

Brooks, A. (2023, November 6). *Who Detects Deepfakes Better: Man or Machine?* MUO. https://www.makeuseof.com/how-reliable-are-deepfake-detection-tools/

Brooks, C. (2024, June 28). *1 in 10 Executives Say Their Companies Have Already Faced Deepfake Threats*. business.com. https://www.business.com/articles/deepfake-threats-study/

Chitrakorn, K. (2021, January 11). How deepfakes could change fashion advertising. *Vogue Business*. https://www.voguebusiness.com/companies/how-deepfakes-could-change-fashion-advertising-influencer-marketing

Christie, A. (2023, October 2). *Rolling in the deepfakes: Generative AI, privacy and regulation*. Market Insight. Published in *LexisNexis Privacy Bulletin*, 2023, Vol. 20, No. 6.

Clark, S. (2023, August 18). Unmasking Deepfakes: How Brands Can Combat AI-Generated Disinformation. *CMSWire.com*. https://www.cmswire.com/digital-experience/unmasking-deepfakes-how-brands-can-combat-ai-generated-disinformation/

Cooper, C. (2024, July 19). Deep fakes: Are you aware of the risk they pose to your brand? *Medium*. https://medium.com/@colin-cooper/deep-fakes-are-you-aware-of-the-risk-they-pose-to-your-brand-42d8d0246cb1

Cruz, B. (2024, September 26). *2024 Deepfakes Guide and Statistics*. Security.org. https://www.security.org/resources/deepfake-statistics/

Deansr. (2023, June 20). *The High Stakes of Deepfakes: The Growing Necessity of Federal Legislation to Regulate This Rapidly Evolving Technology*. Princeton Legal Journal. https://legaljournal.princeton.edu/the-high-stakes-of-deepfakes-the-growing-necessity-of-federal-legislation-to-regulate-this-rapidly-evolving-technology/

Deepfake Technology Using Gans | Restackio. (n.d.). https://www.restack.io/p/adversarial-networks-knowledge-deepfake-technology-cat-ai

. *Deepfake: The new digital threat and strategies for protection*. (2024, October 21). News & Events.

Deepfakes Pose Businesses Risks—Here's What to Know. (2024, November 8). https://www.boozallen.com/insights/ai-research/deepfakes-pose-businesses-risks-heres-what-to-know.html

Deepfakes Pose Businesses Risks—Here's What to Know. (2024b, November 8). https://www.boozallen.com/insights/ai-research/deepfakes-pose-businesses-risks-heres-what-to-know.html

Deepfakes: What They Are & How Your Business Is at Risk. (n.d.). Bank of America. https://business.bofa.com/en-us/content/cyber-security-journal/deepfakes-business-risks.html

Engler, A. (2019, November 14). Fighting deepfakes when detection fails. *Brookings*. https://www.brookings.edu/articles/fighting-deepfakes-when-detection-fails/

Fisher Phillips. (n.d.). *You Can No Longer Believe What You See: 5 Ways Employers Can Guard Against Deepfakes*. https://www.fisherphillips.com/en/news-insights/5-ways-employers-can-guard-against-deepfakes.html

Foundation Labs. (2024, September 4). *Deepfakes at work: Why AI videos are the future of marketing*. Foundation Inc. Retrieved from https://www.foundationinc.co

Frank, K. (2022b, June 22). *Deepfake Technology Pros & Cons For Digital Marketing*. Search Engine Journal. https://www.searchenginejournal.com/deepfake -technology-digital-marketing/454395/

Frank, K. (2022b, June 22). *Deepfake Technology Pros & Cons For Digital Marketing*. Search Engine Journal. https://www.searchenginejournal.com/deepfake -technology-digital-marketing/454395/

Frank, K. (2022b, June 22). *Deepfake Technology Pros & Cons For Digital Marketing*. Search Engine Journal. https://www.searchenginejournal.com/deepfake -technology-digital-marketing/454395/

Frank, K. (2022b, June 22). *Deepfake Technology Pros & Cons For Digital Marketing*. Search Engine Journal. https://www.searchenginejournal.com/deepfake -technology-digital-marketing/454395/

Frank, K. (2022d, June 22). *Deepfake Technology Pros & Cons For Digital Marketing*. Search Engine Journal. https://www.searchenginejournal.com/deepfake -technology-digital-marketing/454395/

Gans In Deepfake Technology | Restackio. (n.d.). https://www.restack.io/p/adversarial -networks-knowledge-gans-deepfake-cat-ai

Goldman-Kalaydin, P. (2024, November 5). New AI tools and training vital to combat deepfake impersonation scams. *TechRadar*. https://www.techradar.com/pro/new-ai -tools-and-training-vital-to-combat-deepfake-impersonation-scams

How to Protect Against Deepfake Attacks and Extortion. (2023, August 23). Security Intelligence. https://securityintelligence.com/articles/how-protect-against-deepfake -attacks-extortion/

Kite-Powell, J. (2023, September 26). Deepfakes Are Here, Can They Be Stopped? *Forbes*. https://www.forbes.com/sites/jenniferkitepowell/2023/09/20/deepfakes-are -here-can-they-be-stopped/

Leighton, N. (2024, November 6). *Ethical AI in marketing: Balancing automation with human values*. Forbes Coaches Council. Retrieved from https://www.forbes.com

Marr, B. (2022, January 12). Deepfakes – The Good, The Bad, And The Ugly. *Forbes*. https://www.forbes.com/sites/bernardmarr/2022/01/11/deepfakes--the-good -the-bad-and-the-ugly/

Marr, B. (2024, November 7). The Dark Side Of AI: How Deepfakes And Disinformation Are Becoming A Billion-Dollar Business Risk. *Forbes*. https://www.forbes.com/sites/bernardmarr/2024/11/06/the-dark-side-of-ai-how-deepfakes-and-disinformation-are-becoming-a-billion-dollar-business-risk/

McFarland, A. (2024, November 5). *7 Best Deepfake Detector Tools & Techniques (November 2024)*. Unite.AI. https://www.unite.ai/best-deepfake-detector-tools-and-techniques/

National Security Agency. (2023, September 12). *NSA, U.S. federal agencies advise on deepfake threats* (U/OO/199197-23 I PP-23-3076 I Ver. 1.0). Press Release.

O'Brien, C. (2024, March 22). *Protecting corporate reputation in the era of the deepfake: Understand how AI is affecting your organisation and how you can adapt.*

Ollie. (2024, July 23). The Rise of Deepfake Videos: Unraveling the Magic Behind GANs. *Medium*. https://medium.com/@ohermans1/the-rise-of-deepfake-videos-unraveling-the-magic-behind-gans-a4d7c03637fa

Ollie. (2024b, July 23). The Rise of Deepfake Videos: Unraveling the Magic Behind GANs. *Medium*. https://medium.com/@ohermans1/the-rise-of-deepfake-videos-unraveling-the-magic-behind-gans-a4d7c03637fa

Oversight Committee Republicans Verified account. (2023, December 7). *Hearing Wrap Up: Action Needed to Combat Proliferation of Harmful Deepfakes - United States House Committee on Oversight and Accountability*. United States House Committee on Oversight and Accountability. https://oversight.house.gov/release/hearing-wrap-up-action-needed-to-combat-proliferation-of-harmful-deepfakes%ef%bf%bc/

Pal, D. (2023, December 4). *The Looming Threat of Deepfakes: How They Can Damage Brand Identity*. https://www.linkedin.com/pulse/looming-threat-deepfakes-how-can-damage-brand-identity-debojyoti-pal-wuwgf

Sahota, N. (2023, March 21). *Deepfake Technology: The Risks, Benefits and Detection Methods*. https://www.linkedin.com/pulse/deepfake-technology-risks-benefits-detection-methods-sahota-%E8%90%A8%E5%86%A0%E5%86%9B-

Sarkhedi. (2024, February 20). *Deceptive or Disruptive: How deepfakes and AI will transform marketing in 2024*. Forbes India. https://www.forbesindia.com/blog/technology/deceptive-or-disruptive-how-deepfakes-and-ai-will-transform-marketing-in-2024/

Schwarz, S. (2023, August 16). *Deepfakes in marketing – from a legal perspective*. DMEXCO. https://dmexco.com/stories/deepfakes-uses-and-legal-implications/

The Rise of AI Deepfake Technology: Transforming Media and Raising Ethical Questions. (n.d.). https://techcosmictales.com/Deepfake-Technology

The Rise of Deepfake Marketing - What Are the Cons and Pros? | Brand Vision. (n.d.). https://www.brandvm.com/post/deepfake-marketing

The Rise of Deepfake Marketing - What Are the Cons and Pros? | Brand Vision. (n.d.-b). https://www.brandvm.com/post/deepfake-marketing

The Rise of Deepfake Marketing - What Are the Cons and Pros? | Brand Vision. (n.d.-b). https://www.brandvm.com/post/deepfake-marketing

The Rise of Deepfake Marketing - What Are the Cons and Pros? | Brand Vision. (n.d.-c). https://www.brandvm.com/post/deepfake-marketing

The Rise of Deepfake Marketing - What Are the Cons and Pros? | Brand Vision. (n.d.-d). https://www.brandvm.com/post/deepfake-marketing

Ughade, N. (2024, September 18). *5 Best Deepfake Detection Tools (2024).* hyperverge.co. https://hyperverge.co/blog/deepfake-detection-tools/

Vyas, K. (2019, August 12). Generative Adversarial Networks: The Tech Behind DeepFake and FaceApp. *Interesting Engineering.* https://interestingengineering.com/innovation/generative-adversarial-networks-the-tech-behind-deepfake-and-faceapp

Webster, G. (2023, July 6). *6 best ad campaigns that use deep fakes.* Big Ideas That Work. https://blog.bigideasthatwork.com/creative-campaigns-that-use-deep-fake-technology/

Week, A. (2024, July 15). *Why the Evolution of Deepfakes Is a Wake-up Call for Brands.* https://advertisingweek.com/why-the-evolution-of-deepfakes-is-a-wake-up-call-for-brands/

Woollcott, E. (2024, March 20). The rise of deepfakes: navigating their impact on reputation and business. *Mishcon de Reya LLP.* https://www.mishcon.com/news/the-rise-of-deepfakes-navigating-their-impact-on-reputation-and-business

Wright, N. (2024, August 19). *Deepfakes and the Ethics of Generative AI | Tepperspectives.* Tepperspectives. https://tepperspectives.cmu.edu/all-articles/deepfakes-and-the-ethics-of-generative-ai/

Wright, W. (2023b, April 3). A marketer's guide to deepfakes. *The Drum.* https://www.thedrum.com/news/2023/04/03/marketer-s-guide-deepfakes

Writer, S. (2023, September 8). *Deepfake AI and Digital Marketing: Pros, Cons and Dangers*. Bold Business. https://www.boldbusiness.com/digital/deepfake-ai-digital -marketing-pros-cons-dangers/

Writer, S. L. C. (2024, November 7). *Regulators Combat Deepfakes With Anti-Fraud Rules*. https://www.darkreading.com/data-privacy/regulators-combat-deepfakes -anti-fraud-rules

Chapter 7
Collaboration and Collective Action:
Addressing the Deepfake Challenge as a Community

Satya Subrahmanyam
https://orcid.org/0000-0003-0441-2742
Holy Spirit University of Kaslik, Lebanon

ABSTRACT

This chapter explores the critical role of collaboration and collective action in addressing the deepfake challenge. As deepfake technology advances, it presents unprecedented risks to businesses, individuals, and society. This chapter examines cross-sector partnerships among governments, tech companies, businesses, academia, and nonprofits to combat deepfakes effectively. It emphasizes the need for legal frameworks, innovative detection technologies, public education, and digital literacy to build resilience. Through case studies, the chapter highlights successful strategies and identifies gaps in current approaches, advocating for proactive solutions to anticipate future technological developments. Ultimately, it calls for continuous, unified efforts to create a safer, more trustworthy digital ecosystem.

1. INTRODUCTION

In recent years, the emergence of deepfakes—highly realistic and manipulated media generated by artificial intelligence (AI)—has presented new and significant challenges for both businesses and communities. Deepfakes, which use techniques such as generative adversarial networks (GANs) to create synthetic but hyper-realistic images, audio, and videos, have far-reaching implications, including the erosion of

DOI: 10.4018/979-8-3693-6890-9.ch007

Copyright © 2025, IGI Global Scientific Publishing. Copying or distributing in print or electronic forms without written permission of IGI Global Scientific Publishing is prohibited.

public trust, brand reputation risks, and the spread of misinformation (Chesney & Citron, 2019). For businesses, deepfakes threaten corporate integrity and consumer confidence, posing risks to brand value and the potential for financial loss. Communities also suffer as deepfakes undermine trust in social institutions and the integrity of public information, which can destabilize the collective perception of truth.

In addressing these threats, it is essential to recognize that no single organization or entity can combat the deepfake challenge alone. The sophistication of these manipulative technologies calls for collaborative solutions that combine technological innovation, legal frameworks, cross-sector partnerships, and community education. A collective approach can strengthen resources, increase knowledge sharing, and enable swift and effective responses to deepfake incidents, ultimately building a stronger defense against these evolving threats (Westerlund, 2019).

This chapter explores the necessity of collective action in confronting the deepfake challenge, detailing roles and responsibilities across different sectors—including government, technology companies, businesses, academic institutions, and communities—and proposing actionable collaborative solutions. The following sections outline the importance of community awareness, cross-sector partnerships, shared technological solutions, policy frameworks, and educational initiatives as vital components in a unified defense against deepfake threats.

1.1 Understanding Deepfakes as a Community Threat

The advancement of deepfake technology has led to concerns that extend beyond individual impacts, affecting society as a whole. Deepfakes have potential applications in malicious activities such as identity theft, corporate espionage, and the manipulation of public opinion (Ajder et al., 2019). Businesses are particularly vulnerable, as deepfake-related incidents can lead to reputational harm and compromised consumer trust. In the context of community impact, deepfakes foster an environment where deception becomes easily accessible, thereby undermining the fundamental trust that binds societies together. Addressing this issue thus requires a coordinated and widespread understanding of deepfakes as a community threat, which must be acknowledged and acted upon collectively (Kietzmann et al., 2020).

1.2 Cross-Sector Collaboration: Roles and Responsibilities

A multi-layered approach to combatting deepfakes involves stakeholders from various sectors, each contributing unique resources and expertise to mitigate the risks.

Government and Regulatory Bodies: Governments play a pivotal role in establishing and enforcing regulations around deepfake usage. By setting legal boundaries, governments can discourage malicious use of the technology, protect vulnerable sectors, and promote the responsible use of AI technologies. Regulatory bodies should coordinate with international partners to create global standards for content authentication, privacy, and accountability (Schwarz, 2020).

Technology Companies: Given their technical expertise, technology firms are essential in developing and refining detection technologies and authentication tools. By creating algorithms that can identify and flag deepfakes, companies can protect consumers and clients while helping businesses monitor their brand presence online. Collaborative efforts between tech companies can also result in open-source databases and shared detection tools, which broaden accessibility and strengthen overall defenses (Nguyen et al., 2021).

Businesses and Corporations: Businesses face considerable brand-related risks from deepfakes and, therefore, should be proactive in adopting detection tools, educating employees, and setting up protocols to respond to deepfake-related incidents. Large corporations can also support smaller businesses by sharing resources and insights, contributing to a broader community-based defense (Chawla et al., 2021).

Academic and Research Institutions: Academic institutions are crucial in advancing deepfake detection research and understanding psychological and societal impacts. By partnering with governments and tech firms, universities can facilitate innovation and the development of new detection frameworks, making the fight against deepfakes a research priority that benefits all sectors (Westerlund, 2019).

Nonprofits and Advocacy Groups: Nonprofit organizations and advocacy groups can play an influential role in raising public awareness and advocating for ethical standards. These groups often serve as intermediaries, bridging gaps between policymakers and the general public to foster understanding and promote responsible media consumption (Kietzmann et al., 2020).

Addressing the deepfake challenge as a community is an urgent and multifaceted endeavor. The collective actions of governments, technology companies, businesses, academic institutions, and communities are essential in creating a resilient defense against deepfakes. Through collaborative partnerships, shared technological solutions, robust legal frameworks, and widespread educational initiatives, society can mitigate the risks associated with deepfakes and preserve the integrity of media, communication, and public trust. As deepfake technology continues to evolve, ongoing cooperation and vigilance are required to adapt to new threats and safeguard the community against the damaging impact of digital manipulation.

2. UNDERSTANDING DEEPFAKES: A COMMUNITY THREAT

2.1 Defining Deepfakes

Deepfakes refer to synthetic media where a person in an existing image or video is replaced with someone else's likeness using artificial intelligence (AI) techniques. This technology primarily employs Generative Adversarial Networks (GANs), which consist of two neural networks—the generator and the discriminator—competing against each other. The generator creates synthetic data, while the discriminator evaluates its authenticity (Goodfellow et al., 2014). Over time, as these networks engage in this adversarial process, the generator improves its ability to produce highly realistic images or videos, effectively fooling the discriminator.

The implications of this technology are vast. GANs have enabled the creation of convincing audio and visual deepfakes that can be indistinguishable from genuine media. This ability has been applied across various fields, from entertainment and art to advertising. However, the same technology has also been exploited for malicious purposes, leading to serious ethical and societal concerns (Chesney & Citron, 2019).

2.2 Impacts on Businesses and Society

The proliferation of deepfakes poses significant risks to both businesses and society at large. Understanding these risks requires an examination of the potential harms associated with deepfakes, including misinformation, brand damage, loss of consumer trust, and psychological impacts.

Misinformation and Disinformation: One of the most pressing threats posed by deepfakes is their potential to disseminate misinformation. Deepfake videos can be manipulated to misrepresent facts, making it appear as though individuals are saying or doing things they never did. This capability can be particularly dangerous in political contexts, where deepfakes can be used to undermine candidates, manipulate public opinion, or incite violence (Westerlund, 2019). Misinformation campaigns leveraging deepfake technology can create confusion and distrust among the public, contributing to polarization and societal division.

Brand Damage: For businesses, the stakes are equally high. A deepfake that falsely depicts a corporate leader making inappropriate remarks could lead to significant reputational damage, stock price fluctuations, and loss of customer loyalty. Organizations invest heavily in brand integrity and public relations, making them particularly vulnerable to deepfake attacks (Chawla et al., 2021). Companies may find it challenging to recover from the negative press generated by such incidents, which could result in long-lasting harm to their brand image.

Loss of Consumer Trust: As deepfakes become more prevalent, public trust in media and information sources is likely to erode. Consumers rely on authentic media for decision-making, whether regarding products, services, or even political issues. When individuals cannot discern between real and fabricated content, their ability to trust any media source diminishes (Ajder et al., 2019). This skepticism can have far-reaching consequences for businesses, as consumers may hesitate to engage with brands that they perceive as vulnerable to manipulation or deceit.

Psychological Impacts: The psychological effects of deepfakes extend beyond individuals directly affected by misinformation or defamation. The general public can experience anxiety, paranoia, and distrust, as the line between reality and fabrication becomes increasingly blurred. The prevalence of deepfakes can create a sense of helplessness among individuals, who may feel overwhelmed by the difficulty of discerning truth in a media landscape inundated with manipulation (Kietzmann et al., 2020). This psychological toll can lead to social disengagement and a general decline in civic participation, undermining the social fabric of communities.

2.3 The Importance of Community Awareness

In light of these risks, community awareness becomes a critical factor in combating the challenges posed by deepfakes. Raising awareness across all levels—business, government, and the general public—can create a collective defense mechanism that empowers individuals and organizations to navigate the deepfake landscape more effectively.

Empowering Businesses: For businesses, awareness of deepfake technology and its implications is essential for proactive risk management. Companies should implement training programs that educate employees about deepfakes, helping them recognize potential threats and respond appropriately. By fostering a culture of vigilance, organizations can mitigate the risks associated with deepfake-related incidents and enhance their overall resilience (Chesney & Citron, 2019). Furthermore, businesses can invest in technology that detects deepfakes and verify the authenticity of media content before distribution.

Government and Regulatory Role: Governments have a vital role in establishing frameworks that promote community awareness. This can include public campaigns aimed at educating citizens about the risks associated with deepfakes and promoting critical media literacy. By implementing regulations that require transparency in media production, governments can help safeguard the public from misleading content. Additionally, they can collaborate with tech companies and academic institutions to develop and disseminate tools that assist in identifying deepfakes, thus fostering a more informed and resilient citizenry (Westerlund, 2019).

Public Education Initiatives: Raising public awareness about deepfakes must also extend to educational institutions. Integrating media literacy programs into school curriculums can equip future generations with the skills necessary to discern credible information from manipulated content. By fostering critical thinking and media analysis skills from an early age, educational institutions can empower students to become discerning consumers of media, capable of navigating an increasingly complex digital landscape (Nguyen et al., 2021).

Collective Action and Collaboration: Community awareness also benefits from collaborative initiatives involving multiple stakeholders. Organizations can form coalitions that bring together businesses, government agencies, and nonprofits to address the challenges posed by deepfakes collectively. These coalitions can work together to share knowledge, resources, and best practices, thereby enhancing overall community resilience. By engaging in collective action, stakeholders can amplify their efforts to combat deepfakes and foster a culture of awareness and vigilance within their communities (Kietzmann et al., 2020).

The Role of Technology in Community Awareness: Finally, technological solutions can play a significant role in enhancing community awareness of deepfakes. For example, social media platforms can develop algorithms to detect and flag potential deepfake content, alerting users to the possibility of manipulation. By integrating these tools into everyday digital experiences, platforms can contribute to a more informed user base. Additionally, public-facing campaigns that utilize engaging content—such as videos and infographics—can effectively communicate the risks of deepfakes and encourage critical media consumption (Ajder et al., 2019).

Understanding deepfakes as a community threat necessitates a comprehensive examination of their defining technology, the wide-ranging impacts on businesses and society, and the importance of awareness at all levels. As deepfake technology continues to evolve, so too must our collective response. Empowering businesses, engaging governments, and fostering public education initiatives are crucial steps toward building a resilient community capable of navigating the challenges posed by deepfakes. Ultimately, a coordinated approach that prioritizes awareness, collaboration, and technological innovation will be essential in combating the threats posed by deepfakes and safeguarding the integrity of information in our digital age.

3. THE ROLE OF CROSS-SECTOR COLLABORATION

The rapid advancement of deepfake technology, while remarkable, has raised ethical, social, and security concerns across multiple sectors. Deepfakes pose significant risks in disinformation, reputation damage, security breaches, and psychological harm, highlighting the need for a multifaceted response that transcends individual sectors. Addressing the deepfake challenge effectively requires a coordinated response from governments, technology companies, businesses, academic institutions, and nonprofit organizations. Each sector brings unique strengths, responsibilities, and approaches to building a more resilient framework against the risks of deepfakes.

3.1 Government and Regulatory Bodies

Governments and regulatory bodies have a critical role in curbing the malicious use of deepfakes by establishing legal frameworks, enforcing penalties, and setting policies that outline acceptable standards and accountability. Recognizing deepfakes as a threat to social stability, democracy, and privacy, governments worldwide are beginning to implement specific legal measures to combat the issue (Hancock, 2020). Through policy-making and regulation, governments can establish boundaries that make it easier to prosecute those who use deepfakes maliciously. For example, the U.S. recently introduced the "DEEP FAKES Accountability Act," aimed at imposing stringent penalties on creators and disseminators of maliciously intended deepfakes (Chesney & Citron, 2019).

In addition to legal measures, regulatory bodies are essential in setting up certification and labeling systems that indicate the authenticity of media content. By mandating transparent labeling for AI-generated or altered content, governments can help establish consumer awareness and trust. Moreover, governments can allocate funds to support law enforcement agencies in their fight against malicious uses of deepfake technology, enhancing their ability to respond to deepfake-related threats and provide protection against abuses (Westerlund, 2019).

However, given the rapid evolution of AI technology, governments must continuously update these frameworks to keep pace with emerging capabilities in deepfake generation. An example of forward-thinking regulation is the European Union's General Data Protection Regulation (GDPR), which has provisions that could apply to AI-driven media manipulation. The GDPR's focus on privacy rights and data transparency helps regulate the ethical use of AI technologies, indirectly influencing the permissible uses of deepfakes (Tolosana et al., 2020).

3.2 Technology Companies

Technology companies, particularly those developing artificial intelligence and machine learning, play a fundamental role in counteracting the harmful effects of deepfakes. As creators and distributors of AI, these companies hold unique responsibilities in advancing tools and methods for detecting manipulated content. Companies like Google, Microsoft, and Facebook have already begun developing and releasing open-source tools for identifying deepfakes. For instance, Facebook's

Deepfake Detection Challenge sought to accelerate innovation in identifying manipulated media by inviting researchers to develop state-of-the-art detection models (Dolhansky et al., 2020).

Another area of responsibility for technology companies lies in establishing industry-wide standards for content verification and authentication protocols. By collaborating with other tech entities and stakeholders, companies can set consistent rules and practices that help end-users verify the integrity of online content. Such collaboration could include the development of blockchain-based systems to create an indelible record of content origin, tracking the lifecycle of media files from creation to final distribution (Kietzmann et al., 2020).

Technology companies can also enhance their role by incorporating deepfake detection technologies directly into their platforms. By detecting manipulated content at the point of upload, companies can prevent its spread and notify users of potentially misleading information. Content moderation, combined with prompt notifications, helps limit the reach of harmful deepfake content and equips users to make informed decisions. This approach not only mitigates the potential for harm but also promotes a culture of digital literacy and skepticism around potentially deceptive media (Nguyen et al., 2021).

3.3 Businesses and Corporations

Businesses and corporations are vulnerable to deepfake attacks, which can damage reputations, compromise security, and erode customer trust. Consequently, organizations must be proactive in implementing measures to safeguard their brands and protect their customers. Investment in deepfake-detection technologies is an essential step, enabling companies to identify manipulated content before it reaches the public. Using these technologies to monitor brand mentions, media reports, and social media posts allows companies to preemptively respond to any deepfake-based disinformation targeting their brand or executives (Chawla et al., 2021).

Employee training programs also play a key role in an organization's defense against deepfakes. By educating employees on the risks associated with deepfakes, businesses can foster a culture of vigilance. Employees trained to recognize deepfakes and understand their implications are better prepared to take appropriate actions, especially in sensitive areas like public relations, corporate communications, and security. As front-line defenders, employees' awareness and knowledge are crucial to an organization's defense strategy (Westerlund, 2019).

In addition to internal defenses, corporations can play a broader role by enhancing consumer awareness. Many organizations already invest in consumer education about cybersecurity and fraud prevention, and adding deepfake awareness can build consumer trust. Companies can inform their customer base about the risks posed by deepfakes and provide resources to help them identify manipulated content. This approach not only protects the brand but also contributes to a more informed and resilient public.

3.4 Academic and Research Institutions

Academic and research institutions are instrumental in advancing the technological and psychological understanding of deepfakes. Research in this field has primarily focused on improving detection capabilities and examining the psychological impact of exposure to deepfake content. Institutions are also conducting essential research on GANs and other AI models, contributing to the development of more accurate detection tools. Continued investment in this research will be crucial to staying ahead of deepfake creators, who continually find ways to bypass current detection methods (Nguyen et al., 2021).

Beyond detection, academic research plays a pivotal role in exploring the psychological and societal impact of deepfakes. Studies that assess the emotional, cognitive, and behavioral effects of exposure to deepfake content can inform public education campaigns and help shape guidelines for content creators and regulators. For example, understanding the psychological mechanisms that lead individuals to believe false information enables researchers to design more effective educational initiatives that promote critical thinking and media literacy (Chesney & Citron, 2019).

Moreover, universities and research centers can play a central role in fostering cross-sector collaboration. By acting as neutral, research-driven conveners, these institutions can bridge the gap between sectors, creating forums where stakeholders can share insights, discuss challenges, and develop collaborative solutions. Such collaboration can catalyze innovation and allow experts from various fields to contribute their unique expertise to the fight against deepfakes (Hancock, 2020).

3.5 Nonprofits and Advocacy Groups

Nonprofits and advocacy groups are vital in raising public awareness and advocating for ethical standards and policy reform related to deepfakes. Nonprofits can organize campaigns to educate the public on recognizing and responding to deepfake content, addressing the urgent need for digital literacy in an age where manipulated media is increasingly prevalent. Initiatives like the "Deep Truth" campaign, which targets disinformation in digital media, exemplify the proactive role advocacy groups can play in fostering a more informed public (Westerlund, 2019).

In addition to public education, advocacy groups provide support for individuals and communities affected by deepfake abuse, including victims of non-consensual pornography and online harassment. By offering legal aid, counseling, and digital safety resources, nonprofits play a direct role in assisting those harmed by deepfakes, helping them seek justice and reclaim their digital autonomy (Hancock, 2020).

Nonprofits are essential in pushing for ethical standards and policy change. Through lobbying efforts and public pressure campaigns, they can advocate for policies that require transparency, accountability, and ethical considerations in the use and dissemination of deepfake technology. By working with policymakers, nonprofits can amplify public demand for protective measures, helping to establish a regulatory environment that upholds both individual rights and public trust (Kietzmann et al., 2020).

Addressing the deepfake challenge requires coordinated efforts across government, technology companies, businesses, academia, and nonprofit organizations. Each sector has a distinct but interconnected role in mitigating the risks associated with deepfakes. Governments and regulatory bodies establish legal boundaries and enforce penalties; technology companies develop detection tools and promote content verification; businesses protect their brands and educate consumers; academic institutions advance research and psychological understanding; and nonprofits drive public awareness and advocacy. Together, these cross-sector efforts can create a more resilient and informed society, better equipped to counter the threats posed by deepfake technology.

4. COLLECTIVE TECHNOLOGICAL SOLUTIONS

The rise of deepfake technology has catalyzed the development of technological solutions that can help mitigate its harmful impact. By leveraging advances in artificial intelligence, blockchain technology, shared databases, and community-driven tools, stakeholders are increasingly equipped to detect, verify, and counter malicious deepfakes. However, effectively combating deepfakes requires not just individual advancements but collaborative, community-centered efforts that draw on the strengths of various sectors. Collective technological solutions foster resilience and enhance the ability to address these threats systematically and comprehensively.

4.1 Advances in Detection Technologies

Detection technology represents the frontline in the fight against deepfakes. Most current detection systems rely on AI algorithms, such as machine learning and deep learning models, specifically trained to identify telltale signs of synthetic media. In particular, Generative Adversarial Networks (GANs) are not only used to create deepfakes but also serve as a basis for detection tools designed to expose manipulated content. GAN-based detection models employ techniques that analyze pixel inconsistencies, unnatural blinking patterns, and lip-sync discrepancies to distinguish between real and manipulated media (Nguyen et al., 2021).

One of the most promising advances in detection technology is the use of multimodal AI systems that can assess multiple signals, such as visual, audio, and metadata, simultaneously. These systems analyze both visual elements (like subtle facial movements) and audio markers (such as voice modulation) to improve detection accuracy. For instance, automated forensic tools developed by AI companies and research institutions combine these markers to identify manipulations that may not be noticeable with traditional single-mode analysis. As deepfakes grow increasingly sophisticated, multimodal detection is expected to play a central role in deepfake countermeasures (Tolosana et al., 2020).

Another innovative approach is blockchain technology, which has emerged as a potential tool for content verification. Blockchain's decentralized nature makes it suitable for tracking the origin, modification history, and distribution pathway of digital content. By storing a unique hash or digital fingerprint for each media file, blockchain can help verify content authenticity, providing a tamper-proof record of the media's lifecycle (Kietzmann et al., 2020). For example, a video or image created and verified as authentic could have its unique fingerprint uploaded to a blockchain. Any manipulation would create a mismatch, allowing users to verify whether the content is original or altered.

Blockchain-based verification systems are gaining attention in industries with high stakes for media authenticity, such as journalism and law enforcement. For instance, the Content Authenticity Initiative, a coalition formed by Adobe, Twitter, and The New York Times, uses blockchain to ensure the authenticity of published images. By expanding such efforts across industries, blockchain could serve as a unifying tool in deepfake detection, making it easier for consumers, businesses, and governments to trust digital content (Chawla et al., 2021).

4.2 Shared Databases and Open-Source Solutions

A centralized or shared database of known deepfakes and suspicious patterns represents a significant step forward in creating collective defenses against this technology. Shared databases can enhance detection capabilities by allowing researchers and developers to access a wide array of deepfake samples. This approach enables the creation of more robust algorithms that can identify deepfake patterns with greater accuracy and adapt to new deepfake trends. For example, the Deepfake Detection Challenge, sponsored by Facebook, has generated vast datasets of real and manipulated videos to support the development of advanced detection tools (Dolhansky et al., 2020).

By storing data on both benign and harmful uses of deepfake technology, shared databases can assist not only in detection but also in understanding how deepfakes evolve and the specific methods used in malicious instances. Such datasets, however, need to be carefully curated to ensure that access is controlled and does not facilitate further misuse of the technology. Open-source initiatives, like FaceForensics++ and DeepFaceLab, already contribute to this mission by providing deepfake datasets and model benchmarks for researchers to test and improve detection tools (Rossler et al., 2019).

Open-source solutions play an essential role by making deepfake detection technologies accessible to the wider public. With open-source tools, developers worldwide can collaborate, adapt, and enhance existing detection methods, providing community-driven improvements and continuous adaptation to new manipulation techniques. The decentralized nature of open-source projects fosters collaboration, transparency, and rapid innovation, as contributors can identify and address flaws more efficiently than in proprietary models (Westerlund, 2019). Moreover, open-source approaches can reduce costs, making detection solutions available to smaller businesses and individuals.

4.3 Community Detection Tools

Publicly accessible detection tools are another crucial element in the collective fight against deepfakes. Most detection technologies are sophisticated and require specialized knowledge, making them difficult for average users to utilize. Developing user-friendly detection tools allows everyday consumers and small businesses to verify content authenticity, empowering them to protect themselves against deepfake-based misinformation and fraud (Nguyen et al., 2021).

Several organizations have already begun creating online platforms where users can upload videos to assess their authenticity. For instance, tools such as Truepic and Deepware Scanner offer user-friendly interfaces that allow individuals to detect manipulated content without needing extensive technical expertise. These tools employ simple machine learning models that analyze uploaded content and report on possible manipulation, providing an accessible solution for both individuals and small businesses (Westerlund, 2019).

Community detection tools also play an educational role by promoting media literacy among the public. These platforms not only detect deepfakes but also educate users about the risks and methods of detection. Informed users are better equipped to question the authenticity of media, reducing the impact of misinformation on society. By involving the public in deepfake detection, community tools contribute to a collective response against malicious media manipulation, building a more resilient digital environment (Chesney & Citron, 2019).

4.4 Collaborative Development and Open Innovation

Collaboration in research and development is fundamental to staying ahead of the rapid advancements in deepfake technology. Partnerships among technology companies, academic institutions, government agencies, and nonprofit organizations foster an environment of open innovation where diverse experts work together to create and refine detection and verification tools. For example, initiatives such as DARPA's Media Forensics program involve researchers and technology companies in a collaborative effort to develop state-of-the-art detection capabilities for digital media authentication (Goodfellow et al., 2020).

Collaborative development is not limited to detection but also encompasses prevention strategies, such as creating ethical guidelines for AI use and disseminating best practices for content creation and verification. By establishing standardized protocols and methodologies, stakeholders can work together to define ethical boundaries for AI-generated content. This collaborative framework benefits from the unique strengths of each sector: governments provide regulatory support, technology companies contribute technical expertise, and academic institutions deliver research insights (Chawla et al., 2021).

In addition to fostering innovation, collaborative development initiatives facilitate knowledge-sharing, which accelerates the development and deployment of new tools. Tech giants like Google and Microsoft have already committed resources to joint research projects with universities, focusing on areas like adversarial machine learning and deepfake detection. Such partnerships exemplify how collective action can harness diverse expertise to advance the understanding of and solutions to the deepfake challenge (Nguyen et al., 2021).

Open innovation through cross-sector collaboration has the potential to not only enhance detection technology but also create a global community committed to mitigating the risks associated with deepfakes. Through conferences, hackathons, and collaborative projects, professionals from different backgrounds can exchange ideas, share research findings, and pool resources to counter emerging threats. Such a collective approach encourages a shared sense of responsibility and empowers all participants to contribute actively to the digital safety of individuals and organizations alike (Hancock, 2020).

The threat of deepfakes necessitates a coordinated, collective response that combines the strengths of detection technologies, shared databases, community tools, and cross-sector collaboration. Recent advances in detection algorithms and blockchain-based content verification provide the technical foundation needed to counteract deepfake abuse, while shared databases and open-source solutions foster an inclusive and adaptable approach to combating these threats. Publicly accessible detection tools enhance digital literacy and empower consumers and small businesses to verify content authenticity. Meanwhile, collaborative development efforts involving tech companies, academic institutions, government bodies, and nonprofits contribute to ongoing innovation in detection and prevention. Together, these collective technological solutions create a more resilient and informed digital community capable of withstanding the evolving risks posed by deepfake technology.

5. POLICY FRAMEWORKS AND LEGAL STANDARDS

As the prevalence of deepfake technology increases, the legal and policy landscape surrounding its use must evolve to address the multifaceted challenges it presents. Existing laws often fall short in effectively regulating the production and dissemination of deepfakes, which can lead to misinformation, fraud, and reputational harm. To combat these issues, there is a pressing need for global cooperation to develop standardized policies and industry-specific guidelines that protect individuals and organizations. Furthermore, ethical considerations surrounding the deployment of deepfake technology must be addressed to foster public trust.

5.1 Current Legal Landscape

The current legal landscape regarding deepfakes is characterized by a patchwork of laws that vary significantly by jurisdiction and often lack specificity regarding the manipulation of digital media. In the United States, for example, existing laws primarily fall under categories such as defamation, fraud, and intellectual property, but they do not explicitly address the unique challenges posed by deepfakes. The First Amendment protects freedom of expression, making it challenging to regulate creative uses of deepfake technology in artistic or entertainment contexts (Chesney & Citron, 2019). However, this protection can complicate efforts to curtail harmful applications, such as revenge porn, misinformation, or political manipulation.

Some states have begun to introduce legislation specifically targeting deepfakes. For instance, California enacted a law in 2019 that makes it illegal to use deepfakes with the intent to harm, defraud, or intimidate. Similarly, Texas passed a law that prohibits the use of deepfake technology to harm or defraud individuals (Goodman, 2020). While these laws represent a step in the right direction, they are limited in scope and often lack clear enforcement mechanisms. Furthermore, many laws focus on criminalizing specific actions rather than addressing the broader implications of deepfake technology, such as its potential impact on democratic processes and public discourse.

The limitations of existing laws highlight the urgent need for comprehensive frameworks that address deepfakes holistically. Current legal approaches tend to be reactive rather than proactive, often responding to specific incidents rather than anticipating future challenges. This reactive stance may leave vulnerable populations unprotected and hinder efforts to build a safer digital environment.

5.2 Developing Global Standards

Given the global nature of the internet, the development of international standards to regulate deepfake technology is crucial. Similar to the General Data Protection Regulation (GDPR) established in the European Union, which sets stringent guidelines for data protection and privacy, a standardized policy framework for deepfakes could offer a unified approach to addressing the challenges associated with this technology. Such a framework would facilitate cooperation among nations to share information, best practices, and regulatory measures that effectively combat the misuse of deepfakes.

The need for international cooperation is underscored by the transnational nature of digital media. A deepfake created in one country can easily spread and cause harm in another, complicating enforcement efforts and creating legal gray areas. By establishing global standards, countries can harmonize their approaches, making it easier to prosecute offenders and protect victims across borders. This collaboration can also help mitigate the risks of regulatory arbitrage, where individuals exploit more lenient laws in certain jurisdictions to escape accountability (Chesney & Citron, 2019).

Developing global standards for deepfake regulation would require engagement from a range of stakeholders, including governments, technology companies, civil society organizations, and academia. Multi-stakeholder dialogues can facilitate the sharing of insights and experiences, helping to create balanced policies that protect individual rights while promoting innovation. Such discussions could also address ethical considerations, ensuring that any regulatory framework incorporates a commitment to responsible technology use.

5.3 Industry-Specific Guidelines

While broad regulatory frameworks are essential, industry-specific guidelines can provide more tailored approaches to address the unique challenges posed by deepfakes in different sectors. Industries such as finance, entertainment, and media face distinct risks and opportunities related to deepfake technology, necessitating customized regulatory frameworks.

In the financial sector, for example, deepfakes can be used to create fraudulent transactions or impersonate executives in phishing attacks. Regulatory bodies such as the Securities and Exchange Commission (SEC) could develop guidelines to help financial institutions mitigate these risks through enhanced verification processes and employee training programs (Farrugia et al., 2021). By establishing specific protocols for identifying and responding to deepfake threats, the financial industry can enhance its resilience against fraudulent activities.

The entertainment industry also faces unique challenges, particularly concerning the unauthorized use of actors' likenesses in deepfake content. Developing guidelines that outline consent protocols, intellectual property rights, and distribution standards can help protect artists while promoting responsible content creation. For instance, guidelines could mandate that any deepfake content featuring an individual's likeness must receive explicit permission, thereby respecting the rights of performers and creators (Chesney & Citron, 2019).

In the media sector, guidelines should focus on transparency and accountability in content creation and dissemination. Media organizations could adopt best practices for verifying sources and authenticity before publishing potentially harmful content. Implementing editorial standards that require fact-checking and transparency regarding the use of deepfakes can help maintain public trust and counter misinformation (Farrugia et al., 2021).

By tailoring guidelines to the specific needs and challenges of various industries, stakeholders can create more effective regulatory frameworks that encourage compliance and foster a culture of responsibility.

5.4 Ethics and Responsibility

As deepfake technology continues to evolve, ethical considerations surrounding its use must take center stage. Companies and governments bear a significant responsibility to curb deepfake misuse and protect public trust. This responsibility encompasses not only compliance with existing laws but also proactive engagement in ethical practices and standards.

Corporations, especially those in the tech sector, must prioritize ethical considerations in the design and deployment of deepfake technology. Companies should conduct thorough impact assessments before releasing new technologies to understand their potential misuse and societal implications. Furthermore, businesses can establish ethical guidelines that emphasize responsible technology use, transparency, and accountability. This commitment can help mitigate the risks of deepfake misuse while reinforcing public trust in technology (Kietzmann et al., 2020).

Governments also have an ethical obligation to protect their citizens from the harms associated with deepfakes. By enacting comprehensive regulations, investing in public awareness campaigns, and collaborating with technology companies, governments can foster an environment that discourages deepfake misuse. Educating the public about the risks and consequences of deepfakes is crucial for empowering individuals to recognize and challenge manipulated content.

Moreover, ethical discussions surrounding deepfakes should extend to the implications for democracy and public discourse. The potential for deepfakes to undermine trust in institutions, spread misinformation, and manipulate public opinion necessitates a commitment from all stakeholders to uphold the integrity of democratic processes. By engaging in ongoing dialogue about the ethical dimensions of deepfake technology, society can work towards creating a safer and more trustworthy digital landscape.

The rapid proliferation of deepfake technology presents significant legal and ethical challenges that require urgent attention. The current legal landscape is insufficient to address the complexities associated with deepfakes, highlighting the need for comprehensive policy frameworks and international cooperation. Developing global standards and industry-specific guidelines can help mitigate risks while promoting responsible technology use. Furthermore, ethical considerations must guide the actions of companies and governments in curbing deepfake misuse and protecting public trust. By fostering collaboration among diverse stakeholders, society can collectively address the challenges posed by deepfakes and build a safer digital environment for all.

6. CASE STUDIES IN COLLABORATIVE ACTION

The rapid rise of deepfake technology has challenged organizations, media outlets, and governments to work together in combating its misuse. Collaborative action has shown promise in mitigating deepfake threats, with real-world case studies offering insights into the success of collective approaches and identifying areas for improvement. This chapter explores several case studies, examining how multi-stakeholder collaborations have responded to deepfake incidents. By analyzing key takeaways and best practices, it highlights both the strengths and limitations of current efforts, while suggesting pathways for more effective future collaboration.

6.1 Real-World Examples

1. The Deepfake Detection Challenge

The Deepfake Detection Challenge (DFC), organized by Facebook in collaboration with Microsoft, the Partnership on AI, and academic institutions, exemplifies a successful multi-stakeholder effort aimed at advancing deepfake detection technology (Dolhansky et al., 2020). Initiated in 2019, this competition provided a large dataset of deepfake videos for researchers and developers worldwide, encouraging them to create algorithms capable of detecting manipulated content with high accuracy. The DFC aimed to accelerate the development of detection tools that would help social media platforms and news organizations identify deepfakes before they spread widely.

The project highlighted the value of collaboration between tech companies, academia, and research organizations. By pooling resources and expertise, the DFC fostered an environment for collective problem-solving and produced several highly accurate algorithms, which are now used by social media platforms to flag potentially harmful content. This case illustrates how competition-based initiatives can motivate and engage diverse stakeholders, fostering innovation that benefits the entire industry.

2. The Collaboration Between Reuters and Facebook

In 2021, Reuters, a global news organization, partnered with Facebook to combat misinformation and deepfakes through a program designed to educate journalists and promote digital literacy. This initiative provided journalists with resources on how to identify deepfake content and respond effectively to misinformation. Reuters trained journalists in over 15 countries, emphasizing the importance of accurate reporting and verifying sources in the digital age (Reuters, 2021).

This collaboration underscores the role of news organizations and social media platforms in combating deepfake proliferation. By equipping journalists with the tools and knowledge to detect and report manipulated content, Reuters and Facebook contributed to a more informed media environment. This case demonstrates the impact of targeted training initiatives and highlights how strategic partnerships can help prevent misinformation from reaching the public.

3. The Partnership on AI (PAI) Framework for Deepfake Responsibility

The Partnership on AI, a non-profit organization consisting of major tech companies, academic institutions, and civil society groups, established a framework for responsible practices around synthetic media, including deepfakes (Partnership on AI, 2021). The framework aimed to set ethical guidelines for deepfake creation and distribution, emphasizing transparency and disclosure in synthetic content production. Key members, including Amazon, Google, and IBM, committed to following these guidelines, aiming to reduce harm and prevent the misuse of deepfake technology.

This initiative highlights the importance of ethical standards in technology development and deployment. By promoting transparency, the framework encourages companies to disclose when content is synthetically generated, helping audiences discern real from manipulated content. This case exemplifies the potential for industry-wide frameworks to set a foundation for ethical deepfake use, creating a shared understanding of responsibility across sectors.

6.2 Lessons Learned

Key Takeaways from the Case Studies

1. **Collaborative Efforts Enhance Resource Sharing**: The DFC exemplifies how pooled resources can accelerate technological advancements. By working together, stakeholders were able to compile a substantial dataset and attract talent from around the world, ultimately producing high-quality deepfake detection tools.
2. **Training and Education are Vital**: The Reuters-Facebook partnership highlights the importance of equipping journalists with digital literacy skills to recognize and combat deepfake threats. Educating those on the front lines of information dissemination is crucial for preventing the spread of misinformation.
3. **Standardized Ethical Guidelines are Effective**: The Partnership on AI's framework demonstrates the value of establishing shared ethical standards. By agreeing on best practices for synthetic media creation, the tech industry can reduce harm and foster trust with the public.

Best Practices in Collaborative Action

- **Encourage Cross-Sector Participation**: Effective deepfake countermeasures require input from various sectors, including government, academia, and private industry. The inclusion of multiple perspectives ensures comprehensive solutions that address technological, ethical, and regulatory challenges.

- **Invest in Public Awareness and Education**: Providing training for journalists and the general public is essential in promoting digital literacy. Initiatives like Reuters' training programs empower individuals to critically evaluate content, reducing the risk of deepfake deception.
- **Develop Open and Transparent Frameworks**: Transparency is essential for building trust in synthetic media. Establishing open frameworks and guidelines, as demonstrated by the Partnership on AI, encourages responsible use of deepfake technology and mitigates risks associated with misuse.

6.3 Opportunities for Improvement

Despite the successes demonstrated in these case studies, certain gaps and limitations remain. Addressing these weaknesses is crucial for creating a more robust framework against deepfake threats in the future.

1. Broader Participation from Smaller Organizations

While large organizations have taken the lead in deepfake countermeasures, smaller media outlets, startups, and non-profit organizations often lack the resources to participate fully. Future initiatives should aim to provide more accessible training, resources, and support for smaller entities that may be more vulnerable to deepfake-related misinformation. Expanding participation can create a more resilient media environment across all levels.

2. Standardizing Detection Technology Across Platforms

Although significant progress has been made in deepfake detection, there is still a lack of standardization in how these tools are applied across platforms. For example, social media platforms may use different detection algorithms with varying levels of accuracy, which can lead to inconsistencies in content moderation. Standardizing detection technology, perhaps through government regulation or industry collaboration, can ensure that all platforms maintain a high level of accuracy in identifying deepfakes.

3. Addressing Ethical and Privacy Concerns in Detection

Deepfake detection tools often require access to large datasets, raising privacy concerns about how personal data is used and stored. As detection technologies evolve, ethical considerations around data usage must be addressed to maintain public trust. Industry groups and policymakers should work together to create frameworks that balance privacy rights with the need for robust detection capabilities.

4. Encouraging Ongoing Innovation in Detection and Response

Deepfake technology is advancing rapidly, making it necessary for detection tools to evolve continuously. While current initiatives, such as the DFC, have fostered innovation, long-term investment in research and development is essential for staying ahead of new deepfake techniques. Government grants, industry funding, and academic partnerships can support ongoing innovation in deepfake detection and mitigation strategies.

These case studies in collaborative action illustrate the power of collective efforts in addressing the challenges posed by deepfake technology. By examining the successes and limitations of initiatives like the Deepfake Detection Challenge, the Reuters-Facebook partnership, and the Partnership on AI's ethical framework, valuable insights emerge regarding best practices and areas for improvement. Future collaborative efforts can build on these lessons to create more comprehensive and resilient defenses against deepfake threats, ensuring a secure and trustworthy digital environment.

7. CHALLENGES AND BARRIERS TO COLLECTIVE ACTION

Addressing the deepfake challenge requires an intricate web of collaboration across governments, private sector entities, academia, and non-profits. However, even with a shared goal of reducing harm from deepfake misuse, achieving effective collective action is complex. This chapter delves into key challenges that hinder collaborative efforts, including technological limitations, privacy concerns, economic constraints, and coordination difficulties. Understanding these barriers is crucial for designing effective strategies to counter deepfake threats.

7.1 Technological Limitations

Deepfake detection technology has made significant progress, yet limitations remain in terms of detection accuracy, speed, and adaptability to emerging threats. Generative Adversarial Networks (GANs), the technology behind deepfakes, are evolving rapidly, often outpacing detection efforts (Chesney & Citron, 2019). As deepfake generation becomes more sophisticated, detection algorithms must continuously adapt to detect new forms of digital manipulation. However, keeping up with advancements in GANs can be challenging, as each new generation often requires novel detection methodologies.

Moreover, real-time detection, particularly on social media platforms, remains a significant challenge. For instance, platforms with millions of users and high volumes of uploaded content may struggle to efficiently filter deepfakes without compromising user experience. High detection accuracy often comes at the expense of processing speed, resulting in potential delays that allow malicious content to circulate before it is flagged or removed. Additionally, deepfake detection algorithms often yield false positives or false negatives, undermining their reliability and raising concerns over automated decision-making (Mirsky & Lee, 2021).

Further complicating matters is the issue of deepfake audio, which is even more challenging to detect than video. While deepfake video detection relies on identifying visual inconsistencies, audio deepfakes may seamlessly imitate a person's voice, making detection more difficult and raising the need for specialized algorithms. Addressing these technological limitations requires sustained research and development investments, collaborative testing of detection tools, and ongoing improvement of algorithmic capabilities to stay ahead of rapidly advancing deepfake technology.

7.2 Privacy and Data Concerns

Privacy and data protection concerns emerge as significant barriers when combating deepfake threats. Detection tools and training datasets often rely on large amounts of data, which may include sensitive information about individuals. For example, databases used to train deepfake detection algorithms may contain personal images, videos, or audio files, raising ethical concerns about consent and the right to privacy (Floridi, 2020). When organizations collect or share such data, questions arise regarding data ownership, compliance with privacy laws, and potential misuse.

To ensure the effectiveness of deepfake detection, organizations often need to share data across borders and sectors. However, inconsistent privacy regulations, such as those seen between the General Data Protection Regulation (GDPR) in Europe and privacy laws in other regions, complicate data-sharing agreements. Privacy concerns can inhibit the free flow of information, which is necessary for coordinated efforts against deepfake threats. For instance, organizations may hesitate to share potentially sensitive datasets with research institutions or detection tool developers if data privacy risks are not adequately addressed (Solove, 2021).

An additional privacy issue stems from the potential misuse of deepfake detection tools. When misused, these tools could be employed to analyze and monitor individuals' activities or create unauthorized biometric profiles, thereby infringing on personal privacy rights. To mitigate these concerns, it is critical to establish transparent data governance protocols, consent frameworks, and legal protections that safeguard privacy while allowing necessary data sharing for deepfake detection and prevention.

7.3 Economic Barriers

Economic constraints present another substantial barrier to collective action against deepfake threats. Developing, implementing, and maintaining deepfake detection and prevention tools is expensive, with research, software development, and deployment costs often extending beyond the budgets of smaller organizations. Large technology companies and government bodies may have the resources to invest in advanced detection technology, but small businesses, non-profits, and some media organizations struggle to afford such investments, leaving them vulnerable to deepfake-related risks.

Implementing deepfake detection technology at scale requires not only initial development costs but also continuous updates, as the detection landscape must evolve alongside advancements in deepfake creation methods. The financial burden can be particularly heavy for social media platforms and news organizations that are expected to monitor and verify vast amounts of user-generated content. Additionally, employing specialized personnel to manage and analyze detection tools contributes to operational costs, making it economically prohibitive for smaller organizations (Vincent, 2021).

Another economic factor is the cost associated with potential legal actions resulting from deepfake incidents. If organizations become victims of deepfake-related harm, such as reputational damage or defamation, they may face costly legal battles. For some businesses, the risk of economic losses due to deepfake threats outweighs the perceived benefits of investing in detection technology. To encourage widespread adoption of deepfake detection tools, policymakers might consider offering subsidies or tax incentives for organizations investing in protective technologies, thereby alleviating some of the economic burdens and fostering more inclusive participation.

7.4 Coordination and Communication Challenges

Coordinating efforts across multiple stakeholders—governments, private sector entities, and civil society organizations—is essential but fraught with challenges. Aligning these diverse groups, each with unique priorities, resources, and ethical stances, is a difficult task. For instance, government bodies may prioritize regulatory measures to safeguard public safety, while technology companies might focus on innovation in detection technology. Such differing priorities can create conflicts and slow down coordinated efforts to address deepfake issues effectively.

Communication challenges further complicate coordination. Efficient information-sharing protocols are crucial, but organizations often operate with proprietary information and limited disclosure, leading to silos that hinder effective collaboration. Additionally, inconsistencies in technical terminology and varying expertise levels among stakeholders can impede clear and productive communication. For instance, government regulators may lack the technical knowledge needed to understand the nuances of deepfake detection, making it difficult for them to establish appropriate guidelines (Gillespie, 2021).

Ethical disagreements also pose significant obstacles to collaboration. For example, disagreements may arise about balancing the need for technological advancement with the ethical obligation to respect individual privacy. Some stakeholders may be cautious about deploying surveillance-based detection tools due to concerns about potential overreach, while others prioritize security measures to combat deepfake threats. Addressing these ethical concerns requires ongoing dialogue, compromise, and a shared ethical framework that aligns stakeholders around core values and mutually beneficial goals.

To overcome coordination and communication challenges, stakeholders might benefit from establishing cross-sector task forces or working groups that foster regular dialogue and facilitate information sharing. Such structures can help develop a shared understanding of challenges, promote transparency, and support collective decision-making. Additionally, creating standardized frameworks for terminology, ethical guidelines, and detection practices can reduce ambiguity and improve coordination among diverse stakeholders.

The fight against deepfake threats relies on collective action from a broad coalition of stakeholders. However, technological, economic, privacy, and coordination challenges present significant barriers to effective collaboration. Recognizing these barriers is crucial for developing strategies that enable organizations to work together more effectively. By addressing technological limitations through continuous R&D, ensuring privacy protections in data-sharing practices, reducing economic barriers, and fostering open communication among stakeholders, it is possible to strengthen collective efforts against deepfake threats.

The deepfake challenge illustrates the complexities of combating digital threats in an interconnected world. As technology continues to evolve, addressing these barriers will be essential for creating a more resilient digital landscape. By understanding and overcoming these challenges, stakeholders can better protect individuals, businesses, and communities from the risks posed by deepfakes.

8. FUTURE DIRECTIONS FOR COLLECTIVE EFFORTS

The deepfake phenomenon has shown how advancing technology can challenge society in unexpected ways, requiring a shift towards collaborative and adaptive responses across sectors. To address the ongoing and evolving threat that deepfakes pose, future directions in collective efforts must focus on fostering innovative partnerships, establishing robust public-private initiatives, building a culture of resilience, and anticipating technological advances.

8.1 Innovative Partnerships

The fight against deepfakes requires a multi-sectoral approach, where technology, finance, government, and academia pool their resources and expertise to develop effective solutions. Technology companies can partner with financial institutions to develop funding strategies that support deepfake research and detection, which can be applied broadly to protect industries from malicious attacks. Academic institutions, known for their groundbreaking research in artificial intelligence, can collaborate with tech companies to develop advanced detection algorithms and tools that can be commercialized or made accessible to the public (Chesney & Citron, 2019).

Governments also play a key role by providing financial support for research and creating a conducive environment for cross-sector collaborations. For instance, they can establish innovation hubs that facilitate interaction between diverse stakeholders focused on combating the deepfake threat. Public policy experts can further collaborate with academics and tech firms to conduct impact assessments of proposed technologies, ensuring that the outcomes address societal concerns about privacy and misuse. By fostering these partnerships, the deepfake detection ecosystem can develop more resilient and practical solutions (Westerlund, 2019).

8.2 Public-Private Initiatives

Public-private initiatives are essential to create scalable, sustainable solutions against deepfake threats. Such initiatives leverage the strengths of both the private sector's innovation capabilities and the regulatory and funding support from the public sector. For example, government-backed grants and incentives can encourage technology companies to develop and deploy deepfake detection technologies that can be integrated across sectors such as media, finance, and healthcare (Kietzmann et al., 2020).

These initiatives can also create frameworks for developing standardized tools and technologies, such as universal APIs for content verification, which would enable a more uniform approach to tackling deepfakes. Public-private collaboration can also focus on creating accessible resources, such as open-source tools and educational programs, which can be distributed to smaller businesses and individuals who may not otherwise have the means to defend against deepfake-related risks. These types of initiatives would help democratize access to tools and knowledge, creating a more resilient public front against malicious actors (Paris & Donovan, 2019).

8.3 Building a Culture of Resilience

Building a culture of resilience is critical to sustaining efforts against deepfakes and related misinformation. Resilience in this context means fostering a community mindset that prioritizes digital literacy, ethical standards, and verification as part of daily interactions with digital media. This requires integrating digital literacy into educational systems, from primary school through university, to empower future generations to recognize and critically assess digital content (Chawla, 2020).

Businesses and organizations can contribute by establishing and promoting guidelines that reinforce the importance of content verification, ethical standards, and transparency when using AI tools. Media organizations, for instance, can implement policies requiring verification of visual content, building trust and reinforcing societal resilience against manipulated media. A culture of resilience also involves public education campaigns, with both private and public sectors educating the public about deepfakes and encouraging responsible consumption and sharing of digital content. As trust in media is crucial to combating misinformation, transparent practices will strengthen resilience in society at large (Diakopoulos & Johnson, 2019).

8.4 Anticipating Technological Advances

The pace of AI and machine learning advancements suggests that deepfake technologies will continue to evolve, potentially creating new challenges that current detection methods cannot address. Therefore, a proactive approach in anticipating and adapting to future technologies is essential. This includes establishing forward-looking research agendas and developing detection techniques that can evolve alongside deepfake generation capabilities. Public and private entities can work together to fund research into "deepfake-proof" content creation methods or watermarking technologies that ensure authenticity (Mirsky & Lee, 2021).

For instance, quantum computing and blockchain offer promising avenues for the development of secure content authentication methods. Blockchain could provide transparent verification of content origin, making it easier to track and identify unauthorized manipulations. Additionally, creating AI-powered anomaly detection systems that leverage large datasets could make it possible to identify fabricated content in real-time. As new detection methods are developed, public-private partnerships should work to ensure these innovations are scalable and accessible, allowing for rapid and widespread adoption (Vaccari & Chadwick, 2020).

The deepfake phenomenon underscores the need for society to develop adaptive, collaborative, and resilient solutions. By fostering innovative partnerships, supporting public-private initiatives, building a culture of resilience, and anticipating technological advances, society can collectively safeguard against the growing risks posed by deepfake technologies. While challenges remain, the combined efforts of tech, finance, government, academia, and the public can create a robust defense against this evolving threat. Addressing deepfakes requires not only technological innovation but also a commitment to fostering a culture of ethical responsibility, transparency, and resilience, ensuring that digital spaces remain trustworthy and secure.

CONCLUSION

The threat of deepfakes presents a unique and complex challenge that cannot be effectively addressed by any single entity. It requires a collective approach that leverages the strengths and resources of various stakeholders—including governments, technology companies, businesses, academia, and nonprofit organizations. Key takeaways from examining these multifaceted efforts emphasize that an effective response to deepfakes relies on collaboration, continuous innovation, and a shared commitment to public trust and safety.

Firstly, cross-sector partnerships are vital in the fight against deepfakes. Government regulatory bodies provide the necessary legal and ethical frameworks, setting boundaries for acceptable AI use and enforcing penalties for malicious actors. Technology companies bring in their technical expertise, developing sophisticated detection tools and adopting industry standards for content verification. Businesses safeguard their brands and customer relationships by investing in detection technologies, training their employees, and educating consumers about potential deepfake threats. Academia contributes through research, which not only advances detection technologies but also helps society understand the social and psychological impacts of deepfakes. Finally, nonprofits and advocacy groups ensure that the public is educated and protected, playing a crucial role in holding other sectors accountable for ethical and responsible practices.

Continuous collaboration and vigilance are necessary as deepfake technology continues to evolve. Technological advances in artificial intelligence and machine learning have enabled the creation of increasingly realistic deepfakes, which means detection and prevention methods must be equally adaptive. By maintaining robust partnerships across sectors, stakeholders can pool resources to stay ahead of these advancements and share knowledge through collective research and innovation. This collaborative effort helps to mitigate risks more effectively than isolated responses, creating a resilient front against the misuse of synthetic media.

In addition, fostering a culture of resilience and digital literacy is essential. Society must prioritize verification, ethical standards, and responsible media consumption as integral aspects of digital engagement. By building this culture within educational institutions, workplaces, and communities, society can become less vulnerable to manipulation, reinforcing public trust and minimizing the impact of deepfake misinformation.

In conclusion, the fight against deepfakes is not a one-time effort but a continuous journey that requires constant vigilance and adaptation. All stakeholders must recognize their unique roles and embrace their responsibilities to build a safer, more trustworthy digital environment. Governments, technology firms, businesses, academic institutions, and nonprofits must work together to create solutions, share best practices, and educate the public on recognizing and responsibly interacting with digital content. By committing to these collaborative efforts, society can transform the deepfake challenge into an opportunity to strengthen digital integrity, protect individuals, and uphold trust in the digital age. This proactive, unified approach is crucial to building a secure, resilient, and ethical digital future.

REFERENCES

Ajder, H., Patrini, G., Cavalli, F., & Cullen, L. (2019). *The state of deepfakes: Landscape, threats, and impacts.* Sensity.

Chawla, D. S. (2020). Deepfakes and synthetic media: What journalists need to know. *Columbia Journalism Review.* Retrieved from https://www.cjr.org

Chawla, Y., Dhir, A., & Misra, A. (2021). Are we safe in the age of synthetic media? An analysis of the deepfake phenomenon and its implications for business. *Journal of Business Research*, 123, 57–68.

Chesney, R., & Citron, D. K. (2019). Deepfakes and the new disinformation war: The coming age of post-truth geopolitics. *Foreign Affairs*, 98(1), 147–156.

Diakopoulos, N., & Johnson, R. (2019). Anticipating and addressing the ethical implications of deepfakes in journalism. *Journalism Practice*, 13(8), 997–1005.

Dolhansky, B., Howes, R., Pflaum, B., Baram, N., & Ferrer, C. C. (2020). The deepfake detection challenge dataset. *arXiv preprint arXiv:2006.07397.*

Farrugia, R., Mohan, N., & Thomas, M. (2021). Protecting financial markets from deepfakes: A comprehensive approach. *Journal of Financial Regulation and Compliance*, 29(3), 345–362.

Floridi, L. (2020). AI and digital ethics: A roadmap for the future. *AI & Society*, 35(2), 531–541. DOI: 10.1007/s00146-019-00947-3

Gillespie, T. (2021). The politics of platforms. In *The social media reader* (pp. 187–204). New York University Press.

Goodfellow, I., Pouget-Abadie, J., Mirza, M., Xu, B., Warde-Farley, D., Ozair, S., & Bengio, Y. (2020). Generative adversarial nets. *Communications of the ACM*, 63(11), 139–144. DOI: 10.1145/3422622

Goodfellow, I., Pouget-Abadie, J., Mirza, M., Xu, B., Warde-Farley, D., Ozair, S., . . . Bengio, Y. (2014). Generative adversarial nets. In *Advances in Neural Information Processing Systems* (pp. 27-42).

Goodman, M. (2020). The deepfake crisis: Can we stop the spread of misinformation? *Harvard Business Review.* Retrieved from https://hbr.org/2020/06/the-deepfake-crisis-can-we-stop-the-spread-of-misinformation

Hancock, J. T. (2020). Technology, trust, and deepfakes. *Technology and Trust Journal*, 6(3), 118–131.

Kietzmann, J., Lee, L. W., McCarthy, I. P., & Kietzmann, T. C. (2020). Deepfakes: Trick or treat? *Business Horizons*, 63(2), 135–146. DOI: 10.1016/j.bushor.2019.11.006

Mirsky, Y., & Lee, W. (2021). The creation and detection of deepfakes: A survey. *ACM Computing Surveys*, 54(1), 1–41. DOI: 10.1145/3425780

Nguyen, T. T., Nguyen, C. M., Nguyen, D. T., Nguyen, D. T., & Nahavandi, S. (2021). Deep learning for deepfakes creation and detection: A survey. *Computer Survey*, 53(11), 1–27.

Paris, B., & Donovan, J. (2019). Deepfakes and cheap fakes: The manipulation of audio and visual evidence. *Data & Society Institute Report*. Retrieved from https://datasociety.net

Partnership on AI. (2021). *Framework for synthetic media responsibility*. Partnership on AI. Retrieved from https://www.partnershiponai.org/synthetic-media-guidelines/

. Reuters. (2021). *Reuters teams up with Facebook to provide digital literacy training for journalists*.

Rössler, A., Cozzolino, D., Verdoliva, L., Riess, C., Thies, J., & Nießner, M. (2019). FaceForensics++: Learning to detect manipulated facial images. *Proceedings of the IEEE/CVF International Conference on Computer Vision (ICCV)*, 1–10. DOI: 10.1109/ICCV.2019.00009

Schwarz, O. (2020). Deepfakes and the social theory of digital falsehood. *Journal of Cultural Analysis and Social Change*, 5(1), 12–23.

Solove, D. J. (2021). The myth of the privacy paradox. *The George Washington Law Review*, 89, 1–48.

Tolosana, R., Vera-Rodriguez, R., Fierrez, J., Morales, A., & Ortega-Garcia, J. (2020). Deepfakes and beyond: A survey of face manipulation and fake detection. *Information Fusion*, 64, 131–148. DOI: 10.1016/j.inffus.2020.06.014

Vaccari, C., & Chadwick, A. (2020). Deepfakes and disinformation: Exploring the impact of synthetic political video on deception, uncertainty, and trust in news. *Social Media + Society*, 6(1), 1–13. DOI: 10.1177/2056305120903408

Vincent, J. (2021). Fighting deepfakes: Is AI keeping up with AI-generated misinformation? *The Verge*. Retrieved from https://www.theverge.com

Westerlund, M. (2019). The emergence of deepfake technology: A review. *Technology Innovation Management Review*, 9(11), 39–52. DOI: 10.22215/timreview/1282

Chapter 8
Financial Fraud and Manipulation:
The Malicious Use of Deepfakes in Business

Pooja Kaushik
https://orcid.org/0009-0009-4853-286X
Galgotias College of Engineering and Technology, India

Vikas Garg
https://orcid.org/0000-0002-1421-5980
Christ University, India

Anu Priya
https://orcid.org/0009-0008-3088-0957
G.L. Bajaj Institute of Technology and Management, India

Shashi Kant
https://orcid.org/0000-0003-4722-5736
College of Business and Economics, Bule Hora University, Ethiopia

ABSTRACT

Advanced technologies like Deepfakes are dispatched more frequently in the financial fraud and manipulation to manipulate the stakeholders and markets. Deepfake is synthetic media created using artificial intelligence techniques; the deep fake can impersonate the person's voice, picture, and videos. As a result posing severe risks to the privacy of financial transactions and corporate communications. This chapter focuses on the emerging area of financial fraud with focus on the use of deepfake for stock manipulation and impersonation and spreading fake information. Last, the author offers a complex approach, which deals with both the regulation and

DOI: 10.4018/979-8-3693-6890-9.ch008

Copyright © 2025, IGI Global Scientific Publishing. Copying or distributing in print or electronic forms without written permission of IGI Global Scientific Publishing is prohibited.

the technology, and instruction levels to prevent the financial industry from this sophisticated fraud. It is our belief that carrying out this analysis will help expand the dialogue on financial fraud prevention during the age of artificial intelligence.

1. INTRODUCTION

New technology in the fast-evolving digital environment has impacted a good number of sectors; one of such is the business and finance. Some of these technologies include deepfakes which have however attracted a lot of attention because it is capable of generating very authentic-looking fake audio, video and pictures. Deepfake technology may be defined as the process of using artificial intelligence to create synthetic media in which someone's image is substituted with the original picture or video. The term ''deepfake'' is a composition of the words ''deep learning'' and ''fake.'' Deep learning is a subset of machine learning that trains large datasets and learns patterns to mimic original content. This technique makes use of Generative Adversarial Networks (GANs), which are composed of two neural networks: It consists of a real and fake discriminator that seeks to determine if the information issued is real or fake and a generator that creates fake images or videos. Iteratively, through different operations, GANs create content that becomes more realistic in terms of media, despite it being artificial. Due to these capabilities, scams now plan to use deepfakes for distorted markets, embezzlement and pyramid fraud among other vices. Market integrity and trust can be threatened by means of changing often the price of stocks, spreading false information, and misleading the investors through using the high-fidelity models of the successful CEOs, heads of companies, and other crucial financial personalities. Deepfake technology is an aspect that has a major impact on the future of financial fraud. Both creators and consumers of deepfake material with malintent hold capacities for instigating severe economic damages and inflicting prejudice on the affected individuals and organizations. Beyond personal fines, deepfake-based fraud cases generate doubt in the authenticity of the markets and systems by which people engage with monetary transactions. Obtainability of deepfake technology and the rate at which designs are produced enhance these anxieties, thus it goes without saying, companies, local governments and tech vendors should develop effective countermeasures and detection strategies.

The emergence of such deepfake can be attributed to various scholarly studies carried out in artificial intelligence and computer vision. It gained a lot of exposure and serious ethical and legal questions arose when amateur producers began to use the method in 2017 to swap faces in adult movies without the two people's consent (Kietzmann, 2020). Since then, the technology has evolved to the extent that it has gained applications extending to financial frauds, corporate spying, and political manipulation. The use of deepfake technology is highly effective in generating nearly real synthetic media, which could be seen as the primary benefit of this particular technique. This has also been used in negative use cases as well as positive ones. Deepfakes are used in the entertainment industry to enhance the visual effects, create realistic virtual characters and even resurrect actors who are not among the living. But when applied futilely, those same characteristics entail serious risks. For instance, deepfakes have been utilized to create fake films in financial scams, mimick speeches of influential personalities and influencing the voters during polls (Chesney & Citron, 2019). The applicability of deepfake technology is a clear threat to society's moral and security fabric. It becomes even more tragic when given the advancement and easy availability of deepfakes, the authenticity of the program is questionable hence eroding the trust people have in digital media. This often makes it almost impossible to counter them due to the social platforms used in their diffusion and the continuous advancements in the Artificial Intelligence field. To prevent the dangers of deepfakes, stickers and probable preventing methods are being developed by scientists and lawmakers alike (Maras & Alexandrou, 2019).

2. SCOPE OF THE CHAPTER

As for the areas of concern in this study, it names and shames analysing the financial fraud and manipulation within the business sphere using the malicious application of deepfakes. The objective of this study is to classify and assess the various ways deepfakes can be used to perpetrate some forms of fraud include mimicking CEOs, disseminating fake financial information, and inflating stock prices. As part of the research showing the specifics of fraud linked with deepfake and the ways it is performed, the work will consider such examples.

Technological advances that have enabled deepfakes; psychological attributes that enable deepfakes sway stakeholders' and deepfake exploits of financial and business domain vulnerabilities are critical considerations. Further, how the detection and preventive strategies are being applied will be examined; the effectiveness of the current procedures will be evaluated and deficiencies that might have been overlooked noted. Besides, the limitations in the use of deepfake technologies for financial fraud will also be explored together with an assessment of the conformity of the present legal framework. This paper aims at providing strategic directions for any business, regulatory body and politician to minimize the risks associated with deepfakes although the paper involves a discussion of the best practices and new strategies. This way, the study will contribute to better understanding of deepfake threats and will assist in developing stronger prevention mechanisms against financial fraud, through such detailed analysis.

3. PURPOSE OF THE STUDY

The chapter "Financial Fraud and Manipulation: The Malicious Use of Deepfakes in Business", seeks to tackle the ever-present danger that deepfakes pose in the business world more specifically in the financial aspect. It examines the role of deepfake technology as a tool in fraud particularly in the doctored document scams and faked financial statements as well as impersonation of executives to the stakeholders. The chapter highlights implications for organisations, investors and financial institutions and underlines requirements of detection tools and the enhanced security systems for the new generation. With the help of various cases the study aims at making the audience more informed and offer precaution measures concerning deepfake-induced financial fraud.

4. EVOLUTION AND ADVANCEMENTS IN DEEPFAKE TECHNOLOGY

The use of deepfake has really grown especially with technological improvement in artificial intelligence and machine learning. First detected in December 2017, deepfakes use generative adversarial networks (GANs) in which two neural networks consist of a generator and a discriminator—battle to create more accurate fake images and videos. The generator generates fake content and the discriminator try to identify it; there is thus, a continuous enhanced generation of deepfakes (Goodfellow et al., 2014). Entertainment and media industries were amongst the first that used deepfake technology to represent certain people in videos, for example, turning acting actors into videos after they are dead. This first stage showed the creative positive and the negative use of deepfakes. With time, deepfakes became even better as they began to have fine details, closer to real life facial features, and facial expressions and even movements. Deepfakes by 2019 had evolved to achieve almost realistic quality thus creating anxiety of their potential use in trickery and identity theft (Chesney & Citron, 2019).

There has also been an increased availability of deepfake technology which has been democratized as another innovation. Most of them earlier consumed a lot of computational power and bestowal of expertise, however with friendly applications and availability of open source tools and programming, it has reached the common populace to use. As the availability of the Apps such as Fake App and Deep Face Lab has made it easy for anyone with at least a little knowledge about technology to create a deepfake, the general problem of determining the authenticity of a content has become even harder (Kietzmann et al.,2020).

At the same time there has been the increased attempts to detect and stop deepfakes. Scientists have proposed different detection techniques that utilize AI and ML to find discrepancies in the entire body of deepfake work. The use of method such as looking at the pixel-space features of image and video, the differences in the blinks that the subjects make and potentially the physics of portrayed scene have been found to be useful in detecting deepfakes (Agarwal et al., 2020). Moreover, the concept of using blockchain for the purposes of proven the genuine identity of the material, creating an unalterable history of the original file within the media.

However, regulatory and ethical perspectives are the key issues that turn to be considerable. Deepfake technology has become a problem for government organizations, hence resulting in introduction of laws that seek to prevent the technology. Hence, the US and EU have put in place measures to sanction the use of deepfake technologies for criminal purposes especially in realms including political manipulation and revenge pornography (Maras & Alexandrou, 2019).

5. IMPORTANCE OF UNDERSTANDING DEEPFAKE IN THE CONTEXT OF FINANCIAL FRAUD

Concerning the financing fraud, there is a need to understand its potential due to the application of the deepfake technology. Deepfake technologies are realistic videos and audio that involve artificial intelligence in fabricating fake content, which can be utilized to con people as well as organizations, resulting in monetarily costly effects. Identity theft is one of the most critical issues caused by the use of deepfakes. Cybercriminals can hack and record videos and/or audio and pose as CEOs or financial officers of organizations. This can be applied in an enterprise to authenticate highly prohibited activities such as conning, manipulation of share prices, or unauthorized access to important enterprise's financial data. For example, in 2019, UK energy firm scammers managed to take €220,000 using the voice cloned of the firm's CEO to talk one of the employees into transferring money to a bogus account (Rosenblatt, 2019).

Deepfakes can destabilize society's confidence in financial systems. Identity verification is widely used in banking institutions as well as other financial holders for the processing of transactions and access to accounts. It affords traditional identification techniques a major twist in such a way that it becomes difficult to identify an individual with certainty. Such loss of trust can affect clients and consumers more by developing doubts The populace, especially clients, employed by firms or as customers of products, will trust less in their companies or products and services they receive or obtain from the companies Consequently, firms' financial markets can be destabilized to a better extent if such fraudulent activities are suspected on a large scale (Kraus, 2020).

The issue with deepfake is equally crucial, given that deepfakes could be utilized in other social engineering attacks. Such events include making a victim reveal sensitive details or make a financial decision that suits the fraudster because the fake videos or audio make them believable. For instance, a video containing a fake message from a well-known consultant concerning investment opportunities that only serve to swindle investors can cost them their money (Nguyen et al., 2020). Thus, the banking institutions need to spend on sophisticated detection mechanisms and should encourage inflexible confirmation procedures. At the same time, even fine discrepancies that can be hardly noticed even at close range can be easily identified by using artificial intelligence and machine learning algorithms to look for, for instance, unnatural movement of the face or some echoes in the audio track. On the other hand, multi-factor authentication and biometric verification can some level of protection against deepfakes and make it harder for deepfake to work effectively for a malicious purpose (Miller et al., 2020).

Another measure that helps to fight the deepfakes' threat in the context of financial fraud is also the activity of regulatory authorities. The solutions would suggest regulation and legislation on the deployment of AI as well as the technology utilized in deepfakes to avoid their utilization in malicious ways and potentially damaging consumers. It must be noted that combined endeavours of the governments, financial organizations, IT companies are crucial in creation of multifaceted plans to address potential threats posed by deepfakes (Chesney & Citron, 2019).

6. DEEPFAKE TECHNOLOGY: MECHANISMS AND APPLICATIONS

Generative Adversarial Networks (GANs)

Deepfake technology is based on Generative Adversarial Networks (GANs) that was proposed by Ian Goodfellow and his colleagues in year 2014. GANs consist of two neural networks: consists of two major components, namely the generator and the discriminator, and both of which learn through adversarial operations. The generator produces fake data (for example, image or video) that is intended to emulate the real data, whereas the discriminator identifies the discrepancy in the data set generated by the generator. The discriminator provides feedback to the generator to make it refine its output which in turn increases the normal's capability to distinguishing real data from synthesized data (Goodfellow et al., 2014).

This process of adversarial training results to the creation of exceptionally realistic synthetic content. The objective of the generator is to generate data that looks like the real data that cannot be distinguished from the discriminator and with the process of iteration, the system presents fresh mediocre results. GANs have been applied in fields other than deepfakes such as image enhancement, data enhancement, and artwork generation. However, the same strength also contribute to the weakness because the nature of GANs, which utilizes realism to power its generative engines, means that fake media produced by it can be quite convincing and easily misused (Creswell et al., 2018).

Machine Learning Techniques

Although GANs are widely used for creating deepfakes, there are a few other technologies in machine learning used as well. Some of the examples include autoencoders which are neural networks that take in input data and compress it into a smaller code and then map the code back to the original input data. When it comes to deepfakes, autoencoders are useful in encoding face textures, and expressions that are later transformed to fake videos (Kingma & Welling, 2013).

Other one is the Recurrent Neural Networks (RNNs) such as Long Short-Term Memory (LSTM) networks are used in the case of sequential data. Compared to raw audio, LSTMs can produce phonetically and semantically related follow-up sequences, which make the use if deepfake audio in and of itself that sounds realistic (Hochreiter & Schmidhuber, 1997). Furthermore, Convolutional Neural Networks (CNNs) are used to draw and produce clear images and image recognition. CNNs can learn the features of the image data well; since the formation of facial expressions in deepfake videos requires the identification of details and derived features, as in (LeCun et al. 2015), CNNs are quite suitable for this task.

These methods along with GANs have increased the level of realism and the probability of deepfakes being real. Every of them assists in defining different facets of creation: synthesis of images and audio signals, feature extraction, and pattern identification that all add up to deepfake technology becoming more complex and imperceptible (Dong et al., 2015).

7. COMMON APPLICATIONS OF DEEPFAKE TECHNOLOGY

Impersonation of Executives

Hackers engage in the application of deepfake technology to produce believable videos or voice messages of company managers, who sign suspicious transactions. For instance, in 2019, the UK energy firm's CEO was impersonated through clone speech AI by which 243000 USD was fraudulently siphoned off (Mondaq). These impersonations sometimes lure the employees into forwarding some amount of money or disclosing some important information.

Synthetic Identity Fraud

Deepfake technology is used by creating new identities from the real and fake persona mixture. These facets make it possible for a person to open an account at the bank or ensure credit or any other transactions. In this way, the synthetic identities leave no trace of biometric recognition and thus cannot be identified as fraudsters by financial institutions (TechRadar).

Manipulation of Financial Markets

Deepfakes can be used to spread false information that surfaces some effect on stock prices. For instance, a fake video of a CEO stating false bankruptcy or other large-scaled news, the company's stock prices immediately decrease which helps the fraudsters make money out of short selling stocks or manipulate the shares and stocks in any other way (Global Initiative) (TechRadar).

Bypassing Security Systems

Financial organisations begin to use biometric security systems, including facial and voice identification. While deepfake technology makes it possible to deploy highly realistic fake biometrics, these can easily bypass the above mechanisms of security and capture people's accounts and other options for performing transactions (TechRadar).

8. EMERGING TRENDS IN DEEPFAKE DEVELOPMENT

In the case of deepfake technology, artificial intelligence and machine learning have made vast improvements which has been a boon and bane. Originally, deepfakes were created for fun and amusement; however, in the present time, they have profound consequences in numerous fields.

1. Technological Sophistication

Deepfakes have proved more advanced mainly because of the progress made in GANs generative adversarial networks. Today's deepfake can produce convincing audio, video, and image alterations that even professionals can hardly tell are fake. Such amendments are wrought by the advancement in algorithms, information volume, and the computational capacity (Goodfellow et al., 2014).

2. Accessibility and Democratization

Technology, another driver that makes deepfakes possible has advanced and the tools needed to make them have been made available. As more and more people gain access to friendly user app and open-source program such as Deep Face Lab and Face Swap, more and more people are creating deepfakes. This democratization holds dangers because these tools can be used for various purposes that are not noble or even unlawful by various actors (Chesney & Citron, 2019).

3. Ethical and Legal Challenges

Due to the emergence of deepfakes, ethic and legal issues have emerged. Some of these are consent, privacy and ownership of ideas in cases where there is intellectual property infringement. Investigating, governments and organizations are trying to determine how to regulate deepfakes while not inhibiting development. Legal requirements are being developed to target the immoral use of deepfakes, which is well illustrated by different legislative measures taken in the global level (Citron, 2019).

4. Detection and Mitigation Efforts

Mainly, deepfake is a particular practice in which artificial intelligence techniques are used to generate new media that makes it virtually impossible to distinguish between the real and fake news. Academics are work on complex detection signal and technologies to detect deepfakes and by using deep learning as well as blockchain.

Organizations such as Facebook and Microsoft have started the effort to improve deepfake detection (Agarwal et al., 2020).

5. Positive Applications

All the same, deepfake also has its benefits or positive use which include the following. They facilitate accurate specal effects in movies, television and other entertainment sources as well as voice impersonation. Similarly in the arena of education and training deepfakes can build realistic scenarios for medical and military trainings. Also they resides in possible areas like, for disabled people they can produce artificial speech (Patel et al., 2020).

As with many technologies, deepfake is a work in progress and as such has risks as well as benefits. Therefore, it is imperative to investigate the combination of the innovation with the principles of ethics and reliable methods for detecting threats in order to maximize its positive effects and minimize its drawbacks.

9. FINANCIAL FRAUDS INVOLVING DEEPFAKE TECHNOLOGY

Historical Context of Financial Frauds

Financial fraud as a phenomenon has a history, it existed and exists together with the finance systems and markets. The history and development of financial fraud dates back to as early civilizations. For instance, in Ancient Greece individuals who performed the functions of a banker were trapezitai at times engaging in activities like embezzlement and fraud (Janssen, 2015). In the course of the 18th century, a speculative affair in England known as South Sea Bubble contributed to the problem of misrepresentation of investments and financial doom. Brought into the society by the South Sea Company which had made a proposal to the government and which had the pretention of yielding fabulous profits, it collapsed in the year 1720 bringing great loss to most of the investors (Dale, 2004).

On the financial crime, the fake explicitly presented the society's twentieth-century conspicuous colonization through an increase in complicated and organized schemes. In this category, one could work on topics like the deceitful roles that led to the 1929 crash fumed by stock manipulation and insider trading in the stock market. Savings and Loan Crisis was experienced in the United States in the 1980s characterized by risky lending and fraud activities which led to a loss in billions of taxpayers' money (Barth, 1991).

The most recent well-publicised fraud case is that of Bernard Madoff who was caught in 2008 with a pyramid scheme, commonly known as a Ponzi scheme. Madoff defrauded investors of about sixty-five billion dollars causing a full-blown scandal to hit the financial markets; he took advantage of trust and used fabricated statements to perpetuate the fraud. Fraud was also reported on a large scale in 2008 global financial crisis for instance the mortgage fraud as well as the misrepresentation of the financial products by some of the biggest firms (Lewis, 2010).

10. EVOLUTION OF FINANCIAL FRAUD TACTICS WITH TECHNOLOGY

The way that financial frauds have been executed has been along the trend of the growth in the technology level of the society. As the century began fraud in finance entailed forgery and embezzlement in which organizational records were altered manually (Geis, 1968). During the mid of 20th century, computers brought new prospects to fraudulent schemes. The first documented incident of using computers for fraudulent activities was reported in 1958 when a programmer employed in a bank situated in New York placed his account numbers into other people's receipts, and succeeded in embezzling some cash (Parker, 1983).

The advancement in the use of information technology particularly through the internet at the end of the twentieth century influenced significantly the techniques of ''financial fraud'. Toward that end, phishing techniques that involved swindling people into divulging their personal details particularly of a financial nature were pronounced by cybercriminals. In the report by The Anti-Phishing Working Group it is evident that phishing has continued to rise and this is because cyber criminals have not relent in seeking better ways to perpetrate the vice (APWG, 2020).

Modern methods such as the AI and machine learning have also advanced financial fraud in the 21st century. Deepfake is the form of AI that can synthesize distorted audio and video reproductions of the people that are being impersonated. This technology has also been applied in complex frauds for instance the fraud of a Hong Kong firm in 2023 whereby deepfake videos were used to sign for fraudulent transactions (NextWeb, 2023).

Blockchain technology, which has constantly used and promised to enhance the security of monetary transactions, has been used for scams. ICO and cryptocurrencies trading markets have continuously been exposed to rampant fraud and hacking. Reports show that crytocurrency thefts equivalents to over $1 billion were recorded in 2018 alone (CipherTrace, 2019).

Table 1. Cases of frauds involving deepfake technology

S.no	Countries	Year	Cases
1	United Kindgdom	2020	The fraudsters used AI-generated voice technology to clone the CEO's voice and instructed an executive in a subsidiary to transfer €220,000 (approximately $243,000) to a Hungarian supplier.
2	Hong-Kong	2023	Fraudsters used a deepfake video to impersonate company executives. The finance department employee was convinced to transfer $25.6 million across 15 transactions to accounts controlled by the fraudsters.
3	India	2023	The fraudsters conducted convincing phone and video calls with junior employees and financial institutions, authorizing unauthorized financial transactions.
4	Europe	2019	The CEO's voice was cloned, and a convincing phone call was made to a senior executive, instructing them to transfer a large sum of money to an external account.

(Source: Internet)

Figure 1. Percentage of deepfake cases across various countries in the world

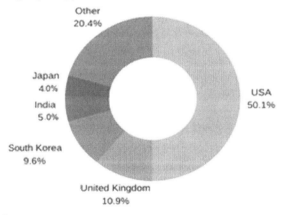

Source: *The Hindu*

According to a recent survey conducted by McAfee, In the last 12 months, more than 75% of Indians who have an online presence have come across some form of deepfake content. In the same survey it was discovered that around 38% of the respondents have encountered a deepfake scam. Scams are done on daily basis specifically related to finance. Few of the scams that have made its way in the news are done to extract money from the innocent public. (McAfee survey 2024)

A case that was registered in kerala highlights the potential danger of deepfake technology. A 73-year-old man named Radhakrishan, received a whatsapp call from an unknown number. On picking the call he heard the voice of one of his former colleagues, Venu kumar. The caller, using deepfake technology, perfectly mimicked

Venu Kumar's voice and appearance. The caller asked Radhakrishnan for a loan of 40,000, claiming that he was in urgent need of money. Without giving a second thought Radhakrishnan transferred the amount to given QR code. (Source: Internet)

Two different incidents that were reported to Bengaluru's Cyber Economic and Narcotics (CEN) South Police Station. Both events included fraudulent schemes in which victims were mislead by films purporting to feature Narayana Murthy and Mukesh Ambani, advertising rich investment possibilities. In the first case, a woman from Banashankari saw a video on social media promoting a trading platform that promised high returns on investment. The film, which included Narayana Murthy, seemed legitimate, boosting her belief in the platform. The woman clicked a suspicious link featured in the video and gave her contact information to a bogus website. Later she received a call from an agent claiming to provide higher returns. Initially she invested 1.4 lakh rupees and got a return of 8000 rupees, on establishing trust she was further asked to invest 6.7 lakh rupees which she ultimately lost without getting any return. Another woman lost 67 Lakh rupees in similar case. (Source: The Times of India)

11. TECHNIQUES USED IN DEEPFAKE-ENABLED FINANCIAL FRAUD

Creation of Realistic Fake Videos and Audio

Deepfake technology is the process of using artificial intelligence, specifically machine learning to synthesize realistic fake videos and audio. Such systems including but not limited to Generative Adversarial Networks (GANs) are trained to learn from large databases of multiple images and recordings of the targeted person. The GANs can then create new synthetic content which looks and sounds like the person in question and imitates his/her behaviour. It has advanced to the level where a person can easily make another say something or even make him/her do something which in real life he/she never did. The availability of the deepfake generator as a tool with the use of which those who do not know anything about it, can create fairly good fakes, puts at great risks privacy, security, and credibility of the materials (Hui, 2023; Harwell, 2020).

Integration With Phishing and Social Engineering Attacks

It is evident that deepfake is being incorporated into phishing and social engineering, thus increasing the impact of such threats. This involves imitating the appearance of genuine people the victim is likely to know personally and trust;

such as executives in a company or members of the victim's family, and using such artificial videos or the fake audio and voice of such people to lure the victim into a form of compliance, such as releasing sensitive information or money. As such, these deepfake-based attacks leverage the trust that people have in familiar voices or faces which make the targets to be in a dilemma between the real and fake messages. When deepfakes are used together with the typical phishing methods such as fake emails or, for instance, phone calls, such scams are much more effective. Organisations are encouraged to use MFA and other tools to contain these threats (Bradshaw, 2022; Newman, 2021).

12. DETECTION AND PREVENTION OF DEEPFAKE FINANCIAL FRAUDS

Current Methods for Detecting Deepfakes

The use of deepfakes, a technology that makes use of machine learning and artificial intelligence, reproduces realistic, high-stakes risks, with one of them being the risk of financial scams. In order to deal with these threats, researchers and security professional have proposed following methods of detection.

AI-Based Detection Systems

Using of AI- Based detection are prominent here, which makes use of a machine learning algorithm to help detect synthetic media. Such systems are able to scrutinize the disparities of moving face, irregular blinking of the eyes, and, the incongruencies of audio-video timeline which are characteristic features of deepfakes (Chesney & Citron, 2019). In the same capacity, pre-determined neural network schemes can be trained on huge sets of data to differentiate between the real and fake content with consideration of artifacts introduced when preparing the fake deep-fakes.

Manual and Traditional Verification Methods

The AI techniques discussed here are not the only ways of identifying deepfakes, but what is important is that in addition to these methodologies, the traditional ways of verifying claims and related manual processes remain relevant. Such methods entail analyzing media content by reviewing experts who may notice peculiarities that a machine cannot observe. For example, analysts can look at alterations in light, shadows, or reflections that do not correspond to the behaviour in genuine footage. Also, traditional methods used entail utilization of the content with other databases of original media to check its credibility (Verdoliva, 2020). These approaches are significant especially when high levels of accuracy are necessary, and the consequences are immense.

13. CHALLENGES IN DETECTING AND PREVENTING DEEPFAKE FINANCIAL FRAUDS

Technological Sophistication and Rapid Evolution

Another variant that can be cited as a compelling factor is that deepfake technology is constantly evolving and becomes more and more difficult to recognize. As these edges are advanced, they are also able to develop more enhanced forms of synthetic media that can easily bypass both technologies and human perception. Deepfakes are, therefore, created using such subsequent generations artificial neural networks like GANs, to manipulate audio, video, and images (Mirsky & Lee, 2021). Since the technologies are still advancing at a fast pace, there is a need to constantly update the method of detecting deepfakes, which entails various forms of imitation with small adjustments to imagery that cannot be easily detected by existing technologies. It creates an obvious trend where makers of deepfakes are continuously devising new ways through which they can bypass the latest designed to detect them which in turn, makes it difficult to keep financial transactions and identity verification honest.

Regulatory and Legal Hurdles

Another major issue is the external environment, which includes the actors and rules in the structure of regulation and law. Today's existing jurisdictions are not entirely prepared to deal with deepfake-related issues that arise with their increased usage, particularly in the sphere of finance. Lack of regulation and eagerness in defining deepfake offences as well as federal practices to prosecute such activities may cause incongruity in the law as well as put a person in unlawful jeopardy. Also, there is usually a problem of coordination at the international level, which is important since the financial markets and the trending use of social media are all global (Schwartz, 2020). Since the concept of deepfakes and its categorization remains legally undefined and unclear, it becomes increasingly difficult to assign responsibility and deter malicious actors; financial institutions and individuals are therefore exposed to highly developed fraudulent schemes.

Implementing Robust Verification Processes

Lack of adequate security measures in mitigating such risks In the light of this new and growing danger of deepfake financial fraud, the highest level of verification must be applied in order to debar such threats. That is why we should welcome such features as the introducing of the artificial intelligence capabilities in the identification of such manipulations in media materials. Some of these tools can also be integrated into the current security technologies to get real time outcomes and look for likely risky content (Maras & Alexandrou, 2019). Likewise, depending on the research, it becomes paramount that organizations most especially when transacting financially adopt multi-factor authentication to address some or most of the existing fraudulent activities on the internet. This could comprise the ID of the sender, employing a secure communication channel, and comparing the acquired data with true data. Therefore, when such approaches are applied in an integrated form, varieties of deepfake scams can be prevented and all the communications and transactions that an organization gets involved in can be closely examined.

Educating Stakeholders About Deepfake Risks

Awareness can also be invoked as one of the components of combating not only deepfake frauds and fake news. Regarding the second recommendation, the organizations and individuals should know what deepfakes are and what risks are connected to them; Any organization's workers, including the management and employees at the operational level, have to complete the training that has to focus on the need to be security-sensitive and not to trust any suspicious messages or calls. The preventive measures could range from employing training programs through which these employees could easily detect the deepfakes, for instance, the inability to properly move facial muscles, poor-quality videos, disparities in sound quality, and disparities in video features. Thus, Deepfakes could be considered as the capability-threat for the persons, particularly if they are celebrities or have something to do with money. The communication can also be targeted at the consumers for promoting the critical approach to the social networks, reviewing the sources of information and refusing to share personal data without the check of the legitimacy of the request.

Figure 2. Deep fake technology

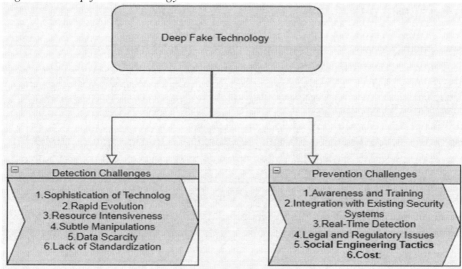

Source: *Author's own*

14. LEGAL AND REGULATORY FRAMEWORKS

Existing Laws and Regulations Addressing Deepfake Technology

Artificially created fake audio and video through Deepfake technology and artificial intelligence bring legal barriers to the test. At the moment, laws that pertain to deepfakes are relatively limited, and quite frequently geographical in their disparities. For instance, certain states in the United States have even legislated on deepfakes depicting their enactment. California and Texas passed laws against the production and dissemination of fatal deepfake intended for the purpose of causing torment to a person or an organization with special reference of elections or pornographic content (California Assembly Bill No. 730, 2019; Texas Senate Bill 751, 2019). Nevertheless, there is no a general federal law that directly regulates the application of deepfakes for fraud in the financial area or in other unlawful activities.

In the case of the European Union, the GDPR indirectly relates to some aspects of deepfakes as it offers protection of personal data that can include biometric data used in the deepfake videos. As for synthetic media, deepfakes are yet again not mentioned in the GDPR and their applicableness is still questionable (Veale, Van Kleek, & Binns, 2018).

Global Strategies in Fighting Sophisticated Fake Financial Scams

Globally, measures for preventing deepfake associated frauds differ in some ways. Currently only a few countries, for example the UK and Australia, are introducing specific mentions of deepfakes under general digital and cybercrime legislation. The UK's Online Safety Bill for example have provisions that could be used to regulate deep few as the government holds duties on the platforms to ensure users are protected from illegal and damaging contents (UK Government, 2021). The intergovernmental approach is also seen in such cooperation as G7, for example, in the fight against deepfakes' misuse in financial fraud and fake news. These initiatives point out the difference in the necessity of cooperation between countries in the development of legislation and its regulation, as digital media and the sphere of fintech are interconnected worldwide (G7 Finance Ministers and Central Bank Governors, 2021).

Proposals for Strengthening Legal Frameworks

To effectively combat deepfake financial fraud, there is a growing consensus on the need for more comprehensive legal frameworks. One proposal is to introduce new regulations that specifically address the creation and distribution of deepfakes, particularly those used for fraudulent purposes. These regulations could include provisions for criminalizing the intentional creation of deepfakes for financial gain, enhancing penalties for using deepfakes in fraudulent activities, and establishing standards for digital forensic analysis in courts. Additionally, existing laws could be amended to better encompass the challenges posed by deepfakes. For instance, expanding definitions of identity theft and fraud in criminal codes to include synthetic media could provide clearer legal grounds for prosecution. Privacy laws could also be updated to explicitly protect individuals from unauthorized use of their likeness in deepfakes, thereby providing a basis for civil litigation. Collaboration Between Governments and Tech Companies.

An essential aspect of combating deepfake frauds is the collaboration between governments and technology companies. Tech companies, particularly those that develop or host digital content, play a crucial role in detecting and preventing the spread of deepfakes. Governments can encourage this by establishing guidelines and best practices for tech companies, which could include implementing robust content verification processes, developing and deploying AI-based detection tools, and providing transparency reports on the prevalence and mitigation of deepfake content. Moreover, public-private partnerships could facilitate the sharing of information and resources. For example, governments could support research into advanced detection technologies or fund public awareness campaigns about the risks of deepfakes. In return, tech companies could cooperate in regulatory compliance and provide expertise to inform policy-making.

15. FUTURE RESEARCH SCOPE

Potential Future Developments in Deepfake Technology

Deepfake technology, which leverages artificial intelligence to create hyper-realistic fake videos or audio, has seen rapid advancements in recent years. This technology has wide-ranging implications, from entertainment to misinformation and cybersecurity. As deepfakes become more sophisticated, understanding their potential future developments and implications, particularly in financial fraud and cybersecurity, is crucial.

Area of future scope Deepfake technology is evolving at a rapid pace, driven by advancements in machine learning and neural networks. The following are some anticipated future developments. Increased Realism and Accessibility: With ongoing improvements in algorithms, deepfakes are expected to become more realistic and harder to detect. The barriers to creating high-quality deepfakes are also decreasing, making the technology accessible to a broader audience. This democratization of technology could lead to more widespread use, both benign and malicious (Chesney & Citron, 2019). Automation and Integration: Future developments may include the integration of deepfake technology with other AI systems, enabling automated creation of deepfakes for various purposes, including entertainment, virtual reality, and online impersonation. This integration could also enhance the ability to generate deepfakes in real-time, further complicating detection efforts (Korshunov & Marcel, 2020). Ethical and Legal Considerations: As deepfakes become more prevalent, there will be increasing demand for ethical guidelines and legal frameworks to govern their use. The challenge lies in balancing the protection of individual rights with freedom of expression and technological innovation (McGlynn, Rackley, & Johnson, 2020).

16. PRACTICAL IMPLICATIONS

For Investors: The implications of this study for investors are significant, as it highlights the growing threat of deepfake-related financial fraud and manipulation. Investors need to be aware that deepfakes can be used to impersonate corporate executives, spread false financial information and manipulate stock prices, potentially leading to substantial financial losses. The study emphasizes the importance of enhanced due diligence and verification processes to identify and mitigate these risks. Investors are urged to press for more regulatory measures to prevent fraud connected to deepfake as well as to promote and lobby for the use of advanced detection technology inside the firms in which they invest. Additionally, investors may support a more robust and secure financial ecosystem by encouraging stakeholders to become more digitally literate and informed. In the end, this study emphasises how important it is for investors to continue being watchful and proactive in safeguarding their money against sophisticated digital fraud.

For Organisation: There are significant organisational ramifications to the research on the malevolent use of deepfakes in financial fraud and manipulation. It emphasises how crucial it is for companies to strengthen their security protocols in order to combat deepfake threats. To make sure that communications and transactions are real, organisations need to build strong verification procedures and invest in cutting-edge detection technology. The report emphasises how critical it is for staff members to participate in awareness and training campaigns in order to identify and handle such deepfake frauds. Establishing thorough incident response procedures is also advised for organisations in order to promptly address and lessen the effects of fraud connected to deepfake. The report also recommends that businesses support and abide by strict regulatory structures intended to prevent digital theft. Organisations may strengthen overall cybersecurity resilience, preserve stakeholder confidence, and better safeguard their financial integrity in the face of more complex types of deception by using these measures.

For Financial Institutions: Financial institutions should take serious note of the research on the fraudulent use of deepfakes in financial fraud. It emphasises how critical it is for banks and other financial institutions to improve their security measures in order to identify and stop fraud connected to deepfakes. To secure the legitimacy of customer communications and transactions, financial institutions need to implement strict verification processes and invest in state-of-the-art detection technology. The study highlights how crucial it is to train staff members how to identify and handle such deepfake risks in order to lower the risk of fraud. Financial institutions are also urged to join with regulatory agencies to create and uphold strong structures intended to combat cybercrime. Additionally, the report recommends that in order to raise consumers' general knowledge of security, financial institutions should cultivate a culture of digital literacy. Financial institutions may strengthen their resilience against sophisticated cyber-attacks, preserve client confidence, and safeguard their assets by putting these precautions into place.

CONCLUSION

Deepfake in the last years enriched with new risks in different fields, and finance industry is not the exception. This summary presents the main points related to the idea of deepfake financial fraud as a dangerous threat and the necessity of action as well as constant research and shared work on the solution of the problem. Deepfake financial fraud entails the employment of high-quality artificial Intelligence generated media to mimic people or even twist data in a way that could contribute to severe monetary loss. These consist of flexibility of these threats, as well as the fails when it comes to identifying deepfakes and strengths that are weak points in current security models. It is important to prevent such a type of frauds as unorganized protection measures won't help as much as planned countermeasures. It will be necessary to raise the issue of the fact that organizations must spend the money on sophisticated detection technologies, including those based on AI, which will be able to recognize deepfake patterns. Moreover, improving the cybersecurity measures and raising the awareness of the employees as well as the public about the dangers of and signs of deepfakes are the preventive steps towards falling for these attacks. Thus, the constant development of deepfake technology creates the need and importance of cybersecurity research, the financial industry, and governmental authorities' further interaction. Thus, collaborating and learning from each other can lead to the implementation of new approaches that would help to mitigate the impact of new threats in the light of rapidly progressing technologies. Joint actions also facilitate the promotion of unified guidelines that shape the industry as well as possible solutions for preventing deepfake fraud. Finally, deepfake related to financial fraud is a current and evolving problem that is extremely dangerous. In many cases, it is possible to prevent risks by providing awareness to the risk, dedicating capital on detection technologies, and incorporating various education to the employees in an organization. Moreover, research is ongoing and interdisciplinary cooperation is required to face these threats which tipped out as a dynamic threat matrix. Altogether, these actions may support the preservation of the financial systems' stability and prevent possible negative consequences of deepfake technologies.

REFERENCES

G7 Finance Ministers and Central Bank Governors. (2021). G7 Finance Ministers' and Central Bank Governors' Statement on Digital Payments and Central Bank Digital Currencies. Retrieved from G7 UK.

Agarwal, S., Farid, H., Gu, Y., He, M., Nagano, K., & Li, H. (2020). Protecting World Leaders Against DeepFakes. *Proceedings of the IEEE Conference on Computer Vision and Pattern Recognition Workshops (CVPRW)*.

Anti-Phishing Working Group (APWG). (2020). Phishing Activity Trends Report.

Barth, J. R. (1991). *The Great Savings and Loan Debacle*. American Enterprise Institute.

Bradshaw, T. (2022). The rise of deepfakes in cybercrime. Financial Times.

California Assembly Bill No. 730, 2019. Retrieved from California Legislative Information

Chesney, R., & Citron, D. K. (2019). Deepfakes and the New Disinformation War: The Coming Age of Post-Truth Geopolitics. *Foreign Affairs*, 98(1), 147–155.

CipherTrace. (2019). Cryptocurrency Anti-Money Laundering Report 2018.

Citron, D. K. (2019). Sexual Privacy. *The Yale Law Journal*, 128(7), 1870–1960.

Creswell, A., White, T., Dumoulin, V., Arulkumaran, K., Sengupta, B., & Bharath, A. A. (2018). Generative Adversarial Networks: An Overview. *IEEE Signal Processing Magazine*, 35(1), 53–65. DOI: 10.1109/MSP.2017.2765202

Dale, R. (2004). *The First Crash: Lessons from the South Sea Bubble*. Princeton University Press.

Deepfake Impersonation Case: TechRadar Synthetic Identity Fraud: TechRadar Market Manipulation: CNBC Security Systems Bypass: TechRadar

Dong, C., Loy, C. C., He, K., & Tang, X. (2015). Image super-resolution using deep convolutional networks. *IEEE Transactions on Pattern Analysis and Machine Intelligence*, 38(2), 295–307. DOI: 10.1109/TPAMI.2015.2439281 PMID: 26761735

Galbraith, J. K. (1954). *The Great Crash 1929*. Houghton Mifflin.

Geis, G. (1968). White-Collar Crime: The Heavy Electrical Equipment Antitrust Cases of 1961. *Journal of Criminal Law and Criminology*, 58(3), 337–354.

Goodfellow, I., Pouget-Abadie, J., Mirza, M., Xu, B., Warde-Farley, D., Ozair, S., . . . Bengio, Y. (2014). Generative adversarial nets. Advances in neural information processing systems, 27. Agarwal, S., Farid, H., Gu, Y., He, M., Nagano, K., & Li, H. (2020). Detecting Deep-Fake Videos from Appearance and Behavior. arXiv preprint arXiv:2003.05696.

Harwell, D. (2020). Faked voices, social media scams: How AI tech is being used to deceive. The Washington Post.

Henriques, D. B. (2011). *The Wizard of Lies: Bernie Madoff and the Death of Trust.* Times Books.

Hochreiter, S., & Schmidhuber, J. (1997). Long short-term memory. *Neural Computation*, 9(8), 1735–1780. DOI: 10.1162/neco.1997.9.8.1735 PMID: 9377276

Hui, M. (2023). *The growing threat of deepfake technology.* Global Initiative.

Janssen, P. (2015). Ancient Greek Bankers: Trapezitai and Their Operations. Journal of Ancient History.

Kietzmann, J., Lee, L. W., McCarthy, I. P., & Kietzmann, T. C. (2020). Deepfakes: Trick or treat? *Business Horizons*, 63(2), 135–146. DOI: 10.1016/j.bushor.2019.11.006

Kingma, D. P., & Welling, M. (2013). Auto-Encoding Variational Bayes. arXiv preprint arXiv:1312.6114.

Korshunov, P., & Marcel, S. (2020). Vulnerability Assessment and Detection of Deepfake Videos. *IEEE International Conference on Image Processing (ICIP),* 226-230.

Kraus, S. (2020). The Growing Threat of Deepfakes and Synthetic Media in Financial Fraud. *Journal of Financial Crime*, 27(3), 877–885.

LeCun, Y., Bengio, Y., & Hinton, G. (2015). Deep learning. *Nature*, 521(7553), 436–444. DOI: 10.1038/nature14539 PMID: 26017442

Maras, M.-H., & Alexandrou, A. (2019). Determining Authenticity of Video Evidence in the Age of Artificial Intelligence and in the Wake of Deepfake Videos. *The International Journal of Evidence & Proof*, 23(3), 255–262. DOI: 10.1177/1365712718807226

https://economictimes.indiatimes.com/, McAfee Survey 2024

https://www.indiancybersquad.org/post/case-study-kerala-s-first-deepfake-fraud

McGlynn, C., Rackley, E., & Johnson, K. (2020). Deepfakes, Pornography, and Privacy. *European Journal of Law and Technology*, 11(1).

Miller, T., Spooner, K., & Landman, T. (2020). Deepfake Detection: Fighting AI with AI. *Financial Times*.

Mirsky, Y., & Lee, W. (2021). The creation and detection of deepfakes: A survey. *ACM Computing Surveys*, 54(1), 1–34. DOI: 10.1145/3425780

Newman, L. H. (2021). *How deepfakes are transforming the fraud landscape*. Wired.

NextWeb. (2023). Deepfake Fraud Attempts are up 3000% in 2023 — Here's Why.

Nguyen, T. T., Nguyen, T. N., Nguyen, D. T., & Hsu, C. H. (2020). Deep Learning for Deepfakes Creation and Detection: A Survey. arXiv preprint arXiv:2007.12084.

Parker, D. B. (1983). *Fighting Computer Crime*. Charles Scribner's Sons.

Patel, P., Chopra, V., & Bakshi, P. (2020). Positive Use Cases of Deepfake Technology. *Journal of Digital Innovation*, 3(1), 45–55.

Rosenblatt, K. (2019). *Scammers Use AI to Mimic CEO's Voice in Unusual Cybercrime Case*. NBC News.

Schwartz, O. (2020). You thought deepfakes were scary? Think again. *Harvard Business Review*.

The Times of India. November 2024, https://timesofindia.indiatimes.com/

Tufekci, Z. (2018). *Twitter and Tear Gas: The Power and Fragility of Networked Protest*. Yale University Press.

UK Government. (2021). *Online Safety Bill*. Retrieved from UK Government Publications.

Veale, M., Van Kleek, M., & Binns, R. (2018). Fairness and accountability design needs for algorithmic support in high-stakes public sector decision-making. *Proceedings of the 2018 CHI Conference on Human Factors in Computing Systems*. DOI: 10.1145/3173574.3174014

Verdoliva, L. (2020). Media forensics and deepfakes: An overview. *IEEE Journal of Selected Topics in Signal Processing*, 14(5), 910–932. DOI: 10.1109/JSTSP.2020.3002101

Chapter 9
Deepfake Prospects, Mitigating Factors, and Deceptions

Uttam Kaur
https://orcid.org/0000-0002-7153-2982
Chandigarh University, India

Prashant Kumar Siddhey
https://orcid.org/0000-0002-4236-0966
ITM University, Gwalior, India

ABSTRACT

Deepfakes, which are synthetic yet incredibly lifelike images, sounds, and video produced by computers, are among the most recent advancements in artificial intelligence technology. Due to the speed and breadth of social media, they can swiftly spread to millions of individuals and lead to a variety of deceptive practices in the marketplace. Nevertheless, current knowledge about the effects of deep fakes on the market is incomplete and dispersed. According to our research, the primary dangers facing businesses are the quick obsolescence of current technologies and harm to their reputation, image, and credibility. On the other hand, customers could also experience identity theft, intimidation, extortion, harassment, slander, and revenge porn. Next, we gather and disseminate information about the tactics and defenses against deep fake-based market manipulation. Additionally, we identify and document the several valid prospects provided by this novel technique. We conclude by outlining a research plan for this rapidly developing and crucial field.

DOI: 10.4018/979-8-3693-6890-9.ch009

Copyright © 2025, IGI Global Scientific Publishing. Copying or distributing in print or electronic forms without written permission of IGI Global Scientific Publishing is prohibited.

1. INTRODUCTION

Deepfakes refer to digitally altered synthetic media content, such as films, photographs, and sound snippets, wherein individuals are depicted doing or saying things that are not real or have never happened (Mustak et al., 2023). Deepfakes are a product of AI advancements, specifically in machine learning (ML) and deep neural networks (DNNs) (Kietzmann et al., 2020). These appear so "true to life" and believable that it can be difficult for a human to tell them apart from real media (Lu & Chu, 2023). They can therefore be employed to deceive the market on a large scale, with unpredictable consequences for businesses and customers alike (Okolie, 2023). Fake audio or video content is actually the most concerning application of AI in terms of possible criminal or terrorist uses (Williamson & Prybutok, 2024). Still, there's also a chance that this new technology will open up significant commercial options for engagement and content production (Murphy et al., 2023).

In customer research and marketing, deception is a major problem since it is so common in the marketplace (Łabuz, 2023). Generally speaking, deception is the intentional attempt or act of providing someone with inaccurate or omitted information in an effort to persuade them of something the communicator believes to be untrue (Sunvy et al., 2023). Therefore, it is deliberate information manipulation intended to lead to erroneous beliefs in the minds of others (i.e., deceiving parties) (Li & Wan, 2023). Deepfakes can exacerbate this effect and harm both businesses and consumers (Murillo-Ligorred et al., 2023). The market is rife with deception, which damages people's health, welfare, and financial resources as well as erodes public confidence in businesses and the market at large (Pawar & Shirsath, 2024). An initial negative outcome could be a sharp decline in the company's stock value if, for instance, a fictitious video purporting to show the CEO acknowledging the business has been hit with a significant regulatory fine (or class-action lawsuit) (Carnevale et al., 2023). Attacks of this kind have already started to happen (Vasist & Krishnan, 2022). The thieves successfully assumed the role of the CEO of the company's parent company by using AI-based voice spoofing software, leading the CEO to believe he was conversing with his boss (Hussain et al., 2022). According to cybersecurity firm Symantec, at least three instances of deepfake-based fraud were reported to them in 2019, costing millions of dollars (Campbell et al., 2022). Customers are also vulnerable to identity theft, sabotage, intimidation, blackmail, harassment, and revenge porn. But there is also good potential for this new technology in terms of various commercialization strategies. In fact, deepfakes might be able to innovate or alter business paradigms (Burgstaller & Macpherson, 2021). As customers spend more time in virtual worlds, the prospects surrounding deepfakes are becoming progressively more pertinent, and this will undoubtedly draw increased attention and investment from businesses of all stripes (Harris, 2022). For instance,

Facebook rebranded itself as Meta and is reportedly investing $10 billion in the Metaverse, a virtual reality environment. The majority of the objects in this virtual environment will be deepfake ones. Thus, new opportunities and risks will come with this latest technology (Kim et al., 2021). The internet and social networking sites have become indispensable to people's personal and professional lives, giving users access to user-friendly platforms for instantaneous discussions, the exchange of ideas, the sharing of emotions and sentiments, and the dissemination of information (Turner, 2022). This is another important factor contributing to the relevance of deepfakes. Therefore, there will be both good and negative effects on the market due to the size, volume, and speed of deepfakes' distribution as well as the growing ubiquity of digital technology in all spheres of society (Kietzmann et al., 2020).

Deepfakes are a complex, emerging technology, and our knowledge of their ramifications is still limited to a few key areas (Chesney & Citron, 2019). The literature currently in publication only provides anecdotal and inconsistent evidence regarding the potential for deepfakes to deceive consumers and businesses (Mirsky & Lee, 2021). As a result, there is a dearth of comprehensive knowledge regarding the unique opportunities that deepfakes can present to both parties (Masood et al., 2023). The majority of research on marketplace deception to date has focused heavily on how it impacts consumers and has been conducted from the viewpoint of the consumer (Hancock & Bailenson, 2021). Researchers have highlighted that organizations are not immune to the effects of deepfakes, although the repercussions on businesses have gotten little attention (Tolosana et al., 2020). To set them apart from other deceptive practices like opinion spam and fake reviews, which solely have negative consequences, deepfakes also have a genuine chance to generate business opportunities (Albahar & Almalki, 2019). Therefore, in order to minimize the harm that deepfakes might cause and take advantage of any benefits they may present, both consumers and businesses need to increase their awareness of and ability to recognize deepfake fraud (De Ruiter, 2021). In light of this, the goal of this research is to provide a comprehensive knowledge of deepfakes in relation to deceit in the marketplace and the opportunities they may present. In this study explicitly address the research questions (RQs) listed below:

RQ1: How might deceptions in the marketplace is aided by deepfakes?
RQ2: How can businesses and customers prevent the harmful impacts of deepfakes?
RQ3: What advantages may consumers and businesses derive from deepfakes?

In order to develop a thorough understanding relevant to our goal, in this study applied an integrative literature review to the analysis of prior studies. To summarize the body of knowledge, we also looked at academic literature from the fields of communications, computer science, information science, journalism, and social sciences, all of which have a presence in deepfake research. This study provides a fundamental knowledge of deepfakes in terms of consumer and company deception through this study. This study also compiles and displays the defenses against their negative impacts, providing information about the acceptable prospects this new technology presents.

2. FOUNDATIONAL IDEAS

2.1 Recognizing Dishonesty in the Marketplace

Misperception, misprediction, non-perception, and non-prediction are the foundations of marketplace deceptions (Shahzad et al., 2022). Marketplace transactions between companies, marketers, customers, and any other entity looking to profit illegally or unethically sometimes involve deception (Karnouskos, 2020). Misrepresentations based on statistics or study findings, information overload and distraction, feigned emotions in sales and service delivery scenarios, brand emulation, and fabrications about the characteristics of products and their effects on users are a few examples of these kinds of deceptions (Johnson & Diakopoulos, 2021). The majority of the early academic research in this field was on marketing and advertising communications deceptions (Kirchengast, 2020). It was proposed as early as 1975 that deception exists if an advertisement (or advertising campaign) gives the consumer an impression, belief, or both that differs from what would be expected if the consumer had reasonable knowledge and that impression, belief, or both are factually false or potentially misleading (Dagar & Vishwakarma, 2022). This argument focuses on how a marketer could mislead consumers in order to get an edge. Since professionals usually create and distribute these kinds of communications, it is logical to assume that the misleading material in question is produced with the intention of making money off of customers (Mustak et al., 2023). As a result, customers develop unfavorable opinions of marketing and advertising in general and become skeptical of claims made in the future due to deceptions in the marketplace through advertising. When it comes to e-commerce, manipulating information generation, content, and presentation can all be considered product-related deceptive information practices (Kietzmann et al., 2020). An e-commerce platform may misrepresent information on a product's packaging or withhold potentially negative information about the product (Lu & Chu, 2023). Software applications known as fake product recommendation agents, which replicate the interests or preferences of certain customers, have the ability to manipulate recommendation systems in order to produce misleading product recommendations (Okolie, 2023). Similar to this, companies might create and disseminate phony product reviews to influence consumers' decisions because consumers depend on them when making decisions about products they want to buy online (Williamson & Prybutok, 2024). Opinion spams, or similar forms of marketplace fraud, can be produced by computers or by humans. Businesses may sponsor human-generated phony reviews by using fictitious online customer accounts (Murphy et al., 2023). Text-generation algorithms are used by computer-generated false reviews to automate the manufacture of bogus reviews (Łabuz, 2023). Regardless of the methods used to produce and disseminate the deceptions, their main goal is to mislead customers and occasionally rival businesses in order to make money or achieve other forms of economic gain (Sunvy et al., 2023).

2.2 Market Manipulation With Fake Media

Synthetic media deception in the marketplace is distinct from conventional deception in a number of ways (Li & Wan, 2023). The phrase "synthetic media'" refers to any artificial production or alteration of media by "machines"—more especially, by programs that make use of AI and ML (Murillo-Ligorred et al., 2023). These days, artificial intelligence (AI) is used to create text, images, videos, voice synthesizing, and music. Deepfakes are by far the most common of these many kinds. In late 2017, a combination of the terms "deep learning" and "fake" was created: "deepfake" (Pawar & Shirsath, 2024). In general, conventional forms of advertising deception involve presenting incorrect material as factual or hiding certain facts (Carnevale et al., 2023). The most contemporary technological manifestations, such opinion spam and bogus reviews, are primarily textual or may contain real photos taken out of context (Vasist & Krishnan, 2022). They are also purpose- and context-specific because of its increased appeal to human cognitive functions and versatility, synthetic media has raised the bar for commercial deception (Hussain et al., 2022). The fact that these media are also far more realistic and enticing, and that they may be used widely in a range of settings, all contribute to the difficulty of protecting against them (Campbell et al., 2022).

Recent technological advancements have reduced or eliminated the availability of visible or nonverbal cues (such as facial expressions and eye contact) for assessing a piece of information, elevating the level of deception in the marketplace to previously unheard-of heights (Burgstaller & Macpherson, 2021). Also, it has become more difficult to assess the veracity of incoming information because computer-mediated deception has previously been applied to language action cues like verbal and non-verbal immediacy (as well as the unnecessary use of words, structured messages, or argument development) and has modified or mimicked interactional exchanges between messages (Harris, 2022). Because hyper-realistic movies and other multimedia deepfakes are so hard to distinguish from the real thing, the recent advent of deepfakes has further increased the harm that may be done to the marketplace through deceit (Kim et al., 2021).

3. METHODOLOGY

This study utilized the integrated literature review (ILR) method, which is defined as "a research approach that integrates, evaluates, and synthesizes representative literature on a topic to generate new frameworks and perspectives on the topic". It's recognized as a specific type of systematic literature review. The SLR method, however, has a tendency to concentrate on a single subject or category of research. On the other hand, ILR aims to be inclusive from a phenomenological standpoint, with less focus on the discipline, venue, and style of study. The inadequate state of investigation into deepfakes in the business and marketing domains has an impact on our decision to employ the ILR strategy. It is worthwhile to pursue information gained in other subjects, such as computer science and political science, while examining any potential implications for the marketing domain, as these fields have more relevant research than the business domain. We were therefore able to combine primary knowledge from many study streams using the ILR approach, producing logical and perceptive responses to our research questions. This study used a three-phase methodology.

> Phase I: Planning the Review Process: Determining the purpose and parameters of the research as well as identifying the critical phenomenon of deepfakes.
> Phase II involves carrying out the review process, which includes selecting research to examine, creating an analytical framework, categorizing and combining pertinent data, and creating a conceptual framework.
> Phase III: Reporting and Disseminating the Research Results: This involves providing a descriptive summary of the findings in accordance with the research questions, going into additional detail about the findings, drawing conclusions from the study, and suggesting directions for future research.

The research's "Phase I"—identifying the crucial phenomena of deepfakes and outlining the purpose and parameters of the study was previously discussed in this article's introduction section. The study then provides a thorough explanation of "Phase II." Sections 4 and 5 present "Phase III," which consists of reporting and disseminating the overall results.

4. FINDINGS

This study developed a conceptual framework to encapsulate the deepfake phenomena in the context of marketplace deception and opportunity based on our thorough investigation of the reviewed literature. In addition to allowing for the collection of a broad overview of the phenomenon, the framework also makes it easier to present the results in an orderly manner. This study proposes that the dualistic character of this powerful and emerging technology presents both radical potential for innovation and risks to businesses and consumers. The results show that applying current defense mechanisms and tactics only provides partial protection and does not completely offset the negative effects of deep fakes. Companies and consumers may still experience some negative consequences. Deepfakes have both beneficial and detrimental implications that extend beyond the realms of businesses and consumers. Instead, they frequently have knock-on effects, meaning that changes that impact businesses can also influence consumers and vice versa. Next, in accordance with the conceptual framework and in response to our research questions, we first outline the different types of potential deepfake marketplace deceptions. This study examines what is currently known about protecting businesses and consumers from their harmful impacts. Subsequently, the present study aims to discover and report on the potential opportunities that this developing technology may offer. The study provides multiple instances that highlight these elements, which enables the establishment of theory-practice ties and an understanding of what these entail in the "real world."

4.1 Deepfakes Used to Deceive the Market

4.1.1 Risks to Businesses

The majority of the available research on deception in the marketplace focuses on consumers who fall prey to dishonest acts and behaviors (Turner, 2022). Nonetheless, our research indicates that deepfakes provide a far wider range of risks than standard deceptions since they can negatively impact enterprises in several ways (Kietzmann et al., 2020). These include harm to a company's reputation, image, and trustworthiness, as well as malicious acts like sabotage and slander (Chesney & Citron, 2019). Due to the widespread use of deepfakes, businesses are becoming targets of malicious acts including sabotage and defamation (Mirsky & Lee, 2021). These actions can jeopardize a company's brand image and reputation by misleading consumers and other stakeholders, which can lead to a loss of confidence (Masood et al., 2023). Deepfake propagation started by an enemy can seriously hurt businesses. These detrimental consequences frequently trickle down from businesses to customers, as our conceptual framework demonstrates (Hancock & Bailenson, 2021). A company's reputation and brand image can be negatively impacted when a senior executive or other prominent figurehead is perceived to be making derogatory or highly contentious remarks (Tolosana et al., 2020).

Deepfake technology has the potential to harm companies with varying capacities and personalities (Albahar & Almalki, 2019). Competitors may, for instance, utilize deepfakes to trick a company's clients or to incite misunderstanding or unfavorable public perceptions regarding a rival's goods, names, and services (De Ruiter, 2021). Deepfakes can also be used to damage a company by fabricating negative reviews of its goods and services (Shahzad et al., 2022). In a virtual brand community (VBC), for example, the appearance of false but incredibly realistic deepfake-based reviews (especially negative reviews) can have an impact on how people interact with other members of the VBC as they start to lose faith in the group and become less interested in interacting with others (Karnouskos, 2020). Developing deepfakes by a company to mislead customers or hide facts from them could make them more distrustful of the company (Johnson & Diakopoulos, 2021). Deepfake technology not only threatens a company's image, reputation, and credibility by engaging in various forms of deceit in the marketplace, but it also poses a threat to business models by upending established technologies in specific sectors (such as entertainment) and essentially making them obsolete (Kirchengast, 2020). But there's also the other way around, as we cover in Section 4.3.1, where these technologies can be leveraged to improve these sectors. For example, the ability of improving technology to change languages and lips correspondingly puts the dubbing and re-voicing sector at risk of going extinct. This industry used to interpret films to guarantee that words in another language matched the actor's original lip movements. Similar to biometric authentication technology, deepfake technologies pose a serious risk and could cause disruptions to companies that offer authentication services (Dagar & Vishwakarma, 2022).

4.1.2. Threats to Customers

Deepfake deception can have serious negative effects on customers that go beyond the confines of business-customer interactions because it can be used for a number of nefarious activities (Mustak et al., 2023). The first report on deepfakes by Europol, the European Union Agency for Law Enforcement Cooperation, lists a number of threats, such as using the internet to harass or humiliate people, commit fraud and extortion, facilitate document fraud, fake online personas and trick "know your customer" systems, engage in non-consensual pornography, exploit online child sexual exploitation, fabricate or manipulate electronic evidence for criminal justice investigations, disrupt financial markets, disseminate false information and manipulate public opinion, support the narratives of extremist or terrorist groups, incite social unrest, and polarization on a political level (Kietzmann et al., 2020). The lack of security, susceptibility, and potential for deepfake exploitation that consumers face are increased by the cognitive limitations and ideological biases of humans (Lu & Chu, 2023). Lack of media literacy or familiarity with contemporary digital technologies, for example, may make consumers more likely to be persuaded by inaccurate or misleading information (Okolie, 2023). This highlights a new manifestation of the digital divide, where consumers who lack the cognitive abilities to recognize deepfakes are structurally inferior to those who do. Stated differently, consumers who lack sophistication may be more susceptible to deepfake deceit (Williamson & Prybutok, 2024).

Similarly, customers who don't know enough about digital technology may be exposed to fake products and spread false information online (Murphy et al., 2023). For example, the website "Random Face Generator" creates fictitious portraits of people that don't actually exist using artificial intelligence. Previous studies suggest that specific demographics are more vulnerable to fraudulent content (Łabuz, 2023). The literature implies that the third-person effect and internet disinformation are related (Sunvy et al., 2023). The fundamental idea behind the third-person effect is that people tend to underestimate the impact of media on their own behaviors while overestimating its influence on the attitudes and behaviors of others (Li & Wan, 2023). From a business perspective, fake technology can contribute to customer mistrust of organizations and psychological pain by creating ambiguity in the marketplace and misleading consumers (Murillo-Ligorred et al., 2023). This can therefore weaken consumers' inclinations to buy and reduce the accuracy of useful technology like recommendation systems (Pawar & Shirsath, 2024). It is reasonable to anticipate that the integration of deepfakes with technologies capable of producing human-like narratives through natural language processing (NLP), such as GPT-3, a text-generation model, will only serve to increase market deception, given the rapid development of these technologies (Carnevale et al., 2023). People find it harder to react to tailored ads when they encounter deepfakes (Vasist & Krishnan, 2022). It can be difficult for consumers to balance the personalization of incoming data from deepfakes with the degree to which they compromise privacy when weighing the perceived value of highly personalized advertisements against a perceived violation of personal privacy (Hussain et al., 2022). Furthermore, customers that engage in diverse virtual communities, such as brand communities, often hold comparable beliefs (Campbell et al., 2022). Because of the perceived similarities between the message and their embraced philosophy, members of these virtual communities would probably consider it to be true (Burgstaller & Macpherson, 2021). As a result, deepfake technologies might be used to initiate naturally disruptive campaigns against these communities.

Deepfakes used in the marketplace can deceive consumers in ways other than those seen in business-to-business transactions (Harris, 2022). For example, these kinds of lies could be harmful to somebody trying to get a job. Hiring applicants who are not stigmatized by perceived unfavorable online reputations is less risky, and the reasons behind these findings are rather obvious. In many cases, incriminating photos and videos of an individual that are posted online for public viewing will severely hurt that individual's chances of finding work (Kim et al., 2021). Employers suffer from this as well, since they run the danger of losing out on prospective talent (Turner, 2022). Beyond the workplace, a number of intelligence services have voiced worry that deepfakes could compromise national security by influencing election campaigns and disseminating political misinformation, which would impair consumers' capacity to remain informed about the real situation (Kietzmann et al., 2020).

4.2 Protection Against Deepfakes and Other Market Deception

Protection methods must be developed and made available due to the seriousness of the threat posed by deepfakes in terms of deceitful marketing and malicious intent (Chesney & Citron, 2019). We then provide our findings in this respect. It's important to remember that the protection mechanisms for consumers and businesses are not mutually exclusive, despite the fact that we display them separately for the sake of presentation and reporting (Mirsky & Lee, 2021). Therefore, preventing harmful impacts from reaching customers and vice versa is commonly achieved by shielding businesses from deepfakes.

4.2.1 Protection of Businesses Against Deepfakes and Other Forms of Market Deception

The majority of research that is now available uses the assumption that using legal action is the main, and frequently the only, defense against conventional kinds of deception in the marketplace (Masood et al., 2023). Nonetheless, our data unequivocally demonstrates that using only legal measures to shield businesses and consumers from the harmful consequences of deepfakes is exceedingly challenging (Hancock & Bailenson, 2021). Instead, three different but related types of protection mechanisms—market, circulation, and technical—as well as associated legal responses, are required to solve the issues raised by deepfakes (Tolosana et al., 2020).

In order to defend themselves, businesses can use processes and strategies to enlighten consumers about their brands, products, and services and assist them in identifying reliable and company-sponsored sources of information (Albahar & Almalki, 2019). Investments in CSR programs aimed at enhancing public media literacy will pay off for companies and the industry at large (De Ruiter, 2021). Developing consumer information, media literacy, critical thinking, and evaluation skills is the goal of this strategy, which can be used to evaluate the veracity and credibility of news reports and other information (Shahzad et al., 2022). It is noted that creating information literacy interventions necessitates a multidisciplinary approach, involving contributions from social psychology, economics, and legal studies in addition to education (Karnouskos, 2020). Businesses can educate customers on opinion-reinforcing versus opinion-challenging information that they can use to assess web material when developing methods to increase consumers' awareness of deceit (Johnson & Diakopoulos, 2021). Information that supports or validates preexisting views or opinions is known as opinion-reinforcing information; on the other hand, material that contradicts preexisting beliefs or opinions of a person or consumer is known as opinion-challenging information (Kirchengast, 2020). Businesses can also use online brand communities to combat deepfakes and other forms of marketplace fraud (Dagar & Vishwakarma, 2022). Engaging with online communities that produce deepfake content is one of these tactics; by doing so, businesses can prevent taking any decisions that could expose them to deepfake attacks (Mustak et al., 2023). The accuracy of information being disseminated through online channels can be established and verified by utilizing resources from specialist group areas, user ratings, and user credibility networks (Kietzmann et al., 2020). In a similar vein, businesses might come up with plans for handling customer relations and feedback in order to encourage brand community members to take precautions against the damage that deepfakes can do to their reputation (Lu & Chu, 2023). Thus, companies can create so-called online good nodes—approved false accounts of actual people—that can spread accurate information to counter or dispute misleading material by working with prominent real-life people and utilizing deepfake technology (Okolie, 2023).

More defenses against the possible harms of deepfakes can be provided by restricting or tightly controlling their dissemination (Williamson & Prybutok, 2024). Posting them on social media sites is also completely prohibited. TikTok, for example, is changing its community guidelines to forbid "synthetic or manipulated content that misleads users by distorting the truth of events in a way that could cause harm. Reddit does not allow content that impersonates individuals or entities in a misleading or deceptive manner," according to an amended version of its impersonation policy (Murphy et al., 2023). The term "video content that has been technically manipulated (beyond clips taken out of context) to fabricate events where there's a serious risk of egregious harm" is used by YouTube to describe the kind of content that is currently prohibited from the platform (Łabuz, 2023). One technical solution is to restrict access to the computer resources required for creating and executing deepfakes (Sunvy et al., 2023). The effective use of deepfake detection technology and additional research and development (R&D) expenditures are equally vital (Li & Wan, 2023). Companies that invest in this way can detect and counteract the content-, context-, and domain-dependent aspects of deepfakes using algorithmic and computational detection approaches like support vector machines and deep learning (Murillo-Ligorred et al., 2023). Companies that invest in this way can detect and combat the content-, context-, and domain-dependent characteristics of deepfakes using algorithmic and computational detection approaches like support vector machines and deep learning (Pawar & Shirsath, 2024). Microsoft, for instance, has released the Microsoft Video Authenticator, which assesses the possibility that a still image or video has been purposefully altered (Carnevale et al., 2023). It is important to acknowledge that the safeguards against deepfake deceptions, which rely on technology, have some constraints because of the rapid advancements in creating artificial media (Vasist & Krishnan, 2022).

The framework takes a risk-based approach to regulating AI and its applications. The term "AI systems used to generate or manipulate image, audio, or video content" is specifically used to describe deepfakes (Hussain et al., 2022). They also have to meet some minimal requirements, like marking content as deepfake to inform consumers that they are dealing with edited footage (Campbell et al., 2022). The framework isn't operational yet; it's currently in the proposal stage. Legislation that forbids fraud, as well as measures against harassment, defamation, copyright infringement, and data protection, can provide businesses and consumers with protection (Burgstaller & Macpherson, 2021). Rules, laws, and regulations are often not imposed by businesses (Harris, 2022). However, given the current situation, they might keep an eye on things and push for laws that defend the rights of organizations that are the targets of damaging deepfake content. Companies and regulators can work together to create, put into effect, and publicize rules or regulations controlling the production and distribution of fake content.

4.2.2 Safeguarding Customers From Being Deceived by Deepfakes in the Marketplace

Research on how customers might safeguard themselves against deepfakes and other forms of market deception is scarce, according to our findings. The deepfake domain has been designated as a "disintermediation" phase (Kim et al., 2021). Protecting against deepfakes is made more difficult by the variety of sources from which they are distributed, the possibility of confidentiality, the lack of information quality standards, the ease with which material can be altered, the absence of contextual information, and the lack of credibility assessment objectives (i.e., subject matter, medium, and source) (Turner, 2022). Developing the skills required to evaluate and assess the reliability of internet content is a fairly broad yet essential safeguard for consumers in their daily lives (Kietzmann et al., 2020). Their protection will be further enhanced by taking into account the credibility of the information source, the involvement of reliable middlemen like experts and/or opinion leaders, and personal confidence based on first-hand knowledge (Chesney & Citron, 2019). Furthermore, buyers who learn about products, companies, and services will be better able to recognize and steer clear of false information (Mirsky & Lee, 2021). In this case, consumers should prioritize developing their critical thinking skills when assessing the veracity or accuracy of the information they receive (Masood et al., 2023). A person's awareness of bogus information can be raised on an individual basis by having a diverse range of social relationships, which are described as the range of offline groups and situations reflected in their online social networks (Hancock & Bailenson, 2021). The study also suggests that raising consumer awareness of fraud-ulent content like deepfakes has a positive impact on network trust and verification behavior (Tolosana et al., 2020). Therefore, a workable individual-level approach to solving the deepfake issue is to actively expose oneself to a variety of ideas and networks in order to counteract the echo chamber effect of social media (Albahar & Almalki, 2019). In an attempt to defend other consumers, consumers may even employ an aggressive coping technique by finding and presenting contradictory proof to the claims made in fraudulent content (De Ruiter, 2021).

4.3 Deepfakes Present Opportunities

There is no denying that deepfakes pose a risk to consumers and businesses alike by misleading the market (Shahzad et al., 2022). But unlike other forms of deception that are only employed for malevolent and unethical intent, deepfake technology is special since it also presents a number of advantageous options (Karnouskos, 2020). Here, we examine and outline the advantages of deepfakes for both customers and companies (Johnson & Diakopoulos, 2021). Similar to the challenges posed by fake technologies, the opportunities they present may also have knock-on implications (Kirchengast, 2020). As a result, the advantages that these technologies provide for businesses are probably also beneficial for customers, and vice versa.

4.3.1 Opportunities for Businesses

The creation of affordable, accessible learning environments and content, the deployment of AI-based solutions for the detection and countering of deepfakes, the creation of new offerings and business models backed by deepfakes, and new forms of marketing campaigns are all opportunities for businesses.

Opportunity 1: Upcoming Marketing Campaign Chances

Businesses can replace or enhance the role of humans in marketing communications with deepfakes to create and implement eye-catching marketing campaigns at a cheap cost (Dagar & Vishwakarma, 2022). Marketing campaigns can use deepfakes to generate artificial human-like models instead of real people in order to draw in and interact with a large number of fans and followers (Mustak et al., 2023). Deepfakes can also help break down language barriers by artificially matching lip movements and facial expressions in videos that are dubbed into other languages (Kietzmann et al., 2020). This enables the construction of multilingual marketing campaigns (Lu & Chu, 2023). This makes it possible for celebrities and business leaders to communicate with people directly, sending personalized messages and even calling clients by name (Okolie, 2023). Text-based customer reviews and testimonials, for example, could benefit from the addition of audiovisual components through the use of deepfakes (Williamson & Prybutok, 2024).

Opportunity 2: Creating Accessible and Reasonably Priced Learning Settings and Content

The literature claims that deepfake technology offers businesses that produce educational content a number of advantages, including the capacity to impart knowledge to students in ways that are more believable than those achieved through conventional methods (Murphy et al., 2023). With the use of this technology, video production that produces original movies or television series or modifies existing ones to provide a variety of educational viewpoints may be done at a reasonable cost and with ease (Łabuz, 2023). Additionally, books can be narrated by celebrities, the author of memoirs can read them aloud, and historical figures can employ AI voice-cloning technologies to tell their stories in their own voices (Sunvy et al., 2023). The outcome is an engaging and excellent listening experience for the listener (Li & Wan, 2023). Also, as raising information literacy has been linked to reducing the harmful effects of false information, the technology itself may be utilized for interventions and education targeted at resolving the issues raised by deepfakes (Murillo-Ligorred et al., 2023).

Opportunity 3: Creating and Implementing AI-Based Methods to Identify and Combat Deepfakes

The proliferation of algorithm-generated false information creates a new market for the development of AI-based products and services that distinguish artificial from human-generated content and alert customers to fraudulent or questionable content (Pawar & Shirsath, 2024). This therefore makes it possible to develop and market services meant to shield businesses and customers from deep-fake fraud

(Carnevale et al., 2023). These technologies have the potential to enhance certain services that have surfaced recently due to consumer worries around identity theft (Vasist & Krishnan, 2022).

Opportunity 4: Creating New Products and Business Plans That Rely on Deepfakes

The research emphasizes how using deepfakes could help companies create new products or perhaps whole new business models (Hussain et al., 2022). Technology has the potential to be an extremely useful tool for personalizing goods, names, and services (Campbell et al., 2022). Viewers were informed in advance by the broadcaster that Kim Joo-Ha was still employed and that the newsreader would be a phony (Burgstaller & Macpherson, 2021). DeepBrain AI, the company that created the deepfake, has said that it is looking for media clients in China and the US, and MBN has said that it will keep using the deepfake for breaking news stories (Harris, 2022) . Extending this idea, image synthesis techniques can be used to simplify or even fully automate the creation of some visual illustrations, such as animated cartoons, comic books, and political cartoons (Kim et al., 2021). The automation procedure reduces product costs and removes the need for teams of designers, artists, and other personnel involved in the entertainment production process (Turner, 2022). As a result, anyone can create content that is on par with the highest-budget manufacturing for a little more than the cost of running a computer (Kietzmann et al., 2020). New frontiers in augmented and virtual reality are made possible by creative applications, which also allow for the generation of value in cyber-physical systems. "Digital humans" are artificially lifelike personalities that can communicate and interact with one another thanks to technology (Chesney & Citron, 2019). This potential has already been shown in the tourism industry at several locations and has been employed in the notion of profound resurrection (Mirsky & Lee, 2021).

4.3.2 Opportunities for Customers

Deepfake technology has been shown to present a number of opportunities for consumers, much like businesses. Two particular opportunities were found in this study: 1) improving the digital consumer experience; and 2) using social goods and medicine.

Opportunity 5: Improving the Online Shopping Experience for Customers

The digital consumer experience could be improved via deepfakes. A high level of personalization is introduced for online customer interactions, such as online apparel purchasing, by combining deepfakes with synthetic AI models (Masood et al., 2023). For example, consumers will be able to enter their primary physical traits into an online clothing store, and the store will be able to create realistic avatars to help them make judgments about what to buy. Deepfakes can be used to make custom materials that turn users into models, so they can virtually try on clothes before buying those (Hancock & Bailenson, 2021). Customized fashion advertising that varies according to audience, weather, and time can be made (Tolosana et al., 2020). Systematic model generation is the name of the technique that fashion advertisers and other virtual communicators can employ (Albahar & Almalki, 2019). Customers may find artificial material to be memorable, enjoyable, or even emotionally compelling in this kind of application, which could provide them with the opportunity to get experience value from deepfakes (De Ruiter, 2021).

Opportunity 6: Applications in Medical and Social Welfare

Deepfakes can be used for good in society as well. Customers will gain from their utilization, for example, in eliminating language hurdles that often obstruct the transmission of cross-cultural content and require the use of subtitle reinforcement (Shahzad et al., 2022). People who have lost their voice due to illnesses like motor neuron disorders will also have one thanks to technology (Karnouskos, 2020). For example, Project Revoice uses voice samples from vocally disabled people to generate video deepfakes with personalized synthetic voices using deep learning methods. Another example is the experimental feature that Amazon has made available for Alexa, which lets the AI assistant pretend to be users' departed family members. In the video's introduction, Amazon's senior scientist for Alexa AI, Rohit Prasad, said that "human attributes" were becoming more and more important for AI systems, especially "in these times of the ongoing pandemic, when so many of us have lost someone we love." "While AI can't make their memories last, it can definitely make that pain of loss go away," he continued (Kirchengast, 2020; Johnson & Diakopoulos, 2021).

5. CONCLUSION

5.1 General Discussion

Deepfakes are artificial media produced by algorithms that appear incredibly realistic and are usually shared on social media. They have the ability to lead to consumer and company deceit in the marketplace. Deepfakes present a number of other potentials. There is currently a dearth of clear information regarding deep fakes. In order to gain insight into the consequences of deepfakes for businesses and consumers, this study evaluated and assessed prior research on the subject from the domains of business, communications, computer science, information science, journalism, and social sciences. Particularly pertinent to conversations about risk management, deception theory may clarify how deepfakes purposefully change facts to affect perception. Understanding deception processes can simplify the analysis of deepfake makers and their impact on the intended audience. Applying this idea, for example, may show how deepfakes deliberately affect people's trust and judgment, which is why it is so important to create safeguards and regulations to reduce these hazards. This research offers an unbiased evaluation of the threats that deepfake-caused market deceptions bring to businesses and customers, as well as the safeguards and countermeasures against negative consequences and the prospects that deepfake technology offers. In a time when a sizable portion of the public is using social media more and more as a source of information, fake news has the potential to spread quickly. Determining credibility in the digital domain is often more complicated than in the "offline" world, where people have traditionally reduced their doubts based on personal first-hand experiences or the reputation of the knowledge source (e.g., experts and/or opinion leaders). Deepfakes are very real and serious threats because of the variety of sources used to distribute false information, the lack of information quality requirements and evaluation, the ease with which information can be altered, the lack of contextual clarity, and the existence of multiple potential credibility evaluation objectives (i.e., content, source, and medium). The distinctions between reality and truth may become less significant in light of how we as humans perceive these ideas when manufactured content in digital environments becomes seamlessly integrated with authentic content. Deepfakes can be used to manipulate the generation, presentation, and content of information in order to trick the market.

The issue lies not only in the rapid advancement of deepfake technology but also in the threat it poses to social processes that enable us to jointly gather information, discern what is real from false, and critically examine the definition of reality itself. People who are frequently exposed to misleading information tend to lose trust in what they see and hear. Put another way, the risk is not so much that individuals would be duped in the marketplace alone, but rather that they would start to see everything as a lie and lose trust in it. Studies of deception should be conducted in the marketplace, especially in light of the advent of powerful new technology. With this work, we expand on the general knowledge about deepfakes and add to the body of research on marketplace deception. The results of this study could, in fact, have wider ramifications for understanding deceit outside of the marketplace. For example, news reports about politicians, celebrities, and influencers acting dishonestly are a constant source of information for the public, and the use of deepfakes will further exacerbate this problem. From the standpoint of society as a whole, our work contributes to a deeper knowledge of various forms of deceit, their effects, and the protective systems involved.

Extending international legal frameworks provides information on how other nations are handling deepfake-related problems, including defamation, misinformation, and invasion of privacy. Comparing current rules in different areas would reveal regulatory shortcomings and provide uniform international solutions. Analyzing legal strategies such as the General Data Protection Regulation (GDPR) of the European Union or the new legislation in the US may offer insightful viewpoints on how to reduce the hazards of deepfakes in various countries. Examining how deepfakes affect customers psychologically might deepen conversations about their consequences on society. Deepfakes frequently cause intense emotional responses, such as mistrust, terror, or perplexity, which might reduce trust in media outlets. Deepfakes are becoming a potent instrument for swaying political beliefs and eroding the credibility of the media. Political deepfakes, such as those used in election campaigns or to disparage prominent people, are included as case studies to show how these fake movies may skew facts, sway public perception, and breed mistrust against both political parties and media outlets. Drawing attention to the consequences of political deepfakes might emphasize how urgent it is to create trustworthy detection techniques. The practical difficulties and effects of these dishonest tactics would be illustrated by presenting case studies of actual political deepfakes. Additionally, a critical evaluation of the detection technologies already in use and their drawbacks would present a fair assessment, demonstrating that although technology has some advantages, it also has drawbacks when it comes to accurately differentiating between genuine and deepfake material.

The majority of earlier research on deepfakes has been industry-, product-, or service-specific. Although our method has provided insightful information about a number of important deepfake topics, more research is obviously needed to fully understand the implications of deepfakes. According to most studies, deep fakes pose a serious risk. This makes sense because deepfakes can definitely pose a major risk to businesses and customers. A non-technical individual may find the technology mysterious and difficult to understand, which could make them feel intimidated or afraid. Our study is among the first to produce and offer a comprehensive explanation of the phenomenon that integrates the viewpoints of various stakeholder groups and considers the perspectives of both businesses and consumers. The ease with which synthetic content can now be created and distributed because of technological improvements has made deepfakes relatively new compared to earlier forms of market deception. Because of this, businesses and customers are moving toward a mixed reality in which elements of the genuine and the fake mix and mingle. Deepfakes, in particular, appear to be a part of the shift in people's lives toward a greater level of digitality, which includes spending more time in virtual and augmented worlds. This patchwork of realities emphasizes the necessity for businesses and customers to acquire new competencies in order to deal with cognitive abilities such as object detection and veracity assessments that were not previously necessary. Paradoxically, individuals may even come to like the deception to some degree due to the deepfake's entertainment value since it has a certain element of magic that amuses and surprises.

5.2 Implications

There are various consequences of our study for managers and businesses. Criminals can more easily commit deceptive practices in the marketplace while avoiding detection thanks to deepfake technologies. This survey provides businesses with a clear picture of how serious these concerns are. An organization's reputation, brand image, and stakeholder trust could all be destroyed by hostile and predatory deepfake campaigns, and deepfake-based deceptions could have a direct financial negative impact. As a result, businesses must make investments in building their capacities and resources to guard against deep-fake-enabled market deceptions. This involves making technological investments that improve a company's capacity for deepfake detection and avoidance. They should also make investments in human resources to improve their capacity to effectively combat the potentially harmful impacts of fake technology. Supervisors need to be aware of any possible harm that their clients might experience and take precautionary steps to keep them safe. This report also recommends that managers be ready to take advantage of the different business opportunities that technology presents. Deepfake-based marketing campaigns and content can be very advantageous for businesses when used in non-deceptive, value-adding ways. Deepfake technology may also be advantageous for advertising, personification of brands, and customer support. This study also suggests that managers should be aware of and take advantage of various forms of synthetic media in their company, in addition to videos. Considering the fast-changing technology landscape and the study's results, it is highly advised to take a proactive rather than reactive approach. Crucially, deepfakes have the ability to upend entire business models in addition to creating new products, and many companies can find themselves caught off guard if they fail to consider these factors. Although the current focus of deepfake applications is on entertainment and humorous jokes, the historical trajectory of technological development has demonstrated that a given technology's performance tends to shift from humor to action. Deepfakes may likewise follow such a trend. As a result, the entertainment-to-value ratio may vary in the future.

5.3 Limitations and Recommendations of This Study

This study has several limitations, just like any other research. Initially, our investigation was limited to scientific papers that were indexed in the Web of Science and Scopus, two distinct databases. Even with their extensive and comprehensive coverage of the literature, we have unavoidably overlooked some important information that is available in other databases. Secondly, the research was limited to English-language publications, leaving out information that was available in other languages. Therefore, any additional research that expands this scope to encompass such material will improve our body of knowledge. Third, we approached the deepfake phenomenon using the conceptual lens of marketplace deception. A lot of research needs to be done because deepfake science is still in its early stages, especially in the commercial sector. We offer some suggestions for more study in these important areas. Studying the causes and precursors of deepfakes can be advantageous for researchers, businesses, and customers alike. Research focused on figuring out what elements influence deepfake visibility on online platforms, that is, how newsfeed ranking and content recommendation systems interact with deepfake content, will also have academic and managerial value.

As our analysis indicates, there are differences among consumers' abilities and aptitudes to identify phony information, as well as their perspectives on artificial content in general. In order to provide more accurate recommendations for consumer education and to better comprehend the complex behaviors and attitudes of customers based on deepfakes, future research should explore these distinctions in greater detail. Comparably, although it should go without saying that deep-fake-based marketing requires some ethical guidelines, these guidelines are presently absent from marketing literature. With the purpose of providing an overview of the subject, this study suggests that the following standards should be met: the use of deepfakes should be fair, transparent, and non-deceptive (i.e., the rights of third parties, whether they be businesses, individuals, or groups of individuals, should not be violated), and customers should be able to opt out of fake content if they so choose. More research is needed to understand the motivations of those producing deepfakes, especially how to separate the good actors from the bad guys. Since deepfake technologies can be used for a variety of objectives, determining and evaluating the moral status of their users remains a difficult task, as is often the case with AI technology. Further examination of the legal ramifications is warranted. Legal experts currently propose amending the law to include identity theft, libel, defamation, and impersonation of public officials. Whether and how rules or enforcements can be made normatively appealing and acceptable is the crucial question to address here.

Lastly, considering the potential that deepfakes offer, more study is required to determine how to use the technology constructively. It might be beneficial to investigate several content modalities for these investigations. While video content is the main target of deepfakes at the moment, other content modalities, like audio, also have significant commercial value. For instance, several deep-learning startups already provide the service of creating synthetic voices. As a result, using a written script as guidance, an individual can type a text they wish to speak and allow an ML model trained on their voice to do the talking. This raises intriguing questions about hybrid forms of communication, in which the writer communicates using a deepfake avatar or a copy of themselves. These and other consequences of deepfakes on business procedures in domains such as sales and consumer service create rich opportunities for experimental study.

REFERENCES

Albahar, M., & Almalki, J. (2019). Deepfakes: Threats and countermeasures systematic review. *Journal of Theoretical and Applied Information Technology*, 97(22), 3242–3250.

Burgstaller, M., & Macpherson, S. (2021). Deepfakes in international arbitration: How should tribunals treat video evidence and allegations of technological tampering? *The Journal of World Investment & Trade*, 22(5-6), 860–890. DOI: 10.1163/22119000-12340232

Campbell, C., Plangger, K., Sands, S., & Kietzmann, J. (2022). Preparing for an era of deepfakes and AI-generated ads: A framework for understanding responses to manipulated advertising. *Journal of Advertising*, 51(1), 22–38. DOI: 10.1080/00913367.2021.1909515

Carnevale, A., Delgado, C. F., & Bisconti, P. (2023). Hybrid Ethics for Generative AI: Some Philosophical Inquiries on GANs. *HUMANA.MENTE Journal of Philosophical Studies*, 16(44), 33–56.

Chesney, B., & Citron, D. (2019). Deep fakes: A looming challenge for privacy, democracy, and national security. *California Law Review*, 107, 1753.

Dagar, D., & Vishwakarma, D. K. (2022). A literature review and perspectives in deepfakes: Generation, detection, and applications. *International Journal of Multimedia Information Retrieval*, 11(3), 219–289. DOI: 10.1007/s13735-022-00241-w

De Ruiter, A. (2021). The distinct wrong of deepfakes. *Philosophy & Technology*, 34(4), 1311–1332. DOI: 10.1007/s13347-021-00459-2

Hancock, J. T., & Bailenson, J. N. (2021). The social impact of deepfakes. *Cyberpsychology, Behavior, and Social Networking*, 24(3), 149–152. DOI: 10.1089/cyber.2021.29208.jth PMID: 33760669

Harris, K. R. (2022). Real fakes: The epistemology of online misinformation. *Philosophy & Technology*, 35(3), 83. DOI: 10.1007/s13347-022-00581-9 PMID: 36059716

Hussain, S., Neekhara, P., Dolhansky, B., Bitton, J., Ferrer, C. C., McAuley, J., & Koushanfar, F. (2022). Exposing vulnerabilities of deepfake detection systems with robust attacks. [DTRAP]. *Digital Threats : Research and Practice*, 3(3), 1–23. DOI: 10.1145/3464307

Johnson, D. G., & Diakopoulos, N. (2021). What to do about deepfakes. *Communications of the ACM*, 64(3), 33–35. DOI: 10.1145/3447255

Karnouskos, S. (2020). Artificial intelligence in digital media: The era of deepfakes. *IEEE Transactions on Technology and Society*, 1(3), 138–147. DOI: 10.1109/TTS.2020.3001312

Kietzmann, J., Lee, L. W., McCarthy, I. P., & Kietzmann, T. C. (2020). Deepfakes: Trick or treat? *Business Horizons*, 63(2), 135–146. DOI: 10.1016/j.bushor.2019.11.006

Kietzmann, J., Lee, L. W., McCarthy, I. P., & Kietzmann, T. C. (2020). Deepfakes: Trick or treat? *Business Horizons*, 63(2), 135–146. DOI: 10.1016/j.bushor.2019.11.006

Kim, B., Xiong, A., Lee, D., & Han, K. (2021). A systematic review on fake news research through the lens of news creation and consumption: Research efforts, challenges, and future directions. *PLoS One*, 16(12), e0260080. DOI: 10.1371/journal.pone.0260080 PMID: 34882703

Kirchengast, T. (2020). Deepfakes and image manipulation: Criminalisation and control. *Information & Communications Technology Law*, 29(3), 308–323. DOI: 10.1080/13600834.2020.1794615

Łabuz, M. (2023). Regulating deep fakes in the artificial intelligence act. *Applied Cybersecurity & Internet Governance*, 2(1), 1–42. DOI: 10.60097/ACIG/162856

Li, M., & Wan, Y. (2023). Norms or fun? The influence of ethical concerns and perceived enjoyment on the regulation of deepfake information. *Internet Research*, 33(5), 1750–1773. DOI: 10.1108/INTR-07-2022-0561

Lu, H., & Chu, H. (2023). Let the dead talk: How deepfake resurrection narratives influence audience response in prosocial contexts. *Computers in Human Behavior*, 145, 107761. DOI: 10.1016/j.chb.2023.107761

Masood, M., Nawaz, M., Malik, K. M., Javed, A., Irtaza, A., & Malik, H. (2023). Deepfakes generation and detection: State-of-the-art, open challenges, countermeasures, and way forward. *Applied Intelligence*, 53(4), 3974–4026. DOI: 10.1007/s10489-022-03766-z

Mirsky, Y., & Lee, W. (2021). The creation and detection of deepfakes: A survey. *ACM Computing Surveys*, 54(1), 1–41. DOI: 10.1145/3425780

Murillo-Ligorred, V., Ramos-Vallecillo, N., Covaleda, I., & Fayos, L. (2023). Knowledge, Integration and Scope of Deepfakes in Arts Education: The Development of Critical Thinking in Postgraduate Students in Primary Education and Master's Degree in Secondary Education. *Education Sciences*, 13(11), 1073. DOI: 10.3390/educsci13111073

Murphy, G., Ching, D., Twomey, J., & Linehan, C. (2023). Face/Off: Changing the face of movies with deepfakes. *PLoS One*, 18(7), e0287503. DOI: 10.1371/journal.pone.0287503 PMID: 37410765

Mustak, M., Salminen, J., Mäntymäki, M., Rahman, A., & Dwivedi, Y. K. (2023). Deepfakes: Deceptions, mitigations, and opportunities. *Journal of Business Research*, 154, 113368. DOI: 10.1016/j.jbusres.2022.113368

Okolie, C. (2023). Artificial intelligence-altered videos (deepfakes), image-based sexual abuse, and data privacy concerns. *Journal of International Women's Studies*, 25(2), 11.

Pawar, S. B., & Shirsath, K. A. (2024). Deep Learning Based Web Data Classification Techniques for Forensic Analysis: An Overview. *International Journal of Intelligent Systems and Applications in Engineering*, 12(4s), 320–334.

Shahzad, H. F., Rustam, F., Flores, E. S., Luis Vidal Mazon, J., de la Torre Diez, I., & Ashraf, I. (2022). A review of image processing techniques for deepfakes. *Sensors (Basel)*, 22(12), 4556. DOI: 10.3390/s22124556 PMID: 35746333

Sunvy, A. S., Reza, R. B., & Al Imran, A. (2023). Media coverage of DeepFake disinformation: An analysis of three South-Asian countries. *Informasi*, 53(2), 295–308. DOI: 10.21831/informasi.v53i2.66479

Tolosana, R., Vera-Rodriguez, R., Fierrez, J., Morales, A., & Ortega-Garcia, J. (2020). Deepfakes and beyond: A survey of face manipulation and fake detection. *Information Fusion*, 64, 131–148. DOI: 10.1016/j.inffus.2020.06.014

Turner, C. (2022). Augmented reality, augmented epistemology, and the real-world web. *Philosophy & Technology*, 35(1), 19. DOI: 10.1007/s13347-022-00496-5

Vasist, P. N., & Krishnan, S. (2022). Deepfakes: An integrative review of the literature and an agenda for future research. *Communications of the Association for Information Systems*, 51(1), 14.

Williamson, S. M., & Prybutok, V. (2024). The Era of Artificial Intelligence Deception: Unraveling the Complexities of False Realities and Emerging Threats of Misinformation. *Information (Basel)*, 15(6), 299. DOI: 10.3390/info15060299

Chapter 10
The Dark Side of Deepfakes:
Fraud and Cybercrime

Svetlana Volkova
ⓘ https://orcid.org/0000-0001-7710-4009
Vologda State University, Russia

ABSTRACT

Even though deepfakes have numerous positive and beneficial applications, such as replacing the faces of deceased actors to complete the movies, creating realistic special effects, visualizing historical events with real figures, or creating personalized advertising materials, deepfakes remain and rightfully associated with fraud and abuse. Since deepfakes are often used unethically and illegitimately, there are a vast number of security threats that they can pose, ranging from invasion of privacy to manipulation of public opinion. The chapter provides a comprehensive overview of the potential targets, domains, and areas where malicious actors might illegitimately utilize deepfake technologies to conduct fraudulent activities and other illegal operations. This chapter thoroughly examines the various ways in which deepfake technology can be abused, co-called its "dark side." Specifically, it delves into the use of deepfakes for committing fraud and financial crimes, corporate espionage, compromising biometric identity, manipulating public opinion, as well as extortion and blackmail.

DOI: 10.4018/979-8-3693-6890-9.ch010

Copyright © 2025, IGI Global Scientific Publishing. Copying or distributing in print or electronic forms without written permission of IGI Global Scientific Publishing is prohibited.

INTRODUCTION

Despite the significant potential for positive applications inherent in deepfake technology, it also harbors serious threats that necessitate careful examination and the development of preventive measures. On the one hand (the so-called bright side), deepfakes can be employed in marketing to create personalized advertising materials, in the entertainment industry to produce unique and, importantly, memorable content, or in education, for instance, to generate realistic simulations and visualizations. On the other hand (the so-called dark side), they can be exploited to create compromising videos, fake news, or breach remote authentication systems.

In the corporate environment, deepfakes can be used to mimic the voices and appearances of executives or employees, thereby gaining access to confidential information or financial resources of a company. The use of deepfakes has the potential to undermine trust in digital and media information sources, complicating the differentiation between truth and falsehood, which is particularly perilous in a political context.

In private life, deepfakes can be used to fabricate video recordings involving people close to the victim, leading to emotional distress, blackmail, or identity theft.

All of these considerations highlight the imperative need for the creation of sophisticated countermeasures against deepfake technology, the formulation and implementation of robust protective measures, and the establishment of comprehensive regulatory frameworks. Nevertheless, to accurately identify the spectrum of threats, develop effective countermeasures and risk mitigation strategies, and enhance public awareness, it is essential to first possess a thorough and detailed overview of the potential targets, domains, and areas wherein malicious actors might illicitly employ deepfake technology.

The primary objective of this chapter is to provide such a comprehensive overview. The chapter is systematically divided into several sections, each of which offers an in-depth analysis of the various so-called "dark sides" of deepfake technology. These sections describe the numerous ways in which this technology can be exploited for illicit and malicious purposes.

In the first section, the various methods and examples of using deepfakes in the realm of fraud are meticulously described. The subsequent section delves into instances where deepfakes are employed to influence public consciousness. Particular attention is devoted to the issue of circumventing biometric information, which is the focus of the next section of the chapter. Another dark aspect of deepfake usage is blackmail and extortion, which is comprehensively examined in the penultimate section. The concluding section emphasizes the critical importance of collective efforts in combating deepfakes and highlights the necessity for collaboration among researchers, companies, and universities. This collaboration is crucial for the development of new detection technologies, the implementation of educational campaigns to raise public awareness about the risks associated with deepfakes, the formulation of ethical standards and guidelines, as well as the creation of resources and support services for victims of deepfakes. Finally, we conclude the whole chapter.

Thus, the chapter demonstrates the broad and diverse spectrum of deepfake abuses, underscoring the necessity for public awareness, legal regulation, and the development of detection and counteraction tools.

Deepfakes for Fraud

In recent years, there has been an explosive and significant growth in the utilization of deepfakes for fraudulent activities (Bateman, 2022; Gambín, 2024; Kshetri, 2023). According to the Sumsub Identity Fraud Report (Sumsub, 2024), within the United States, the proportion of deepfake-related frauds in the overall number of fraud cases surged from 0.2% to 2.6% over the period from 2022 to 2023. Similarly, in Canada, this proportion escalated from 0.1% to 4.6%, representing an increase of over 3000%.

Fraud involving the use of deepfakes is not confined solely to America or Europe. In the Asia-Pacific region, during the same period, there was a staggering 1530% increase in the number of cases of deepfake fraud. Similarly, in Africa, the increase was recorded at 452%, and in Latin America, it was 411% (Sumsub, 2024).

This trend is not surprising, as advancements in technologies for generating fake images, audio, and video recordings have significantly reduced the cost associated with producing a single deepfake attack. The average expense incurred for creating a deepfake in 2024 is merely $1.33, whereas the potential damage inflicted can amount to tens of millions of dollars (Kshetri, 2023).

Table 1 presents several well-known incidents in which malicious actors have used Deepfakes for fraudulent activities (or attempted fraud). This includes examples such as the creation of fake videos to impersonate company executives or officials, through which the perpetrators compelled employees and clients to transfer large sums of money or disclose confidential information. Additionally, it describes instances where deepfakes were utilized for corporate espionage, with fake calls and videos aimed at gaining access to secured data.

All the presented incidents were meticulously selected from the AI Incident Database (AIID), which serves as an extensive and comprehensive repository of incidents related to artificial intelligence. This portal facilitates users in searching, submitting, and analyzing detailed reports on AI-related incidents. The platform offers a variety of tools for data exploration, including spatial and tabular views, taxonomies, and word analysis. The primary objective of the AIID is to enhance the understanding, management, and mitigation of risks associated with artificial intelligence (Artificial Intelligence Incident Database, n.d.).

Table 1. Selected cases of fraud involving deepfake technology

Incident Number. Date. Incident Reference.	Description	Victim	Consequences
#147 2020-01-01 https://incidentdatabase.ai/cite/147/	Fraudsters utilized deepfake technology to forge the voice of a company director. They called a bank manager in Hong Kong and demanded authorization for a transfer of $35 million.	Bank manager in Hong Kong	The transfer of $35 million. A significant financial loss for the bank.
#422 2022-11-22 https://incidentdatabase.ai/cite/422/	A visual and audio deepfake of former FTX CEO Sam Bankman-Fried was posted on Twitter to deceive victims of the FTX exchange collapse, urging them to transfer funds to an anonymous cryptocurrency wallet.	Victims of the FTX exchange collapse	Transfer of funds by users affected by the FTX collapse to a fraudulent account. Significant financial losses.
#390 2022-06-28 https://incidentdatabase.ai/cite/390/	Voice and video Deepfakes were used to pass online interviews for remote job positions.	Interviewers and employers of remote positions	Illegitimate acquisition of remote job positions
#564 2023-08-30 https://incidentdatabase.ai/cite/564/	Florida investor Clive Kabatznik was targeted in an attempted fraud involving a voice Deepfake that mimicked his own voice. The fraudster, using generated speech, contacted a representative of Bank of America, attempting to trick them into transferring funds to another account. The transfer attempt was unsuccessful.	Clive Kabatznik and Bank of America	Financial losses were averted.
#509 2023-03-23 https://incidentdatabase.ai/cite/509/	In Vietnam, fraudsters employed deepfake technology to create fake messages requesting money transfers, purportedly from the friends and families of the victims.	Facebook users in Vietnam	Victims suffered significant financial losses, amounting to thousands of US dollars.

continued on following page

Table 1. Continued

Incident Number. Date. Incident Reference.	Description	Victim	Consequences
#567 2023-08-27 https://incidentdatabase.ai/cite/ 567/	A hacker managed to breach Retool, an IT company specializing in business software solutions, affecting 27 cloud customers. The hacker initiated the attack by sending phishing SMS messages to employees, and subsequently used an AI-generated voice deepfake during a phone call to obtain multi-factor authentication codes.	Retool, Google, and 27 Retool clients	The breach exposed vulnerabilities in the Google Authenticator app, particularly in its cloud sync feature, which allowed unauthorized access to the company's internal systems.
#626 2023-12-26 https://incidentdatabase.ai/cite/ 626/	Fraudsters created and disseminated fake videos on social media featuring Taylor Swift, Selena Gomez, and several other celebrities, in which they claimed users could receive free cookware by paying a small shipping fee.	Several celebrities and their fans	Financial losses for fans who unknowingly subscribed to an expensive monthly service.
#634 2024-02-02 https://incidentdatabase.ai/cite/ 634/	Fraudsters employed deepfake technology during a video call, impersonating the Chief Financial Officer of a multinational company in Hong Kong and convincing an employee to transfer $25 million.	Financial department employee of a diversified company in Hong Kong, the unnamed company itself.	The company suffered a loss of $25 million.
#715 2024-03-01 https://incidentdatabase.ai/cite/ 715/	Australians lost over $8 million due to scams involving deepfakes and fake news articles promoting investment platforms. The total number of incidents exceeded 400.	The population of Australia	Collective losses of over $8 million, with one individual losing more than $80,000 in cryptocurrency.

Even a limited number of examples illustrates that individual across a broad spectrum, ranging from an ordinary person to a director of a large corporation, or even a well-known politician or public figure, can fall victim to the schemes of fraudsters. According to forecasts by Bitget, global financial losses resulting from this type of fraud could potentially reach a staggering $1 trillion in 2024 (Bitget Research, 2024).

Each year, cybercriminals devise increasingly sophisticated and intricately detailed schemes for committing fraud using deepfakes. Nevertheless, certain common features and patterns can be identified across all such fraudulent schemes:

- In the initial phase of orchestrating the attack, fraudsters gather comprehensive data about the victim and their social circle, including managers, relatives, and friends. This information encompasses photographs, video clips, or voice recordings, typically sourced from social networks or public platforms.
- Next, employing the gathered data alongside specialized software tools, fraudsters create a deepfake. This manipulated content can take the form of an image, audio clip, or video recording that convincingly imitates the victim's superior, relative, or friend.
- In the subsequent stage, the attackers meticulously design a fraudulent scheme that leverages the generated deepfake. This scheme could involve a counterfeit video requesting a money transfer, a fraudulent voice message for a phone call, or a falsified identification document.
- Finally, the most critical stage involves direct engagement with the victim, where manipulation techniques are employed to fulfill the fraudsters' objectives. The attackers initiate contact with the victim through various channels such as email, social networks, messaging apps, or phone calls. Utilizing the deepfake, they impersonate a trusted figure, such as a boss, relative, or friend. By establishing the victim's trust, the fraudsters manipulate the victim into performing specific actions, such as transferring funds to a designated account or divulging confidential information. As a result, the fraudsters successfully obtain access to the victim's money or sensitive data.

Social engineering plays a significant and influential role in the success of cyber attacks. Therefore, it is of utmost importance to educate and train employees and users to recognize and identify the indicators of deepfakes and to exercise a high degree of caution when dealing with or responding to suspicious requests. Adherence to the security policies and protocols adopted and implemented by the organization is essential, as is the strict observance of established procedures for processing financial transactions and transferring confidential information (Nicholls et al., 2023).

Equally important is the need to maintain and uphold personal digital hygiene. Individuals should be diligent in avoiding the unnecessary posting of personal information on social networks, refrain from publicly sharing videos and photographs that reveal their faces and documents, and make full use of the privacy settings available on social media profiles to protect their information from unauthorized access.

Deepfakes for the Manipulation of Public Consciousness

This section is dedicated to the issue of utilizing deepfakes to influence public consciousness. This includes political manipulations, where fake clips may be created to discredit opponents, manipulate public opinion, and, in some cases, even influence election outcomes. Such instances can have a profound impact on political stability.

Another so-called "dark side" of influencing public opinion that needs to be highlighted is the proliferation of disinformation and fake news through social networks using deepfakes. The dissemination of fake videos via social media platforms such as Facebook, Twitter, Instagram, and TikTok can provoke public outcry, erode trust in information sources, and exacerbate social divisions (Veerasamy et al., 2022; Walker et al., 2024, Samoilenko et al., 2023; Ray, 2021; Byman et al., 2023; Verdoliva, 2020).

Table 2 illustrates a range of examples and incidents where deepfakes were employed to manipulate public consciousness. All the examples presented were meticulously sourced from the AI Incident Database (Artificial Intelligence Incident Database, n.d.).

Table 2. Selected cases of attempts to influence public consciousness using deepfake technology

Incident Number. Date. Incident Reference.	Description	Victim	Consequences
#201 2020-04-14 https://incidentdatabase.ai/cite/201/	A group of climate change activists published a fake video in which the Prime Minister of Belgium calls for urgent action to address the climate crisis.	Sophie Wilmès (Prime Minister of Belgium), the government of Belgium	Erosion of trust in public figures and political institutions.
#481 2023-02-12 https://incidentdatabase.ai/cite/481/	A deepfake video circulated on TikTok featuring podcast host Joe Rogan promoting a supplement that "enhances libido." Although TikTok removed the video along with the account that posted it, a large number of users had already viewed the clip.	Joe Rogan, his fans, TikTok users	Creation of a fake advertising campaign and the spread of misinformation.
#547 2023-06-05 https://incidentdatabase.ai/cite/547/	Ron DeSantis' presidential campaign shared a video on Twitter containing several AI-generated images of Donald Trump hugging former White House coronavirus advisor Anthony Fauci. These images were presumably used as part of a smear campaign.	Donald Trump, Anthony Fauci, American voters	This incident represents one of the first examples of using deepfakes in a U.S. presidential campaign to deliberately mislead voters.
#669 2024-02-11 https://incidentdatabase.ai/cite/669/	The Golkar Party in Indonesia created and disseminated a deepfake video featuring the long-deceased dictator Suharto ahead of the February 2024 elections. The purpose of the video was to influence voter perception, urging them to recall Suharto's legacy and support the party.	Indonesian voters	Persuasive misinformation for political propaganda.
#673 2024-02-19 https://incidentdatabase.ai/cite/673/	At least 129 fake deepfake videos and images undermining the integrity of elections were identified in the lead-up to the parliamentary elections in South Korea.	South Korean voters	Threat to the integrity of the electoral process. Increased monitoring and control of digital media to prevent further attempts at voter manipulation through AI technologies.

continued on following page

Table 2. Continued

Incident Number. Date. Incident Reference.	Description	Victim	Consequences
#676 2024-04-24 https://incidentdatabase.ai/cite/ 676/	A deepfake falsely depicting Philippine President Ferdinand Marcos Jr. ordering an attack on China circulated online. The video was debunked and refuted by the Presidential Communications Office.	Ferdinand Marcos Jr.	Increased tensions between the Philippines and China. Misinformation. Threat to national security and international relations.
#675 2024-01-15 https://incidentdatabase.ai/cite/ 675/	The Athletic Director of Pikesville High School in Baltimore utilized AI to create a deepfake audio clip, imitating the school principal making racist and antisemitic remarks.	Principal of Pikesville High School in Baltimore	Discreditation of the principal, threats, and administrative dismissal of the principal.
#697 2023-06-23 https://incidentdatabase.ai/cite/ 697/	A fake image circulated on social media purportedly showing Donald Trump with an underage girl on Jeffrey Epstein's private island in 1992.	Donald Trump, American voters	Discreditation of Donald Trump. Misleading the electorate.
#698 2023-09-02 https://incidentdatabase.ai/cite/ 698/	In September 2023, a deepfake video circulated on social media, falsely depicting Ron DeSantis (a presidential candidate) announcing his withdrawal from the 2024 presidential race. In reality, DeSantis did not suspend his campaign until January 2024.	Ron DeSantis, American voters	Misleading voters. Threat to the integrity of political processes and erosion of trust in the candidate and his campaign.
#703 2024-01-13 https://incidentdatabase.ai/cite/ 703/	A deepfake audio clip spread online, falsely featuring President Joe Biden allegedly threatening to deploy F-15 fighter jets to Texas. The audio mimicked Biden's voice and falsely informed Texans that Joe Biden planned military action against Texas.	Joe Biden, residents of Texas	Escalation of tensions between Texas residents and the presidential administration. Spread of misinformation, undermining public trust, and incitement of political conflicts.

The steps involved in utilizing deepfakes to influence public consciousness are more or less always the same, and adhering to the following similar pattern:

- Initially, advanced artificial intelligence technologies are employed to create realistic forgeries. Moreover, with each passing year, the tools for generating deepfakes are becoming increasingly accessible to a wider audience, which inevitably leads to a rise in the number of fake materials being created and disseminated.

- Once the fake material has been created, it is disseminated through social networks or messaging applications. Frequently, news portals either intentionally or inadvertently pick up on these fake news stories, thereby amplifying their impact.
- The first reaction people experience when encountering a deepfake is often intense emotional responses (such as surprise, outrage, or fear), which can vary depending on the content of the fake. Some individuals may suspect that the video or audio is fake, but the quality of fake content generation is improving, making it increasingly difficult to detect forgeries each year.
- Following the initial reaction, users begin actively discussing the fake content on social networks, sharing it in chats and groups. In some cases, deepfakes become the basis for memes and jokes, which further increases their popularity.
- Ultimately, people begin to believe in the veracity of the false information and construct erroneous conclusions and beliefs based on it. This process eventually leads to the formation of public opinion grounded in inaccurate data.

This means that deepfakes pose a significant threat. The advancement of modern deepfake creation technologies allows for the production of videos and images that are virtually indistinguishable from real ones, making attacks highly plausible and convincing, and enabling the dissemination of false information. The spread of such content through social networks allows for the rapid and efficient reach of a wide audience, thereby increasing its danger. According to Statista, 67% of Americans report encountering false information on social media (Statista, n.d.).

Detecting and thoroughly debunking deepfakes necessitates a significant investment of time and resources. By the point at which a fabricated video or audio recording is definitively exposed as fraudulent, it may have already inflicted considerable damage. This scenario is especially perilous during critical junctures, such as electoral periods, where the element of timing is of paramount importance.

In addition to the potential utilization of deepfakes for discrediting opponents or orchestrating political attacks, it is crucial to emphasize the erosion of trust in information sources. The proliferation of deepfakes significantly undermines confidence in genuine information. As the public becomes increasingly aware of the existence of deepfakes and frequently encounters seemingly plausible yet fraudulent clips followed by their subsequent debunking, it engenders a growing skepticism towards the authenticity of any information, including legitimate videos and audio recordings. This phenomenon, in turn, erodes the fundamental basis of public trust, diminishes the authority of established institutions, and fosters a climate of panic and mistrust within society.

This is why it is of utmost importance to develop and advance technologies specifically designed for the detection and identification of deepfakes. Additionally, there is a pressing need to enhance media literacy among the general population, enabling individuals to critically evaluate and scrutinize the information they receive. Equally significant is the introduction and implementation of new laws and regulations specifically aimed at combating the creation, proliferation, and dissemination of deepfakes. The discussion on addressing the Deepfake Challenge as a community effort will be elaborated upon in the concluding section of this chapter.

Deepfakes for Biometric Systems Attack

With the increasing frequency of use and the growing popularity of digital payment methods and remote banking services, there has been a notable and substantial rise in the number of fraudulent transactions and cyberattacks. In the year 2023, the total amount of fraudulent operations escalated to $485.6 billion on a global scale (Sopra Banking, n.d.).

Therefore, special attention should be given to the issue of using deepfakes to bypass biometric information in biometric identification and authentication systems, which is the focus of this section. Biometric authentication systems are vulnerable to spoofing attacks, where unauthorized clients (malicious actors) may attempt to deceive the system by substituting a "live" facial image or voice recording of an authorized client with a photograph or video/audio file. The issue of detecting digital manipulations in face substitution is particularly pressing. Deepfakes can be used to forge biometric data, allowing malicious actors to bypass biometric authentication systems and gain unauthorized access to secure systems and data (Salko et al., 2024).

Face and voice substitution technologies have already reached a level where malicious actors can create such realistic forgeries that not only the human eye is unable to distinguish the fake from the original image, but even software specifically designed to detect deepfakes struggles to do so, often resulting in false positives and allowing successful attacks. This poses a significant threat to banks, government institutions, and other organizations that utilize biometric security systems.

According to the iProov Biometric Threat Intelligence Report (iProov, 2024), instances of fraudsters using deepfakes to create fake voice recordings to deceive voice authentication systems have already led to significant financial losses in several cases. The same report also indicates that the cost of conducting an attack to forge facial images is decreasing, and the technology itself is becoming more accessible, allowing low-skilled criminals to launch sophisticated attacks.

We will not discuss attacks on all possible components of a biometric system here. Attacks on the communication channel, the database, and the decision-making system can be mitigated by employing communication channel encryption methods and digital encoding techniques. Within this section, we will focus exclusively on attacks targeting the component of the system responsible for acquiring biometric samples. It is precisely for the substitution of biometric characteristics that deepfakes can be utilized. Malicious actors can use digital modifications of facial images or voice recordings to compromise the entire system.

To enhance the resilience of biometric systems against digital spoofing attacks targeting the biometric input module, it is imperative that a quality control check be performed to ascertain whether the acquired biometric sample is genuine and has not been subjected to tampering by a malicious actor. In other words, the process of classifying whether the facial image or voice recording that is input into the system is fraudulent or authentic must be conducted during the biometric sample analysis phase, prior to the commencement of the biometric feature extraction stage.

In the event that the acquired biometric sample is determined to be fraudulent, the processes of biometric registration, verification, and identification are immediately terminated. Consequently, the fraudulent sample is prevented from entering both the data storage subsystem and the comparison and decision-making subsystem. Therefore, the incorporation of a module designed to detect the use of facial image or voice recording manipulation technologies at the biometric sample quality control stage facilitates the identification and interception of attempts to masquerade as an authorized client by means of digital identity manipulation methods, thereby significantly enhancing the security of biometric systems.

In this manner, the principal strategy for countering deepfake-based attacks on biometric information fundamentally involves the ongoing and continuous improvement of software tools, alongside the advancement and refinement of artificial intelligence methods which specifically aimed at detecting and identifying anomalies in video and audio that may be indicative of forgeries.

The methodologies for detecting deepfakes can be broadly categorized into two principal types: those directed towards the identification of artifacts and those aimed at the development of universal classifiers. Methods focused on artifact detection strive to highlight characteristics that are inherently generated by the digital manipulation tools themselves, as the techniques used to create deepfakes can leave behind defects and distortions that may not be apparent to the human eye. For instance, generative adversarial networks (GANs) might leave texture-specific fingerprints (Patel, 2023).

Conversely, methods aimed at constructing universal classifiers do not concentrate on isolated features left by deepfake creation tools. The latter category of methodologies has been the focus of significant advancements in recent times. This is largely due to the progress in AI techniques for generating highly realistic text, audio, and video, designed to deceive both victims and security systems, which have evolved to the point where they leave virtually no visible defects or distortions. Consequently, artifact-based detection methods fail to deliver the requisite quality of recognition. Hence, the detection of forgeries necessitates the integration of AI methodologies, which, at present, predominantly involve the construction of global neural network classifiers (Tolosana et al., 2020; Rana et al., 2022; Akhtar, 2023; Volkova, 2023; Pei et al., 2024; Singh & Kumar, 2024).

Furthermore, beyond the refinement of deepfake detection methodologies, it is of paramount importance to conduct thorough and comprehensive testing of biometric systems. Prior to their deployment, these systems should be subjected to a variety of assessments, which may include performance evaluations (measured in terms of error probabilities and operational efficiency), reliability assessments, as well as evaluations of availability, usability, security, and safety. These assessments should also encompass evaluations of user acceptability, the impact of human factors, and the degree of compliance with established privacy regulations.

Deepfakes for Blackmail and Extortion

Another "dark side" aspect of utilizing deepfakes is blackmail and extortion. Victims of blackmail and extortion involving fake videos can face severe legal and psychological consequences. Thus, raising awareness about the potential use of deepfakes for creating such content, the necessity for developing effective protection methods, and the need for legal regulation are critical aspects that must be addressed. The number of instances where fake videos are used to compromise and extort money or other resources from victims is steadily increasing. Criminals may exploit deepfakes to create counterfeit videos containing compromising materials. These videos are then directly sent to the victim with threats of publication if a ransom is not paid (SlashNext, 2023).

Often, the target image or video involves pornographic content or sexualized images. According to a report by Home Security Heroes (Home Security Heroes, n.d.), from 2022 to 2023, the production of pornographic deepfakes increased by 464%, becoming a significant issue. The National Security Agency (NSA), the Federal Bureau of Investigation (FBI), and the Cybersecurity and Infrastructure Security Agency (CISA) in their Cybersecurity Information Sheet (CSI) titled "Contextualizing deepfake threats to organizations" (U.S. Department of Defense, 2023) reported more than 7,000 cases of online sextortion (using deepfakes in sexualized images and videos for blackmail), with teenagers among the victims.

In June 2023, the FBI issued a public service announcement numbered I-060523-PSA titled "Malicious Actors Manipulating Photos and Videos to Create Explicit Content and Sextortion Schemes," which highlighted the activities of malicious actors who utilize advanced techniques to produce synthetic content (deepfakes) by manipulating innocuous photos or videos with the intent to exploit victims (Federal Bureau of Investigation, 2023).

In this advisory, the FBI reports that malicious actors utilize content manipulation technologies and services to exploit photos and videos, typically sourced from a person's social media account, publicly accessible on the Internet, or obtained through victim solicitation, into sexually explicit images that appear realistic and resemble the victim. These manipulated images are then disseminated across social media platforms, public forums, or pornographic websites. Many victims, including minors, are unaware that their images have been copied, manipulated, and distributed until someone else brings it to their attention. Subsequently, the perpetrators send these photos directly to the victims for purposes of sextortion or harassment, or until they are discovered independently on the Internet. Once disseminated, victims may encounter significant challenges in preventing the continued spread of the altered content or its removal from the Internet (Federal Bureau of Investigation, 2023).

In the same recommendations, the FBI urges the public to exercise caution when posting personal photos and videos on the internet, as they can be exploited by malicious actors for criminal activities. The rapid evolution of technologies facilitates perpetrators in locating and targeting potential victims, which may result in incidents of harassment, extortion, and financial losses.

A typical deepfake-based blackmail scheme encompasses several common stages similar to those found in a deepfake fraud scheme, yet it also possesses its own distinct characteristics. Analogous to fraudulent activities, the initial phase of blackmail and extortion involves the malicious actor selecting a target, who is often an individual with publicly available images and videos that can be utilized to generate a deepfake. In this stage, the malicious actor meticulously gathers photographs, video footage, and audio recordings of the victim from social media platforms, public appearances, or other accessible sources. Subsequently, the actor employs specialized software to fabricate a deepfake that depicts the victim in compromising or illegal scenarios.

The next step involves the perpetrator contacting the victim and threatening to release the deepfake unless the victim complies with specific demands, typically of a monetary nature. If the victim succumbs to the blackmail, the malicious actor receives the demanded sum or other benefits. Depending on the victim's actions, the perpetrator may either continue the extortion, demanding more, or cease their activities if a significant benefit has been obtained. If the victim does not yield to the blackmail, the perpetrator may either carry out their threats or move on to another victim.

In the event that an individual is confronted with blackmail or extortion involving deepfakes, the FBI advises against panicking and paying the extortionists. Paying the ransom does not resolve the issue and may encourage further blackmail attempts. It is essential to preserve all information related to the incident (such as usernames, email addresses, websites, or platform names used for communication, photos, videos, etc.), as this will aid law enforcement agencies in their investigation. One should promptly contact law enforcement, as they can provide necessary support and initiate an investigation.

If the deepfake has been published on a social platform (such as a social network, public forum, channel or group in messaging apps, specialized website, etc.), it is recommended to immediately contact the platform's support and report the violation. It is also advisable to inform close ones, so they are aware that it is a fake and do not fall for provocations. Additionally, it is recommended to review and enhance the privacy and security settings of social media accounts and other online resources. If necessary, one should seek advice from a lawyer specializing in cybersecurity.

All these recommendations will help protect against the consequences of the incident and minimize them. The FBI also recommends familiarizing oneself with the security guidelines on their official website and regularly updating knowledge about current threats and protection methods. It is important to remember that deepfakes can be used in various spheres of life, often for nefarious purposes. It is advisable to be prepared, monitor children's online activities, use privacy settings, avoid sharing personal information with strangers, and secure accounts with strong passwords and multi-factor authentication.

ADDRESSING THE DEEPFAKE CHALLENGE AS A COMMUNITY

At the conclusion of this chapter, it is pertinent to engage in a comprehensive deliberation on addressing the Deepfake problem as a unified community. In this final section, it is essential to underscore the critical importance of collective and collaborative efforts in combating the proliferation and impact of deepfakes.

In the context of countering and combating deepfakes, it is crucial to foster collaboration among researchers, companies, and universities to develop innovative technologies for Deepfake detection. To enhance transparency and improve interaction, it is necessary to establish and maintain open databases and platforms for testing deepfake detection methods and algorithms. We must not overlook the importance of conducting educational campaigns to raise public awareness about the risks associated with deepfakes, as well as developing ethical standards and guidelines for AI technology. Additionally, it is imperative to consider the creation of resources and support services for victims of deepfakes (Birrer & Just, 2024).

Undoubtedly, the utilization of advanced technologies for detecting deepfakes, such as machine learning algorithms and specialized software solutions, can significantly mitigate the risks posed by the malicious use of deepfakes. However, without enhancing the level of digital literacy among the population, technological measures alone will not suffice in countering these threats. Unfortunately, according to a survey conducted by iProov, 71% of respondents admit that they do not know what a deepfake is. Furthermore, 43% of those who are aware of deepfakes acknowledge that they would not be able to distinguish a fake video from a real one (iProov Blog, 2024).

The FBI consistently issues recommendations containing valuable information on preventing and responding to threats associated with deepfakes. For instance, in March 2021, the FBI released public service announcement number 210310-001, titled "Malicious actors almost certainly will leverage synthetic content for cyber and foreign influence operations" (Federal Bureau of Investigation, 2021), highlighting the increasing threat posed by synthetic content, including deepfakes used to create compromising videos. Subsequently, in 2023, the FBI issued public service announcement number I-060523-PSA, titled "Malicious Actors Manipulating Photos and Videos to Create Explicit Content and Sextortion Schemes" (Federal Bureau of Investigation, 2023), reporting on malicious actors creating synthetic content. This advisory noted that the FBI regularly receives reports from victims, including minors and adults, whose photographs or videos have been altered into explicit content and publicly disseminated on social media platforms or adult websites without their consent, often to harass victims or engage in sextortion schemes.

Therefore, when addressing deepfakes, it is essential first and foremost to enhance one's level of digital literacy (by regularly updating knowledge about current threats and their potential implementations) and digital hygiene (by using multi-factor authentication, setting appropriate privacy settings on social networks, not sharing personal or confidential information through unsecured sources, and not trusting unverified sources of information).

Another measure to address the problem of deepfakes is legal regulation and the introduction of strict penalties for those involved in the production and distribution of fake content. Already, several U.S. states, such as California and Georgia, have enacted legislation prohibiting deepfakes, with fines for distributing synthetic media without proper disclosure. Other states are considering similar bills. In Europe, new laws and regulations are also being introduced, such as the European Commission's plan to fine social networks for inadequate moderation of content created using AI. In Asian countries, strict rules are also being introduced for labeling synthetically created images and videos (U, 2024; Ramluckan, 2024).

In addition to introducing and implementing a combination of technological, educational, and legal measures aimed at countering deepfakes, the effectiveness of these countermeasures can be significantly enhanced through active collaboration and partnership with social networks and content-sharing platforms. Such cooperation will facilitate the rapid and efficient detection and removal of deepfake content. Establishing transparent and clearly defined content moderation policies, coupled with the improvement and refinement of filtering algorithms, will further contribute to reducing the potential negative impacts arising from deepfakes. At present, major technology companies are already acknowledging and addressing the threats posed by the creation of synthetic content. For example, the team behind the YouTube video service has started to accept and process complaints regarding videos generated by artificial intelligence that can be mistaken for genuine footage, featuring the victim of the forgery in the primary role (YouTube, n.d.-a; YouTube, n.d.-b).

Therefore, to counteraction deepfakes effectively, it is necessary to implement a comprehensive and multifaceted approach that encompasses a wide range of strategies. This approach should include not only technological measures, which are directed towards the development and implementation of sophisticated tools and methodologies for the automatic detection and identification of Deepfakes, but also legal measures, which involve the formulation and enforcement of stringent legislation and regulatory frameworks to govern the use and distribution of Deepfake technologies. Furthermore, it is imperative to incorporate educational initiatives aimed at significantly enhancing the level of digital literacy among the general population and raising public awareness about the potential threats posed by deepfakes, and the various methods and techniques available for protecting against these threats. Additionally, proactive collaboration with social media networks and content-sharing platforms is essential for the timely and efficient detection and removal of deepfake content. This multi-tiered and holistic approach will significantly advance society's efforts to effectively counter the menace of deepfakes and mitigate their adverse effects on public trust and safety.

CONCLUSION

The technology of deepfakes, without a doubt, constitutes one of the most remarkable achievements in the domain of computer vision and machine learning over recent years. This technology harbors an enormous potential for positive and beneficial applications; however, similar to any technological innovation, it brings with it significant threats that necessitate thorough analysis and the formulation of strategies aimed at their prevention.

The present chapter provides a detailed examination of the primary threats associated with deepfakes, which encompass fraudulent activities and financial crimes, the influence on public consciousness, breaches of biometric security, as well as blackmail and extortion. Deepfakes are being actively utilized to forge the voice and appearance of individuals familiar to the victim in order to gain unauthorized access to financial resources and confidential information, for political manipulation, the creation of false news and dissemination of misinformation, to circumvent biometric authentication systems, and to produce compromising videos intended for the purposes of blackmail and extortion. The examples illustrated in the article demonstrate the extent to which malicious actors can easily manipulate security systems, the trust relationships between individuals, and public opinion to achieve their malicious objectives.

The conclusion of the article underscores the critical importance of collective efforts in addressing the threats posed by deepfakes. To effectively counteract the threats associated with deepfakes, it is imperative to adopt a holistic approach that integrates technological, educational, and legal measures. Only through concerted efforts at all levels will it be possible to mitigate the adverse impact of deepfakes on society and ensure security and trust within the digital world.

REFERENCES

Akhtar, Z. (2023). Deepfakes generation and detection: A short survey. *Journal of Imaging*, 9(1), 18. DOI: 10.3390/jimaging9010018 PMID: 36662116

Artificial Intelligence Incident Database. (n.d.). Retrieved July 8, 2024, from https://incidentdatabase.ai/

Bateman, J. (2022). *Deepfakes and synthetic media in the financial system: Assessing threat scenarios*. Carnegie Endowment for International Peace.

Birrer, A., & Just, N. (2024). What we know and don't know about deepfakes: An investigation into the state of the research and regulatory landscape. *New Media & Society*, •••, 14614448241253138. DOI: 10.1177/14614448241253138

Bitget Research. (2024). Deepfakes may reach 70% of crypto crimes in two years. *Bitget*. Retrieved July 8, 2024, from https://www.bitget.com

Byman, D. L.. (2023). *Deepfakes and international conflict*. Brookings Institution.

Federal Bureau of Investigation. (2021). Malicious actors almost certainly will leverage synthetic content for cyber and foreign influence operations (210310-001). Retrieved July 8, 2024, from https://www.ic3.gov/Media/News/2021/210310-2.pdf

Federal Bureau of Investigation. (2023). I-060523-PSA: Malicious actors manipulating photos and videos to create explicit content and sextortion schemes. Retrieved July 8, 2024, from https://www.ic3.gov/Media/Y2023/PSA230605

Gambín, Á. F., Yazidi, A., Vasilakos, A., Haugerud, H., & Djenouri, Y. (2024). Deepfakes: Current and future trends. *Artificial Intelligence Review*, 57(3), 64. DOI: 10.1007/s10462-023-10679-x

Home Security Heroes. (n.d.). State of deepfakes. Retrieved July 8, 2024, from https://www.homesecurityheroes.com/state-of-deepfakes/

iProov. (2024). Biometric threat intelligence report 2024: The impact of generative AI on remote identity verification. *iProov*. Retrieved July 8, 2024, from https://www.iproov.com/reports/iproov-threat-intelligence-report-2024

iProov Blog. (2024). How To Protect Against Deepfakes – Statistics and Solutions. Retrieved July 8, 2024, from https://www.iproov.com/blog/deepfakes-statistics-solutions-biometric-protection

Kshetri, N. (2023). The economics of deepfakes. *Computer*, 56(8), 89–94. DOI: 10.1109/MC.2023.3276068

Nicholls, J., Kuppa, A., & Le-Khac, N. A. (2021). Financial cybercrime: A comprehensive survey of deep learning approaches to tackle the evolving financial crime landscape. *IEEE Access: Practical Innovations, Open Solutions*, 9, 163965–163986. DOI: 10.1109/ACCESS.2021.3134076

Patel, Y., Tanwar, S., Gupta, R., Bhattacharya, P., Davidson, I. E., Nyameko, R., Aluvala, S., & Vimal, V. (2023). Deepfake generation and detection: Case study and challenges. *IEEE Access: Practical Innovations, Open Solutions*, 11, 143296–143323. DOI: 10.1109/ACCESS.2023.3342107

Pei, G., ... (2024). Deepfake generation and detection: A benchmark and survey. *arXiv preprint* arXiv:2403.17881.

Ramluckan, T. (2024). Deepfakes: The legal implications. *International Conference on Cyber Warfare and Security*, 19(1), 282-288.

Rana, M. S., Nobi, M. N., Murali, B., & Sung, A. H. (2022). Deepfake detection: A systematic literature review. *IEEE Access: Practical Innovations, Open Solutions*, 10, 25494–25513. DOI: 10.1109/ACCESS.2022.3154404

Ray, A. (2021). Disinformation, deepfakes and democracies: The need for legislative reform. *The University of New South Wales Law Journal*, 44(3), 983–1013. DOI: 10.53637/DELS2700

Salko, M., Firc, A., & Malinka, K. (2024). Security implications of deepfakes in face authentication. *Proceedings of the 39th ACM/SIGAPP Symposium on Applied Computing*, 1376-1384. DOI: 10.1145/3605098.3635953

Samoilenko, S. A., & Suvorova, I. (2023). Artificial intelligence and deepfakes in strategic deception campaigns: The US and Russian experiences. In *The Palgrave handbook of malicious use of AI and psychological security* (pp. 507–529). Springer International Publishing. DOI: 10.1007/978-3-031-22552-9_19

Singh, S., & Kumar, R. (2024). Image forgery detection: Comprehensive review of digital forensics approaches. *Journal of Computational Social Science*, 7(1), 1–39. DOI: 10.1007/s42001-024-00265-8

SlashNext. (2023). Listen to these recordings: Deepfake social engineering scams are scaring victims. Retrieved July 8, 2024, from https://slashnext.com/blog/deepfake -scaring-victims-into-submission/?utm_content=252103511&utm_medium=social &utm_source=linkedin&hss_channel=lcp-10572287

Sopra Banking. (n.d.). Digital banking fraud: Latest challenges faced by banks. Retrieved July 8, 2024, from https://www.soprabanking.com/insights/digital-banking -fraud-challenges-banks/

Statista. (n.d.). False news in the U.S. - statistics & facts. Retrieved July 8, 2024, from https://www.statista.com/topics/3251/fake-news/

Sumsub (2024) Sumsub Identity Fraud Report. A comprehensive, data-driven report on identity fraud dynamics and innovative prevention methods. Retrieved July 8, 2024, from https://sumsub.com/fraud-report-2023/

Teneo. (2024). Deepfakes in 2024 are suddenly deeply real: An executive briefing on the threat and trends. Retrieved July 8, 2024, from https://www.teneo.com

Tolosana, R., Vera-Rodriguez, R., Fierrez, J., Morales, A., & Ortega-Garcia, J. (2020). Deepfakes and beyond: A survey of face manipulation and fake detection. *Information Fusion*, 64, 131–148. DOI: 10.1016/j.inffus.2020.06.014

U.S. Department of Defense. (2023). Contextualizing deepfake threats to organizations: Cybersecurity information sheet. Retrieved July 8, 2024, from https://media .defense.gov/2023/Sep/12/2003298925/-1/-1/0/CSI-DEEPFAKE-THREATS.PDF

Veerasamy, N., & Pieterse, H. (2022). Rising above misinformation and deepfakes. *International Conference on Cyber Warfare and Security*, 17(1), 340-348.

Verdoliva, L. (2020). Media forensics and deepfakes: An overview. *IEEE Journal of Selected Topics in Signal Processing*, 14(5), 910–932. DOI: 10.1109/ JSTSP.2020.3002101

Volkova, S. S. (2023). A method for deepfake detection using convolutional neural networks. *Scientific and Technical Information Processing*, 50(5), 475–485. DOI: 10.3103/S0147688223050143

Walker, C. P., Schiff, D. S., & Schiff, K. J. (2024). Merging AI incidents research with political misinformation research: Introducing the political deepfakes incidents database. *Proceedings of the AAAI Conference on Artificial Intelligence*, 38(21), 23053–23058. DOI: 10.1609/aaai.v38i21.30349

YouTube. (n.d.-a). Community guidelines. Retrieved July 8, 2024, from https:// www.youtube.com/intl/ALL_in/howyoutubeworks/policies/community-guidelines/

YouTube. (n.d.-b). Fighting misinformation. Retrieved July 8, 2024, from https:// www.youtube.com/howyoutubeworks/our-commitments/fighting-misinformation/

Chapter 11
The Future of Deepfakes:
Emerging Trends and Potential Applications

T. Venkat Narayana Rao
https://orcid.org/0000-0002-1996-1819
Sreenidhi Institute of Science and Technology, India

Maithri Koppula
Sreenidhi Institute of Science and Technology, India

Goboori Harsh Vardhan
Sreenidhi Institute of Science and Technology, India

Sangers Bhavana
https://orcid.org/0009-0005-6134-1081
Sreenidhi Institute of Science and Technology, India

Bolla Sujith Kumar
Sreenidhi Institute of Science and Technology, India

ABSTRACT

Deepfakes is a new generation of machine learning algorithms, which has demonstrated the possibility of creating audacious synthetic media and raised serious concerns. Firstly, we discuss the evolution of deep fake technology in terms of algorithmic development, the size of the dataset and the way the technology is trained – which has led to a generation of even more convincing fake videos or fake images. It explores the creation of deepfake tools and the emergence of deepfake platform platforms in making synthetic media more accessible and democratic. Deepfakes use including misinformation, identity theft, and privacy infringements and efforts to contain regulation violations given the fluidity of this digital world are also dis-

DOI: 10.4018/979-8-3693-6890-9.ch011

Copyright © 2025, IGI Global Scientific Publishing. Copying or distributing in print or electronic forms without written permission of IGI Global Scientific Publishing is prohibited.

cussed. This study focus on the technology of deepfakes can be applied including both entertainment and advertising and also education and medicine. This chapter offers a general insight into deepfakes, future developments, and trends in deepfake usage, as well as precautionary measures for the future.

1. INTRODUCTION TO DEEPFAKES

Deepfakes are fake images and videos which are generated through artificial intelligence technology wherein a person in a particular image or in a video is replaced with a different person. The very term 'deepfake' – derives from 'deep learning', and 'fake', which is an apt description for these examples of highly sophisticated artificial portrayals, frequently designed to deceive. Machine learning is a profound technique among which deep learning is one of the most popular ones; it implies the use of algorithms that simulate the functioning of the human brain and recognize data as well as generate patterns for decision-making. In the case of deepfakes, these algorithms learn and transform the content of sound and picture in order to synthesize fake media that resembles the existing recordings as closely as possible.

Some of the applications which deepfake technology posses includes; It can manipulate facial expressions regarding the audio tracks, it can perfectly match the lip movements with the particular sounds it has, and even mimic voice patterns, which are possible makes fake videos where people look like they talked or acted in ways they never did. As much as there is strength in the use of the technology in making entertainment, education, and accessibility a reality, there is even more strength in the possible vices of the technology as an ethical and security concern.

1.1 Brief History and Development of Deepfake Technology

It is possible to note that the roots of deepfake technology can be linked to the development of artificial intelligence and computer graphics during recent decades. Some of the rudimentary CG and special effects seen in movies acted as precursors to what would later become deepfakes. But in the case of deepfakes, they advanced from CGI, they needed to make some progress in artificial intelligence and machine learning.

In the later part of the decade of 2010, the deep learning and particularly generational adversarial network brought about a major shift in how synthetic media could be produced. GANs are made up of two lengthy neural networks known as the generator and the discriminator, which interact and learn to produce more natural images or videos. The generator delivers the fake content, and the discriminator comes in to determine the accuracy of the fake content. The way both networks are trained is that they gradually improve the quality of the generated media to nearly natural originals(Westerlund et.al,2019).

The term 'deepfake' in fact came to public notice for the first time in the year 2017, which was created by a Reddit user who used to post the fake videos. Many of the first cases involved the use of celebrities' photos where the face of a popular actor/actress was grafted onto the body of an adult film star, this demonstrated how the technology could be used for harassment and other malicious purposes. Access to deepfake tools and gradual enhancement of the deep fake quality made a significant number of people generate both low-quality and increasingly high quality deep fakes.

That said, like all modern innovations, new uses for the technology soon emerged. For instance in the entertainment sector, deepfake technology have been used to animate dead actors, young actors for certain scenes or roles and generally create more convincing looks in a movie. For instance, the Star Wars employed deepfake to mimic the younger version of the actress who died recently, Carrie Fisher. In education and training, they can give realistic look and feel for practice and learning situations, e. g. simulated operations in healthcare or emergency management (T. Venkat Narayana Rao et. al, 2019).

2. EVOLUTION OF DEEPFAKE TECHNOLOGY

2.1 Algorithmic Advancements in Deepfake Technology

Deepfake technology by extension the evolution of deepfake technology traces its origins in the continued development of artificial intelligence and features primarily in modern applications involving the use of machine learning especially the deep learning algorithms. Machine learning, in short, is a subset of AI that enables computers to learn from data automatically without being explicitly programmed, thereby performing better with time. In other words, machine learning algorithms allow systems to identify patterns and use them to make predictions or to take decisions. Another important advancement that has occurred in this line of research is the implementation of Generative Adversarial Networks (GANs). Introduced by Ian Goodfellow and his colleagues in 2014, GANs consist of two competing neural networks: Previously, there were two primary models including the generator and the discriminator(Sharma et.al,2022). The generator produces generalized data and the discriminator is responsible for determining the plausibility or authenticity of the generated data. This type of approach and feedback loop help the generator refine the quality of the fake data over time while producing highly realistic results.

Ideas for the subsequent improvement of GANs have involved stability of the algorithms and time reduction of training. There are also various improvement methods developed previously, which has also enhanced the ability of GANs including Progressive Growing of GANs (ProGAN) and StyleGAN. ProGAN is an approach that helps to learn simple structures at first and then add layers of complexity gradually, and hence, it added layers of complexity in generations images also. StyleGAN, in contrast, presents a adaptive style structure that divides the image synthesis into multiple layers of the abstraction to provide more explicit control over the output attributes.

Another territory of generating work is generating models, specifically Variational Autoencoders or VAEs, which are basically different from GANs. VAEs learn features of the input data and map it into a latent space, and then map it back into the input format adding distortions that can seem realistic when generating synthetic data. Considering decompositions of both Generative Adversarial Networks and Variational Autoencoder, there are Hybrid models that complement the advantages of each type, improving the realism and quality of deepfakes (T. Venkat Narayana Rao et. al, 2019).

2.2 Impact of Dataset Size on the Quality of Synthetic Media

The quality of the artificial synthetic media produced by deepfake technology therefore, depends very much on the size and the geographical spread of the dataset that is used for training. It is advisable to work with big volumes of data as they can offer a great amount of details in order the model to converge to a great number of features and intricacies. For instance, deepfake models, that are trained using a range of pictures with a unique facial feature of the individual, in various poses, lighting conditions and emotions, will generate much more realistic and diversified fake content (Millière et.al,2022).

Such large-scale datasets as CelebA that host more than 200,000 images of celebrities while providing various annotations are rather helpful to develop deepfake techniques. These large datasets make it possible to generalize the model better, thus decrease the overfitting and increase the strength of media produced by the generation models. On the other hand, fewer images in a dataset give a worse quality of outputs because the model fails to learn about variability of target domain and the(fake) generates artifacts and less believable impostures.

The basic kinds of data augmentation include rotation, cropping of images and even alteration of color of images so as to make the data sets bigger artificially. These techniques make models more robust and, thus, produce better synthetic materials, adding to the quality of the models that are employed.

2.3 Training Methods Employed in Deepfake Technology

There are techniques and different methods for training deep fake models for a purpose of achieving a high quality of the output. There is one of those learning methodologies, known as the supervised learning, and it involves a model being trained through available datasets. This is usually the case with deepfake where it entails image or videos pairs of original and target images. The model becomes capable of training itself so as to establish correspondence between the features in source as well as in the target and the parameters of the model are optimized in order to get as closer as possible towards real content.

Other methods that are also being employed in unsupervised learning are also starting to be used in deepfake technology. Unlike standard supervised learning techniques, these methods do not use labeled data and instead have the model search for patterns and structures of the program data. This approach is especially helpful when it is hard or when there are few labeled datasets that are available for the language in question.

Transfer learning is another significant approach, in which last layers of the model are trained on an existing large data set, while the last layers are trained on a small domain specific data set. This makes it easier for the model to use previously learned features and in the process, saves on time and performs well specifically on tasks that the model is trained to do(Heidari et.al,2024).

Besides the mentioned methods, a number of regularization techniques that contribute to reduction in data overfitting and improve the generalization of deepfake models. The regularizations including dropout, weight decay, and data augmentation are often employed to control the over-fitting of the models so that instead of memorizing the training set, the models create realistic fake media that can pass real data checks in fresh, unseen data(T.Venkat Narayana Rao et. al, 2020).

3. ACCESSIBILITY AND DEMOCRATIZATION

3.1 Role of Deepfake Tools in Making Synthetic Media More Accessible

Deepfake technology has played a major role in the expansion of 'synthetic media' as it has opened up the idea into new possibilities that people can use in their everyday lives. At the beginning of AI development, fashioning appealing artificial avatars called synthetic media was possible only with comprehensive expertise in AI and high-performance computing systems. Previous deepfake tools only allowed the heavy modification of a single frame, which was a complex process; progress in deepfake has made this an easy task (Barnes et.al,2020).

Among these, one could include the advancement of interfaces and apps that make it possible for people with no programming skills to create deepfakes. There are many other programs for creation of deep fakes, which offer friendly interface and allow making fake videos with minimal efforts: DeepFaceLab, FaceSwap, Reface app. These tools often provide default models and detailed help guides that allow users who don't have prior coding knowledge. Such democratization has allowed hobbyists, artists, writers, and other small creators to tinker with synthetic media and practice without much need for assets or profound computational expertise (T. Venkat Narayana Rao et. al, 2016).

Furthermore, cloud-based services have helped in development of the deep fake technology in one way or another. Some of these are easy to use interfaces like Google Colab and some takes subscription charge like Amazon Web Services (AWS) and so the users do not have to invest some big bucks on computing hardware in order to train and develop their deepfake models. This structure includes some downsides, as there is no need to buy any service with a large amount; however, it adds flexibility and allows those users who have a small amount of money in their accounts to get all the computing resources required for deepfake generation.

Deepfake technologies should also be discussed as they have enabled work in different areas be progress in numerous ways. As for entertainment, the tools are applied by directors, producers, game designers, and other professionals to develop realistic characters and unique environment. For instance, technology used in deep fake has been used in making documentaries featuring the dramatic stories of great people who are now dead or portrayal of actors who could be alive, but their death brought an aspect of creativity in performance.

According to educators, deepfakes can be used to enhance the training process and help to create highly interesting and individualized educational materials. Synthetic media could be employed in the creation of educational content such as animated lessons or history representations, and communication learning applications. For instance, a lecture by one of the historical characters in a course could be created using deepfake technology to make classes more engrossing for learners.

3.2 Increased Deepfake Platform Popularity and Its Repercussions

This is mainly due to emergence of dedicated deepfake platforms as well as general rise of synthetic media's influence and availability. Such platforms provide a development environment, as well as a file-sharing and distribution system for deepfakes, thus increasing the development and user base. Deepfake generation platforms such as Deepfakes Web and ZAO offer people to use the required tools and mechanisms for deepfake generation based on cloud computing to handle the most demanding calculations as the process of deepfake generation can be rather heavy in terms of computational power required to solve this problem.

As we have seen, the existence of these platforms has extensive ramifications for both the constructive and destructive uses of deepfake technology (Hancock et.al,2021). On the positive side, they democratize content creation,, enabling persons or small business firms to develop contents that used to demand lot of capital and technical input. This can result in a more diverse and richer form of narrative because the synthetic media has the capability of being used by people of different demographics with various ideas on what they wish to describe through visuals.

Nevertheless, the availability of deepfake platforms is of a quite questionable nature to say the least as far as ethics and security of such technology are concerned. It is worrisome to observe that they can be misused since deepfake technology can be utilized in making fake content that is misleading or even harmful. For instance, the political deepfakes present on social media can include fake news, and the dox pop up deepfakes sex as a tool of sexual assault.

Since deepfake tools have become widely available, there is a need for intervention as well as standards to prevent the misuse of this technology in artificial intelligence. This means that legal scholars, computer scientists, and policymakers need to work together in search of regulation that would minimize/Prevent the negative effects of deepfake technology while maintaining the positive impacts. These would involve actions like imprinting of watermarks to easily identify synthetic content from actual content, legal consequences of use of deepfakes, and creating general public awareness that such contents exist and are being produced.

Few of the high profile and real-world examples are:

Political deepfakes: Deepfakes were seen circulating false information related to the 2020 U.S. presidential election, including re-encoded video of Nancy Pelosi-altered to make her appear drunk and blur words-to manipulate message and confused.

Manipulation through Corporate and Social Media: With deepfakes, cases involving corporate espionage or celebrity impersonation for fraudulent purposes such as tricking employees into doing wire transfers using deepfaked videos may also indicate the wider financial and social ramifications.

4. REGULATORY ENVIRONMENT

4.1 Current Regulatory Landscape for Deepfakes

Regulations concerning deepfakes remain Today, there are no universally agreed upon regulations regarding deepfakes as different countries are still in the process of attempting on how to address the risks posed by this relatively new innovation. As applied to deepfake technology, there are concerns that such technology can be utilized for the purpose of posting fake news, fraud, or making adult videos without the consent of the people involved, and stricter regulation has been discussed in recent years (Birrer et.al,2024).

In the United States, the legal measures that have been taken toward deepfakes have so far mainly taken a reactive approach, where both federal and state legislation has been enacted. At the federal level, the national defense authorization act FY 2020 made provisions to have the department of homeland security to carry out annual reviews on the deepfake technology and its impacts on the nation's security. There is also the DEEPFAKES Accountability Act which is a proposed bill that would begin the session of Deepfakes by labeling them as synthetic and making it unlawful to produce and disseminate deepfakes that are specifically meant to manipulate or deceive.

Some of the U. S. state laws have also been passed aiming at prohibiting and regulating specific uses of deepfakes. For instance, in California the law was enacted prohibiting the dissemination of deepfakes that are created for purposes involving elections manipulation or for producing pornographic content without the consent of the involved subjects. This makes the use of deepfakes to defame or deceive people or for shaping the outcome of a selection criminal in Texas to ensure that the generation and sharing of synthetic media are done rightfully.

In Europe there is no specific law regulating AI but instead there are wider digital and data protection laws. The EU law has the GDPR, which gives guidelines that would be implementable in the case of deepfakes, particularly on the issue of consent and the right to private life. In GDPR terms, there is the power of the person to control the use of his or her personal data including a likeness and this could be applied to unauthorized deepfake. EU has also stressed upon reporting and ethical uses of AI especially of deepfakes through approaches such as the European AI Strategy and the Ethics Guidelines for Trustworthy Artificial Intelligence.

The Chinese government has shown more assertiveness in regulating deepfake videos by enacting measures that mandate a disclaimer be placed on the video content that is deemed as deepfake. Starting January 2020, the Cyberspace Administration of China required that deepfake videos and audio must declare their deceptive content so that their malefaction does not go unmitigated in deceiving the citizenry (Van der Sloot et.al,2022).

4.2 Changes and Updates in Policies Addressing Ethical Concerns

As for deepfakes, the ethical risks, which include privacy violations, spreading fake news, and creating psychological distress, continue to evolve, and, therefore, updates and changes are made to policies all over the world. There has been recent attempts to regulate deepfake technology by policymakers and regulation authorities due to change in capabilities and availability of application for deepfake.

Technology advancement is another category that has seen the development of policies that strengthen the digital identification procedures. Effort is currently underway to create technological tools that can ensure they identify deep fake and ensure the actuality of the content. Companies like the Partnership on AI have been actively involved in trying to outline the common practices and technical specifications essential for fake media detection so as to enhance a better and safer virtual world environment (T.Venkat Narayana Rao et. al, 2019).

Continuing with the disclosable policies, another policy area that has recently undergone significant changes is the integration of ethical standards in AI and deep fake studies. Deepfake technology has prompted research institutions and governments to consider ethical concerns with reference to the development and use of the advanced software. This is consideration of getting consent from individuals who are depicted in synthetic media and also ensuring that necessary measures of not using them in the wrong way are taken.

Some educational measures towards emphasizing the problem of deep fakes and possible consequences are being launched as well. Policymakers believe that, by engaging citizens in understanding how to identify fake news spreads within social media platforms, the impacts of such fake news dissemination will be reduced besides improving the general public's digital literacy (Diakopoulos et.al,2021).

Besides that, there is the development of international cooperation concerning the threats of deepfake technology due to the globalization of the phenomenon. Since deep fakes can be produced and shared globally, there is a need for global collaboration in finding a cohesive and effective approach to the regulation of these products. The United Nations and the European Commission are but among the organizations that are mediating in discussions and partnerships with a view to improve policies and exchange of good practice (T.Venkat Narayana Rao et. al, 2011).

5. MISUSE OF DEEPFAKES

5.1 Instances of Misuse: Misinformation, Identity Theft, and Privacy Infringements

Even though the Deepfake technology has the potential to generate natural seeming synthetic media, it has been abused most of the times, therefore, causing many challenges in the realm of ethics and law (Farid et.al,2022). Misleadership is one of the most unpleasant methods of misuse because it involves providing the public with false information. The deep fakes can even build live-like videos or sound clips of any person, including politicians, uttering fake statements or performing things they have never done. These manipulated media clips are also suitable for political advertisements, manipulation of elections, or even creation of societal riots and revolutions.

a. **Misinformation**: The potential of deepfakes is illustrated by a peculiar example of a deepfake video employing former U. S. President Barack Obama; the video was developed by filmmaker Jordan Peele in 2018. It depicting Obama making statements that he never made in his life, this was to show how deepfake could be used in spreading fake news and changing people's opinions, and even the 2020 US presidential elections. Another example can be seen in May of 2020 when a deep fake video with Belgium's Prime Minister Sophie Wilmès was created and spread across the internet where she claimed that COVID-19 is caused by environmental issues, even though the video was immediately removed and the politician recognized that she has never made such statement, this example shows how political deep fakes are damaging and dangerous.

b. **Identity Theft:** For instance, in 2019, the fraudsters employed a deepfake sound and a voice imitation of the CEO of a UK-based energy firm, and coerced an executive of the firm to transfer €220,000 to a fake account. The deepfake was so realistic that the CEO could barely distinguish the call as fake, this made him/ she act in a particular fashion he/she believed was rightful. This case illustrated the loophole that deepfakes possess, masterminding clear phishing campaigns and cases of fraud.

c. **Privacy Infringements:** Deepfake is not just a technology that can be used for pranking or entertainment purposes — there are its dangerous implications, and one of the most significant and mischievous use cases of deepfake is non-consensual pornography. The year 2019 seen an application known as DeepNude through which people are capable to generate fake naked images of women from their images while they are fully dressed. The app was removed subsequently from the market due to immense backlash from the general public, but the event served to draw attention to the numerous instances of privacy violations and emotional abuse which occur through misuse, especially where women and girls' images are concerned, and with no consent given.

5.2 Challenges in Regulating Deepfake Use and Mitigating Violations

This paper has discussed that controlling the use of deepfake technology and avoiding its violations present many difficulties. One of the keys challenges is the shortening of technology adoption cycle which makes an organization put under pressure its competitors. The discrete generation of deepfake algorithms gives out realistic contents and then slow detection technologies cannot handle it. The technologies used by deepfake producers and the measures to prevent them create an ever-evolving underground and classification, which makes it challenging for regulators to implement solutions and threats that are swiftly changing because of technological progression.

The other issue is the internet is a global platform where products can easily flood a country and push out local products. These are some of the potential ways of deepfake production and sharing that do not necessarily require a specific country and assets, which means that it is hard to regulate such content solely by using a certain country's resources. As a result, it is high time to seek global partnerships and build supranational legal requirements to prevent the manipulation of deepfakes. Nevertheless, it can be difficult to reach consensus in such regulations; some cases may be rooted in the opposite legal systems, cultural differences, or political ambitions of countries.

Legal and ethical issues which surround the use of ransomware are also a problem for regulating authorities. Determining whether deepfake content is risky or nefarious can be challenging mainly when determining the limits of speech and self-representation rights (Kugler et.al,2021). To this end, laws have to be written in such a way that they do not pre-empt the formulation of other laws that may be necessary for properly safeguarding its citizens but at the same time, the laws have to be drafted in a manner that guarantees the safety of people from certain harms. However, these laws must be accompanied by sound approaches for enforcing those laws, which may entail practical difficulties and demands considerable time and resources, particularly in cases with anonymous or semipseudonymous offenders.

In addition, the continuous spread of fake news and awareness about deepfakes, remain vital ingredients in fighting against deepfakes abuse. The problem of deepfakes, as seen from the survey, is that many people are yet to know about them or how to spot them. The first defense method that could significantly reduce the harm that such fake information might have is to raise people's digital literacy levels as well as familiarizing them with not only the risks but also the signs of deepfake content.

6. APPLICATIONS IN ENTERTAINMENT AND ADVERTISING

Technological advancements in deep fake have advanced to new levels, with the creative applications arising in the film industry and the advertisement industry. Open sourcing artificial intelligence, deep fakes have taken on the mantle of changing the way content, marketing, and audiences look at the process. While this technology holds much promise, there is a clear need to look at possible ethical issues and other concerns that it can bring.

6.1 Using Deepfake Technology in Entertainment Industry

The entertainment industry has been quick to seize upon deepfake technology for its realizations of altering multiple domains of filmmaking, television, and artistic production (Campbell et.al,2022).

a. **De-aging and Resurrecting Actors:** Perhaps, the oddest and fully utilized use of deepfake technology in entertainment is in the process of de-aging actors. This technology makes it easier for directors and cinematographers to portray actors at different ages in the production without hiring different actors or having to make use of elaborate makeup and body suits. For instance, when Manufacturing Scorsese created "The Irishman", which was released recently, the deepfake tech was employed to age reduce De Niro, Pacino, and Pesci since the characters play across different periods in the film. Similarly, deepfakes can bring actors back such that their decals can be used in motion pictures even in those years which they were not part of the movie industry. This was demonstrated in "Rogue One: Specifically, here – in 'Solo: A Star Wars Story,' where the Spanish company performed digital reconstruction of the actor Peter Cushing to cast him back as Grand Moff Tarkin.

b. **Voice Cloning and Dubbing:** It is important to note that beyond face and image synthesis, deepfake technology is applicable to audio domain by leveraging voice cloning. AI can mimic the human voice superbly thus making it easier to have natural voices and lip movement synched to the dialogue in foreign films. This technology is also useful when the actors themselves cannot come for the recording session due to some reasons or any ailments. Thus, when a filmmaker wants to achieve continuity or retain authenticity in the performed scenes, a cloned voice can be used in the film. However, voice cloning can also be obvious for creating new dialogues from scratch to improve characters' narrative outcomes.

c. **Creative Expression and Special Effects:** To the filmmakers, deepfakes are just tools that can be used to make movies while at the same time offering ways in which special effects can be done. To be more precise, it allows directors to try out new faceswap or establish a surrealistic scene which can be impossible in the regular way. Thus, it can be said that with the help of the deepfake technology, it is possible to improve the special effects and make the fantastic and science-fiction images look more realistic. It enables designers and developers to build engaging and aesthetically beautiful interactive apps that engage users.

6.2 Consequences of Picturing Deepfakes on Advertising Models

In this sense, analyzing the role that deepfake technology plays in the advertising industry, it can be concluded that it opens up specific opportunities for interacting with consumers, individualizing and optimizing advertising messages.

a. **Personalized Advertising:** Personalized advertisements can be created using deepfakes, making the content more relevant to the targeted consumers with respect to their preference and mode of response. Marketing professionals can make videos with the likes of celebrities or brand influencers directly speaking to the consumers using names or talking about their favorite things. Such specific appeal enhances the brand identity with the audience and may lead to the higher interest in the product and purchasing rates. For instance, in advertising, a skincare brand may leverage deepfake to produce unique advertisements in which a celebrity speaks directly to the audience and gives information about the skin type and issues that the viewer might be experiencing (Karpinska-Krakowiak et.al,2024).

b. **Dynamic and Interactive Campaigns:** The use of deep fake technology in advertising enables advertising to create dynamic and engaging campaigns. Brand can develop a technology where ads are interactive in the sense they change depending on the user's input or any other stimuli. For instance, a sports equipment company might create an ad where the product is presented by an athlete and the athlete interacts with the viewer or answers their questions. To this extent, the flexibility of advertisements ensures that they are captivating as well as useful in grabbing the attention of the audience.

c. **Cost-Effective Content Creation:** Other forms of advertising is conventional, they may require huge capital to fund product's shooting for example hiring actors or even shooting in particular locations. Thus, Deepfake technology can significantly bring down these costs as it creates videos involving the actors using an avatar. This cost-effectiveness kind of opens the possibility for many companies to create a wider and more frequent range of content, ensuring their constant dissemination in the market. Companies can still produce professional ads even without the need to spent time and money on taping and shooting the commercials as always, giving brands the opportunities for more frequent and quicker reaction.

7. APPLICATIONS IN EDUCATION AND MEDICINE

7.1 Potential Applications of Deepfakes in the Education Sector

In the following section, we will particularly discuss deepfakes which are synthetic media generated through AI. Deepfakes have the potential to transform the education sector. Perhaps the most significant form is in the application of personalized learning environments. In this respect, having learnt that deepfakes can be implemented in education, it is possible to deliver educational material to students in a more individualized manner that is congruent with the learning modalities of the learners that are being targeted. For example, real people, specific personalities from history classes could appear and perform as teachers or engage the students in discussions and other forms of teaching, which would be far more effective in terms of educating the learners. Just think about the power of history when you're learning about the formation of the United States from President Lincoln himself, or the thrill of science as you listen to Einstein explain relativity. Such cases are capable of engaging the students' interest and improve their grasp of subjects or course (Krishna et.al,2020).

Second, language learning: In learning a second language, translation searches are conducted on translated paradigms or similar texts to identify corresponding words in the other language. Deepfakes can create genuine imitations of native speakers, which gives students a chance to speak with real accent, thus enhancing the level of conversation in learning. This can however serve as a great benefit to learners who may not get opportunity to practice with actual speakers from the region. Also, deepfake can be used to create virtual teachers who could assist students and scribe necessary information concerning their difficulties or the way toward improvement in their academic performance.

Moreover, it is possible to use deepfakes, and create virtual classrooms and campuses which may provide an illusion of presence and interaction to students that may be noticed beyond the mere online courses. Although it is quite possible to use physical presence in lessons, there can be cases when it is impossible to do so, for example, during a pandemic, and in such cases, it is possible to provide continuity and high quality of education through deepfake-enabled virtual environments. These experiences can be designed to replicate the real-life scenarios such as interaction between teacher and students, students and peers, and smaller group discussions, and various quizzes and knowledge-checks in the form of group activities and projects, therefore providing a complete educational experience.

7.2 Role of Deepfakes in Medical Training and Diagnosis Simulations

In the medical field, deepfakes provide potential change in training and simulation can have positive effects. Permanent professional education is frequently based on the practical use of devices and equipment, and this may be difficult due to difficulties in accessing the required volume of pathological cases or possible negative impact on the patient's state. Applications of Deepfake technology can include scanning models and developing very realistic representations of diseases, disorders etc where learners and practitioners can rehearse on the simulacra. For instance, patients that have been produced with deepfake technology exhibit any possible symptoms and respond with any possible reaction, which lets trainees practice various situations. This can be particularly useful in teachings of students/rare diseases that clinicians can hardly encounter in practice.

Additionally, deep fakes can be used in surgical training to learn various surgeries that would be difficult to try out on human beings. Specialists can rehearse complex procedures on virtual patients that stimulate the body part and mimic its response to distinct actions or treatments by the operator. This not only assists in establishing a routine practice, but also minimizes the likelihood of complications occurring during actual surgeries. In essence, the nature of skill development that allows surgical and related professionals to practice and receive performance review in the safety of a controlled database enhances skill acquisition and results in better overall surgical outcomes.

In diagnostics, deep learning technologically aids in the development of more precise counterfeit images required for specific medical imaging. In this way, radiologists and other healthcare professionals can apply synthetic images to train ML algorithms to achieve more accurate diagnostic outcomes (Qureshi et.al,2024). For instance, images of tumors or fractures created through deep fake technology can be employed in increasing the efficiency in which algorithms are set to discern and categorize medical conditions. Some of them can enhance the understanding of diseases and contribute to earlier and more precise diagnosis, which is important for treatment outcomes.

In addition, deepfakes can help engage patients and educate them about their conditions and or treatment regimens. The outcomes are closely connected with the methods of treatment and it is considered that with the help of realistic exemplifications of the patients' conditions and suggested treatments, clients will be able to take a better understanding of the nature of their disease and the ways it will be cured. This can help in situations where people are not fully aware of the implications of a decision they are making or a treatment they are receiving and in situations where patient compliance to her prescribed treatment plans is required.

8. FUTURE DEVELOPMENTS AND TRENDS

8.1 Emerging Trends in Deepfake Usage

AI-generated synthetic media, commonly known as deepfakes, are advancing with incredible speed, and several distinctive trends indicate the path through which this realm of technology is heading. One somewhat curious aspect is the fact that deepfakes have been commonly employed in media and entertainment. With deepfakes, it is possible to generate lifelike avatars of actors, which will enable the filmmakers and producers to age down or bring back actors for other roles. It has been observed in such contexts as giving a background of actors younger than the others, or even in cases where new scenes with the actors who are late have to be put in by morphing and implementing the same to give the viewer a real life feeling.

Another trend tied to the process is ads and marketing messages containing individualized content (Gil et.al,2023). Some firms have decided to apply the deepfakes in making sensitive adverts, of/about celebrities or influential personalities based on specified age groups. Such a level of personalization can increase enrollment and the chances of making a purchase because consumers prefer content from sources that they deem close to them. In the same way, in the case of customer services, deepfakes could be adopted to create virtual solutions offering tailored interactions due to the collected customer information and enhancing the consumer satisfaction level.

In the world of social media marketing, deepfakes have gradually started appearing not only as pranks and jokes but as tools for content creation and attracting users. The deep fake technology is being tested on the platforms that allows users to develop more comprehensive posts. For example, someone can become an actor in the famous films' scenes, replace a face with someone else's face in the real scenario or even receive a letter from a movie star. Not only does this increase the amount of interactions users have with the content, but it increases the likelihood of the content being shared on additional platforms.

Education and training applications are also increasing where the deepfakes are being incorporated. As mentioned earlier, deep fake technology can be used for creating simulations that are hard to distinguish between the real and fake for purposes of training and practicing especially in realms such as medical practice and military training. Also, educators are also attempting to use deepfakes to enhance and diversify the learning experience so that instead of, for instance, having a guest speaker, one could have a speech from Abraham Lincoln or an entire language learning environment with depictions of people of the given language (Jones et.al,2020).

8.2 Global Forecast for the Deepfake Technology

Analyzing developments and trends of future deepfake technology several factors should be named. Some of them are; The former is an article from Vice News Dot Com which predicts that in the future, deepfakes will be more realistic and of even better quality. Deepfakes are also going to get tougher to distinguish and improve with the improvement of the algorithms and computing capacity of AI. This has implications or positive and negative effects which can make entertainment and education more pleasant but there are also difficulties with fake news and cybersecurity.

Another prediction is that the mainstreaming of deepfakes to home devices and gadgets will occur soon. Be it movies and TV shows and advertisements to business conference and virtual meetings or virtual assistants, deep fakes are the future of our interactions with the technology. For instance, applications which employ VR and AR could consequently employ deepfakes to deliver more engaging as well as customized user experiences across several industries.

It is for this reason that there are initial anticipations of changes in the ethical and regulatory structures as the deepfake technology becomes more widespread. As for the foreseeable legislative measures that are going to be applied with regard to this innovation, it is possible to predict several trends: Governments and organizations will introduce more tight restrictive measures in order to prevent the negative use of deepfake technology in such spheres as misinformation, violation of privacy and rights to intellectual property. This will include creating ways by which deepfakes presents in the social media platforms can be identified and ensure that whoever is behind them is known (Kwok et.al,2021).

Deepfake technology can be used to create realistic videos to simulate medical conditions and help patients explain their symptoms to doctors and therapists. In keeping with the fact that patient-simulating virtual avatars as deepfakes are even close to real-interaction with doctors and nurses, it can enhance the authenticity of distant consultations. Furthermore, the advancement of deep fake technology can also be applied to the medical field such as in medical imaging and diagnostic tools which are useful in diagnose and treating a disease at the initial stages.

Last but not the least, deepfake industry is predicted to be a major revolution and influence the future of interaction and communications. Teleconferencing and social networks could possibly employ deepfakes to offer people more a more immersive and increased savoring of communication methods and means. This could act as a meeting point, which connects the physical touch with the digital touch; turn the phase around to welcome a new paradigm of touch.

9. PRECAUTIONARY MEASURES AND RECOMMENDATIONS

9.1 Mitigation Strategies for Potential Misuse of Deepfakes

The growth rate of deepfake technology is escalating with the advantage of many benefits, coming with the disadvantage of potential exploitation thus require proper management. Another threat is that the deepfakes can be employed for either producing fake news, defamation, or staged evidence, which is all considered unauthorized uses of the technology (Albahar et.al,2019).

a. **Technological Solutions for Detection:** It is imperative to build concrete and efficient deepfake detectors. These tools employed artificial intelligence to analyze the videos and signs of manipulation which have been overlooked by human eyes. It is as a result of such advanced methods of machine learning that the current detection systems can continue to pose detection challenges to more enhanced deepfake generation models. It is crucial to note that the tech firms, researchers, and cybersecurity practitioners' cooperation is vital to refine these detection abilities constantly.

b. **Digital Watermarking and Authentication:** Sometimes, it is possible to use digital watermarks or signatures within genuine media in order to effectively guarantee their authenticity. Blockchain technology is considered to be a unique concept that can be effectively used to ensure media authentication since it can provide an unaltered and transparent record of the original and subsequent data.

This can help reveal the origin of media files and guarantee customers that they are original.

c. **Public Awareness and Education**: Awareness of the public regarding the presence and risks of deepfakes is a key need. The participants' awareness-raising campaigns can contribute to individuals realizing that the content that has been presented to them is a deepfake and that it is necessary to check the source of information. Effective education programs in media literacy for people in schools, community, and religious institutions will give them a tool to assess content in media and the internet.

d. **Legal and Regulatory Frameworks:** To start with, Deepfakes require well-defined legal frameworks and policies that are within the jurisdiction of government and regulatory authorities. Such regulations should incorporate sanctions for misuse of deep fake particularly in the defamation, fraudulent activities, and electoral manipulation. It is also important to recall the world aspects of digital media as a reason for international collaboration.

e. **Collaborative Efforts:** Shared efforts of the technology firms, authorities, and the CSOs are needed to form the cohort policies with the view of dealing with deepfakes. To enhance the utilization of deepfake technology while at the same time reducing its improper use in the society, the industry should set standards and employ best practices that address the questionable application of deepfakes.

9.2 Suggestions for Strategy in Relation to Deepfake Technology for Various Stakeholders

Therefore, due to the nature of deepfake technology as a phenomenon that encompasses both threats and possibilities, a set of measures, which should be collectively and comprehensively addresses by governments, technology companies, academic institutions, and the public. Here are some recommendations for each group (Leibowicz et.al,2021):

Governments:

a. **Policy Development:** To curb the misuse of deepfake technology, the existing laws and policies should be developed, and severe consequences ordered against any act of malice.

b. **Support Research:** Invest in and drive research toward new and better deepfake forensics and personal identity verification.

c. **International Collaboration:** Call for international cooperation so that different countries focus on dealing with deepfakes as one interrelated problem (Syed Jahangir Badashah et.al, 2023).

Technology Companies:

a. **Invest in Detection Tools:** Invest in further research towards replicating advanced and complex deepfake detection tools and then incorporate such tools in social media applications.
b. **Transparency and Accountability:** Therefore, community standards, policies and procedures for moderating deepfake content must be unambiguous, so that users understand how such content is distinguished and controlled.
c. **Ethical Guidelines:** In other words, cultural norms should be set and followed when using deepfake and its consequential technologies so that it is properly utilized in the benefit of society(T Venkat Narayana Rao et.al,2022).

Academic Institutions:

a. **Research and Innovation:** Focus on the new resources to create deepfakes and the methods to identify the threats that have not been used widely yet.
b. **Educational Programs:** It is crucial to create and provide educational courses about the influence and use of media, AI existence and its possible misuse, and the technical side of deep fake as an educational platform for the next generations.

General Public:

a. **Media Literacy:** reduce the instances of fake content by involving everyone especially the youth in media literacy training to recognize originality.
b. **Critical Thinking:** Encourage users to exercise caution before posting any information on social media platforms by demanding critical thinking and reinforcing the notion that, while the information circulating online may be true, its source should be questioned.
c. **Advocacy:** Call for the right application and governance of deep fake and stand for any programs that would try to curb the misuse of deep fake.

10. CONCLUSION

In conclusion, deepfake technology is a brilliant advancement in machine learning that could produce highly realistic synthetic media. Such advancements have arisen from serious algorithmic advancements, training methodologies, and the availability of large datasets, which make it more convincing to produce fake images and videos. Deepfakes have therefore rapidly transitioned from experimental concepts to tools for wider democratization in content creation. Although this opens new potential avenues for creative industries such as entertainment, advertising, and media, it also raises serious ethical and security issues.

Deepfake tools have become ubiquitous, and it has been spurred on the one hand by mainstream use, on the other hand, by malicious ones. Deepfakes hold great potential for good. First, in the entertainment industry, it is doing better storytelling, hence immersing experiences. They create highly personalized and interactive advertisements in advertising that can touch the hearts of all sorts of different audiences. Moreover, deepfake technology promises to find many practical applications in the field of medicine and education by producing highly realistic simulations for the purpose of training and learning. Such applications reveal a great potential for good that may be realized by utilizing deepfakes: improving creativity, efficiency, and knowledge transfer across different fields (Dr Syed Jahangir Badashah et.al,2022).

However, this potential threat of misuse remains one of the pressing concerns. This possibility of making fake but very convincing content will unleash malicious activities, such as misinformation campaigns, identity theft, and privacy violations. Deepfakes can be employed to affect public opinions, produce fake news, or even cause harm. For instance, revenge porn or cyberbullying can start taking place through such manipulations. Risks therefore imply that deepfakes would need the proper legal frameworks and rules to ensure that it is responsibly and ethically used.

As the challenges are being listened to, governments and policymakers begin addressing them proactively through legislative actions. The aim is to fight the harms created by deepfakes. Deepfakes are found in laws to punish malicious creation and distribution of deepfakes as well as efforts on technological solutions like deepfake detection systems. However, given that technological development is explosive in nature, innovation in legal, technical, and ethics standard will be global, critical in being ahead of potential threats in deepfakes.

In the future therefore, the general public and developers of technology must use deepfakes responsibly. Without being innately harmful in its nature, the current risks and dangers that misuse of this technology entails create a need for very strong guidelines. It should be a joint effort aimed at enhancing deepfake detection methods and the enforcement of laws that try to maintain a boundary on its use, as well as education pertaining to its ethical applicability. This is done to enjoy the fruits of deepfake technology without any adverse effects that could be seriously resultant enough for social harm.

In a nutshell, deepfake technology has the tremendous ability to improve human welfare; development and dissemination require, however, maximum consideration of ethical implications. Perfecting this innovative technology and exercising responsible oversight over its development and application can ensure that such deepfake technology will advance society instead of damaging it.

REFERENCES

Albahar, M., & Almalki, J. (2019). Deepfakes: Threats and countermeasures systematic review. *Journal of Theoretical and Applied Information Technology*, 97(22), 3242–3250.

Barnes, C., & Barraclough, T. (2020). Deepfakes and synthetic media. In *Emerging technologies and international security* (pp. 206–220). Routledge. DOI: 10.4324/9780367808846-16

Birrer, A., & Just, N. (2024). What we know and don't know about deepfakes: An investigation into the state of the research and regulatory landscape. new media & society, 14614448241253138.

Campbell, C., Plangger, K., Sands, S., & Kietzmann, J. (2022). Preparing for an era of deepfakes and AI-generated ads: A framework for understanding responses to manipulated advertising. *Journal of Advertising*, 51(1), 22–38. DOI: 10.1080/00913367.2021.1909515

Diakopoulos, N., & Johnson, D. (2021). Anticipating and addressing the ethical implications of deepfakes in the context of elections. *New Media & Society*, 23(7), 2072–2098. DOI: 10.1177/1461444820925811

Farid, H. (2022). Creating, using, misusing, and detecting deep fakes. *Journal of Online Trust & Safety*, 1(4). Advance online publication. DOI: 10.54501/jots.v1i4.56

Gil, R., Virgili-Gomà, J., López-Gil, J. M., & García, R. (2023). Deepfakes: Evolution and trends. *Soft Computing*, 27(16), 11295–11318. DOI: 10.1007/s00500-023-08605-y

Hancock, J. T., & Bailenson, J. N. (2021). The social impact of deepfakes. *Cyberpsychology, Behavior, and Social Networking*, 24(3), 149–152. DOI: 10.1089/cyber.2021.29208.jth PMID: 33760669

Heidari, A., Jafari Navimipour, N., Dag, H., & Unal, M. (2024). Deepfake detection using deep learning methods: A systematic and comprehensive review. *Wiley Interdisciplinary Reviews. Data Mining and Knowledge Discovery*, 14(2), e1520. DOI: 10.1002/widm.1520

Jones, V. A. (2020). Artificial intelligence enabled deepfake technology: The emergence of a new threat (Doctoral dissertation, Utica College).

Karpinska-Krakowiak, M., & Eisend, M. (2024). Realistic Portrayals of Untrue Information: The Effects of Deepfaked Ads and Different Types of Disclosures. *Journal of Advertising*, ●●●, 1–11. DOI: 10.1080/00913367.2024.2306415

Krishna, D. (2020). Deepfakes, online platforms, and a novel proposal for transparency, collaboration, and education. *Rich. JL & Tech.*, 27, 1.

Kugler, M. B., & Pace, C. (2021). Deepfake privacy: Attitudes and regulation. *Nw. UL Rev.*, 116, 611.

Kwok, A. O., & Koh, S. G. (2021). Deepfake: A social construction of technology perspective. *Current Issues in Tourism*, 24(13), 1798–1802. DOI: 10.1080/13683500.2020.1738357

Leibowicz, C. R., McGregor, S., & Ovadya, A. (2021, July). The deepfake detection dilemma: A multistakeholder exploration of adversarial dynamics in synthetic media. In Proceedings of the 2021 AAAI/ACM Conference on AI, Ethics, and Society (pp. 736-744). DOI: 10.1145/3461702.3462584

Millière, R. (2022). Deep learning and synthetic media. *Synthese*, 200(3), 231. DOI: 10.1007/s11229-022-03739-2

Qureshi, J., & Khan, S. (2024). *Artificial Intelligence (AI) Deepfakes in Healthcare Systems: A Double-Edged Sword?* Balancing Opportunities and Navigating Risks.

Robot Using Raspberry Pi. Journal of Algebraic Statistics Web of Science, Volume 13, Issue 2, e-ISSN: 1309-3452, June 2022, pages 2165-2172.

Sharma, M., & Kaur, M. (2022). A review of Deepfake technology: An emerging AI threat. Soft Computing for Security Applications. *Proceedings of ICSCS*, 2021, 605–619.

Badashah, S. J., Basha, S. S., Ahamed, S. R., Subba Rao, S. P. V., Janardhan Raju, M., & Mallikarjun, M. (2023). Taylor-Gorilla troops optimized deep learning network for surface roughness estimation. *Network (Bristol, England)*, 34(4), 221–249.

Van der Sloot, B., & Wagensveld, Y. (2022). Deepfakes: Regulatory challenges for the synthetic society. *Computer Law & Security Report*, 46, 105716. DOI: 10.1016/j.clsr.2022.105716

Rao, T. V. N., Govardhan, A., & Badashah, S. J. (2011). Statistical analysis for performance evaluation of image segmentation quality using edge detection algorithms. *International Journal of Advanced Networking and Applications*, 3(3), 1184.

Rao, T. V. N., Unnisa, A., & Sreni, K. (2020). Medicine recommendation system based on patient reviews. *Int J Sci Technol Res*, 9, 3308–3312.

Rao, T. V. N., & Manasa, S. (2019). Artificial neural networks for soil quality and crop yield prediction using machine learning. *International Journal on Future Revolution in Computer Science & Communication Engineering*, 5(1), 57–60.

Rao, T. V. N., & Reddy, G. R. (2019). Prediction Of Soil Quality Using Machine Learning Techniques. *International Journal of Scientific & Technology Research*, 8(11), 1309–1313.

Sharma, L. (Ed.). (2020). *Towards smart world: homes to cities using internet of things*. CRC Press.

Rao, T. V. N., Unnisa, A., & Sreni, K. (2020). Medicine recommendation system based on patient reviews. *Int J Sci Technol Res*, 9, 3308–3312.

Venkat Narayana Rao, T., & Yellu, K. R. (2016). Automatic Safety Home Bell System with Message Enabled Features, International Journal of Science. *Engineering and Computer Technology*, 6, 10.

Westerlund, M. (2019). The emergence of deepfake technology: A review. *Technology Innovation Management Review*, 9(11), 39–52. DOI: 10.22215/timreview/1282

Chapter 12
Preventing Deepfakes From Being Used for Impersonation and Defamation

Ashu M. G. Solo
https://orcid.org/0000-0002-1810-9974
Maverick Trailblazers Inc., USA

ABSTRACT

As technology advances, deepfakes have become a problem. Deepfakes can be used for impersonation and defamation, two of the major problems of the information age. Deepfakes for impersonation have been used to create fake intimate images. This research paper makes 9 recommendations for website policies, 17 recommendations for public policies, and 7 recommendations for public education to combat the use of deepfakes for impersonation and defamation. The author of this research paper previously proposed a field called misinformation identification engineering involving the development of algorithms and software to find, flag, or remove misinformation and disinformation on websites and in other documents.

INTRODUCTION

Deepfakes are videos featuring humans manipulated by computational intelligence. Deepfakes can be used to impersonate individuals while conveying disinformation or defamatory information (Blankenship, 2021). The use of deepfakes to impersonate politicians while conveying misinformation is an unethical form of political engineering or computational politics (Solo, 2011, 2014, 2017, 2019d).

DOI: 10.4018/979-8-3693-6890-9.ch012

Copyright © 2025, IGI Global Scientific Publishing. Copying or distributing in print or electronic forms without written permission of IGI Global Scientific Publishing is prohibited.

As technology advances, more sophisticated means can be used to fool people with defamation or impersonation.

Deepfakes can be used for defamation (Collins, 2011; Sternberg, 2019; Truth vs. Lies, 2022) and impersonation (Cox, 2014; Koch, 2016; Reznik, 2013), which are two forms of cyberbullying (Esteban et al., 2022; Guarini et al., 2023; Longobardi et al., 2022, 2023; Mc Guckin & Corcoran, 2015; Navarro, 2019; Rey et al., 2021; Schultze-Krumbholz, 2022; Smith et al., 2019; Smith et al., 2023). Impersonation with deepfakes can include fake intimate images (Cyberbullying and the Non-consensual Distribution of Intimate Images, 2023).

Defamation against an individual involves the communication of false statements that harm the individual's reputation. Internet defamation, inter alia, severely harms people's reputations; prevents them from getting gainful employment; ruins romantic relationships; causes depression, anxiety, and distress; causes mental health problems; etc.

People can be impersonated for many purposes such as to harm their reputations, to gain personal information on them, to cause them to lose business, to cause them to lose friends, to write exams for them, to vote for them, to spread false information about them, etc. Internet impersonation, inter alia, severely harms people's reputations; prevents them from getting gainful employment; ruins romantic relationships; causes depression, anxiety, and distress; causes mental health problems; etc.

Now fake intimate images are being created of people, especially famous actors and singers. People frequently assume that fake intimate images are real intimate images. Distribution of fake intimate images, can, inter alia, violate privacy; humiliate people; harm reputations; cause depression, anxiety, and distress; cause mental health problems; etc. Therefore, nonconsensual distribution of synthetic or fake intimate images should be prohibited.

In the old days, it was hard to spread false information or private information about people. It had to be done by telling people face to face, handing out flyers, putting up posters, etc. Only the mainstream media had the means to reach a lot of people. The mainstream media is generally more careful in what it says, although it has crossed the line into defamation many times too, but usually not nearly as bad as people can commit defamation on the world wide web. Now deepfakes can be used to spread false information about people on the web for the world to see (Banerjee & Chua, 2019; Chiluwa, 2019; Hage et al., 2020; Pal & Banerjee, 2019; Reynard, 2019; Solo, 2019a, 2019b, 2019e, 2020, 2021, 2023c). Defamation, impersonation, and nonconsensual distribution of intimate images are three of the major new problems of the information age.

Social networks like *Facebook* and *Twitter* can be used to spread deepfakes and defamatory information. New software can be used to detect cyberbullying on social networks (Balakrishnan et al., 2019) .

Fake news, which is used to spread disinformation or defamatory information, is a growing problem (Bradshaw & Howard, 2019; Chiluwa & Samoilenko, 2019; Dalkir & Katz, 2020; Rezayi et al., 2018; Stengel, 2019; Watts, 2018). Deepfakes can be used to spread fake news.

Deepfakes, online fake news, and online defamation targeting politicians are an unethical type of network politics (Solo & Bishop, 2011, 2014, 2016, 2017). The development of deepfakes to spread disinformation on politics is an unethical form of political engineering or computational politics (Solo, 2011, 2014, 2017, 2019d). Also, the development of spambots to spread disinformation on politics with or without deepfakes is an unethical form of political engineering or computational politics.

Most private employers these days do web searches on prospective employees to see what turns up. If they have a bunch of people applying for one position, as is usually the case, they aren't going to risk selecting the candidate with a bunch of injurious claims about him on the web whether or not they can determine if it's true.

Humans have a hard time distinguishing between true and false information (Kaufman, 2018; Marsh et al., 2016; O'Connor & Weatherall, 2022; Vosoughi et al., 2018). Andrew Butler, an associate professor of psychological and brain sciences at Washington University in St. Louis, said, "Even when people have knowledge that directly contradicts false information, they fail to detect that it is false information (Kaufman, 2018)." Furthermore, humans are predisposed to believing false information. Butler said, "People have a bias to assume truth (Kaufman, 2018)." A research study found that *Twitter* users are twice as likely to repost fake news as they are to repost real news (Kaufman, 2018; Vosoughi et al., 2018).

The civil remedies for dealing with defamation are extremely inadequate. Lawyer fees for a defamation claim in the United States are typically in the range of $30,000 USD or more. The vast majority of defamation victims can't afford the legal costs. A civil lawyer with expertise in defamation law said that he got inquiries from a bunch of people defamed on an online hate group, but none could afford to retain him. Most lawyers charge more than this lawyer who has been practicing for a few years. When someone is defamed on the web, the defamation typically remains on the Internet until a civil court judgment is obtained and this usually takes years. In the mean time, the victim continues to accumulate all kinds of damages. The author of this research paper has seen people being defamed on the web contemplate criminal violence as the only means they have to get the defamation removed.

Website policies need to be updated as recommended in this research paper to stop defamation, impersonation, and sharing of intimate images. Also, as recommended in this research paper, laws need to be updated for fighting online defamation, impersonation, and sharing of intimate images. Furthermore, as recommended in this research paper, there needs to be better public education for fighting online defamation and impersonation.

WEBSITE POLICY RECOMMENDATIONS

Following are nine recommendations for responsible website policies to prevent and fight defamation, impersonation, and sharing of intimate images (Solo, 2023c):

1. Websites must require users to provide proof of their real identities either by providing identification or by making a payment with a credit card or bank card. Websites should not allow anonymous payments with cryptocurrency. Identity verification will prevent most cases of defamation and impersonation because people will be more likely to be held accountable for their actions. People who get banned from websites often rejoin with another name. Identity verification will prevent this too.
2. Websites should require users to use their real names on their accounts. This will prevent most cases of defamation and impersonation because subpoenas or search warrants won't be needed to determine the identities of users.
3. Websites must require users to provide proof of their addresses either by providing identification or by making a payment with a credit card or bank card. Users should be required to provide addresses where they can be served with civil claims, subpoenas, search warrants, etc. for content on their profiles. This information might be required by law enforcement for defamation or impersonation. This information might also be required by people suing for defamation or impersonation. Address information must be turned over with search warrants or subpoenas.
4. Websites should record the Internet protocol (IP) addresses of its website users for five years. For each post made on an online forum, websites should record the IP address of the individual who made the post and should be required to store this information for five years. This information might be required by law enforcement for defamation or impersonation. This information might also be required by people suing for defamation or impersonation. IP address information must be turned over with search warrants or subpoenas. If websites want to avoid dealing with search warrants and subpoenas, it can publish a user's IP address with every post that she makes.
5. Websites should ban real and fake pornography and nudity so people can't share real or fake intimate images of others. This should include real and fake intimate images. If anyone reports nudity or pornography on the website, an administrator should immediately delete it after verifying that it's there. Any user who posts pornography or nudity should be immediately banned. Any user who posts pornography or nudity of a minor should be immediately reported to the police.

6. If disinformation isn't indexed by search engines, then it will do much less damage to a person's reputation. Websites should block search engines from indexing user posts on its website. This can easily be done with a no index metatag on each webpage with a user post.
7. If disinformation is removed from a website, it will still appear in search engine caches until they are updated. If a webpage is changed or taken down, archiving websites shouldn't be making old information available to the public. Therefore, websites should block web archiving systems and search engines from archiving user posts on its website. This can easily be done with noarchive and nosnippet metatags on each webpage with a user post.
8. If someone complains about a defamatory statement on a website and administrators for the website can't verify that a statement is not defamatory, website administrators should remove that content.
9. If someone complains about impersonation on a website, then website administrators should remove that content.

PUBLIC POLICY RECOMMENDATIONS

Laws and public policies need to be updated to deal with online defamation and impersonation in the information age. Below are 17 recommendations for public policies to effectively combat online defamation, impersonation, and nonconsensual distribution of intimate images on websites (Solo, 2019a, 2019b, 2019c, 2019e, 2020, 2021, 2023c):

1. Criminal laws for defamation need to be enforced. These laws are rarely enforced in the U.S. and Canada.
2. Defamation should be a criminal offense in every country.
3. Defamation should be a civil tort in every country.
4. Impersonation should be a criminal offense in every country.
5. Impersonation should be a civil tort in every country.
6. Nonconsensual distribution of an intimate image that is real or fake should be a criminal offense in every country.
7. Nonconsensual distribution of an intimate image that is real or fake should be a civil tort in every country.
8. Small claims courts must be equipped to deal with defamation and impersonation lawsuits and must be able to order preliminary and permanent injunctions. Most victims do not have the expertise for pro se legal representation in higher courts and can't afford the costs of lawyers to represent them in higher courts.

9. Every website owner should be required to record the IP addresses of its website users for five years. For each post made on an online forum, the website owner should be required to record the IP address of the individual who made the post and should be required to store this information for five years. This information might be required by law enforcement for defamation, impersonation, or nonconsensual distribution of intimate images. This information might also be required by people suing for defamation, impersonation, or nonconsensual distribution of intimate images. IP address information must be turned over with search warrants or subpoenas.

10. No website owner should be able to hide her identity in a domain name registration. Every website owner should be required to provide an address in a domain name registration where he can be served with civil claims, subpoenas, search warrants, etc. for content on the website.

11. A website owner should be liable for defamation, impersonation, or nonconsensual distribution of intimate images by a website user if the website owner doesn't delete the defamation, impersonation, or intimate image after it's complained about by the subject of the defamation, impersonation, or nonconsensual distribution of intimate images. In the United States, courts have interpreted section 230 of the Communications Decency Act (CDA) to give website owners immunity from defamation by website users (Browne-Barbour, 2015; Communications Decency Act, 1996). In the United Kingdom, under the Defamation Act 2013, a website owner can be liable for defamation by a website user if it isn't deleted after being complained about (Defamation Act 2013, 2013).

12. Search engines should be stopped from indexing and displaying hyperlinks to websites notorious for defamation. There should also be public pressure on search engine companies to stop indexing and displaying hyperlinks to websites notorious for defamation.

13. Archiving websites including Google should be stopped from caching or archiving websites notorious for defamation. There should also be public pressure on archiving website companies to stop caching or archiving websites notorious for defamation. If disinformation is removed from a website, it will still appear in search engine caches until they are updated. If a webpage is changed or taken down, archiving websites shouldn't be making old information available to the public.

14. Search engines should be required to follow injunctions to remove hyperlinks to defamation, impersonation, or nonconsensual intimate images on third party websites as well as snippets of defamation, impersonation, or nonconsensual intimate images on third party websites from search engine return pages.

15. Governments should block access to websites that don't comply with the policies above.

16. Foreign judgments for defamation, impersonation, or nonconsensual distribution of intimate images must be enforceable in the U.S. It would be impossible for a middle class or poor person in a developing country who is being defamed or impersonated on an American website to afford a lawyer in the U.S. to handle a civil claim. People should be able to sue for defamation, impersonation, or nonconsensual distribution of intimate images in their own countries and get judgments enforced in the U.S. A defamation judgment in one country should be enforceable in all other countries.

17. There needs to be an international Internet safety commission to quickly determine that content should be removed from the world wide web. If a website administrator doesn't comply with removal orders, then the international Internet safety commission should be able to order a website removed from the world wide web. The international Internet safety commission is needed because it takes a long time for court cases to be adjudicated, most people can't afford the legal fees for court cases, and most people don't have the legal expertise for court cases. Until there is an international Internet safety commission, each country should have its own Internet safety commission to determine if content should be removed from the world wide web and order the website to be blocked within the country if the website administrator doesn't comply with removal orders. Court cases can still be filed to seek awards of monetary damages for unlawful content on the web.

PUBLIC EDUCATION RECOMMENDATIONS

The public needs to be better educated on how to fight back against online defamation and impersonation. Following are seven recommendations on educating the public to combat online defamation and impersonation (Solo, 2021, 2023c):

1. Courthouses, police departments, libraries, and government offices should have free literature available to the public on how to fight online defamation, impersonation, and other violations of torts. The literature should provide sample documents for civil claims related to defamation and impersonation so that people know how to prepare civil claim documents.

2. Civil courts should have free lawyers available to provide guidance and legal advice to self-represented plaintiffs and defendants in civil litigation including litigation for defamation and impersonation. At a civil court, one lawyer could assist plaintiffs and a different lawyer could assist defendants so there is no conflict of interest.

3. Governments should have software developed that can ask users questions about their cases and then generate civil claim documents for them for defamation, impersonation, and other cases. This software should be made available online for free.
4. The courts should offer on-demand noncredit courses on how to sue someone for defamation, impersonation, and other violations of the law. These courses should be made available for free online.
5. American and Canadian law degrees should be four-year undergraduate degrees that can be done right out of high school like in most other countries. Because a law degree is a graduate degree in the U.S. and Canada, there aren't enough lawyers in these countries. As a result, there is a lack of legal knowledge among the general public and lawyers charge exorbitant fees. A lot of people don't want to or can't afford to do a four-year undergraduate degree before doing a three-year law degree. Someone doesn't need years of study in another field or a degree in another field to study law. If someone can start a bachelor's degree in engineering, science, or math right out of high school, there's no reason she can't start a law degree right out of high school. If law degrees were four-year undergraduate degrees, they could include three years of law courses and one year of courses in other subjects. Law degrees should be as pervasive as business degrees, arts degrees, and education degrees. In the United Kingdom, anyone who gets a law degree should be able to become a barrister and solicitor.
6. Universities should offer individual courses on civil litigation and lawsuit document preparation for students who aren't doing degrees in law. The author of this research paper included a university course on civil litigation and lawsuit document preparation in the proposed curriculum of new academic programs that he designed for published research papers (Solo, 2023a, 2023b). Including a course like this in the curriculum will give people the basic knowledge they need to sue for online defamation, online impersonation, nonconsensual distribution of intimate images, and other illegal acts.
7. Each high school should offer a course on civil litigation and lawsuit document preparation.

CONCLUSION

Online defamation (Solo, 2019a, 2019b, 2019e, 2020, 2021, 2023c) and online impersonation (Solo, 2019c, 2020, 2021, 2023c) are two of the major problems of the information age. Another major problem of the information age is online doxing (Solo, 2019a, 2019b, 2019e, 2020,2021, 2023c). Websites need to reform their policies as described with 9 recommendations in this research paper. Also, the laws and public policies need to be updated as described with 17 recommendations in this research paper. Finally, the public needs to be better educated on how to fight back against these problems as described with 7 recommendations in this research paper.

New research and development fields are needed to develop algorithms and software that can find, flag, or remove misinformation and disinformation. The author of this research paper previously proposed a field called *misinformation identification engineering* (Solo, 2021; Solo, 2023c) to develop algorithms and software to find, flag, or remove misinformation and disinformation on websites and in other documents.

REFERENCES

Balakrishnan, V., Khan, S., Fernandez, T., & Arabnia, H. R. (2019). Cyberbullying Detection on Twitter Using Big Five and Dark Triad Features. *Elsevier Journal of Personality and Individual Differences* (The Official Journal of the International Society for the Study of Individual Differences (ISSID)), *141*, 252-257. URL: https://www.sciencedirect.com/science/article/pii/S0191886919300364

Banerjee, S., & Chua, A. Y. K. (2019). Toward a Theoretical Model of Authentic and Fake User-Generated Online Reviews. In Chiluwa, I. E., & Samoilenko, S. A. (Eds.), *Handbook of Research on Deception, Fake News, and Misinformation Online* (pp. 104–120). IGI Global., URL https://www.igi-global.com/chapter/toward-a-theoretical-model-of-authentic-and-fake-user-generated-online-reviews/230748 DOI: 10.4018/978-1-5225-8535-0.ch007

Blankenship, R. J. (Ed.). (2021). *Deep Fakes, Fake News, and Misinformation in Online Teaching and Learning Technologies*. IGI Global., URL https://www.igi-global.com/book/deep-fakes-fake-news-misinformation/255423 DOI: 10.4018/978-1-7998-6474-5

Bradshaw, S., & Howard, P. N. (2019). *The Global Disinformation Order: 2019 Global Inventory of Organised Social Media Manipulation*. Computational Propaganda Research Project. Oxford Internet Institute, University of Oxford. URL: https://comprop.oii.ox.ac.uk/wp-content/uploads/sites/93/2019/09/CyberTroop-Report19.pdf

Browne-Barbour, V. S. (2015). Losing Their Licence to Libel: Revisiting § 230 Immunity. *Berkeley Technology Law Journal*, 30(2), 1505–1560. https://btlj.org/data/articles2015/vol30/30_2/1505-1560_Browne%20Barbour.pdf

Chiluwa, I. E., & Samoilenko, S. A. (Eds.). (2019). *Handbook of Research on Deception, Fake News, and Misinformation Online*. IGI Global., URL https://www.igi-global.com/book/handbook-research-deception-fake-news/218293 DOI: 10.4018/978-1-5225-8535-0

Collins, M. (2011). *The Law of Defamation and the Internet* (3rd ed.). Oxford University Press.

Communications Decency Act, United States, 47 U.S.C. § 230. (1996). URL: https://uscode.house.gov/view.xhtml?req=communications+decency+act+section+230

Cox, C. (2014). Protecting Victims of Cyberstalking, Cyberharassment, and Online Impersonation through Prosecutions and Effective Laws. *Jurimetrics*, 54(3), 277–302. https://www.jstor.org/stable/24395601?seq=1#page_scan_tab_contents

Cyberbullying and the Non-consensual Distribution of Intimate Images, Government of Canada. (2023). URL: https://www.justice.gc.ca/eng/rp-pr/other-autre/cndii-cdncii/p6.html

Dalkir, K., & Katz, R. (2020). *Navigating Fake News, Alternative Facts, and Misinformation in a Post-Truth World.* IGI Global. URL: https://www.igi-global.com/book/navigating-fake-news-alternative-facts/236998

Defamation Act 2013, United Kingdom. (2013). URL: https://www.legislation.gov.uk/ukpga/2013/26

Ebrahimi, M. (Ed.). (2022). *Information Manipulation and Its Impact Across All Industries.* IGI Global., URL https://www.igi-global.com/book/information-manipulation-its-impact-across/268790 DOI: 10.4018/978-1-7998-8235-0

Esteban, C. R., Mateo, I. M., & Fernández-Sogorb, A. (Eds.). (2022). Special Issue "Research in Cyberbullying and Cybervictimization." *European Journal of Investigation in Health, Psychology and Education.* MDPI. URL: https://www.mdpi.com/journal/ejihpe/special_issues/cyberbulling_victimization

Guarini, A., Brighi, A., Skrzypiec, G., & Slee, P. T. (Eds.). (2023). Special Issue "Bullying and Cyberbullying: Definition, Prevalence Rates, Risk/Protective Factors, and Interventions." *International Journal of Environmental Research and Public Health.* MDPI. URL: https://www.mdpi.com/journal/ijerph/special_issues/bullying_interventions

Hage, H., Aimeur, E., & Guedid, A. (2020). Understanding the Landscape of Online Deception. In Dalkir, K., & Katz, R. (Eds.), *Navigating Fake News, Alternative Facts, and Misinformation in a Post-Truth World* (pp. 290–317). IGI Global., URL https://www.igi-global.com/book/navigating-fake-news-alternative-facts/236998 DOI: 10.4018/978-1-7998-2543-2.ch014

Information Resources Management Association. (2021). *Research Anthology on Fake News, Political Warfare, and Combatting the Spread of Misinformation.* IGI Global. URL: https://www.igi-global.com/book/research-anthology-fake-news-political/262491

Kaufman, M. (2018, March 8). Twitter users are twice as likely to retweet fake news stories than authentic ones. *Mashable.* URL: https://mashable.com/2018/03/08/twitter-users-retweet-fake-news-study/

Koch, C. M. (2016). To Catch a Catfish: A Statutory Solution for Victims of Online Impersonation. *University of Colorado Law Review*, 88(1). http://lawreview.colorado.edu/wp-content/uploads/2017/01/12.-88.1-Koch_FinalRevised.pdf

Longobardi, C., Jungert, T., & Badenes-Ribera, L. (Eds.). (2022). Special Issue "Cyberbullying, Mental Health and Behavioral Difficulties in Early Adolescents." *International Journal of Environmental Research and Public Health.* MDPI. URL: https://www.mdpi.com/journal/ijerph/special_issues/Cyberbullying_Adolescents

Longobardi, C., Jungert, T., & Badenes-Ribera, L. (Eds.). (2023). Special Issue "2nd Edition: Bullying and Cyberbullying, Mental Health and Behavioral Difficulties." *International Journal of Environmental Research and Public Health.* MDPI. URL: https://www.mdpi.com/journal/ijerph/special_issues/QVK4XMRQ64

Marsh, E. J., Cantor, A. D., & Brashier, N. M. (2016). Believing that Humans Swallow Spiders in Their Sleep: False Beliefs as Side Effects of the Processes that Support Accurate Knowledge. *Psychology of Learning and Motivation*, 64, 93–132. https://www.sciencedirect.com/science/article/pii/S0079742115000341. DOI: 10.1016/bs.plm.2015.09.003

Mc Guckin, C., & Corcoran, L. (Eds.). (2015). Special Issue "Cyberbullying: Where Are We Now? A Cross-National Understanding." *Societies.* MDPI. URL: https://www.mdpi.com/journal/societies/special_issues/cyberbulling

Navarro, R. (Ed.). (2019). Special Issue "Family, Bullying and Cyberbullying." *Social Sciences.* MDPI. URL: https://www.mdpi.com/journal/socsci/special_issues/family_bullying_and_cyberbullying

O'Connor, C., & Weatherall, J. O. (2022). Why We Trust Lies. *Scientific American.*

Pal, A., & Banerjee, S. (2019). Understanding Online Falsehood from the Perspective of Social Problem. In Chiluwa, I. E., & Samoilenko, S. A. (Eds.), *Handbook of Research on Deception, Fake News, and Misinformation Online* (pp. 1–17). IGI Global., URL https://www.igi-global.com/chapter/understanding-online-falsehood-from-the-perspective-of-social-problem/230742 DOI: 10.4018/978-1-5225-8535-0.ch001

Rey, L., Peláez-Fernández, M. A., & Quintana-Orts, C. (Eds.). (2021). Special Issue "Psychological Well-being: Cyberbullying & Internet Use." *International Journal of Environmental Research and Public Health.* MDPI. URL: https://www.mdpi.com/journal/ijerph/special_issues/Cyberbullying

Reynard, L. J. (2019). Troll Farm: Anonymity as a Weapon for Online Character Assassination. In Chiluwa, I. E. (Ed.), *Handbook of Research on Deception, Fake News, and Misinformation Online* (pp. 392–419). IGI Global., URL https://www.igi-global.com/chapter/troll-farm/230765 DOI: 10.4018/978-1-5225-8535-0.ch021

Rezayi, S., Balakrishnan, V., Arabnia, S., & Arabnia, H. R. (2018). Fake News and Cyberbullying in the Modern Era. In *Proceedings of the International Conference on Computational Science and Computational Intelligence (CSCI 2018)*. IEEE., URL https://ieeexplore.ieee.org/document/8947876 DOI: 10.1109/CSCI46756.2018.00010

Reznik, M. (2013). Identity Theft on Social Networking Sites: Developing Issues of Internet Impersonation. *Touro Law Review*, 29(2), 12. https://digitalcommons.tourolaw.edu/cgi/viewcontent.cgi?article=1472&context=lawreview

Schultze-Krumbholz, A. (Ed.). (2022). Special Issue "Bullying and Cyberbullying: Challenges toward a Sustainable Campus." *Sustainability*. MDPI. URL: https://www.mdpi.com/journal/sustainability/special_issues/BCCSC

Smith, P., Bauman, S., & Wong, D. (Eds.). (2019). Special Issue "Interventions to Reduce Bullying and Cyberbullying." *International Journal of Environmental Research and Public Health*. MDPI. URL: https://www.mdpi.com/journal/ijerph/special_issues/bullying_cyberbullying

Smith, P., Varela, J., & Barlett, C. (Eds.). (2023). Special Issue "Cyberbullying from a Lifespan Perspective." *International Journal of Environmental Research and Public Health*. MDPI. URL: https://www.mdpi.com/journal/ijerph/special_issues/Cyberbullying_sensors

Solo, A. M. G. (2011). The New Fields of Public Policy Engineering, Political Engineering, Computational Public Policy, and Computational Politics. In *Proceedings of the 2011 International Conference on e-Learning, e-Business, Enterprise Information Systems, and e-Government (EEE'11)*. CSREA. URL: http://worldcomp-proceedings.com/proc/p2011/EEE5211.pdf

Solo, A. M. G. (2014). The New Interdisciplinary Fields of Political Engineering and Computational Politics. In Solo, A. M. G. (Ed.), *Political Campaigning in the Information Age* (pp. 226–232). IGI Global., URL https://www.igi-global.com/chapter/the-new-interdisciplinary-fields-of-political-engineering-and-computational-politics/109123 DOI: 10.4018/978-1-4666-6062-5.ch013

Solo, A. M. G. (2017). An Overview of the New Interdisciplinary Fields of Political Engineering and Computational Politics for the Next Frontier in Politics. In *Proceedings of the 2017 International Conference on Computational Science and Computational Intelligence (CSCI'17)*. IEEE. URL https://ieeexplore.ieee.org/document/8561084 DOI: 10.1109/CSCI.2017.319

Solo, A. M. G. (2019a). *Brief on Effectively Combatting Cyberbullying and Cyber-libel by Online Hate Groups for the Study on Online Hate of the Standing Committee on Justice and Human Rights for the House of Commons of Canada.* Standing Committee on Justice and Human Rights, House of Commons of Canada. URL: https://www.ourcommons.ca/Content/Committee/421/JUST/Brief/BR10520155/br -external/SoloAMG-e.pdf

Solo, A. M. G. (2019b). Combating Online Defamation and Doxing in the United States. In *Proceedings of the 2019 International Conference on Internet Computing and Internet of Things (ICOMP'19)*. CSREA.

Solo, A. M. G. (2019c). Combating Online Impersonation in the United States. In *Proceedings of the 6th Annual Conference on Computational Science and Computational Intelligence (CSCI 2019)*. IEEE. URL https://ieeexplore.ieee.org/document/ 9071354 DOI: 10.1109/CSCI49370.2019.00292

Solo, A. M. G. (2019d). The Interdisciplinary Fields of Political Engineering, Public Policy Engineering, Computational Politics, and Computational Public Policy. In Solo, A. M. G. (Ed.), *Handbook of Research on Politics in the Computer Age.* IGI Global. URL https://www.igi-global.com/book/handbook-research-politics -computer-age/228093

Solo, A. M. G. (2019e). *Mémoire sur la lutte efficace contre les actes de cyber-intimidation et de diffamation en ligne commis par des groupes haineux présenté au Comité permanent de la justice et des droits de la personne de la Chambre des communes du Canada dans le cadre de son étude sur la haine en ligne.* Standing Committee on Justice and Human Rights, House of Commons of Canada. URL: https://www.noscommunes.ca/Content/Committee/421/JUST/Brief/BR10520155/ br-external/SoloAMG-10061182-f.pdf

Solo, A. M. G. (2020). Fighting Online Defamation, Doxing, and Impersonation. In *Proceedings of the International Conferences: Internet Technologies & Society and Sustainability, Technology and Education 2020.* IADIS. URL: https://www.iadisportal .org/digital-library/fighting-online-defamation-doxing-and-impersonation

Solo, A. M. G. (2021). Educating the Public to Combat Online Defamation, Doxing, and Impersonation. In J. Bishop (Ed.), *Cases on Technologies in Education from Classroom 2.0 to Society 5.0* (pp. 231-242). IGI Global. URL: https://www .igi-global.com/chapter/educating-the-public-to-combat-online-defamation-doxing -and-impersonation/289193

Solo, A. M. G. (2023a). Curriculum for a New Five-Year Academic Program in Intelligent Systems Engineering and Software Engineering. In *2023 International Conference on Computational Science and Computational Intelligence (CSCI 2023)*. IEEE. DOI: 10.1109/CSCI62032.2023.00280

Solo, A. M. G. (2023b). *Curriculum for a New Four-Year Bachelor's Degree in Intelligent Systems Engineering. In 2023 Congress in Computer Science, Computer Engineering, and Applied Computing (CSCE 2023)*. IEEE. URL https://ieeexplore .ieee.org/document/10487418

Solo, A. M. G. (2023c). Preventing Twitter from Being Used for Defamation, Doxing, Impersonation, Threats of Violence, and Intimate Images. In *Proceedings of the 2023 Congress in Computer Science, Computer Engineering, and Applied Computing (CSCE 2023)*. IEEE. URL https://ieeexplore.ieee.org/document/10487355 DOI: 10.1109/CSCE60160.2023.00369

Solo, A. M. G., & Bishop, J. (2011). The New Field of Network Politics. In *Proceedings of the 2011 International Conference on e-Learning, e-Business, Enterprise Information Systems, and e-Government (EEE'11)*. URL: http://worldcomp -proceedings.com/proc/p2011/EEE5223.pdf

Solo, A. M. G., & Bishop, J. (2014). Conceptualizing Network Politics following the Arab Spring. In Solo, A. M. G. (Ed.), *Handbook of Research on Political Activism in the Information Age* (pp. 231–239). IGI Global. URL https://www.igi-global .com/chapter/conceptualizing-network-politics-following-the-arab-spring/110681 DOI: 10.4018/978-1-4666-6066-3.ch014

Solo, A. M. G., & Bishop, J. (2016). Network Politics and the Arab Spring. *International Journal of Civic Engagement and Social Change (IJCESC)*, *3*(1), 23-27. URL: https://www.igi-global.com/article/network-politics-and-the-arab-spring/149855

Solo, A. M. G., & Bishop, J. (2017). Conceptualizing Network Politics following the Arab Spring: An African Perspective. In J. Bishop (Ed.), *The Digital Media Reader* (pp. 205-212). Crocels.

Stengel, R. (2019). *Information Wars: How We Lost the Global Battle Against Disinformation and What We Can Do About It*. Grove Press.

Sternberg, P. M. (2019). *The Guide to Internet Defamation and Website Removal*. AuthorHouse.

(2022). Truth vs. Lies: The Science of Misinformation and Deception and How to Know What's Real. *Scientific American*.

Vosoughi, S., Roy, D., & Aral, S. (2018). The spread of true and false news online. *Science*, 359(6380), 1146–1151. https://science.sciencemag.org/content/359/6380/1146. DOI: 10.1126/science.aap9559 PMID: 29590045

Watts, C. (2018). *Messing with the Enemy: Surviving in a Social Media World of Hackers, Terrorists, Russians, and Fake News*. Harper.

KEY TERMS AND DEFINITIONS

Defamation: Defamation against an individual involves the communication of one or more false statements that harm the individual's reputation.

Doxing: Doxing of an individual involves the publication of an individual's private information such as his home address or family members.

Impersonation: Impersonation of an individual involves pretending to be that individual. This can be done to harm their reputations, to gain personal information on them, to cause them to lose business, to cause them to lose friends, to write exams for them, to vote for them, to spread false information about them, etc.

Cyberlibel: Cyberlibel involves the online communication of one or more false statements that harm an individual's reputation. The cyberlibel can be communicated by email, a bulletin board, an online chat, an article, a message board, a forum, a blog, a social network, another website, text messaging, etc.

Cyberbullying: Cyberbullying includes online defamation, doxing, impersonation, threats of violence, mocking, etc. This can occur by email, a bulletin board, an online chat, an article, a message board, a forum, a blog, a social network, another website, text messaging, etc.

Fake News: Fake news includes misinformation or disinformation presented as news. The fake news can be presented by a website, newspaper, magazine, radio station, television station, etc.

Deepfakes: Deepfakes are videos featuring humans manipulated by computational intelligence. Deepfakes can be used to impersonate individuals while conveying disinformation or defamatory information.

Misinformation: Misinformation is false information presented as factual information. There may or may not be an intent to deceive with this false information.

Disinformation: Disinformation is false information presented as factual information. There is an intent to deceive with this false information. All disinformation is misinformation.

Misinformation Identification Engineering: Misinformation identification engineering is a term coined by Ashu M. G. Solo for a new field to develop algorithms and software to find, flag, or remove misinformation and disinformation on websites and in other documents.

Chapter 13
Building Resilience:
Strategies for Business to Mitigate Deepfake Risks

Manjeet Singh
Amity University, Noida, India

Deepshikha Bhargava
https://orcid.org/0000-0001-7017-1372
Amity University, Noida, India

Amitabh Bhargava
Amity University, Noida, India

Kirti Singh
Amity University, Noida, India

ABSTRACT

This chapter discusses deepfake and delves into its potential benefits and inherent risks. Contrary to the negative perception generally created about deepfake technology, the authors have given evidence to highlight its positive applications and advantages. This chapter also gives equal discussion to the associated dangers in its use, particularly violations which may arise from criminal activities. With that in view, a review of the networks and applications both utilized in the creation of deepfakes, while assessing state-of-the-art open-source tools presently available, has been performed. The chapter goes further to detail the actual process for creating a deepfake video; hence, this provides some first-hand overview of the technology. The main task of this work is to contribute to enhanced resilience against deepfake-related threats by critically reflecting on various factors, such as: relevant rules and regulations within the EU and North Macedonia; an overview of the regulatory

DOI: 10.4018/979-8-3693-6890-9.ch013

Copyright © 2025, IGI Global Scientific Publishing. Copying or distributing in print or electronic forms without written permission of IGI Global Scientific Publishing is prohibited.

landscape.

INTRODUCTION

DeepFake AI is one of the most impressive achievements in machine learning and technology development. It allows the creation of incredibly realistic web images, audio, and video. The term "DeepFake" comes from a combination of "Deep Learning" and "Fake" Using generative anti-networks (GANs), the technology can accurately replicate the appearance, sound, and actions of a person, as (Kietzmann et al., 2020) highlight. Although This innovation has exciting potential in creative industries such as entertainment and advertising. But it also comes with serious risks. This includes misinformation, fraud, and privacy violations, as (Chesney and Citron, 2019) noted, as deepfake technology becomes more advanced and more widely accessible. There is therefore an urgent need for a strong ethical and legal framework to address these challenges. The rise of DeepFakes has also created significant legal and communications issues. According to the law They challenge traditional standards of honesty and responsibility. This raises difficult questions about defamation. invasion of privacy and liability (Renda, 2021) warns that creating fake, but believable situations or statements can damage reputations. destroys the integrity of the organization and even threaten national security. Make it clear that stricter regulations are needed. From a communication perspective, DeepFakes undermine trust between content creators and viewers. They accelerate the spread of misinformation. undermines the credibility of the media and this makes it more difficult to build trust in public conversations. It emphasizes that reducing the risks posed by Deepfakes will require a combination of legal measures and strategic communications efforts. With AI deepfakes, associated serious ethical, social, and regulatory challenges are emerging. A closer look into these issues, their greater implications, and some feasible solutions to this growing concern follows (Altuncu, 2022).

ETHICAL CONCERNS OF DEEPFAKES

Deepfakes often involve people without their permission and involve serious privacy violations. Where manipulated media involves explicit or defamatory content, the results can be disastrous: social stigma, career damage, and emotional harm. Current privacy laws offer victims not much recourse so far. As (Langvardt, 2020) discusses, the lack of legal redress underlines the urgent need for deepfake misuse laws that effectively take care of the victims.

Manipulation of Reality and Erosion of Truth

Deepfakes have chipped away at our ability to believe any evidence of what we see and hear, which has made it even harder to differentiate between what is fact or what is fiction. Fake quotes of public figures can deceive people, interfere with democratic processes, and undermine the confidence in institutions. On the other hand, mechanisms should be set up regarding media source verification and informed education of the public for critical evaluation of the content provided, so they could filter real information out of fabricated material (Esezoobo, 2023).

REAL-WORLD IMPACTS OF DEEPFAKES

The losses perpetuated by deepfakes are not solely experienced at the individual level; they can further destabilize institutions and even nations. According to (Paris and Donovan, 2019), deepfakes, in most instances, have been associated with fabricated news purposed for misleading societies through false information. Such RNs have the potential to spur unrest or financial market manipulation by showing a political leader uttering inflammatory remark.

Building Ethical and Regulatory Solutions

The deepfake problem cannot be tackled by any single entity; it requires much-needed collaboration with well-designed frameworks that take up both ethical and legal challenges:

1. Obtaining Consent:

Implement systems that acquire consent for using a person's likeness through blockchain-based digitized identity verification.

2. Improved Detection and Prevention:
    - Developing high-level AI tools that can trace out manipulated media.
    - Encourage tech giants to work together to establish common standards and methods for deepfake detection.
    - Integrate the detection software directly into platforms such as social media—where deepfakes are widely distributed (Busacca, 2023).
3. Establish Accountability:
    - Clearly outline the responsibilities of a person creating, disseminating, or hosting deepfakes.

- Pass legislation similar to "revenge porn" legislation that illegalizes nefarious uses of deepfakes.
4. Educating the Public:
   - Design and conduct media literacy campaigns that allow citizens to correctly recognize potential deepfakes and raise eyebrows regarding such content.
   - Introduce education programs on digital ethics and manipulation in content.

RECOMMENDATIONS FOR MOVING FORWARD

The designers of AI systems need to think in ethical terms, considering fairness and accountability, and policymakers must work hand in hand. In the same vein, clear guidelines regarding the development of AI, supported by strong legal protection, would help mitigate risks associated with deepfakes and unlock its positive potential—in the sphere of entertainment, for instance, or improving accessibility. Would you rather learn more about the development of technologies for the detection of deepfakes, or explore specific legal precedents and proposals that have to do with the subject at hand?

Deepfakes: Threats and Associated Criminal Activities

Deepfakes pose serious risks when misused for malicious purposes that amplify several threats (Nenovski, 2023). These include:

Disinformation Campaigns: Deepfakes can be utilized to spread disinformation that would further erode trust and create confusion.
Defamation: Manipulated videos show an individual saying words that they never uttered. These harms one's reputation.
Identity Theft: Deepfake technology greens lights personal identity theft for fraud.
Scams: Deepfake videos use the faces of celebrities or public figures to endorse certain products or services that are not true.

Political Manipulation: AI-generated content could turn out to be one of the forgers of political discourses and decisions. For example, after the Russian invasion of Ukraine, there was a deepfake video of President Zelensky that surfaced online, showing him in surrender and calling on Ukrainian forces to lay down their arms. Ukrainian officials quickly discredited it via official channels. A deepfake video of

President Putin also declared martial law, calling for mobilization, and played on several different Russian media platforms. Deepfakes become even more dangerous when used in combination with other criminal activities. For example, Indian journalist Rana Ayyub reported a case where she was victimized with targeted harassment, starting with fake social media profiles and culminating in a deepfake pornographic video featuring her likeness. The video went viral after it was shared on a political party's Facebook page, with over 40,000 shares. The attack was completed with her personal information being doxxed (Ayyub, 2018). Deepfakes can also lead to numerous other major risks in the backdrop of surveillance systems. Cyberattacks could insert fake footage aiming to implicate innocent people for crimes that in essence hit at the integrity of video evidence. Cyber Violence and Gender-Based Harm Deepfakes are increasingly becoming weapons against women and girls, exacerbating gender-based violence both in the physical and digital spaces. Cyber-based violence, woefully rooted in societal power imbalances, further results in silencing the victims and hindering their freedom of speech. Women in public or political life are easy victims of disinformation campaigns aimed at discrediting and intimidating them. (Powell and Henry, 2017) describe "technology-facilitated sexual violence" as acts where technology facilitates committing an act of gender-based harm, and it includes criminal and abusive behavior such as non-consensual sharing of explicit content. That is also quite disturbing, because several studies note that 98% of deepfake videos online are pornographic, and 99% involve women. These examples show how much is urgently required to take every possible measure to counter the misuse of deepfake technology in order to save individuals, particularly women, from its harmful results.

Deepfake Software

There are many software tools available for creating deepfakes, such as Deep-Swap, FaceMagick, SwapStream, Reface, FaceApp and FaceSwapper, among many others. Some sections can be accessed through a web browser. Some are available as apps for iOS and Android devices. These tools are marketed primarily for entertainment, humor, or satire. And advanced features generally require payment with credits or tokens. Although these tools provide adequate results for general purposes, but more complex and realistic in-depth outbreaks are often created using open source software. Open-source tools provide important benefits. including transparency Because everyone can publicly inspect, edit, or improve the code. Advanced users can improve functionality or fix bugs. And these tools are generally free. Unlike professional applications and websites, open-source projects also often have supportive communities that help other users use and improve the software (Fraga-Lamas, 2020). The most popular open-source tools for creating deepfakes are Faceswap and DeepFaceLab, both of which are Python-based and use deep learning frameworks. These tools are released under the GPL 3.0 license, making them available with confidence. Their popularity is evidenced by metrics on GitHub such as "stars" (project favorites), "viewers" (users following updates). and "fork" (where the information was originally found). Although there are other tools such as DeepFaceLive (from the same developer as DeepFaceLab), FaceFusion and SimSwap, Faceswap and DeepFaceLab are more powerful, and community based. Show off bigger users…. In general. These tools require a training dataset with multiple images. This is usually drawn from the source and target (Rosa Gil, 2023).

Figure 1. Screenshot from the original video (left); and the deepfaked version (right)

Building Robust Defenses Against Deepfakes

Countering the rising danger of deepfakes calls for a coherent strategy that employs technological, legislative, and societal measures. The authors point to four main pillars in achieving this resilience: increased public awareness, sophisticated detection tools and systems, sound media and social media policies, and smart government regulation and legal infrastructures. The pillars are mutually dependent. For example, increased public awareness can stimulate better recognition tools to develop, while better tools can improve public perception. Recognition technologies may be produced by different companies, but tools made by media and social media corporations provide the benefit of easy integration with their services (Lad, 2024). Legislation by the government can push these companies to create such tools, further reinforcing a cycle of better technology and better awareness. Such awareness can be achieved through targeted public education campaigns, by media coverage of the issue, and by workshops and public service announcements tailored to various demographic, social, and cultural contexts using a variety of media channels and approaches. A strong legal framework will be essential to establish clear responsibilities and penalties for the creation or circulation of malicious deepfakes. The other part is international and industry collaboration, sharing information, collaborating on research, and developing new countermeasures (Saima Waseem, 2024). This is part of an integrated approach for defending society not only from deepfakes but on a much wider scope. The needed action will be implemented through ongoing research and development activities, enhancing technology that gives users more control over their use of available material and allowing greater transparency.

Regulation and Legislation in the European Union

Insights which are considered a means of distorting information are in sharp contrast to the legal framework for resolving this issue. Creating a defax often involves processing personal data. Especially when they represent an identifiable person. According to the General Data Protection Regulation (GDPR), personal data can only be processed in specific legal situations. Respecting every individual's right to privacy and data protection, GDPR requires the processing of personal data to have a valid legal basis and gives individuals the right to rectification or delete incorrect information Each EU member state has at least one independent regulatory body to ensure that these rules are followed (Chenhao Lin, 2024). In 2018, the European Commission introduced a comprehensive strategy to combat disinformation. It focuses on increasing media knowledge. Support for quality news reporting Ensuring transparency in online forums and protection of personal information One of the cornerstones of this strategy is False Information Code of Conduct. Established as a voluntary framework for online platforms, advertisers and the advertising industry (Cabral, 2019). Its aim is to:

1. Reduce revenue streams for misinformation providers through advanced ad placement verification.
2. Increase transparency in political and issue-based advertising by requiring identification and funding of supporters.
3. Label automated accounts clearly.
    4. Promote media literacy and prioritize trustworthy content.

5. Provide researchers with access to platform data to analyze and track the impact of disinformation. The 2022 Updated Code of Conduct on False Information builds on the 2018 framework with more ambitious measures. Expand participation across industries and it includes commitments such as preventing the spread of misinformation.

Countering Disinformation in North Macedonia

Foreign malicious disinformation campaigns in Northern Macedonia and the Western Balkans have fluctuated in frequency. This often corresponds to the political climate in a certain region or country. Disinformation is a major challenge for North Macedonia. by affecting the political landscape social cohesion, public health and security (Meskys, 2019). The government is aware of the seriousness of this threat. Therefore, tackling disinformation is a top priority. In 2019, the Prime Minister launched "Revised Action Plan to Combat Disinformation," which outlines initiatives non-binding document aimed at resolving the issue. But it emphasizes the urgent need to revise and strengthen plans to meet new and evolving challenges. to ensure effectiveness The government should involve various stakeholders Come take part (Hancock, 2021). including media organizations Civil society and experts in the open consultation process. Using the broader context of hybrid threats, the government adopted a "Strategy for Building Resilience and Addressing Hybrid Threats" in October 2021 with the 2021-2025 Action Plan. Provisions for parliamentary oversight and the creation of communication channels between informal parliamentary groups and civil society to increase coordination and transparency.

How to Identify Deepfake Videos

To effectively detect deepfake videos It is necessary to look at both general indicators and specific indicators that signal possible distortions. The authors of the study on this topic analyzed several deepfake videos to understand the current capabilities and challenges in detecting them. Here is a summary of their recommendations (Shaji George, 2023).

> **Trust your conscience.** If something in a video feel "off" visually, auditorily, or contextually, it may indicate distortion.
> **Conscience is often the first line of defense.** Specific indicators light and shadow Inconsistencies in the silhouette of the face relative to the background or body (such as the neck) may indicate spoofing.
> **Blurred or pixelated areas Look for blurry or pixelated images**. Especially in the cheek area There may be less detail in areas such as the eyes, nose, and mouth. Face and background details uneven level of detail between faces and backgrounds (Exaggerated or understated facial features) **indicate distortion.** Multiple faces in one video If many people are seen Inconsistent levels of facial detail between them or across scenes It may be a sign of intensive use (Seng, 2024).

Eyes blinked. Abnormal blinking patterns, such as not blinking for long periods of time or blinking too frequently may indicate intense blinking. eye movement eye movement facial expression and body language must be naturally consistent. His eyes fixed with curiosity as he turned his head. Pupil size Irregular pupil shape While this is commonly seen in AI-generated still images, it can also be seen in deepfake videos.

Reflections in the eyes. The picture should match the environment in which it is painted. Discrepancies are more noticeable in still images. But they can still appear in the video. sound quality High quality picture coupled with poor sound quality.

CONCLUSIONS

As deepfake technology continues to evolve, it is poised to disrupt most businesses in various sectors. How AI-generated manipulation undermines a brand's reputation Spreads false information and disruption of the operation The development of business resilience against profound threats There is a growing need for most businesses to build resilience against profound threats. Fighting such a complex and fluid challenge can be approached only in various ways. This approach may include new ideas in terms of technology, law, security, and combined communication strategies. and employee training In this regard They can minimize the risks involved with Deepfakes and safeguard their businesses, reputation and trust with clients and other concerned parties (Sandoval, 2024).

To begin with Businesses should invest in deep tech to detect and prevent deep tech. Using AI and machine learning tools that are specifically meant to identify digital fraud, companies can monitor and protect their content from distortion. Such real-time detecting systems can warn businesses. Regarding video or photo editing and audio file editing This would enable prompt corrective action before misinformation is spread. And organizations should embrace digital watermarking and metadata surveillance, through which any legitimate content can be traced back to the source. And this is an investment in a full cybersecurity strategy, keeping the integrity of digital assets intact. In addition to technology, though, businesses must further strengthen their legal frameworks for themselves to be able to deal with the risks associated with deepfakes. Preparedness does not merely encompass familiarity with the regulatory landscape-it also involves proactive policy advocacy work in shaping future legislation. Since deepfakes are still a novelty in the realm of laws and regulations, the enterprises need to engage their legal experts to come up with strict internal policies regarding content development, application, and authenticity. Any lawsuit that will arise from defamation, fraud, and identity theft needs to be based on a legal policy. This can be collaborated by cooperating with various law enforcement agencies and cybercrime units in identifying and pursuing individuals who carry out malicious campaigns of deepfakes. Businesses can prevent any litigation and reputational issues by establishing an environment to actively fight deepfake abuse through the rule of law and regulation (Langa, 2021).

Communication-level strategies are also critical in helping companies deal with the deepfake risks. Clear and proactive communications from businesses regarding their position with respect to deepfakes technology and misinformation; amongst that is stating what the company will be doing regarding instances of occurrence and communicating with stakeholders regarding what the company is doing to detect and prevent manipulation. Business companies can reduce the possible surging cases of panics or confusions linked to deepfakes by creating a culture of trust through transparent and consistent communication. In the meantime, business companies can utilize media literacy campaigns to make their workforce, customers, or even wider communities aware of how to identify such manipulated content and challenge it. This would therefore make it easier for their stakeholders to critically evaluate digital content and make them harder to fool by deepfakes.

REFERENCES

Altuncu, E., Franqueira, V. N., & Li, S. (2022). Deepfake: definitions, performance metrics and standards, datasets and benchmarks, and a meta-review. arXiv preprint arXiv:2208.10913.

Ayyub, R. (2018) I Was the Victim of A Deepfake Porn Plot Intended To Silence Me. HuffPost UK. Available at: HTTPs://www.huffi ngtonpost.co.uk/entry/deepfake porn_uk_5bf2c126e4b0f32bd58ba316 (Access 9.10.2023).

Busacca, A., & Monaca, M. A. (2023). Deepfake: Creation, Purpose, Risks. In Marino, D., & Monaca, M. A. (Eds.), *Innovations and Economic and Social Changes due to Artificial Intelligence: The State of the Art. Studies in Systems, Decision and Control* (Vol. 222). Springer., DOI: 10.1007/978-3-031-33461-0_6

Cabral, T. S. (2019). Ai Regulation in the European Union: Democratic Trends, Current Instruments and Future Initiatives (Master's thesis, Universidade do Minho (Portugal)).

Chesney, R., & Citron, D. K. (2019). Deepfakes and the New Disinformation War: The Coming Age of Post-Truth Geopolitics. *Foreign Affairs*, 98(3), 147–155.

Dr.A.Shaji George, & A.S.Hovan George. (2023). Deepfakes: The Evolution of Hyper realistic Media Manipulation. Partners Universal Innovative Research Publication (PUIRP), 01(02), 58–74. DOI: 10.5281/zenodo.10148558

Esezoobo, S. O., & Braimoh, J. J. (2023). *Integrating Legal, Ethical, and Technological Strategies to Mitigate AI Deepfake Risks through Strategic Communication. International Journal of Scientific Research and Management.* IJSRM.

Fraga-Lamas, P., & Fernandez-Carames, T. M. (2020). Fake news, disinformation, and deepfakes: Leveraging distributed ledger technologies and blockchain to combat digital deception and counterfeit reality. *IT Professional*, 22(2), 53–59.

Gil, R., Virgili-Gomà, J., López-Gil, J.-M., & García, R. (2023). Journal. *Soft Computing*, 27(16), 11295. DOI: 10.1007/s00500-023-08605-y

Jeffrey, T. (2021). Hancock and Jeremy N. Bailenson. The Social Impact of Deepfakes. *Cyberpsychology, Behavior, and Social Networking*, 24(3), 149–152. DOI: 10.1089/cyber.2021.29208.jth PMID: 33760669

Kietzmann, J., Lee, L. W., McCarthy, I. P., & Kietzmann, T. C. (2020). Deepfakes: Trick or treat? *Business Horizons*, 63(2), 135–146. DOI: 10.1016/j.bushor.2019.11.006

Lad, S. (2024). Adversarial Approaches to Deepfake Detection: A Theoretical Framework for Robust Defense. Journal of Artificial Intelligence General Science (JAIGS) ISSN:3006-4023, 6(1), 46–58. https://doi.org/DOI: 10.60087/jaigs.v6i1.225

Langa, J. (2021). Deepfakes, real consequences: Crafting legislation to combat threats posed by deepfakes. *BUL Rev.*, 101, 761.

Langvardt, K. (2020). Regulating the Deadliest Technology of All: Deepfakes, Free Speech, and the Long Road Ahead. *Georgetown Law Technology Review*, 5(2), 204–231.

Law Kian Seng, M. A. M. A. T. (2024). AI Integrity Solutions for Deepfake Identification and Prevention. *Open International Journal of Informatics*, 12(1), 35–46. DOI: 10.11113/oiji2024.12n1.297

Lin, C., Yi, F., Wang, H., Deng, J., Zhao, Z., Li, Q., & Shen, C. (2024). Exploiting Facial Relationships and Feature Aggregation for Multi-Face Forgery Detection. *IEEE Transactions on Information Forensics and Security*, 19, 8832–8844. DOI: 10.1109/TIFS.2024.3461469

Meskys, E., Kalpokiene, J., Jurcys, P., Liaudanskas, A., & Fakes, R. D. Legal and Ethical Considerations (December 2, 2019). Journal of Intellectual Property Law & Practice, Volume 15, Issue 1, January 2020, Pages 24–31., Available at SSRN: https://ssrn.com/abstract=3497144

Nenovski, B., Ilijevski, I., & Stanojoska, A. (2023). Strengthening Resilience Against Deepfakes as Disinformation Threats. In *Poland's Experience in Combating Disinformation* (pp. 127–142). Inspirations for the Western Balkans. Oficyna Wydawnicza ASPRA-JR.

Paris, B., & Donovan, J. (2019). Deepfakes and cheap fakes.

Powell, A., & Henry, N. (2017). *Sexual Violence in a Digital Age*. Palgrave Macmillan. DOI: 10.1057/978-1-137-58047-4

Renda, A., Arroyo, J., Fanni, R., Laurer, M., Sipiczki, A., Yeung, T., & de Pierrefeu, G. (2021). *Study to support an impact assessment of regulatory requirements for artificial intelligence in Europe*. European Commission.

Sandoval, M. P., de Almeida Vau, M., Solaas, J., & Rodrigues, L. (2024). Threat of deepfakes to the criminal justice system: A systematic review. *Crime Science*, 13(1), 41. DOI: 10.1186/s40163-024-00239-1

Waseem, S., Abu, S. A. R. B. S., & Ahmed, B. A. (2024, September). Attention-Guided Supervised Contrastive Learning for Deepfake Detection. In 2024 IEEE 8th International Conference on Signal and Image Processing Applications (ICSIPA) (pp. 1-6). IEEE.

Chapter 14
Demystifying Deepfakes:
Understanding, Implications, and Safeguards

Manjeet Singh

Amity University, Noida, India

Deepshikha Bhargava

https://orcid.org/0000-0001-7017-1372

Amity University, Noida, India

Amitabh Bhargava

Amity University, Noida, India

Kirti Singh

Amity University, Noida, India

ABSTRACT

Deepfakes are a new generation of AI-manufactured, hyper-realistic synthetic media that is rapidly evolving into a disruptive technology with novel ways of harming others. From its initial use in entertainment and advertising, the misuse of deepfake technology will result in revenge porn, cyberstalking, dissemination of disinformation, and political manipulation, especially during elections, causing huge concern about the erosion of trust in social institutions. While deepfake methods are getting improved and more accessible, the urge for measures to be taken against their negative impacts is getting more pressing. This paper presents the dual nature of deepfakes, both potential benefits and risks. While the deepfake technology can protect intellectual property positively, such as enabling the protection system FORGE, it's dangerous applications create outstanding threats. This becomes all the more ominous with tools available that allow people to create fake identities.

DOI: 10.4018/979-8-3693-6890-9.ch014

Copyright © 2025, IGI Global Scientific Publishing. Copying or distributing in print or electronic forms without written permission of IGI Global Scientific Publishing is prohibited.

1.INTRODUCTION

Deepfakes are a type of artificially manufactured video, image, or audio that is incredibly realistic, generated through AI algorithms. Such manipulations might make it seem like a person is saying or doing something they never actually did. With kits like FaceSwap, one without any technical experience can make very realistic deepfakes in under five minutes. This has brought up concerns regarding possible misuse with deepfakes. While deepfakes promise some intriguing uses, they carry immense ethical and legal risks when used maliciously. As deepfakes grow increasingly easy to make, there have been increasing debates on their social implications and the ensuing regulatory imperatives. We discuss the issues in this paper, underlining how deepfakes make us aware of our cognitive vulnerabilities, which may contribute to an overall tendency of being more manipulable. The ability to understand why deepfakes do their effects on us psychologically will provide a basis for developing ways of spotting them and, further, for developing educational campaigns against misinformation. This research attempts to establish ethical guidelines for the responsible use of deepfake technology in ways that benefit society with minimum harm (Takruri, 2023).

Deepfake technologies are based on advanced AI, namely Generative Adversarial Networks, or GANs—a pair of neural networks pitted against each other in competition, one generates realistic images or audio, while the other evaluates authenticity. The result is astoundingly convincing media. Deepfake algorithms study source material to imitate such subtleties as speech patterns, facial expressions, and lip movements so it can produce flawless overlays. While basic face-swapping began in the 1990s, significant strides took place in 2018 when Hao Li combined computer vision with CGI to create realistic deepfakes (L., 2023). The invention of GANs and user-friendly tools like FakeApp and DeepFaceLab further democratized deepfake creation to almost any arbitrary user. As deepfakes grow in prevalence, researchers develop watermarking of media, verification by blockchain and other types of artifact analysis to detect manipulated media. Social media platforms are considering policies related to the moderation of deepfakes. Developments in generative AI are outpacing many of these efforts. Combating the harmful use of deepfakes requires a holistic approach—a common cause taken up by technology companies, legislators, journalists, and the public (Shaji George, 2023).

Deepfakes use AI to create astoundingly realistic manipulations of media. What began as a somewhat experimental technology has rapidly evolved into one used for deception, humor, and entertainment. In any case, generative algorithms have outrun protective measures in place by a long shot. As the process for creating deepfakes becomes more accessible, it will require sustained vigilance, education, and technological innovation to respond to the manipulation of media for the protection of truth and society (Y., 2023).

With these in mind, deepfakes can present major social harms, most of which have to do with explicit content creation, blackmail, and the facilitation of spreading false news. To date, this has led to the erosion of public confidence in any form of news and visual evidence through the introduction of wide measures of doubt, raising the ante for deception. Deepfake videos distort memories more titanically and alter how people view others in manners upon which there is no valid basis in reality. Understanding this technology is important to addressing the ethical and legal issues it brings into today's digital world. (Shaji George, 2023)

The life cycle of deepfake content, described by Figure 1, involves creation and social media circulation, detection, and mitigation stages, where policies intervene. Indeed, effective monitoring of the spread of deepfakes can rely on a feedback loop between detection and mitigation. Deepfake impacts are not only more holistic but go deep in societal contexts. For instance, deepfakes in critical events, such as elections, can undermine public trust with serious results; if there is no effective control, it might take a long time for future generations to trust online information at a time when social trust will be more weakened with negative consequences in many industries (Aldredge, 2020).

Figure 1. Deep-fake content workflow

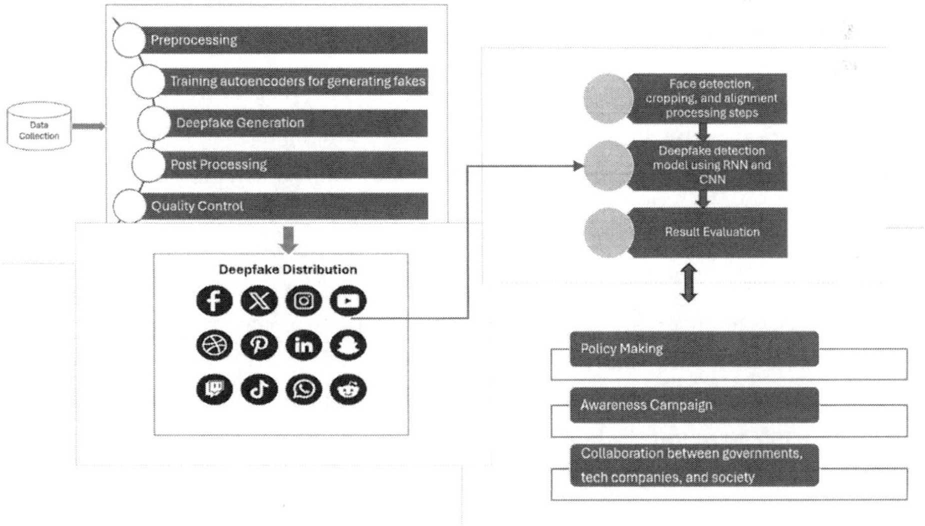

2.LITERATURE REVIEW

2.1 Social Impact of Deepfake

At first, deepfake videos were done in the context of entertainment, because others hoped to elicit amusement for the creators and the ones featured in videos. Social media users adopted the technology, too, creating animated versions of historical figures, deceased loved ones, and objects of nostalgia via apps like Deep Nostalgia. Deepfake technology has also been used for more commercial content of an advertising nature, including making famous artworks like the Mona Lisa capable of movement (Shaji George, D. A., 2023). Deepfakes were increasingly being exploited by film studios for editing scenarios far quicker and cheaper than having to reshoot scenes.

However, as deepfake use grew, the technology began to be misused, such as in creating explicit content and materials that could be leveraged for blackmail. A significant social issue resulting from deepfakes is the erosion of public trust in news, leading social media users to verify information across multiple sources to ensure credibility . Deepfakes make it easier to deceive people, creating doubt about the authenticity of videos and images. They can even affect personal relationships by implanting false memories, influencing a person's perception of others without any real basis (C. Wilpert., 2022).

2.2 How Deepfakes Influence Our Perception

With deepfakes becoming increasingly intelligent, the way we look at and perceive information changes; it even changes the way we judge reality from deception. The section shall, therefore, review some research on the effects of deepfakes on perception and attention with regard to the mental processes involved in dealing with synthetic media. Visual Processing and Cognitive Effort: Deepfakes, especially face expression changers or body language, disrupt natural visual processing. For example, studies using eye-tracking have found that manipulated regions are dwelled on for longer periods of time, suggesting that more cognitive work has to be done in order to resolve the inconsistency in information. In fact, Zhao et al. (2022) state that participants look longer at manipulated parts compared to the genuine ones. In addition, brain scans using functional magnetic resonance imaging scans reveal that decision-making and conflict-resolution regions of the brain are most active during the detection of deepfakes. However, individuals also differ in their capabilities to spot deepfakes; factors such as age and thinking style make people variously vulnerable. Memory and False Memories: A number of early studies have suggested that deepfakes may also create false memories. Researchers have documented that manipulated videos result in distorted recollections; this has developed concerns about how easily our memories could be altered due to synthetic media. Further research is needed regarding how the brains of individuals store and retrieve memories influenced by deepfakes, including such influencing factors as emotional content of the memory and source of the memory (M. Zhang., 2021).

2.3 Uncovering the Risks: Investigating the Harmful Uses of Deepfakes

Because there is public information about celebrities, politicians, and public figures, it is easy for deepfakes to be used against them. Such misuse threatens global security because generative AI creates fake videos of world leaders making false statements or producing fake satellite images showing nonexistent objects. Outside social media, such intelligence agencies might also use deepfakes to influence presidential advisors and international policy decisions. The EU Charter of Fundamental Rights ensures voting rights through Article 39. Similarly, the EU AI Act does it by pointing out which AI applications have the potential to affect elections, referendums, and vote patterns as high-risk activities. Clarkson v. OpenAI brought fears about the implications of deepfakes in affecting elections, eroding trust, and debilitating public discourse. Deepfakes also impact all people of all classes. This case, along with FBI reports, highlighted an increasing "sextortion" scheme in which generative AI and public images were used to create fake pornography, where some even involved minors. In most cases, this content is usually disseminated on adult sites as a form of harassment (S. Alanazi, 2023). Some culprits used these video clips for extortion purposes, claiming that they would distribute it throughout their family and friends' networks if their demands were not met. Another example is Clarkson v. OpenAI, which demonstrated the potential for DALL-E to produce hate speech (N. El-Hadi., 2021). The model was trained on a vast dataset and sometimes created images of children that were sexual in nature, causing significant further harm to those affected by them. Deepfakes have been used to commit financial frauds, for example, the fake video of Money Saving Expert's Martin Lewis. Cyber fraudsters, using AI, created a fake endorsement for a fraudulent Elon Musk-backed investment called "Quantum AI". Another space where AI-generated pictures are on the rise is on dating apps. Users can use their tool, Midjourney, to change their appearance, an act of catfishing where they exploit other people's vulnerabilities (Mahmud, 2020).

2.4 Legal Implications of Deepfake Technology

There is a match between the rapid pace of emerging new forms of criminal activity and the rapidly changing technological landscape. Traditional legal systems often catch up slowly with such emerging threats. This necessitates strong, more advanced, and comprehensive laws that undertake to be matched with the causality of cybercrime, coupled with deterrence through liabilities imposed on offenders. Deepfake technology is also the most promising type of technology in terms of widespread destruction, such as the Rohingya genocide in Myanmar in 2018, where deepfake videosy were believed to have spurred the genocide, in Kenya's elections, it was alleged that deepfake content portraying a presidential candidate's illness was released to sway popular opinion, causing further confusion on the candidate's health status (Hancock, 2021).

While other acts, such as murder or theft, are clearly morally wrong and have direct victims, there are also acts whose enormity is not inherently criminal but that may bring about horrific consequences. In this vein, driving under the influence is considered a crime because potentially intoxicated drivers may cause accidents that endanger drivers and passengers alike (Oliveira, 2021). Similarly, deepfakes can result in damage that cannot be undone to an individual's reputation. Mass disseminating deepfakes can at least propagate the manifestation of false news on issues of public interest, and may degrade the discourse in public and the basis of democracy. Fake videos bring along high levels of public panic and distortion of peoples' confidence in the government and law enforcement agencies (Jaiman, 2020).

This has seen the developed world recognize the dangers emanating from deepfakes and appropriate impact that such content has, both socially and in the legal arena, hence ushering in a series of legal and non-legal measures in a bid to address these issues. With courts increasingly showing concern about the incidence of deepfakes as a form of evidence, there is a clear need for mechanisms to assess the reliability of such evidence (Khurana, 2023). In the European Union, although there is no specific legislation enacted for regulating deepfakes, regulatory efforts currently exist in the creation of AI regulations, demanding more transparency in the way an AI system communicates. Other proposed legislation that has been responsible for the dragging attention towards stopping the use of deepfakes in crimes like identity theft, age fraud, illegal immigration, and espionage continues to attract attention. It is, therefore, critical that such measures be taken, as the International Journal of Social Science and Humanity has observed, since the far-reaching consequences that such activities bear on individuals, business, social trust, and political processes hold in high regard (Sidere, 2017). The General Data Protection Regulation (GDPR) currently affords some regulatory oversight that intersects with the issue of deepfakes. However, it is important to mention here that the GDPR does offer some protection, but still does not speak clearly on the circulation of fabricated information through deepfakes if the person in the content can very easily be identified. The data protection institution is called the European Data Protection Board, to which relevant laws are established and implemented. EDPB's main functions include guidance on the application of the General Data Protection Regulation to organizations outside the EU. The guidelines from the EDPB are particularly helpful for companies operating in the region of the Middle East as they can be assessed whether they are in conformity with the implementing standards of GDPR. All leading technologies and processes may be utilized with the aim of ensuring data integrity. For instance, on 14 September 2021, the Kingdom of Saudi Arabia implemented its Personal Data Protection System, which is very indicative of an intention behind data protection using very developed frameworks responding to technological developments (Inscribe., 2021).

In the UK, the laws were established to ensure that the creators of deepfake content have a course for liability. However this would depend on how aware the legal practitioners are of the issue related to deepfake technology. Deepfakes bring forward the need for the UK government to enact laws which regulate different kinds of deepfakes; these include face reenactment, face generation, and speech synthesis. As deepfake technology advances, it is difficult to recognize and punish content. For such reasons, laws discouraging the making of these deepfakes for political and social manipulation must come into creation because its significance goes beyond the level of the individual or organization it may affect to the side of political groups (Han, 2022). Such laws would be based on a proper ground founded on prior legal constructions; one concrete ground for taking legal action would be the spread of misinformation through deepfakes. For such an aim, the UK government is in touch with think tanks, media experts, parliamentary committees, and technical professionals to enact laws that can effectively stop the misuse of deepfakes. This means criminalizing the share of pornographic non-consensual deepfakes and developing systems in favor of complainants with suitable punishment in terms of imprisonment for the perpetrator. In this regard, the EU's AI Act will also provide clarity to users who engage with AI systems, also to create or modify content like deepfakes. Indeed, such detail is intended to have specific steps depend on risks actually associated with certain AI systems, whereas minimum requirements of transparency are applicable to low-risk AI systems, thereby safeguarding users and letting them make decisions in the best ways on AI applications (Ajder, 2021).

Based on these foundational principles of freedom and protecting personal privacy, the case in the United States forms the basis for further law development around deepfake content. These are perceptions of citizen rights to privacy even as deepfake technology threatens these very rights by fabricating videos that harm reputations through people, celebrities, or politicians. Freedom of speech is protected by the

First Amendment, but that needs to be balanced by right to privacy so no one can claim right to intrude into others' privacy or civil rights. So far as the U.S. goes, two Tort laws may provide some relevance to deepfake prevention: "intrusion upon seclusion" and "publicity given to private life" (Barrington, 2023). More obviously relevant would be "appropriation of name or likeness" and "false light publicity" statutes, which protect against the unauthorized use of a person's likeness with resulting harm to that person. The key weakness of Tort laws is that they require the victim to prove that the deepfake has caused damage or that it was likely that public distribution of the deepfake would or did cause harm. As such, whilst speech falls within the protection of the First Amendment, it must be weighed against the need to also protect privacy and reputations against harm created by deepfakes-a technology both capable of causing severe reputational damage and undermining rights to otherwise valid privacy claims (Biometric Update., 2024).

2.5 Algorithms That Detect Deepfake Artifacts and Distortions

Among the highly manipulative media, increasingly realistic threats are impacting the aspects of truth online and even trust. It is in the development of AI-powered detection systems that researchers work on the establishing of AI-powered systems scanning for small inconsistencies and anomalies announcing manipulation (Brookings, 2024).

Detection Techniques

Visual Analysis: Algorithms begin searching for facial landmarks, for light reflections, and pixel anomalies-all these may point to a deepfake.

Biometric Analysis: Techniques such as pulse signal analysis may detect that there is no realistic physiological cue.

Artifact Detection: Involves patterns and inconsistencies in the making of a deep fake which include warping artifacts, unnatural light reflections, and a horizontally presented pattern of artifacts.

Increasing threat: Deepfakes just get better. So good that a deep fake can easily appear to be genuine in case it has to be detected. Training methods using adversarial techniques can be used on generative models so that these do not include forensic artifacts in deepfakes. Others even synthesize realistic heartbeat and blood flow signals to by-pass biometric detectors (Brown, 2022).

The Need for a Holistic Approach

Keeping up with this chameleon enemy requires a multi-layered approach:

Constant Improvement: Algorithms require constant improvements to stay ahead of new techniques.

Hybrid Approach: Detection signals through hybrid methods combining different signals of detections with authenticating techniques along with a review by a human will be the best hope to succeed. Besides technological protection, proactive strategies should be designed from the macro-level with education, regulations, verification, and social resistance against information fraud. Deepfake detection algorithms have only appeared on the market relatively recently, but the war over truth and media manipulation is far from being won. This demands a holistic and adaptive approach for defense of the truth in the digital age (CEDPO, 2023).

3. THE ROLE OF EDUCATION AND SKEPTICISM: A POWERFUL DUO TO UNDERSTAND DEEPFAKE

Education and skepticism go hand in glove; each performs a very important function in the complex world that lies ahead. Good education thus equips us with the ability to understand the world around us. It gives us knowledge, thinking, and a pattern of how to analyze information. There are greater chances for the individuals to question things which have been quite normal, seek evidence for it, and form an opinion. Skepticism basically involves questioning claims and demanding evidence. It's just a healthy dose of doubt that aids in keeping us from merely accepting everything that comes our way (CFR, 2018). With a skeptical mindset, it's so much easier to pick up on any biases, faulty logic, and misinforming. Together, education and skepticism make a very powerful combination in critical thinking and problem-solving. Edu Olorunda Skeptical Knowledge: The educated mind of an individual can then use knowledge to critically judge claims, observe whether anything is biased or inconsistent. Critical thinking: Through skepticism, we put brains to work by calling assumptions into question and seeking alternative explanations. A basis of evidence-based decision-making can be achieved by marrying education and skepticism in such a way that we can arrive at a logical decision concerning evidence, rather than emotional feelings or beliefs. Education and skepticism become much more imperative nowadays, with the falsehood and misinformation gracing this age of information. We will develop these skills to learn to be informed consumers of information and better citizens. Let us cherish education and skepticism: together we shall face whatever life throws our way with confidence and clarity in the modern world (Defense One, 2019).

3.1 Empowering the Public: Spotting the Signs of Deepfakes

Public education in how to recognize visual cues for manipulated media is a priority now that deepfake technology has diffused so rapidly. With enhancements continuously being made to synthesis algorithms, it is increasingly challenging to rely solely on detection technology. However, people's innate perceptiveness may still pick up on subtle behavior cues associated with deception. People can learn to trust intuition aimed at pointing out potentially manipulated content with some training (EDPS, 2010). Most casual viewers remain unaware of the common pitfalls associated with deepfakes that always introduce definite artifacts. In-depth tutorials and courses, as well as broad awareness campaigns, make experts and laypeople aware of important visual clues for determining media authenticity. This empowers people through making them more self-sufficient due to a basis of observation as opposed to the passive acceptance of unverified content. Programs in education should focus on general deep fake flaws: unnatural patterns of blinking, distorting around the mouth, inconsistent lighting, and smoothing of skin—all are artifacts derived from limited source images (EDPS, 2023). This is where critical observation skills will allow all these irregularities to pop into view. Major tech companies, including Facebook, Microsoft, and Google, have developed online resources and trainings designed to help everyday users learn to spot deepfakes. Nonprofit organizations provide tutorials targeting vulnerable groups in the building of detection skills: youth and seniors. Short online games that challenge the user to find real versus fake videos provide an interactive learning experience. Academic settings also include more formal training: some universities have now started introducing courses on how to live in a post-truth world with synthetic media—such courses build critical thinking by assessing techniques of media manipulation and source evaluation. Delivered pervasively, such curricula can enhance the capability of society to resist deception. However, once-imparted education has little effect. Long-term practice is possible only in various contexts. Media literacy campaigns through games, resources, and training on a permanent basis help people be alert as methods of manipulation constantly change. Public awareness is needed to sustain the detection abilities together with the rapid development of devious technologies.

3.2 Practicing Informed Skepticism Over Blind Trust

Conscious skepticism has to be cultivated in order to make one's way through a time when appearances can be so misguiding due to deepfakes and disinformation. Now, more than ever, it is required that people exercise their critical sense upon media authenticity rather than impulsive trusts or shares of sensational content. This means verification of the source, motives, plausibility, and corroborative evidence other than just the content itself. By making healthy skepticism a habit, people can avoid the manipulation trap and make wiser choices pertaining to consuming information. Skepticism is all about questioning and not taking the claims for granted. It mitigates the so-called confirmation bias, or belief in information because it comes out to be congenial to one's beliefs. Deep skepticism raises critical questions: Who is behind this information, and for what reason? Is the information in tune with facts established or veers to sensationalism? What can be the necessary missing links? Verification with credible and independent sources would give a better context for suspicious content. Skepticism makes one investigate further before forwarding unverified media. When was the footage shot? Is the time and location verified? Generally, are the people and scenes depicted naturally or posed? Does the content seek to demean an opposing viewpoint rather than to foster good information? It really pays in taking the time for considering context and not giving credence to manipulated material. Skepticism isn't cynicism—they shouldn't dismiss all media as fake; that's just serving the purpose of disengagement. Healthy skepticism is open to variable thought and is evidenced through credible sources. Conclusions are based on fact and ethics, not simply doubt or emotion. Skepticism, therefore, is best exercised on an individual basis and that too as a constant process rather than some sort of panacea that was applied once and for all. With the emerging techniques of manipulation, there also comes a need for updated diligence. To these ends, one develops one's ability for keeping guard and critically reasoning one's way through situations. Society-wide, inculcated values of healthy skepticism—tempered with trusting—can serve to create resilience. Transparency of sources and accountability therein build the trust level within fodder from credible media and institutions, while deepfakes awareness warns against blind faith. The thinking people who are engaged make use of discernment to guard against manipulative efforts but are open to truths. Summary: Such skepticism, consistently applied and healthily so, is extremely important in today's digital world. It means one has to learn not to take as true media-featured material supportive of one's belief system, lest one reacts to bad information. Verify sources, believe in positive intent, look for common grounds—all of which takes time and helps build resilience. Only vigilance and discernment can help the truth—as understood, anchored in facts, compassion, and justice—contrast with disinformation.

3.3 Implementing Cybersecurity Best Practices to Reduce Manipulation Risks

Besides being cautious about media manipulation, cybersecurity best practices are some of the most important lines of defense against deepfakes. Since deepfakes have something in common with cybercrime, social engineering, and hacking, good digital hygiene and data privacy practices go a long way in minimizing vulnerability. Accordingly, by building cybersecurity infrastructure along with the best practices of responsible data sharing, individuals and organizations can reduce the risk of identity theft and, hence, the possibility of malicious deepfake creation. At the individual level, multi-factor authentication restricts access to data by forcing others to produce multiple pieces of information. Using password managers and keeping software up to date are also effective means to prevent unauthorized access. Frauds related to stolen identities or scams performed by using synthetic voices can be avoided by monitoring financial statements issued by banks or any other source and verifying credentials. Backing up the data securely in an offline location protects from personal deepfake misuse. Sharing personal images and videos online inherently opens up one to deepfake exploitation. Adjust social media privacy settings to make accounts private, report inappropriate accounts, and limit sharing sensitive media to reduce exposure to the sites. The same cautious measures applied while spotting misleading deepfakes should extend to sharing personal content that might get misused. This is proactive reputation management that involves either monitoring where images of themselves have cropped up online or buying up image rights. Public figures, like politicians and celebrities, are at a heightened risk regarding deepfakes that shape public perception. Monitoring unauthorized content and fake accounts dampens reputational harm. Poor data governance increases organizational vulnerability to breaches. Poor access controls, weak security testing, and poor compartmentalization will give malicious actors entry points. A structured framework such as the NIST Cybersecurity Framework will help harden infrastructure against intrusion. Data encryption can also limit the capacity to misuse stolen datasets to create deepfakes.

4.THE FUTURE OF DEEPFAKE TECHNOLOGY

4.1 Projections on Improvements in Deepfake Technology

As deepfakes proliferate, advancements in generative AI are expected to accelerate their creation capabilities, potentially outpacing current safeguards. Experts predict that deepfakes will soon reach photorealistic quality indistinguishable from reality, become accessible via easy-to-use apps, and develop sophisticated techniques to evade detection algorithms. This trajectory underscores an urgent need for proactive measures before we hit a tipping point of rampant disinformation. Deepfake algorithms are rapidly improving in image and video quality through advancements in training frameworks, neural architectures, and data.

Startups are now integrating GANs with 3D modeling, physics-based rendering, and animation to enhance realism. These developments allow for new creative uses: deepfakes have generated synthetic news anchors, fictional celebrities, and realistic personas, enabling unprecedented levels of manipulation. Accessibility is also increasing through consumer apps, web tools, and automatic generation platforms. Apps like Zao offer consumer-grade face-swapping based on cutting-edge research, while new tools make video creation as simple as entering text prompts, allowing users to generate custom images with just a description. Personalized media creation is becoming as seamless as posting on social media.

At the same time, adversarial techniques are evolving to bypass detection. Methods like attention masking, image blending, distortion removal, and antiforensics are making detection more difficult. Startups like Lyrebird have trained voice synthesis systems against detection models, enhancing audio realism and evasion capabilities. Similar methods may eventually bypass biometric safeguards, blockchain fingerprints, and other verification tools, likely outpacing static detection models and rules.

These improvements suggest a future where deepfake technology is widely available, increasingly impervious to human and machine detection. Soon, real-time video generation, continuous voice cloning, and lifelike VR avatars may redefine trust in digital interactions. Although these innovations promise creative possibilities, they also carry risks that require major initiatives across technology, law, and society to mitigate harm before reaching a critical threshold.

In summary, deepfakes are poised for exponential growth in quality, accessibility, and evasive abilities, driven by rapid AI innovation. As barriers fall, an inflection point may approach where preserving authenticity and truth across media becomes exceedingly difficult. To prevent this breakdown, urgent action is needed in governance frameworks, reliable verification systems, public education, and comprehensive monitoring—before the technological genie escapes the bottle.

4.2 Concerns About Potential Large-Scale Disinformation Campaigns

When deep effects are more accessible and realistic There is therefore growing concern about the potential for weaponization of large-scale disinformation campaigns. The ability to create believable and manufactured videos can lead to unprecedented levels of mass distortion through viral myths. If there is no appropriate countermeasure The size and reliability of deepfakes can overwhelm the due diligence required to distinguish real media from fake media. The risk extends to political unrest. market manipulation identity theft and even clinical evidence in trials Experts warn that deepfakes could fuel social division and instability in the years to come. The breadth of fake video tricks tailored to different audiences can cause confusion and conflict. Domestic and international actors can use this insight to undermine public trust in institutions. by broadcasting plausible but false footage which is difficult to refute on a large scale The democratic process is especially vulnerable: shortly before an election. Opponents may disrupt political campaigns by portraying leaders in compromising or inflammatory situations. Thousands of targeted, in-depth fact-checks that show candidates disparage certain demographics may spread before the damage can be mitigated. Deepfakes pose an increasing threat to financial markets and corporate reputations. Synthetic videos showing executives making false announcements can trigger market shifts before their authenticity is questioned. While deep allegations alone can harm companies in industries that depend on their reputation, including law enforcement and the judicial system may face significant challenges. Because falsified evidence undermines trust, deepfakes may show a person in a given situation. which influences the decision unfairly.

4.3 Ongoing 'Arms Race' Between Deepfake Generation and Detection

As deep technology advances an increasing "arms race" has emerged between the creation of synthetic media and the ways to explore it. Each new technique for creating genuine counterfeits encourages the development of forensic methods to reveal them. and vice versa This cycle of innovation is likely to persist as capabilities continue to evolve on both fronts. Building Resilience Against Deepfake Without Revolutionizing will require a sustained commitment to this cycle of adaptation. rather than a single, comprehensive solution. The dynamics of this arms race arise from the dual nature of generative AI: The same advances that improve deepfake design also reveal new signals for detection algorithms, such as GAN fingerprints. created during training has been used to detect the origins of neural synapses. The new model... now deletes these fingerprints they are searching for. Detecting it early by exploiting similar optical realism signals and avoiding facial geometry analysis, it has been very successful. But new models for these analyzes are more specialized in frame stability and response search algorithms. Time cues are now included in the frame. This continuous cycle spans domains such as audio, video, and image synthesis and authentication, with each area rapidly adapting in response to the other. Trade incentives are driving progress in two areas. This is because the startup is working on deepfake technology and competing with anti-deepfake tools. In the absence of research plateau Maintaining insights that go beyond in-depth design alone Continuous innovation is required. Society can be better served by adapting to cycles of continuous improvement.

5. CONCLUSION

Deepfake technology presents significant challenges to truth and trust in the digital age. As AI-powered synthesis capabilities increase rapidly, enhanced video, audio, and images are becoming nearly indistinguishable from real content. This development threatens to undermine trust in online information. This creates new forms of incorrect information. and inhibit social participation Addressing the potential dangers of deepfex requires a comprehensive and coordinated response from technology, education, law, and governance. To understand technology, we explored how deepfexes leverages Generative Adversarial Networks (GAN) to produce realistic results. By analyzing facial expressions skin details and speech patterns, GAN algorithms can transfer a person's likeness and voice to other media. Initial bugs in DeepFex such as visual anomalies and poorly coordinated speech Decreases with advances in movement dynamics and visualization... Creating deepfakes has become easier through consumer apps. Tools like DeepFaceLab, FakeApp, and Zao allow users to create realistic celebrity videos and photos with little technical knowledge. This ease of use portends a future where false content spreads quickly before it is verified. We also examine the protection that occurs in deep-lying birds. Digital authentication methods such as blockchain, encryption, and video watermarking help establish the origins of the medium. AI recognition algorithms can identify subtle differences in faces, voices, and images that indicate distortion. However, these technical solutions remain locked in an ongoing arms race with deepfake models being developed. Promotion Public awareness and skepticism are another important safeguard. Educational campaigns can help identify individuals.

REFERENCES

Ajder, H., & Glick, J. (2021). Just joking! Deepfakes, satire and the politics of synthetic media. WITNESS and MIT Open Documentary Lab. Retrieved April, 13, 2022.

Alanazi, S., & Asif, S. (2023). Understanding deepfakes: A comprehensive analysis of creation, generation, and detection. Artificial Intelligence and Social Computing, 72(72).

Aldredge, J. (2020, June 9). Is Deepfake Technology the Future of the Film Industry? The Beat: A Blog by Premium Beat. https://www.premiumbeat.com/blog/deepfake-technology-future-of-film-industry/

Barrington, S. Romit Barua, Gautham Koorma, and Hany Farid. 2023. "Single and Multi-Speaker Cloned Voice Detection: From Perceptual to Learned Features." ArXiv. https://arxiv.org/abs/2307.07683

Biometric Update. 2024. "Deepfake Videos Looked So Real that an Employee Agreed to Send Them $25 Million." https://www.biometricupdate.com/202402/deepfake-videos-looked-so-real-thatan-employee-agreed-to-send-them-25-million

Brookings. 2024. "Detecting AI Fingerprints: A Guide to Watermarking and Beyond." https://www. brookings.edu/articles/detecting-ai-fingerprints-a-guide-to-watermarking-and-beyond/

Brown, H., Katherine Lee, Fatemehsadat Mireshghallah, Reza Shokri, and Florian Tramèr. 2022. "What Does It Mean for a Language Model to Preserve Privacy?" 2280–2292. .DOI: 10.1145/3531146.3534642

CEDPO (Confederation of European Data Protection Organisations). 2023. "Generative AI: The Data Protection Implications." https://cedpo.eu/generative-ai-the-data-protection-implications/

CFR (Council of Foreign Relations). 2018. "Disinformation on Steroids: The Threat of Deep Fakes." https://www.cfr.org/report/deep-fake-disinformation-steroids#:~:text=A%20well%2Dtimed%20a nd%20thoughtfully,political%20divisions%20in%20a%20society.

Coalition for Content Provenance and Authenticity. 2024. "Introducing Content Credentials Icon." https://c2pa.org/post/contentcredentials/

de Oliveira, N. R., Pisa, P. S., Lopez, M. A., de Medeiros, D. S. V., & Mattos, D. M. (2021). Identifying fake news on social networks based on natural language processing: Trends and challenges. *Information (Basel)*, 12(1), 38.

Deepfake - Wikipedia. (2021, November 1). Deepfake - Wikipedia. https://en.m.wikipedia.org/wiki/Deepfake

Defense One. 2019. "The Newest AI-Enabled Weapon: 'Deep-Faking' Photos of the Earth." https:// www.defenseone.com/technology/2019/03/next-phase-ai-deep-faking-whole-world-and-chinaahead/155944/

Demystifyin'g deepfake videos: The powerful fusion of technology and data science | Data Science Dojo. (n.d.). Data Science Dojo. https://datasciencedojo.com/blog/deepfake-videos-technology/

EDPS (European Data Protection Supervisor). 2010. "Opinion of the European Data Protection Supervisor on the Current Negotiations by the European Union of an Anti-Counterfeiting Trade Agreement (ACTA)." https://www.edps.europa.eu/data-protection/our-work/publications/ opinions/anti-counterfeiting-trade-agreement-acta-0_en

EDPS (European Data Protection Supervisor). 2023. "Deepfake Detection." https:// www.edps. europa.eu/data-protection/technology-monitoring/techsonar/deepfake-detection_en

El-Hadi, N. (2021). Faces of histories the 'Deep Nostalgia' face animator conflates the desire to honor the past with an impulse to appropriate it. [Online]. Available: https://reallifemag.com/faces-of-histories/

Han, Q., Molinaro, C., Picariello, A., Sperli, G., Subrahmanian, V. S., & Xiong, Y. (2022). Generating fake documents using probabilistic logic graphs. *IEEE Transactions on Dependable and Secure Computing*, 19(4), 2428–2441. DOI: 10.1109/TDSC.2021.3058994

Hancock, J. T., & Bailenson, J. N. (2021). The social impact of deepfakes. *Cyberpsychology, Behavior, and Social Networking*, 24(3), 149–152. DOI: 10.1089/cyber.2021.29208.jth PMID: 33760669

Inscribe. (2021). Identifying fake documents: A complete overview. [Online]. Available: https://www.inscribe.ai/document-processing/fake-documents

Jaiman, A. (2020). Debating the ethics of deepfakes. In *Tackling Insurgent Ideologies in a Pandemic World* (pp. 75–79). ORF and Global Policy Journal.

Khurana, D., Koli, A., Khatter, K., & Singh, S. (2023). Natural language processing: State of the art, current trends and challenges. *Multimedia Tools and Applications*, 82(3), 3713–3744. DOI: 10.1007/s11042-022-13428-4 PMID: 35855771

L. (2023, May 3). What is Deepfake Technology? All You Need To Know. Forensics Insider. https://www.forensicsinsider.com/digital-forensics/what-is-deepfake-technology/

Mahmud, B. U., & Sharmin, A. (2020). Deep insights of deepfake technology. *RE:view*.

Shaji George, D. A. (2023, October 25). Evolving with the Times: Renaming the IT Department to Attract Top Talent | Partners Universal International Innovation Journal. Evolving With the Times: Renaming the IT Department to Attract Top Talent | Partners Universal International. *The Innovation Journal*. Advance online publication. DOI: 10.5281/zenodo.8436646

Shaji George, D. A. (2023, September 25). Future Economic Implications of Artificial Intelligence | Partners Universal International Research Journal. Future Economic Implications of Artificial Intelligence | Partners Universal International Research Journal. https://doi.org/DOI: 10.5281/zenodo.8347639

Shaji George, D. A., & Hovan George, A. S. (2023, October 11). The Rise of Robotic Children: Implications for Family, Caregiving, and Society | Partners Universal Innovative Research Publication. The Rise of Robotic Children: Implications for Family, Caregiving, and Society | Partners Universal Innovative Research Publication. https://doi.org/DOI: 10.5281/zenodo.10045270

Shaji George, D. A., Hovan George, A. S., Baskar, D. T., & Gabrio Martin, A. S. (2023, March 31). Human Insight AI: An Innovative Technology Bridging The Gap Between Humans And Machines For a Safe, Sustainable Future | Partners Universal International Research Journal. Human Insight AI: An Innovative Technology Bridging the Gap Between Humans and Machines for a Safe, Sustainable Future | Partners Universal International Research Journal. https://doi.org/DOI: 10.5281/zenodo.7723117

Sidere, N., Cruz, F., Coustaty, M., & Ogier, J. M. "A dataset for forgery detection and spotting in document images," in *Proc. 2017 Seventh International Conference on Emerging Security Technologies (EST)*, 2017. DOI: 10.1109/EST.2017.8090394

Takruri, L. (2023, July 19). What are deepfakes and how do fraudsters use them? | Onfido. Onfido. https://onfido.com/blog/what-are-deepfakes/

The Dangers of Manipulated Media and Video: Deepfakes and More. (2021, February)

Understanding the Technology Behind Deepfake Voices. (2023, April 28). Understanding the Technology Behind Deepfake Voices. https://murf.ai/resources/deepfake-voices/

Wilpert, C. (2022). 7 best deepfake software apps of 2022 (50 Tools Reviewed). [Online]. Available: https://contentmavericks.com/best-deepfake-software/

Y. (2023, May 17). The Rise of Deepfakes: Navigating Legal Challenges in Synthetic Media. CBA's @theBar.

Zhang, M. (2021). 'Deep Nostalgia' brings people in old photos back to life. [Online]. Available: https://petapixel.com/2021/03/01/deep-nostalgia-brings-people-in -old -photos-back-to-life-with-movement/

Compilation of References

Abbas, A. (2024, June 25). *Hyperrealistic Deepfakes: A Growing Threat to Truth and Reality*. Unite.AI. https://www.unite.ai/hyperrealistic-deepfakes-a-growing-threat-to-truth-and-reality/

Abdul Hussein, M. & Bogren, W. (2023). Social Media's Take on Deepfakes: Ethical Concerns in the Public Discourse. diva-portal.org

Academy, E. (2024, May 7). Understanding the Impact of Deepfakes on Brand Trust - Online Business School. *Best Courses in Digital marketing*. https://esoftskills.com/dm/understanding-the-impact-of-deepfakes-on-brand-trust/

Academy, E. (2024b, May 7). Understanding the Impact of Deepfakes on Brand Trust - Online Business School. *Best Courses in Digital marketing*. https://esoftskills.com/dm/understanding-the-impact-of-deepfakes-on-brand-trust/

Agarwal, S., Farid, H., Gu, Y., He, M., Nagano, K., & Li, H. (2020). Protecting World Leaders Against DeepFakes. *Proceedings of the IEEE Conference on Computer Vision and Pattern Recognition Workshops (CVPRW)*.

Ahmed, S. (2023). Navigating the maze: Deepfakes, cognitive ability, and social media news skepticism. New Media & Society. researchgate.net

Ahmed, S. (2023a). Examining public perception and cognitive biases in the presumed influence of deepfakes threat: Empirical evidence of third person perception from three studies. *Asian Journal of Communication*, 33(3), 308–331. DOI: 10.1080/01292986.2023.2194886

Ahmed, S. (2023b). Navigating the maze: Deepfakes, cognitive ability, and social media news skepticism. *New Media & Society*, 25(5), 1108–1129. DOI: 10.1177/1461444821
1019198

Ahmed, S., & Chua, H. W. (2023). Perception and deception: Exploring individual responses to deepfakes across different modalities. *Heliyon*, 9(10), e20383. DOI: 10.1016/j.heliyon.2023.e20383 PMID: 37810833

Ajder, H., & Glick, J. (2021). Just joking! Deepfakes, satire and the politics of synthetic media. WITNESS and MIT Open Documentary Lab. Retrieved April, 13, 2022.

Ajder, H., Patrini, G., Cavalli, F., & Cullen, L. (2019). The state of deepfakes: Landscape, threats, and impact. *Amsterdam: Deeptrace, 27.*

Ajder, H., Patrini, G., Cavalli, F., & Cullen, L. (2019). *The state of deepfakes: Landscape, threats, and impacts.* Sensity.

Akhtar, Z. (2023). Deepfakes generation and detection: A short survey. *Journal of Imaging*, 9(1), 18. DOI: 10.3390/jimaging9010018 PMID: 36662116

Alanazi, S., & Asif, S. (2023). Understanding deepfakes: A comprehensive analysis of creation, generation, and detection. Artificial Intelligence and Social Computing, 72(72).

Alanazi, S., Asif, S., & Moulitsas, I. (2024). Examining the societal impact and legislative requirements of deepfake technology: a comprehensive study. researchgate.net

Albahar, M., & Almalki, J. (2019). Deepfakes: Threats and countermeasures systematic review. *Journal of Theoretical and Applied Information Technology*, 97(22), 3242–3250.

Aldredge, J. (2020, June 9). Is Deepfake Technology the Future of the Film Industry? The Beat: A Blog by Premium Beat. https://www.premiumbeat.com/blog/deepfake-technology-future-of-film-industry/

Alhammadi, S., Alotaibi, K. O., & Hakam, D. F. (2022). Analysing Islamic banking ethical performance from Maqā id al-Sharī'ah perspective: Evidence from Indonesia. *Journal of Sustainable Finance & Investment*, 12(4), 1171–1193. DOI: 10.1080/20430795.2020.1848179

Ali, H., Ahmad, I., & Kamaruddin, B. H. (2020). Efficiency performance of smes firms: A case study of islamic financing guarantee scheme of credit guarantee corporation. *Malaysian Journal of Consumer and Family Economics*, 24(S2), 120–134. https://www.scopus.com/inward/record.uri?eid=2-s2.0-85094199040&partnerID=40&md5=dc630d9fc4ec36051821a66ce6964737

Al-kfairy, M., Mustafa, D., Kshetri, N., Insiew, M., & Alfandi, O. (2024). Ethical Challenges and Solutions of Generative AI: An Interdisciplinary Perspective. Informatics. mdpi.com

Allen, C., Payne, B., Abegaz, T., & Robertson, C. (2022). What You See Is Not What You Know: Deepfake Image Manipulation.

Allen, C., Payne, B., Abegaz, T., & Robertson, C. (2023). What you see is not what you know: Studying deception in deepfake video manipulation. *Journal of Cybersecurity Education Research and Practice*, 2024(1). Advance online publication. DOI: 10.32727/8.2023.25

Altuncu, E., Franqueira, V. N., & Li, S. (2022). Deepfake: definitions, performance metrics and standards, datasets and benchmarks, and a meta-review. arXiv preprint arXiv:2208.10913.

Alwi, Z., Parmitasari, R. D. A., & Syariati, A. (2021). An assessment on Islamic banking ethics through some salient points in the prophetic tradition. *Heliyon*, 7(5), e07103. Advance online publication. DOI: 10.1016/j.heliyon.2021.e07103 PMID: 34124400

Andreadakis, Z. (2020). Deep fakes and intelligence in the digital landscape - preliminary systematic review findings. SSRN *Electronic Journal*. DOI: 10.2139/ssrn.3516344

Anti-Phishing Working Group (APWG). (2020). Phishing Activity Trends Report.

Apolo, Y., & Michael, K. (2024). Beyond A Reasonable Doubt? Audiovisual Evidence, AI Manipulation, Deepfakes, and the Law. [HTML]. *IEEE Transactions on Technology and Society*, 5(2), 156–168. DOI: 10.1109/TTS.2024.3427816

Arato, A. & Cohen, J. L. (2022). Populism and civil society: The challenge to constitutional democracy. [HTML]

Artificial Intelligence Incident Database. (n.d.). Retrieved July 8, 2024, from https://incidentdatabase.ai/

Assagaf, A. S. A. (2023). Legal analysis of freedom of expression and online humour in Indonesia. The European Journal of Humour Research. europeanjournalofhumour.org

Asyiqin, I. Z., & Alfurqon, F. F. (2024). Musyarakah Mutanaqisah: Strengthening Islamic Financing in Indonesia and Addressing Murabahah Vulnerabilities. *Jurnal Media Hukum*, 31(1), 1–18. DOI: 10.18196/jmh.v31i1.20897

Ayyub, R. (2018) I Was the Victim of A Deepfake Porn Plot Intended To Silence Me. HuffPost UK. Available at: HTTPs://www.huffingtonpost.co.uk/entry/deepfake porn_uk_5bf2c126e4b0f32bd58ba316 (Access 9.10.2023).

Badashah, S. J., Basha, S. S., Ahamed, S. R., Subba Rao, S. P. V., Janardhan Raju, M., & Mallikarjun, M. (2023). Taylor-Gorilla troops optimized deep learning network for surface roughness estimation. *Network (Bristol, England)*, 34(4), 221–249.

Balakrishnan, V., Khan, S., Fernandez, T., & Arabnia, H. R. (2019). Cyberbullying Detection on Twitter Using Big Five and Dark Triad Features. *Elsevier Journal of Personality and Individual Differences* (The Official Journal of the International Society for the Study of Individual Differences (ISSID)), *141*, 252-257. URL: https://www.sciencedirect.com/science/article/pii/S0191886919300364

Banerjee, S., & Chua, A. Y. K. (2019). Toward a Theoretical Model of Authentic and Fake User-Generated Online Reviews. In Chiluwa, I. E., & Samoilenko, S. A. (Eds.), *Handbook of Research on Deception, Fake News, and Misinformation Online* (pp. 104–120). IGI Global., URL https://www.igi-global.com/chapter/toward-a-theoretical-model-of-authentic-and-fake-user-generated-online-reviews/230748 DOI: 10.4018/978-1-5225-8535-0.ch007

Barber, A. (2023). Freedom of expression meets deepfakes. Synthese. springer.com

Barnes, C., & Barraclough, T. (2020). Deepfakes and synthetic media. In *Emerging technologies and international security* (pp. 206–220). Routledge. DOI: 10.4324/9780367808846-16

Barrington, S. Romit Barua, Gautham Koorma, and Hany Farid. 2023. "Single and Multi-Speaker Cloned Voice Detection: From Perceptual to Learned Features." ArXiv. https://arxiv.org/abs/2307.07683

Barth, J. R. (1991). *The Great Savings and Loan Debacle*. American Enterprise Institute.

Basaran-Brooks, B. (2022). Money laundering and financial stability: Does adverse publicity matter? *Journal of Financial Regulation and Compliance*, 30(2), 196–214. DOI: 10.1108/JFRC-09-2021-0075

Bateman, J. (2022). *Deepfakes and synthetic media in the financial system: Assessing threat scenarios*. Carnegie Endowment for International Peace.

Battista, D. (2024). Political communication in the age of artificial intelligence: an overview of deepfakes and their implications. Society Register. amu.edu.pl

Bazarkina, D. Y., & Pashentsev, Y. N. (2019). Artificial intelligence and new threats to international psychological security. *Russia in Global Affairs*, 17(1), 147–170. DOI: 10.31278/1810-6374-2019-17-1-147-170

Belhumeur, P., Hespanha, J., & Kriegman, D. (1997). Eigenfaces vs. fisherfaces: Recognition using class specific linear projection. *IEEE Transactions on Pattern Analysis and Machine Intelligence*, 19(7), 711–720. DOI: 10.1109/34.598228

Bellini, A. (2023b, October 18). Deepfakes Tools for Detection - Abe Bellini - Medium. *Medium*. https://medium.com/@abebellini/deepfakes-tools-for-detection-20c24cde976b

Beltramini, R. F. (1988). Perceived believability of warning label information presented in cigarette advertising. *Journal of Advertising*, 17(2), 26–32. https://www.jstor.org/stable/4188673. DOI: 10.1080/00913367.1988.10673110

Berzinski, M. (2024, September 27). Three essential steps for organizations to safeguard against deepfakes. *TechRadar*. https://www.techradar.com/pro/three-essential-steps-for-organizations-to-safeguard-against-deepfakes

Biduri, S., & Tjahjadi, B. (2024). Determinants of financial statement fraud: The perspective of pentagon fraud theory (evidence on Islamic banking companies in Indonesia). *Journal of Islamic Accounting and Business Research*. Advance online publication. DOI: 10.1108/JIABR-08-2022-0213

Biometric Update. 2024. "Deepfake Videos Looked So Real that an Employee Agreed to Send Them $25 Million." https://www.biometricupdate.com/202402/deepfake-videos-looked-so-real-thatan-employee-agreed-to-send-them-25-million

Birrer, A., & Just, N. (2024). What we know and don't know about deepfakes: An investigation into the state of the research and regulatory landscape. new media & society, 14614448241253138.

Birrer, A., & Just, N. (2024). What we know and don't know about deepfakes: An investigation into the state of the research and regulatory landscape. *New Media & Society*, ●●●, 14614448241253138. DOI: 10.1177/14614448241253138

Bitget Research. (2024). Deepfakes may reach 70% of crypto crimes in two years. *Bitget*. Retrieved July 8, 2024, from https://www.bitget.com

Blankenship, R. J. (Ed.). (2021). *Deep Fakes, Fake News, and Misinformation in Online Teaching and Learning Technologies*. IGI Global., URL https://www.igi-global.com/book/deep-fakes-fake-news-misinformation/255423 DOI: 10.4018/978-1-7998-6474-5

Blanz, V., & Vetter, T. (2003). Face recognition based on fitting a 3d morphable model. *IEEE Transactions on Pattern Analysis and Machine Intelligence*, 25(9), 1063–1074. DOI: 10.1109/TPAMI.2003.1227983

Bligen, R. (2024, August 8). *Spotting the Deepfake - IEEE Transmitter*. IEEE Transmitter. https://transmitter.ieee.org/spotting-the-deepfake/

Bond, S. (2023, April 27). AI-generated deepfakes are moving fast. Policymakers can't keep up. *NPR*. https://www.npr.org/2023/04/27/1172387911/how-can-people -spot-fake-images-created-by-artificial-intelligence

Bondy, M. (2023, October 6). https://www.ageofdisruptionblog.com/2023/10/ deepfakes-digital-humans-and-the-future-of-entertainment-in-the-age-of-ai/

Bowie, J., & Kajal. (2024, November 6). *Deepfake: Navigating the Future of Innovation and Privacy Risks*. Pickl.AI. https://www.pickl.ai/blog/deepfake-facing-the -future-with-intrusion-and-innovation/

Bradshaw, S., & Howard, P. N. (2019). *The Global Disinformation Order: 2019 Global Inventory of Organised Social Media Manipulation*. Computational Propaganda Research Project. Oxford Internet Institute, University of Oxford. URL: https://comprop.oii.ox.ac.uk/wp-content/uploads/sites/93/2019/09/CyberTroop -Report19.pdf

Bradshaw, T. (2022). The rise of deepfakes in cybercrime. Financial Times.

Breen, D. C. (2021). Silent no more: How deepfakes will force courts to reconsider video admission standards. *J. High Tech. L.*, 21, 122.

Bregler, C., Covell, M., & Slaney, M. (1997). Video rewrite: Driving visual speech with audio. *Seminal Graphics Papers: Pushing the Boundaries, Volume 2*. https:// api.semanticscholar.org/CorpusID:2341707

Bronk, C. (2018). Blown to Bits. *Understanding Cybersecurity: Emerging Governance and Strategy*, 109.

Brookings. 2024. "Detecting AI Fingerprints: A Guide to Watermarking and Beyond." https://www. brookings.edu/articles/detecting-ai-fingerprints-a-guide-to -watermarking-and-beyond/

Brooks, A. (2023, November 6). *Who Detects Deepfakes Better: Man or Machine?* MUO. https://www.makeuseof.com/how-reliable-are-deepfake-detection-tools/

Brooks, C. (2024, June 28). *1 in 10 Executives Say Their Companies Have Already Faced Deepfake Threats*. business.com. https://www.business.com/articles/deepfake -threats-study/

Brown, H., Katherine Lee, Fatemehsadat Mireshghallah, Reza Shokri, and Florian Tramèr. 2022. "What Does It Mean for a Language Model to Preserve Privacy?" 2280–2292. .DOI: 10.1145/3531146.3534642

Brown, I. & Marsden, C. T. (2023). Regulating code: Good governance and better regulation in the information age. [HTML]

Brown, T. B. (2020). Language models are few-shot learners. *arXiv preprint arXiv:2005.14165.*

Browne-Barbour, V. S. (2015). Losing Their Licence to Libel: Revisiting § 230 Immunity. *Berkeley Technology Law Journal*, 30(2), 1505–1560. https://btlj.org/data/articles2015/vol30/30_2/1505-1560_Browne%20Barbour.pdf

Bughin, J., Seong, J., Manyika, J., Chui, M., & Joshi, R. (2018). Notes from the AI frontier: Modeling the impact of AI on the world economy. *McKinsey Global Institute, 4*(1).

Buijzen, M. (2013). Media, advertising, and consumerism: children and adolescents in a commercialized media environment. In Lemish, D. (Ed.), *The Routledge International Handbook of Children, Adolescents and Media* (pp. 297–304). Routledge.

Burgstaller, M., & Macpherson, S. (2021). Deepfakes in international arbitration: How should tribunals treat video evidence and allegations of technological tampering? *The Journal of World Investment & Trade*, 22(5-6), 860–890. DOI: 10.1163/22119000-12340232

Busacca, A., & Monaca, M. A. (2023). Deepfake: Creation, Purpose, Risks. In Marino, D., & Monaca, M. A. (Eds.), *Innovations and Economic and Social Changes due to Artificial Intelligence: The State of the Art. Studies in Systems, Decision and Control* (Vol. 222). Springer., DOI: 10.1007/978-3-031-33461-0_6

Byman, D. L.. (2023). *Deepfakes and international conflict*. Brookings Institution.

Cabral, T. S. (2019). Ai Regulation in the European Union: Democratic Trends, Current Instruments and Future Initiatives (Master's thesis, Universidade do Minho (Portugal)).

California Assembly Bill No. 730, 2019. Retrieved from California Legislative Information

Campbell, C., Plangger, K., Sands, S., & Kietzmann, J. (2022). Preparing for an Era of Deepfakes and AI-Generated Ads: A Framework for Understanding Responses to Manipulated Advertising. *Journal of Advertising*, 51(1), 22–38. DOI: 10.1080/00913367.2021.1909515

Campbell, C., Plangger, K., Sands, S., Kietzmann, J., & Bates, K. (2022). How Deepfakes and Artificial Intelligence Could Reshape the Advertising Industry The Coming Reality of AI Fakes and Their Potential Impact on Consumer Behavior. *Journal of Advertising Research*, 62(3), 241–251. DOI: 10.2501/JAR-2022-017

Cardenuto, J. P., Yang, J., Padilha, R., Wan, R., Moreira, D., Li, H., ... & Rocha, A. (2023). The age of synthetic realities: Challenges and opportunities. APSIPA Transactions on Signal and Information Processing, 12(1). nowpublishers.com

Carnevale, A., Delgado, C. F., & Bisconti, P. (2023). Hybrid Ethics for Generative AI: Some Philosophical Inquiries on GANs. *HUMANA.MENTE Journal of Philosophical Studies*, 16(44), 33–56.

Cartwright, R. F., & Opree, S. J. (2016). All that glitters is not gold: Do materialistic cues in advertising yield resistance? *Young Consumers*, 17(2), 183–196. DOI: 10.1108/YC-12-2015-00573

CEDPO (Confederation of European Data Protection Organisations). 2023. "Generative AI: The Data Protection Implications." https://cedpo.eu/generative-ai-the -data-protection-implications/

Ceolin, F. (2023). Beyond deepfakes: The positive applications of ai-enhanced video synthesis [Accessed: 2024-10-02].

CFR (Council of Foreign Relations). 2018. "Disinformation on Steroids: The Threat of Deep Fakes." https://www.cfr.org/report/deep-fake-disinformation-steroids#: ~:text=A%20well%2Dtimed%20a nd%20thoughtfully,political%20divisions%20 in%20a%20society.

Chambers, S. (2021). Truth, deliberative democracy, and the virtues of accuracy: Is fake news destroying the public sphere? *Political Studies*, 69(1), 147–163. DOI: 10.1177/0032321719890811

Chan, C., Ginosar, S., Zhou, T., & Efros, A. A. (2019). Everybody dance now. *Proceedings of the IEEE/CVF international conference on computer vision*, 5933–5942.

Chang, C. (2003). Party bias in political-advertising processing—Results from an experiment involving the 1998 Taipei mayoral election. *Journal of Advertising*, 32(2), 55–67. DOI: 10.1080/00913367.2003.10639129

Chawla, D. S. (2020). Deepfakes and synthetic media: What journalists need to know. *Columbia Journalism Review*. Retrieved from https://www.cjr.org

Chawla, Y., Dhir, A., & Misra, A. (2021). Are we safe in the age of synthetic media? An analysis of the deepfake phenomenon and its implications for business. *Journal of Business Research*, 123, 57–68.

Chesney, R., & Citron, D. K. (2019). Deep fakes: A looming challenge for privacy, democracy, and national security. *California Law Review*, 107, 1753–1820.

Chesney, R., & Citron, D. K. (2019). Deepfakes and the New Disinformation War: The Coming Age of Post-Truth Geopolitics. *Foreign Affairs*, 98(1), 147–155.

Chesney, R., & Citron, D. K. (2019). Deepfakes and the new disinformation war: The coming age of post-truth geopolitics. *Foreign Affairs*, 98(1), 147–156.

Chitrakorn, K. (2021, January 11). How deepfakes could change fashion advertising. *Vogue Business*. https://www.voguebusiness.com/companies/how-deepfakes-could -change-fashion-advertising-influencer-marketing

Christie, A. (2023, October 2). *Rolling in the deepfakes: Generative AI, privacy and regulation*. Market Insight. Published in *LexisNexis Privacy Bulletin*, 2023, Vol. 20, No. 6.

CipherTrace. (2019). Cryptocurrency Anti-Money Laundering Report 2018.

Citron, D. K. (2019). Sexual Privacy. *The Yale Law Journal*, 128(7), 1870–1960.

Citron, D. K., & Franks, M. A. (2014). Criminalizing revenge porn. *Wake Forest Law Review*, 49, 345. https://api.semanticscholar.org/CorpusID:153729297

Clark, S. (2023, August 18). Unmasking Deepfakes: How Brands Can Combat AI-Generated Disinformation. *CMSWire.com*. https://www.cmswire.com/ digital-experience/unmasking-deepfakes-how-brands-can-combat-ai-generated -disinformation/

Clarke, C., Xu, J., Zhu, Y., Dharamshi, K., McGill, H., Black, S., & Lutteroth, C. (2023). FakeForward: Using Deepfake Technology for Feedforward Learning. *Proceedings of the 2023 CHI Conference on Human Factors in Computing Systems*. DOI: 10.1145/3544548.3581100

Coalition for Content Provenance and Authenticity. 2024. "Introducing Content Credentials Icon." https://c2pa.org/post/contentcredentials/

Coeckelbergh, M. (2024). Why AI Undermines Democracy and what to Do about it. [HTML]

Collins, M. (2011). *The Law of Defamation and the Internet* (3rd ed.). Oxford University Press.

Communications Decency Act, United States, <u>47 U.S.C. § 230</u>. (1996). URL: https://uscode.house.gov/view.xhtml?req=communications+decency+act+section+230

Cooper, C. (2024, July 19). Deep fakes: Are you aware of the risk they pose to your brand? *Medium*. https://medium.com/@colin-cooper/deep-fakes-are-you-aware-of-the-risk-they-pose-to-your-brand-42d8d0246cb1

Cortes, C., & Vapnik, V. N. (1995). Support-vector networks. *Machine Learning*, 20(3), 273–297. https://api.semanticscholar.org/CorpusID:52874011. DOI: 10.1007/BF00994018

Cox, C. (2014). Protecting Victims of Cyberstalking, Cyberharassment, and Online Impersonation through Prosecutions and Effective Laws. *Jurimetrics*, 54(3), 277–302. https://www.jstor.org/stable/24395601?seq=1#page_scan_tab_contents

Craig, A. W., Loureiro, Y. K., Wood, S., & Vendemia, J. M. C. (2012). Suspicious minds: Exploring neural processes during exposure to deceptive advertising. *JMR, Journal of Marketing Research*, 49(3), 361–372. DOI: 10.1509/jmr.09.0007

Creswell, A., White, T., Dumoulin, V., Arulkumaran, K., Sengupta, B., & Bharath, A. A. (2018). Generative Adversarial Networks: An Overview. *IEEE Signal Processing Magazine*, 35(1), 53–65. DOI: 10.1109/MSP.2017.2765202

Cruz, B. (2024, September 26). *2024 Deepfakes Guide and Statistics*. Security.org. https://www.security.org/resources/deepfake-statistics/

Cyberbullying and the Non-consensual Distribution of Intimate Images, Government of Canada. (2023). URL: https://www.justice.gc.ca/eng/rp-pr/other-autre/cndii-cdncii/p6.html

Dagar, D., & Vishwakarma, D. K. (2022). A literature review and perspectives in deepfakes: Generation, detection, and applications. *International Journal of Multimedia Information Retrieval*, 11(3), 219–289. DOI: 10.1007/s13735-022-00241-w

Dale, R. (2004). *The First Crash: Lessons from the South Sea Bubble*. Princeton University Press.

Dalkir, K., & Katz, R. (2020). *Navigating Fake News, Alternative Facts, and Misinformation in a Post-Truth World*. IGI Global. URL: https://www.igi-global.com/book/navigating-fake-news-alternative-facts/236998

Danielle, K. (2022). *Citron, & Robert Chesney*. Deepfakes and the New Disinformation War.

de Oliveira, N. R., Pisa, P. S., Lopez, M. A., de Medeiros, D. S. V., & Mattos, D. M. (2021). Identifying fake news on social networks based on natural language processing: Trends and challenges. *Information (Basel)*, 12(1), 38.

De Ruiter, A. (2021). The distinct wrong of deepfakes. *Philosophy & Technology*, 34(4), 1311–1332. DOI: 10.1007/s13347-021-00459-2

Deansr. (2023, June 20). *The High Stakes of Deepfakes: The Growing Necessity of Federal Legislation to Regulate This Rapidly Evolving Technology*. Princeton Legal Journal. https://legaljournal.princeton.edu/the-high-stakes-of-deepfakes-the-growing-necessity-of-federal-legislation-to-regulate-this-rapidly-evolving-technology/

Deepfake - Wikipedia. (2021, November 1). Deepfake - Wikipedia. https://en.m.wikipedia.org/wiki/Deepfake

Deepfake Impersonation Case: TechRadar Synthetic Identity Fraud: TechRadar Market Manipulation: CNBC Security Systems Bypass: TechRadar

Deepfake Technology Using Gans | Restackio. (n.d.). https://www.restack.io/p/adversarial-networks-knowledge-deepfake-technology-cat-ai

Deepfakes Pose Businesses Risks—Here's What to Know. (2024, November 8). https://www.boozallen.com/insights/ai-research/deepfakes-pose-businesses-risks-heres-what-to-know.html

Deepfakes Pose Businesses Risks—Here's What to Know. (2024b, November 8). https://www.boozallen.com/insights/ai-research/deepfakes-pose-businesses-risks-heres-what-to-know.html

Deepfakes: What They Are & How Your Business Is at Risk. (n.d.). Bank of America. https://business.bofa.com/en-us/content/cyber-security-journal/deepfakes-business-risks.html

Defamation Act 2013, United Kingdom. (2013). URL: https://www.legislation.gov.uk/ukpga/2013/26

Defense One. 2019. "The Newest AI-Enabled Weapon: 'Deep-Faking' Photos of the Earth." https:// www.defenseone.com/technology/2019/03/next-phase-ai-deep-faking-whole-world-and-chinaahead/155944/

Demir, I., & Ciftci, U. A. (2021, May). Where do deep fakes look? synthetic face detection via gaze tracking. In ACM symposium on eye tracking research and applications (pp. 1-11).

Demystifyin'g deepfake videos: The powerful fusion of technology and data science | Data Science Dojo. (n.d.). Data Science Dojo. https://datasciencedojo.com/blog/deepfake-videos-technology/

Diakopoulos, N., & Johnson, D. (2019). Anticipating and addressing the ethical implications of deepfakes in the context of elections. SSRN *Electronic Journal*. DOI: 10.2139/ssrn.3474183

Diakopoulos, N., & Johnson, D. (2021). Anticipating and addressing the ethical implications of deepfakes in the context of elections. *New Media & Society*, 23(7), 2072–2098. DOI: 10.1177/1461444820925811

Diakopoulos, N., & Johnson, R. (2019). Anticipating and addressing the ethical implications of deepfakes in journalism. *Journalism Practice*, 13(8), 997–1005.

Dolhansky, B., Howes, R., Pflaum, B., Baram, N., & Ferrer, C. C. (2020). The deepfake detection challenge dataset. *arXiv preprint arXiv:2006.07397*.

Dong, C., Loy, C. C., He, K., & Tang, X. (2015). Image super-resolution using deep convolutional networks. *IEEE Transactions on Pattern Analysis and Machine Intelligence*, 38(2), 295–307. DOI: 10.1109/TPAMI.2015.2439281 PMID: 26761735

Do, T.-L., Tran, M.-K., Nguyen, H. H., & Tran, M.-T. (2022). Potential Attacks of DeepFake on eKYC Systems and Remedy for eKYC with DeepFake Detection Using Two-Stream Network of Facial Appearance and Motion Features. *SN Computer Science*, 3(6), 464. Advance online publication. DOI: 10.1007/s42979-022-01364-x

Dr.A.Shaji George, & A.S.Hovan George. (2023). Deepfakes: The Evolution of Hyper realistic Media Manipulation. Partners Universal Innovative Research Publication (PUIRP), 01(02), 58–74. DOI: 10.5281/zenodo.10148558

Duke, J. C., Allen, J. A., Eggers, M. E., Nonnemaker, J., & Farrelly, M. C. (2016). Exploring differences in youth perceptions of the effectiveness of electronic cigarette television advertisements. *Nicotine & Tobacco Research: Official Journal of the Society for Research on Nicotine and Tobacco*, 18(5), 1382–1386. DOI: 10.1093/ntr/ntv264 PMID: 26706908

Duong, T. V., Vy, V. P. T., & Hung, T. N. K. (2024). Artificial intelligence in plastic surgery: advancements, applications, and future. Cosmetics. mdpi.com

Ebrahimi, M. (Ed.). (2022). *Information Manipulation and Its Impact Across All Industries*. IGI Global., URL https://www.igi-global.com/book/information-manipulation-its-impact-across/268790 DOI: 10.4018/978-1-7998-8235-0

EDPS (European Data Protection Supervisor). 2010. "Opinion of the European Data Protection Supervisor on the Current Negotiations by the European Union of an Anti-Counterfeiting Trade Agreement (ACTA)." https://www.edps.europa.eu/data -protection/our-work/publications/ opinions/anti-counterfeiting-trade-agreement- acta-0_en

EDPS (European Data Protection Supervisor). 2023. "Deepfake Detection." https:// www.edps. europa.eu/data-protection/technology-monitoring/techsonar/deepfake -detection_en

Efthymiou-Egleton, I. P., Egleton, T. W. E., & Sidiropoulos, S. (2020). Artificial Intelligence (AI) in Politics: Should Political AI be Controlled? *International Journal of Innovative Science and Research Technology*, 5(2).

Efthymiou, I. P., & Egleton, T. E. (2023). Artificial intelligence for sustainable smart cities. In *Handbook of research on applications of AI, Digital Twin, and Internet of Things for sustainable development* (pp. 1–11). IGI Global. DOI: 10.4018/978- 1-6684-6821-0.ch001

El-gayar, M., Abouhawwash, M., Askar, S., & Sweidan, S. (2024). A novel approach for detecting deep fake videos using graph neural network. *Journal of Big Data*, 11(1), 22. Advance online publication. DOI: 10.1186/s40537-024-00884-y

El-Hadi, N. (2021). Faces of histories the 'Deep Nostalgia' face animator conflates the desire to honor the past with an impulse to appropriate it. [Online]. Available: https://reallifemag.com/faces-of-histories/

Emami, J. (2022). Social Media Victimization: Theories and Impacts of Cyberpun-ishment. [HTML]

Engler, A. (2019, November 14). Fighting deepfakes when detection fails. *Brookings*. https://www.brookings.edu/articles/fighting-deepfakes-when-detection-fails/

Esezoobo, S. O., & Braimoh, J. J. (2024). Integrating Legal, Ethical, and Techno-logical Strategies to Mitigate AI Deepfake Risks through Strategic Communication. Valley International Journal Digital Library, 914-928. vipublisher.com

Esezoobo, S. O., & Braimoh, J. J. (2023). *Integrating Legal, Ethical, and Techno-logical Strategies to Mitigate AI Deepfake Risks through Strategic Communication. International Journal of Scientific Research and Management*. IJSRM.

Esteban, C. R., Mateo, I. M., & Fernández-Sogorb, A. (Eds.). (2022). Special Issue "Research in Cyberbullying and Cybervictimization." *European Journal of Investigation in Health, Psychology and Education*. MDPI. URL: https://www.mdpi.com/ journal/ejihpe/special_issues/cyberbulling_victimization

Farid, H. (2022). Creating, using, misusing, and detecting deep fakes. *Journal of Online Trust & Safety*, 1(4). Advance online publication. DOI: 10.54501/jots.v1i4.56

Farouk, M. A., & Fahmi, B. M. (2024). Deepfakes and Media Integrity: Navigating the New Reality of Synthetic Content. Journal of Media and Interdisciplinary Studies, 3(9). ekb.eg

Farrugia, R., Mohan, N., & Thomas, M. (2021). Protecting financial markets from deepfakes: A comprehensive approach. *Journal of Financial Regulation and Compliance*, 29(3), 345–362.

Federal Bureau of Investigation. (2021). Malicious actors almost certainly will leverage synthetic content for cyber and foreign influence operations (210310-001). Retrieved July 8, 2024, from https://www.ic3.gov/Media/News/2021/210310-2.pdf

Federal Bureau of Investigation. (2023). I-060523-PSA: Malicious actors manipulating photos and videos to create explicit content and sextortion schemes. Retrieved July 8, 2024, from https://www.ic3.gov/Media/Y2023/PSA230605

Feldman, O. (2024). Communicating political humor in the media: How culture influences satire and irony. [HTML]

Filimowicz, M. (2022). Deep fakes: algorithms and Society. [HTML]

Fisher Phillips. (n.d.). *You Can No Longer Believe What You See: 5 Ways Employers Can Guard Against Deepfakes*. https://www.fisherphillips.com/en/news-insights/5-ways-employers-can-guard-against-deepfakes.html

Fleming, K., Thorson, E., & Atkin, C. K. (2004). Alcohol advertising exposure and perceptions: Links with alcohol expectancies and intentions to drink or drinking in underaged youth and young adults[1]. *Journal of Health Communication*, 9(1), 3–29. DOI: 10.1080/10810730490271665 PMID: 14761831

Fletcher, G. G. S. (2020). Macroeconomic consequences of market manipulation. Law & Contemp. Probs.. duke.edu

Floridi, L. (2020). AI and digital ethics: A roadmap for the future. *AI & Society*, 35(2), 531–541. DOI: 10.1007/s00146-019-00947-3

Foundation Labs. (2024, September 4). *Deepfakes at work: Why AI videos are the future of marketing*. Foundation Inc. Retrieved fromhttps://www.foundationinc.co

Fraga-Lamas, P., & Fernandez-Carames, T. M. (2020). Fake news, disinformation, and deepfakes: Leveraging distributed ledger technologies and blockchain to combat digital deception and counterfeit reality. *IT Professional*, 22(2), 53–59.

Frank, K. (2022b, June 22). *Deepfake Technology Pros & Cons For Digital Marketing*. Search Engine Journal. https://www.searchenginejournal.com/deepfake-technology-digital-marketing/454395/

Frank, K. (2022d, June 22). *Deepfake Technology Pros & Cons For Digital Marketing*. Search Engine Journal. https://www.searchenginejournal.com/deepfake-technology-digital-marketing/454395/

G7 Finance Ministers and Central Bank Governors. (2021). G7 Finance Ministers' and Central Bank Governors' Statement on Digital Payments and Central Bank Digital Currencies. Retrieved from G7 UK.

Gaillard, S., Oláh, Z. A., Venmans, S., & Burke, M. (2021). Countering the cognitive, linguistic, and psychological underpinnings behind susceptibility to fake news: A review of current literature with special focus on the role of age and digital literacy. *Frontiers in Communication*, 6, 661801. Advance online publication. DOI: 10.3389/fcomm.2021.661801

Galbraith, J. K. (1954). *The Great Crash 1929*. Houghton Mifflin.

Gambín, Á. F., Yazidi, A., Vasilakos, A., Haugerud, H., & Djenouri, Y. (2024). Deepfakes: Current and future trends. [springer.com]. *Artificial Intelligence Review*, 57(3), 64. DOI: 10.1007/s10462-023-10679-x

Gans In Deepfake Technology | Restackio. (n.d.). https://www.restack.io/p/adversarial-networks-knowledge-gans-deepfake-cat-ai

Geis, G. (1968). White-Collar Crime: The Heavy Electrical Equipment Antitrust Cases of 1961. *Journal of Criminal Law and Criminology*, 58(3), 337–354.

Gevaert, C. M. (2022). Explainable AI for earth observation: A review including societal and regulatory perspectives. *International Journal of Applied Earth Observation and Geoinformation*, 112, 102869. DOI: 10.1016/j.jag.2022.102869

Gillespie, T. (2021). The politics of platforms. In *The social media reader* (pp. 187–204). New York University Press.

Gil, R., Virgili-Gomà, J., López-Gil, J. M., & García, R. (2023). Deepfakes: Evolution and trends. *Soft Computing*, 27(16), 11295–11318. DOI: 10.1007/s00500-023-08605-y

Gioti, A. (2024). Advancements in Open Source Intelligence (OSINT) Techniques and the role of artificial intelligence in Cyber Threat Intelligence (CTI). unipi.gr

Goldman-Kalaydin, P. (2024, November 5). New AI tools and training vital to combat deepfake impersonation scams. *TechRadar*. https://www.techradar.com/pro/new-ai-tools-and-training-vital-to-combat-deepfake-impersonation-scams

Goodfellow, I., Pouget-Abadie, J., Mirza, M., Xu, B., Warde-Farley, D., Ozair, S., . . . Bengio, Y. (2014). Generative adversarial nets. Advances in neural information processing systems, 27. Agarwal, S., Farid, H., Gu, Y., He, M., Nagano, K., & Li, H. (2020). Detecting Deep-Fake Videos from Appearance and Behavior. arXiv preprint arXiv:2003.05696.

Goodfellow, I., Pouget-Abadie, J., Mirza, M., Xu, B., Warde-Farley, D., Ozair, S., . . . Bengio, Y. (2014). Generative adversarial nets. In *Advances in Neural Information Processing Systems* (pp. 27-42).

Goodfellow, I., Pouget-Abadie, J., Mirza, M., Xu, B., Warde-Farley, D., Ozair, S., & Bengio, Y. (2020). Generative adversarial nets. *Communications of the ACM*, 63(11), 139–144. DOI: 10.1145/3422622

Goodfellow, I., Pouget-Abadie, J., Mirza, M., Xu, B., Warde-Farley, D., Ozair, S., Courville, A., & Bengio, Y. (2014). Generative adversarial nets. *Advances in Neural Information Processing Systems*, ●●●, 27.

Goodman, M. (2020). The deepfake crisis: Can we stop the spread of misinformation? *Harvard Business Review*. Retrieved from https://hbr.org/2020/06/the-deepfake-crisis-can-we-stop-the-spread-of-misinformation

Guarini, A., Brighi, A., Skrzypiec, G., & Slee, P. T. (Eds.). (2023). Special Issue "Bullying and Cyberbullying: Definition, Prevalence Rates, Risk/Protective Factors, and Interventions." *International Journal of Environmental Research and Public Health*. MDPI. URL: https://www.mdpi.com/journal/ijerph/special_issues/bullying_interventions

Guarnera, L., Giudice, O., & Battiato, S. (2020). Fighting deepfake by exposing the convolutional traces on images. *IEEE Access : Practical Innovations, Open Solutions*, 8, 165085–165098. DOI: 10.1109/ACCESS.2020.3023037

Guarnera, L., Giudice, O., & Battiato, S. (2024). Mastering deepfake detection: A cutting-edge approach to distinguish gan and diffusion-model images. *ACM Transactions on Multimedia Computing Communications and Applications*, 20(11), 1–24. Advance online publication. DOI: 10.1145/3652027

Gupta, K. (2023). *The Future of Deepfakes: Need for Regulation*. Nat'l LU Delhi Stud. LJ. [HTML]

Hage, H., Aimeur, E., & Guedid, A. (2020). Understanding the Landscape of Online Deception. In Dalkir, K., & Katz, R. (Eds.), *Navigating Fake News, Alternative Facts, and Misinformation in a Post-Truth World* (pp. 290–317). IGI Global., URL https://www.igi-global.com/book/navigating-fake-news-alternative-facts/236998 DOI: 10.4018/978-1-7998-2543-2.ch014

Hameleers, M., van der Meer, T. G. L. A., & Dobber, T. (2022). You won't believe what they just said! The effects of political deepfakes embedded as Vox populi on social media. *Social Media + Society*, 8(3), 205630512211163. DOI: 10.1177/20563051221116346

Hancock, J. T. (2020). Technology, trust, and deepfakes. *Technology and Trust Journal*, 6(3), 118–131.

Hancock, J. T., & Bailenson, J. N. (2021). The social impact of deepfakes. *Cyberpsychology, Behavior, and Social Networking*, 24(3), 149–152. DOI: 10.1089/cyber.2021.29208.jth PMID: 33760669

Han, Q., Molinaro, C., Picariello, A., Sperli, G., Subrahmanian, V. S., & Xiong, Y. (2022). Generating fake documents using probabilistic logic graphs. *IEEE Transactions on Dependable and Secure Computing*, 19(4), 2428–2441. DOI: 10.1109/TDSC.2021.3058994

Hao, H., Bartusiak, E. R., Güera, D., Mas Montserrat, D., Baireddy, S., Xiang, Z., . . . Delp, E. J. (2022). Deepfake detection using multiple data modalities. In Handbook of digital face manipulation and Detection: From DeepFakes to morphing attacks (pp. 235-254). Cham: Springer International Publishing. oapen.org DOI: 10.1007/978-3-030-87664-7_11

Harris, K. R. (2022). Real fakes: The epistemology of online misinformation. *Philosophy & Technology*, 35(3), 83. DOI: 10.1007/s13347-022-00581-9 PMID: 36059716

Harwell, D. (2020). Faked voices, social media scams: How AI tech is being used to deceive. The Washington Post.

Hasan, H. R., & Salah, K. (2019). Combating Deepfake Videos Using Blockchain and Smart Contracts. *IEEE Access : Practical Innovations, Open Solutions*, 7, 41596–41606. DOI: 10.1109/ACCESS.2019.2905689

Heidari, A., Jafari Navimipour, N., Dag, H., & Unal, M. (2024). Deepfake detection using deep learning methods: A systematic and comprehensive review. *Wiley Interdisciplinary Reviews. Data Mining and Knowledge Discovery*, 14(2), e1520. DOI: 10.1002/widm.1520

Helmus, T. C. (2022). Artificial intelligence, deepfakes, and disinformation. *RAND Corporation*, 1-24.

Henriques, D. B. (2011). *The Wizard of Lies: Bernie Madoff and the Death of Trust*. Times Books.

Henry Ajder, Giorgio Patrini, Francesco Cavalli, & Laurence Cullen. (2019). *THE STATE O F DEEPFAKES LANDSCAPE, THREATS, AND IMPACT*.

Hight, C. (2022). Deepfakes and documentary practice in an age of misinformation. [HTML]. *Continuum (Perth)*, 36(3), 393–410. DOI: 10.1080/10304312.2021.2003756

Hirsanudin, H., & Martini, D. (2023). Good Corporate Governance Principles in Islamic Banking: A Legal Perspective on the Integration of TARIF Values. *Journal of Indonesian Legal Studies*, 8(2), 935–974. DOI: 10.15294/jils.v8i2.70784

Hochreiter, S., & Schmidhuber, J. (1997). Long short-term memory. *Neural Computation*, 9(8), 1735–1780. DOI: 10.1162/neco.1997.9.8.1735 PMID: 9377276

Hoek, S., Metselaar, S., Ploem, C., & Bak, M. (2024). Promising for patients or deeply disturbing? The ethical and legal aspects of deepfake therapy. Journal of Medical Ethics. bmj.com

Holly Ann Garnett and Michael Pal. Judge, E. F., & Korhani, A. M. (2021).

Home Security Heroes. (n.d.). State of deepfakes. Retrieved July 8, 2024, from https://www.homesecurityheroes.com/state-of-deepfakes/

Homer, P. M. (1995). Ad size as an indicator of perceived advertising costs and effort: The effects on memory and perceptions. *Journal of Advertising*, 24(4), 1–12. DOI: 10.1080/00913367.1995.10673485

Hornikx, J., & O'Keefe, D. J. (2009). Adapting consumer advertising appeals to cultural values A meta-analytic review of effects on persuasiveness and ad liking. *Annals of the International Communication Association*, 33(1), 39–71. DOI: 10.1080/23808985.2009.11679084

How to Protect Against Deepfake Attacks and Extortion. (2023, August 23). Security Intelligence. https://securityintelligence.com/articles/how-protect-against-deepfake-attacks-extortion/

https://economictimes.indiatimes.com/, McAfee Survey 2024

https://www.indiancybersquad.org/post/case-study-kerala-s-first-deepfake-fraud

Hui, M. (2023). *The growing threat of deepfake technology*. Global Initiative.

Hu, J., Liao, X., Wang, W., & Qin, Z. (2022). Detecting Compressed Deepfake Videos in Social Networks Using Frame-Temporality Two-Stream Convolutional Network. *IEEE Transactions on Circuits and Systems for Video Technology*, 32(3), 1089–1102. DOI: 10.1109/TCSVT.2021.3074259

Hussain, S., Neekhara, P., Dolhansky, B., Bitton, J., Ferrer, C. C., McAuley, J., & Koushanfar, F. (2022). Exposing vulnerabilities of deepfake detection systems with robust attacks. [DTRAP]. *Digital Threats : Research and Practice*, 3(3), 1–23. DOI: 10.1145/3464307

Hutson, J., & Smith, A. (2024). AI Satire and Digital Dystopia: The Dor Brothers Crafting Imperfection and Political Commentary in Contemporary Video Art. ISRG Journal of Arts, Humanities and Social Sciences, 2(5). lindenwood.edu

Hwang, Y., Ryu, J. Y., & Jeong, S.-H. (2021). Effects of disinformation using deepfake: The protective effect of media literacy education. *Cyberpsychology, Behavior, and Social Networking*, 24(3), 188–193. DOI: 10.1089/cyber.2020.0174 PMID: 33646021

Iacobucci, S., De Cicco, R., Michetti, F., Palumbo, R., & Pagliaro, S. (2021). Deepfakes unmasked: The effects of information priming and bullshit receptivity on deepfake recognition and sharing intention. *Cyberpsychology, Behavior, and Social Networking*, 24(3), 194–202. DOI: 10.1089/cyber.2020.0149 PMID: 33646046

Ienca, M. (2023). On Artificial Intelligence and Manipulation. Topoi. springer.com

Information Resources Management Association. (2021). *Research Anthology on Fake News, Political Warfare, and Combatting the Spread of Misinformation*. IGI Global. URL: https://www.igi-global.com/book/research-anthology-fake-news -political/262491

Inscribe. (2021). Identifying fake documents: A complete overview. [Online]. Available: https://www.inscribe.ai/document-processing/fake-documents

iProov Blog. (2024). How To Protect Against Deepfakes – Statistics and Solutions. Retrieved July 8, 2024, from https://www.iproov.com/blog/deepfakes-statistics -solutions-biometric-protection

iProov. (2024). Biometric threat intelligence report 2024: The impact of generative AI on remote identity verification. *iProov*. Retrieved July 8, 2024, from https://www .iproov.com/reports/iproov-threat-intelligence-report-2024

Ishak, M. S. I. (2019). The principle of ma la ah and its application in Islamic banking operations in Malaysia. *ISRA International Journal of Islamic Finance*, 11(1), 137–146. DOI: 10.1108/IJIF-01-2018-0017

Jaiman, A. (2020). Debating the ethics of deepfakes. In *Tackling Insurgent Ideologies in a Pandemic World* (pp. 75–79). ORF and Global Policy Journal.

Janssen, P. (2015). Ancient Greek Bankers: Trapezitai and Their Operations. Journal of Ancient History.

Jevne, F. L., Hauge, Å. L., & Thomassen, M. K. (2023). User evaluation of a national web portal for climate change adaptation – A qualitative case sstudy of the Knowledge Bank. *Climate Services*, 30, 100367. Advance online publication. DOI: 10.1016/j.cliser.2023.100367

Jin, X., Zhang, Z., Gao, B., Gao, S., Zhou, W., Yu, N., & Wang, G. (2023). Assessing the perceived credibility of deepfakes: The impact of system-generated cues and video characteristics. [HTML]. *New Media & Society*, ●●●, 14614448231199664. DOI: 10.1177/14614448231199664

Johnson, D. G., & Diakopoulos, N. (2021). What to do about deepfakes. *Communications of the ACM*, 64(3), 33–35. DOI: 10.1145/3447255

Jones, V. A. (2020). Artificial intelligence enabled deepfake technology: The emergence of a new threat (Doctoral dissertation, Utica College).

Judge, E. F., & Korhani, A. M. (2021). *A Moderate Proposal for a Digital Right of Reply for Election-Related Digital Replicas: Deepfakes.* Disinformation, and Elections.

Juefei-Xu, F., Wang, R., Huang, Y., Guo, Q., Ma, L., & Liu, Y. (2022). Countering malicious deepfakes: Survey, battleground, and horizon. [springer.com]. *International Journal of Computer Vision*, 130(7), 1678–1734. DOI: 10.1007/s11263-022-01606-8 PMID: 35528632

Kamarck, E. & West, D. M. (2024). Lies that Kill: A Citizen's Guide to Disinformation. [HTML]

Kar, S. (2023, February 27). *How Advertisements Are Using Deepfake: Is There A Cause For Concern?* Tom Lydon. (2023, November 20). *How AI will make payments more efficient and reduce fraud.*

Karnouskos, S. (2020). Artificial intelligence in digital media: The era of deepfakes. *IEEE Transactions on Technology and Society*, 1(3), 138–147. DOI: 10.1109/TTS.2020.3001312

Karpinska-Krakowiak, M., & Eisend, M. (2024). Realistic portrayals of untrue information: The effects of deepfaked ads and different types of disclosures. *Journal of Advertising*, ●●●, 1–11. DOI: 10.1080/00913367.2024.2306415

Karras, T., Laine, S., & Aila, T. (2019). A style-based generator architecture for generative adversarial networks. *Proceedings of the IEEE/CVF conference on computer vision and pattern recognition*, 4401–4410. DOI: 10.1109/CVPR.2019.00453

Karras, T., Laine, S., Aittala, M., Hellsten, J., Lehtinen, J., & Aila, T. (2020). Analyzing and improving the image quality of stylegan. *Proceedings of the IEEE/CVF conference on computer vision and pattern recognition*, 8110–8119. DOI: 10.1109/CVPR42600.2020.00813

Kaufman, M. (2018, March 8). Twitter users are twice as likely to retweet fake news stories than authentic ones. *Mashable.* URL: https://mashable.com/2018/03/08/twitter-users-retweet-fake-news-study/

Kaur, S., & Arora, S. (2021). Role of perceived risk in online banking and its impact on behavioral intention: Trust as a moderator. *Journal of Asia Business Studies*, 15(1), 1–30. DOI: 10.1108/JABS-08-2019-0252

Khoo, B., Phan, R. C. W., & Lim, C. H. (2022). Deepfake attribution: On the source identification of artificially generated images. [HTML]. *Wiley Interdisciplinary Reviews. Data Mining and Knowledge Discovery*, 12(3), e1438. DOI: 10.1002/widm.1438

Khurana, D., Koli, A., Khatter, K., & Singh, S. (2023). Natural language processing: State of the art, current trends and challenges. *Multimedia Tools and Applications*, 82(3), 3713–3744. DOI: 10.1007/s11042-022-13428-4 PMID: 35855771

Kietzmann, J., Lee, L. W., McCarthy, I. P., & Kietzmann, T. C. (2020). Deepfakes: Trick or treat? *Business Horizons*, 63(2), 135–146. DOI: 10.1016/j.bushor.2019.11.006

Kietzmann, J., Mills, A. J., & Plangger, K. (2021). Deepfakes: Perspectives on the future "reality" of advertising and branding. *International Journal of Advertising*, 40(3), 473–485. DOI: 10.1080/02650487.2020.1834211

Kim, B., Xiong, A., Lee, D., & Han, K. (2021). A systematic review on fake news research through the lens of news creation and consumption: Research efforts, challenges, and future directions. *PLoS One*, 16(12), e0260080. DOI: 10.1371/journal.pone.0260080 PMID: 34882703

Kingma, D. P., & Welling, M. (2013). Auto-Encoding Variational Bayes. arXiv preprint arXiv:1312.6114.

Kirchengast, T. (2020). Deepfakes and image manipulation: Criminalisation and control. *Information & Communications Technology Law*, 29(3), 308–323. DOI: 10.1080/13600834.2020.1794615

Kismawadi, E. R. (2024a). Blockchain technology and islamic finance: Empowering small businesses for financial sustainability. In *Technopreneurship in Small Businesses for Sustainability* (pp. 50–77). DOI: 10.4018/979-8-3693-3530-7.ch004

Kismawadi, E. R. (2023). *Islamic Banking And Economic Growth: A Panel Data Approach*. Iranian Economic Review., DOI: 10.22059/ier.2023.365739.1007815

Kismawadi, E. R. (2024b). Contribution of Islamic banks and macroeconomic variables to economic growth in developing countries: Vector error correction model approach (VECM). *Journal of Islamic Accounting and Business Research*, 15(2), 306–326. DOI: 10.1108/JIABR-03-2022-0090

Kismawadi, E. R., Irfan, M., Al Muddatstsir, U. D., & Abdulkarim, F. M. (2023). Fintech innovations: Risk mitigation strategies in Islamic finance. In *Fintech Applications in Islamic Finance* (pp. 35–58). AI, Machine Learning, and Blockchain Techniques., DOI: 10.4018/979-8-3693-1038-0.ch003

Kite-Powell, J. (2023, September 26). Deepfakes Are Here, Can They Be Stopped? *Forbes*. https://www.forbes.com/sites/jenniferkitepowell/2023/09/20/deepfakes-are-here-can-they-be-stopped/

Köbis, N. C., Doležalová, B., & Soraperra, I. (2021). Fooled twice: People cannot detect deepfakes but think they can. *iScience*, 24(11), 103364. DOI: 10.1016/j.isci.2021.103364 PMID: 34820608

Koch, C. M. (2016). To Catch a Catfish: A Statutory Solution for Victims of Online Impersonation. *University of Colorado Law Review*, 88(1). http://lawreview.colorado.edu/wp-content/uploads/2017/01/12.-88.1-Koch_FinalRevised.pdf

Kopecky, S. (2024). Challenges of Deepfakes. *Science and Information Conference*. [HTML]

Korshunov, P., & Marcel, S. (2020). Vulnerability Assessment and Detection of Deepfake Videos. *IEEE International Conference on Image Processing (ICIP)*, 226-230.

Kozyreva, A., Herzog, S. M., Lewandowsky, S., Hertwig, R., Lorenz-Spreen, P., Leiser, M., & Reifler, J. (2023). Resolving content moderation dilemmas between free speech and harmful misinformation. [pnas.org]. *Proceedings of the National Academy of Sciences of the United States of America*, 120(7), e2210666120. DOI: 10.1073/pnas.2210666120 PMID: 36749721

Kraus, S. (2020). The Growing Threat of Deepfakes and Synthetic Media in Financial Fraud. *Journal of Financial Crime*, 27(3), 877–885.

Krishna, D. (2020). Deepfakes, online platforms, and a novel proposal for transparency, collaboration, and education. *Rich. JL & Tech.*, 27, 1.

Kshetri, N. (2023). The economics of deepfakes. *Computer*, 56(8), 89–94. DOI: 10.1109/MC.2023.3276068

Kugler, M. B., & Pace, C. (2021). Deepfake privacy: Attitudes and regulation. *Nw. UL Rev.*, 116, 611.

Kumar, A. (2024). Submission of Written Evidence to the House of Lords Communications and Digital Committee Inquiry on The Future of News: Impartiality, Trust, and Technology. gold.ac.uk

Kunnumpurath, B., Menon, V. A., & Paul, A. (2024). ChatGPT and virtual experience: Student engagement in online script writing - an experimental investigation among media students. In *Advances in Computational Intelligence and Robotics* (pp. 32–50). IGI Global.

Kwok, A. O., & Koh, S. G. (2021). Deepfake: A social construction of technology perspective. *Current Issues in Tourism*, 24(13), 1798–1802. DOI: 10.1080/13683500.2020.1738357

L. (2023, May 3). What is Deepfake Technology? All You Need To Know. Forensics Insider. https://www.forensicsinsider.com/digital-forensics/what-is-deepfake-technology/

Laas, O. (2023). Deepfakes and trust in technology. [HTML]. *Synthese*, 202(5), 132. DOI: 10.1007/s11229-023-04363-4

Łabuz, M. (2023). Regulating deep fakes in the artificial intelligence act. Applied Cybersecurity & Internet Governance. acigjournal.com

Łabuz, M. (2023). Regulating deep fakes in the artificial intelligence act. *Applied Cybersecurity & Internet Governance*, 2(1), 1–42. DOI: 10.60097/ACIG/162856

Lad, S. (2024). Adversarial Approaches to Deepfake Detection: A Theoretical Framework for Robust Defense. Journal of Artificial Intelligence General Science (JAIGS) ISSN:3006-4023, 6(1), 46–58. https://doi.org/DOI: 10.60087/jaigs.v6i1.225

Langa, J. (2021). Deepfakes, real consequences: Crafting legislation to combat threats posed by deepfakes. *BUL Rev.*, 101, 761.

Langmia, K. (2023). Black Communication in the Age of Disinformation: DeepFakes and Synthetic Media. [HTML]

Langvardt, K. (2020). Regulating the Deadliest Technology of All: Deepfakes, Free Speech, and the Long Road Ahead. *Georgetown Law Technology Review*, 5(2), 204–231.

Lankes, R. (2023). Corrosive AI: Emerging Effects of the Use of Generative AI on Political Trust. corrosiveai.com

Lastovicka, J. L. (1983). Convergent and Discriminant Validity of Television Rating Scales. *Journal of Advertising*, 12(2), 14–23. DOI: 10.1080/00913367.1983.10672836

Laux, J., Wachter, S., & Mittelstadt, B. (2024). Trustworthy artificial intelligence and the European Union AI act: On the conflation of trustworthiness and acceptability of risk. *Regulation & Governance*, 18(1), 3–32. DOI: 10.1111/rego.12512 PMID: 38435808

Law Kian Seng, M. A. M. A. T. (2024). AI Integrity Solutions for Deepfake Identification and Prevention. *Open International Journal of Informatics*, 12(1), 35–46. DOI: 10.11113/oiji2024.12n1.297

LeCun, Y., Bengio, Y., & Hinton, G. (2015). Deep learning. *Nature*, 521(7553), 436–444. DOI: 10.1038/nature14539 PMID: 26017442

Lee, Y., Huang, K.-T., Blom, R., Schriner, R., & Ciccarelli, C. A. (2021). To believe or not to believe: Framing analysis of content and audience response of top 10 deepfake videos on YouTube. *Cyberpsychology, Behavior, and Social Networking*, 24(3), 153–158. DOI: 10.1089/cyber.2020.0176 PMID: 33600225

Leibowicz, C. R., McGregor, S., & Ovadya, A. (2021, July). The deepfake detection dilemma: A multistakeholder exploration of adversarial dynamics in synthetic media. In Proceedings of the 2021 AAAI/ACM Conference on AI, Ethics, and Society (pp. 736-744). DOI: 10.1145/3461702.3462584

Leighton, N. (2024, November 6). *Ethical AI in marketing: Balancing automation with human values*. Forbes Coaches Council. Retrieved from https://www.forbes.com

Li, C., & Cui, J. (2021). Intelligent Sports Training System Based on Artificial Intelligence and Big Data. *Mobile Information Systems*, 2021, 1–11. DOI: 10.1155/2021/1430512

Li, M., & Wan, Y. (2023). Norms or fun? The influence of ethical concerns and perceived enjoyment on the regulation of deepfake information. [HTML]. *Internet Research*, 33(5), 1750–1773. DOI: 10.1108/INTR-07-2022-0561

Lin, C., Yi, F., Wang, H., Deng, J., Zhao, Z., Li, Q., & Shen, C. (2024). Exploiting Facial Relationships and Feature Aggregation for Multi-Face Forgery Detection. *IEEE Transactions on Information Forensics and Security*, 19, 8832–8844. DOI: 10.1109/TIFS.2024.3461469

Longobardi, C., Jungert, T., & Badenes-Ribera, L. (Eds.). (2022). Special Issue "Cyberbullying, Mental Health and Behavioral Difficulties in Early Adolescents." *International Journal of Environmental Research and Public Health*. MDPI. URL: https://www.mdpi.com/journal/ijerph/special_issues/Cyberbullying_Adolescents

Longobardi, C., Jungert, T., & Badenes-Ribera, L. (Eds.). (2023). Special Issue "2nd Edition: Bullying and Cyberbullying, Mental Health and Behavioral Difficulties." *International Journal of Environmental Research and Public Health*. MDPI. URL: https://www.mdpi.com/journal/ijerph/special_issues/QVK4XMRQ64

Lu, H., & Chu, H. (2023). Let the dead talk: How deepfake resurrection narratives influence audience response in prosocial contexts. *Computers in Human Behavior*, 145, 107761. DOI: 10.1016/j.chb.2023.107761

Lyu, S. (2024). DeepFake the menace: mitigating the negative impacts of AI-generated content. Organizational Cybersecurity Journal: Practice, Process and People. emerald.com

Mahmud, B. U., & Al Sharmin, A. (2021). Deep Insights of Deepfake Technology : A Review. *ArXiv, abs/2105.00192*. https://api.semanticscholar.org/CorpusID: 233481934

Mahmud, B. U., & Sharmin, A. (2020). Deep insights of deepfake technology. *RE:view*.

Mai, K. T., Bray, S., Davies, T., & Griffin, L. D. (2023). Warning: Humans cannot reliably detect speech deepfakes. *PLoS ONE, 18*(8 August). DOI: 10.1371/journal. pone.0285333

Malik, S., Surbhi, A., & Roy, D. (2024). *Blurring boundaries between truth and illusion: Analysis of human rights and regulatory concerns arising from abuse of deepfake technology*. AIP Conference Proceedings. [HTML]

Maras, M.-H., & Alexandrou, A. (2018). Determining authenticity of video evidence in the age of artificial intelligence and in the wake of Deepfake videos. *The International Journal of Evidence & Proof*, 23(3), 255–262. DOI: 10.1177/1365712718807226

Marr, B. (2022, January 12). Deepfakes – The Good, The Bad, And The Ugly. *Forbes*. https://www.forbes.com/sites/bernardmarr/2022/01/11/deepfakes--the-good -the-bad-and-the-ugly/

Marr, B. (2024, November 7). The Dark Side Of AI: How Deepfakes And Disinformation Are Becoming A Billion-Dollar Business Risk. *Forbes*. https://www.forbes.com/sites/bernardmarr/2024/11/06/the-dark-side-of-ai-how-deepfakes-and-disinformation-are-becoming-a-billion-dollar-business-risk/

Marsh, E. J., Cantor, A. D., & Brashier, N. M. (2016). Believing that Humans Swallow Spiders in Their Sleep: False Beliefs as Side Effects of the Processes that Support Accurate Knowledge. *Psychology of Learning and Motivation*, 64, 93–132. https://www.sciencedirect.com/science/article/pii/S0079742115000341. DOI: 10.1016/bs.plm.2015.09.003

Masood, M., Nawaz, M., Malik, K. M., Javed, A., Irtaza, A., & Malik, H. (2023). Deepfakes generation and detection: State-of-the-art, open challenges, countermeasures, and way forward. [PDF]. *Applied Intelligence*, 53(4), 3974–4026. DOI: 10.1007/s10489-022-03766-z

Matamoros Fernandez, A., Bartolo, L., & Troynar, L. (2023). Humour as an online safety issue: Exploring solutions to help platforms better address this form of expression. *Internet Policy Review*, 12(1). Advance online publication. qut.edu.au. DOI: 10.14763/2023.1.1677

Matza, M. (2024, January 23). *Fake Biden robocall tells voters to skip New Hampshire primary election*.

Mc Guckin, C., & Corcoran, L. (Eds.). (2015). Special Issue "Cyberbullying: Where Are We Now? A Cross-National Understanding." *Societies*. MDPI. URL: https://www.mdpi.com/journal/societies/special_issues/cyberbulling

McFarland, A. (2024, November 5). *7 Best Deepfake Detector Tools & Techniques (November 2024)*. Unite.AI. https://www.unite.ai/best-deepfake-detector-tools-and-techniques/

McGlynn, C., Rackley, E., & Johnson, K. (2020). Deepfakes, Pornography, and Privacy. *European Journal of Law and Technology*, 11(1).

Mekkawi, M. H. (2023). The challenges of Digital Evidence usage in Deepfake Crimes Era. Journal of Law and Emerging Technologies. jolets.org

Meskys, E., Kalpokiene, J., Jurcys, P., Liaudanskas, A., & Fakes, R. D. Legal and Ethical Considerations (December 2, 2019). Journal of Intellectual Property Law & Practice, Volume 15, Issue 1, January 2020, Pages 24–31., Available at SSRN: https://ssrn.com/abstract=3497144

Miksa, N., & Hodgson, R. (2021). The Persuasion Knowledge Model within Instagram Advertisements. *Journal of Student Research*, 10(4). Advance online publication. DOI: 10.47611/jsrhs.v10i4.1821

Miller, T., Spooner, K., & Landman, T. (2020). Deepfake Detection: Fighting AI with AI. Financial Times.

Millière, R. (2022). Deep learning and synthetic media. *Synthese*, 200(3), 231. DOI: 10.1007/s11229-022-03739-2

Mirsky, Y., & Lee, W. (2021). The creation and detection of deepfakes: A survey. *ACM Computing Surveys*, 54(1), 1–41. DOI: 10.1145/3425780

Mitra, A., Mohanty, S. P., Corcoran, P., & Kougianos, E. (2021). A machine learning based approach for deepfake detection in social media through key video frame extraction. *SN Computer Science*, 2(2), 98. DOI: 10.1007/s42979-021-00495-x

Mohammad, S. J., Tahtamouni, A., Aldaas, A. A., & Sumadi, M. A. (2022). Preventing money laundering during the placement stage: The Jordanian commercial banks case. *International Journal of Public Law and Policy*, 8(1), 37–51. DOI: 10.1504/IJPLAP.2022.120663

Momeni, M. (2024). Artificial Intelligence and Political Deepfakes: Shaping Citizen Perceptions Through Misinformation. Journal of Creative Communications. sagepub.com

Moravec, P., Minas, R., & Dennis, A. R. (2018). Fake news on social media: People believe what they want to believe when it makes no sense at all. SSRN *Electronic Journal*. DOI: 10.2139/ssrn.3269541

Mullen, M. (2022). A new reality: deepfake technology and the world around us. Mitchell Hamline L. Rev.. mitchellhamline.edu

Murillo-Ligorred, V., Ramos-Vallecillo, N., Covaleda, I., & Fayos, L. (2023). Knowledge, Integration and Scope of Deepfakes in Arts Education: The Development of Critical Thinking in Postgraduate Students in Primary Education and Master's Degree in Secondary Education. *Education Sciences*, 13(11), 1073. DOI: 10.3390/educsci13111073

Murphy, G., Ching, D., Twomey, J., & Linehan, C. (2023). Face/Off: Changing the face of movies with deepfakes. *PLoS One*, 18(7), e0287503. DOI: 10.1371/journal.pone.0287503 PMID: 37410765

Musa, M. A., Sukor, M. E. A., Ismail, M. N., & Elias, M. R. F. (2020). Islamic business ethics and practices of Islamic banks: Perceptions of Islamic bank employees in Gulf cooperation countries and Malaysia. *Journal of Islamic Accounting and Business Research*, 11(5), 1009–1031. DOI: 10.1108/JIABR-07-2016-0080

Mustak, M., Salminen, J., Mäntymäki, M., Rahman, A., & Dwivedi, Y. K. (2023). Deepfakes: Deceptions, mitigations, and opportunities. [sciencedirect.com]. *Journal of Business Research*, 154, 113368. DOI: 10.1016/j.jbusres.2022.113368

Myers, M. (2020, June 12). *The Last of Us Part 2 review: We're better than this.*

Nagendra Rao. (2024, February 29). *Deepfakes: Healthcare's Future is Here, and It's Not What You Expect.*

Nakamura, T., Nagata, Y., Nitta, G., Okata, S., Nagase, M., Mitsui, K., Watanabe, K., Miyazaki, R., Kaneko, M., Nagamine, S., Hara, N., Lee, T., Nozato, T., Ashikaga, T., Goya, M., & Sasano, T. (2021). Prediction of premature ventricular complex origins using artificial intelligence–enabled algorithms. *Cardiovascular Digital Health Journal*, 2(1), 76–83. https://doi.org/https://doi.org/10.1016/j.cvdhj.2020.11.006. DOI: 10.1016/j.cvdhj.2020.11.006 PMID: 35265893

Napshin, S., Paul, J., & Cochran, J. (2024). Individual responsibility around deepfakes: It's no laughing matter. *Cyberpsychology, Behavior, and Social Networking*, 27(2), 105–110. DOI: 10.1089/cyber.2023.0274 PMID: 38265805

National Security Agency. (2023, September 12). *NSA, U.S. federal agencies advise on deepfake threats* (U/OO/199197-23 | PP-23-3076 | Ver. 1.0). Press Release.

Navarro Martínez, O., Fernández-García, D., Cuartero Monteagudo, N., & Forero-Rincón, O. (2024). Possible Health Benefits and Risks of DeepFake Videos: A Qualitative Study in Nursing Students. [mdpi.com]. *Nursing Reports*, 14(4), 2746–2757. DOI: 10.3390/nursrep14040203 PMID: 39449440

Navarro, R. (Ed.). (2019). Special Issue "Family, Bullying and Cyberbullying." *Social Sciences*. MDPI. URL: https://www.mdpi.com/journal/socsci/special_issues/family_bullying_and_cyberbullying

Nenovski, B., Ilijevski, I., & Stanojoska, A. (2023). Strengthening Resilience Against Deepfakes as Disinformation Threats. In *Poland's Experience in Combating Disinformation* (pp. 127–142). Inspirations for the Western Balkans. Oficyna Wydawnicza ASPRA-JR.

Newman, L. H. (2021). *How deepfakes are transforming the fraud landscape.* Wired.

NextWeb. (2023). Deepfake Fraud Attempts are up 3000% in 2023 — Here's Why.

Nguyen, T. T., Nguyen, T. N., Nguyen, D. T., & Hsu, C. H. (2020). Deep Learning for Deepfakes Creation and Detection: A Survey. arXiv preprint arXiv:2007.12084.

Nguyen, T. T., Nguyen, C. M., Nguyen, D. T., Nguyen, D. T., & Nahavandi, S. (2021). Deep learning for deepfakes creation and detection: A survey. *Computer Survey*, 53(11), 1–27.

Nicholls, J., Kuppa, A., & Le-Khac, N. A. (2021). Financial cybercrime: A comprehensive survey of deep learning approaches to tackle the evolving financial crime landscape. *IEEE Access: Practical Innovations, Open Solutions*, 9, 163965–163986. DOI: 10.1109/ACCESS.2021.3134076

NickBryantNY. (2020, December 19). *The year 2020: A time when everything changed*.

Nieweglowska, M., Stellato, C., & Sloman, S. A. (2023). Deepfakes: Vehicles for radicalization, not persuasion. *Current Directions in Psychological Science*, 32(3), 236–241. DOI: 10.1177/09637214231161321

O'Connor, C., & Weatherall, J. O. (2022). Why We Trust Lies. *Scientific American*.

O'Brien, C. (2024, March 22). *Protecting corporate reputation in the era of the deepfake: Understand how AI is affecting your organisation and how you can adapt*.

Ojala, T., Pietikäinen, M., & Harwood, D. (1996). A comparative study of texture measures with classification based on featured distributions. *Pattern Recognition*, 29(1), 51–59. https://doi.org/https://doi.org/10.1016/0031-3203(95)00067-4. DOI: 10.1016/0031-3203(95)00067-4

Okolie, C. (2023). Artificial intelligence-altered videos (deepfakes), image-based sexual abuse, and data privacy concerns. *Journal of International Women's Studies*, 25(2), 11.

Ollie. (2024, July 23). The Rise of Deepfake Videos: Unraveling the Magic Behind GANs. *Medium*. https://medium.com/@ohermans1/the-rise-of-deepfake-videos-unraveling-the-magic-behind-gans-a4d7c03637fa

Ollie. (2024b, July 23). The Rise of Deepfake Videos: Unraveling the Magic Behind GANs. *Medium*. https://medium.com/@ohermans1/the-rise-of-deepfake-videos-unraveling-the-magic-behind-gans-a4d7c03637fa

Oversight Committee Republicans Verified account. (2023, December 7). *Hearing Wrap Up: Action Needed to Combat Proliferation of Harmful Deepfakes - United States House Committee on Oversight and Accountability*. United States House Committee on Oversight and Accountability. https://oversight.house.gov/release/hearing-wrap-up-action-needed-to-combat-proliferation-of-harmful-deepfakes%ef%bf%bc/

Pal, D. (2023, December 4). *The Looming Threat of Deepfakes: How They Can Damage Brand Identity*. https://www.linkedin.com/pulse/looming-threat-deepfakes-how-can-damage-brand-identity-debojyoti-pal-wuwgf

Paris, B., & Donovan, J. (2019). Deepfakes and cheap fakes.

Paris, B., & Donovan, J. (2019). Deepfakes and cheap fakes. data & society.

Paris, B., & Donovan, J. (2019). Deepfakes and cheap fakes: The manipulation of audio and visual evidence. *Data & Society Institute Report*. Retrieved from https://datasociety.net

Parker, D. B. (1983). *Fighting Computer Crime*. Charles Scribner's Sons.

Partnership on AI. (2021). *Framework for synthetic media responsibility*. Partnership on AI. Retrieved from https://www.partnershiponai.org/synthetic-media-guidelines/

Pastor Galindo, J. (2023). Opportunities, risks and applications of open source Intelligence in cybersecurity and cyberdefence. Proyecto de investigación. um.es

Patel, P., Chopra, V., & Bakshi, P. (2020). Positive Use Cases of Deepfake Technology. *Journal of Digital Innovation*, 3(1), 45–55.

Patel, Y., Tanwar, S., Gupta, R., Bhattacharya, P., Davidson, I. E., Nyameko, R., Aluvala, S., & Vimal, V. (2023). Deepfake generation and detection: Case study and challenges. *IEEE Access: Practical Innovations, Open Solutions*, 11, 143296–143323. DOI: 10.1109/ACCESS.2023.3342107

Patz, J. (2024). The Dual Nature of Deepfakes: An Analysis of the Deepfake Discourse in the USA: Benefits, Threats, Challenges, and Solutions. utwente.nl

Pawar, S. B., & Shirsath, K. A. (2024). Deep Learning Based Web Data Classification Techniques for Forensic Analysis: An Overview. *International Journal of Intelligent Systems and Applications in Engineering*, 12(4s), 320–334.

Pawelec, M. (2022). Deepfakes and democracy (theory): How synthetic audio-visual media for disinformation and hate speech threaten core democratic functions. Digital society. springer.com

Pei, G., ... (2024). Deepfake generation and detection: A benchmark and survey. *arXiv preprint* arXiv:2403.17881.

Pennycook, G., & Rand, D. G. (2017). Who falls for fake news? The roles of analytic thinking, motivated reasoning, political ideology, and bullshit receptivity. SSRN *Electronic Journal*. DOI: 10.2139/ssrn.3023545

Portrait, A. (2023). The Cyberspace Administration of China. *The Emergence of China's Smart State*, 9.

Powell, A., & Henry, N. (2017). *Sexual Violence in a Digital Age*. Palgrave Macmillan. DOI: 10.1057/978-1-137-58047-4

Preu, E., Jackson, M., & Choudhury, N. (2022). *Perception vs. Reality: Understanding and evaluating the impact of synthetic image deepfakes over college students. 2022 IEEE 13th Annual Ubiquitous Computing, Electronics & Mobile Communication Conference*. UEMCON.

Qureshi, J., & Khan, S. (2024). *Artificial Intelligence (AI) Deepfakes in Healthcare Systems: A Double-Edged Sword?* Balancing Opportunities and Navigating Risks.

Qureshi, J., & Khan, S. (2024). Artificial Intelligence (AI) Deepfakes in Healthcare Systems: A Double-Edged Sword? Balancing Opportunities and Navigating Risks. *preprints.org*

Rafique, R., Gantassi, R., Amin, R., Frnda, J., Mustapha, A., & Alshehri, A. (2023). Deep fake detection and classification using error-level analysis and deep learning. *Scientific Reports*, 13(1), 7422. Advance online publication. DOI: 10.1038/s41598-023-34629-3 PMID: 37156887

Raina, P. (2024, August 6). *Year of elections: Lessons from India's fight against AI-generated misinformation*.

Rama, A. (2020). Strategic pricing by Islamic banks and the impact on customer satisfaction and behavioral intention. *Journal of Islamic Accounting and Business Research*, 11(9), 2017–2033. DOI: 10.1108/JIABR-04-2019-0078

Ramesh, A., Dhariwal, P., Nichol, A., Chu, C., & Chen, M. (2022). Hierarchical text-conditional image generation with clip latents. *ArXiv, abs/2204.06125*. https://api.semanticscholar.org/CorpusID:248097655

Ramluckan, T. (2024). Deepfakes: The legal implications. *International Conference on Cyber Warfare and Security*, 19(1), 282-288.

Rana, M. S., Nobi, M. N., Murali, B., & Sung, A. H. (2022). Deepfake Detection: A Systematic Literature Review. In *IEEE Access* (Vol. 10, pp. 25494–25513). Institute of Electrical and Electronics Engineers Inc. DOI: 10.1109/ACCESS.2022.3154404

Rao, T. V. N., Govardhan, A., & Badashah, S. J. (2011). Statistical analysis for performance evaluation of image segmentation quality using edge detection algorithms. *International Journal of Advanced Networking and Applications*, 3(3), 1184.

Rao, T. V. N., & Manasa, S. (2019). Artificial neural networks for soil quality and crop yield prediction using machine learning. *International Journal on Future Revolution in Computer Science & Communication Engineering*, 5(1), 57–60.

Rao, T. V. N., & Reddy, G. R. (2019). Prediction Of Soil Quality Using Machine Learning Techniques. *International Journal of Scientific & Technology Research*, 8(11), 1309–1313.

Rao, T. V. N., Unnisa, A., & Sreni, K. (2020). Medicine recommendation system based on patient reviews. *Int J Sci Technol Res*, 9, 3308–3312.

Ray, A. (2021). Disinformation, deepfakes and democracies: The need for legislative reform. *The University of New South Wales Law Journal*, 44(3), 983–1013. DOI: 10.53637/DELS2700

Raza, A., Munir, K., & Almutairi, M. (2022). A Novel Deep Learning Approach for Deepfake Image Detection. *Applied Sciences (Basel, Switzerland)*, 12(19), 9820. Advance online publication. DOI: 10.3390/app12199820

Renda, A., Arroyo, J., Fanni, R., Laurer, M., Sipiczki, A., Yeung, T., & de Pierrefeu, G. (2021). *Study to support an impact assessment of regulatory requirements for artificial intelligence in Europe*. European Commission.

Rey, L., Peláez-Fernández, M. A., & Quintana-Orts, C. (Eds.). (2021). Special Issue "Psychological Well-being: Cyberbullying & Internet Use." *International Journal of Environmental Research and Public Health*. MDPI. URL: https://www.mdpi.com/journal/ijerph/special_issues/Cyberbullying

Rezayi, S., Balakrishnan, V., Arabnia, S., & Arabnia, H. R. (2018). Fake News and Cyberbullying in the Modern Era. In *Proceedings of the International Conference on Computational Science and Computational Intelligence (CSCI 2018)*. IEEE., URL https://ieeexplore.ieee.org/document/8947876 DOI: 10.1109/CSCI46756.2018.00010

Reznik, M. (2013). Identity Theft on Social Networking Sites: Developing Issues of Internet Impersonation. *Touro Law Review*, 29(2), 12. https://digitalcommons.tourolaw.edu/cgi/viewcontent.cgi?article=1472&context=lawreview

Ridho Kismawadi, E., Irfan, M., & Shah, S. M. A. R. (2023). Revolutionizing islamic finance: Artificial intelligence's role in the future of industry. In *The Impact of AI Innovation on Financial Sectors in the Era of Industry 5.0* (pp. 184–207). DOI: 10.4018/979-8-3693-0082-4.ch011

Riemer, K. & Peter, S. (2024). Conceptualizing generative AI as style engines: Application archetypes and implications. International Journal of Information Management. sciencedirect.com

Robot Using Raspberry Pi. Journal of Algebraic Statistics Web of Science, Volume 13, Issue 2, e-ISSN: 1309-3452, June 2022, pages 2165-2172.

Roe, J., & Perkins, M. (2024). *Deepfakes and Higher Education: A Research Agenda and Scoping Review of Synthetic Media.* https://doi.org/DOI: 10.13140/RG.2.2.17544.02562

Roemmich, K., Schaub, F., & Andalibi, N. (2023, April). Emotion AI at work: Implications for workplace surveillance, emotional labor, and emotional privacy. In Proceedings of the 2023 CHI Conference on Human Factors in Computing Systems (pp. 1-20). acm.org DOI: 10.1145/3544548.3580950

Rombach, R., Blattmann, A., Lorenz, D., Esser, P., & Ommer, B. (2021). High-resolution image synthesis with latent diffusion models. *2022 IEEE/CVF Conference on Computer Vision and Pattern Recognition (CVPR)*, 10674–10685. https://api.semanticscholar.org/CorpusID:245335280

Rosenblatt, K. (2019). *Scammers Use AI to Mimic CEO's Voice in Unusual Cybercrime Case.* NBC News.

Rössler, A., Cozzolino, D., Verdoliva, L., Riess, C., Thies, J., & Nießner, M. (2019). FaceForensics++: Learning to detect manipulated facial images. *Proceedings of the IEEE/CVF International Conference on Computer Vision (ICCV)*, 1–10. DOI: 10.1109/ICCV.2019.00009

Rothbart, D., & Bere, M. (2024). Political narcissism of right-wing extremists: Understanding aggression of the proud boys. [HTML]. *Peace and Conflict.* Advance online publication. DOI: 10.1037/pac0000759

Routledge John, L. E. E. (2022). Cyberspace Governance in China.

Sahota, N. (2023, March 21). *Deepfake Technology: The Risks, Benefits and Detection Methods.* https://www.linkedin.com/pulse/deepfake-technology-risks-benefits-detection-methods-sahota-%E8%90%A8%E5%86%A0%E5%86%9B-

Salem, M. Z., Baidoun, S., & Walsh, G. (2019). Factors affecting Palestinian customers' use of online banking services. *International Journal of Bank Marketing*, 37(2), 426–451. DOI: 10.1108/IJBM-08-2018-0210

Salko, M., Firc, A., & Malinka, K. (2024). Security implications of deepfakes in face authentication. *Proceedings of the 39th ACM/SIGAPP Symposium on Applied Computing*, 1376-1384. DOI: 10.1145/3605098.3635953

Samoilenko, S. A., & Suvorova, I. (2023). Artificial intelligence and deepfakes in strategic deception campaigns: The US and Russian experiences. In *The Palgrave handbook of malicious use of AI and psychological security* (pp. 507–529). Springer International Publishing. DOI: 10.1007/978-3-031-22552-9_19

Sample, M., Sattler, S., Blain-Moraes, S., Rodríguez-Arias, D., & Racine, E. (2019). Do Publics Share Experts' Concerns about Brain–Computer Interfaces? A Trinational Survey on the Ethics of Neural Technology. *Science, Technology & Human Values*, 45(6), 1242–1270. DOI: 10.1177/01622439919879220

Samuel-Okon, A. D., Akinola, O. I., Olaniyi, O. O., Olateju, O. O., & Ajayi, S. A. (2024). Assessing the Effectiveness of Network Security Tools in Mitigating the Impact of Deepfakes AI on Public Trust in Media. Archives of Current Research International, 24(6), 355-375. manu2sent.com

Sandoval, M. P., de Almeida Vau, M., Solaas, J., & Rodrigues, L. (2024). Threat of deepfakes to the criminal justice system: A systematic review. *Crime Science*, 13(1), 41. DOI: 10.1186/s40163-024-00239-1

Sanghvi, H., & Rai, D. U. (2015). Internet Addiction and its relationship with Emotional Intelligence and Perceived Stress experienced by Young Adults. *International Journal of Indian Psychology*, 3(1). Advance online publication. DOI: 10.25215/0301.061

Santoso, A. L., Kamarudin, F., Amin Noordin, B. A., & Wei Theng, L. (2023). Islamic ethics commitment and bank outcomes: Evidence in South East Asia. *Cogent Economics & Finance*, 11(1), 2175458. Advance online publication. DOI: 10.1080/23322039.2023.2175458

Sareen, M. (2022). *Threats and challenges by DeepFake technology*. DeepFakes. [HTML] DOI: 10.1201/9781003231493-8

Sarkhedi. (2024, February 20). *Deceptive or Disruptive: How deepfakes and AI will transform marketing in 2024*. Forbes India. https://www.forbesindia.com/blog/technology/deceptive-or-disruptive-how-deepfakes-and-ai-will-transform-marketing-in-2024/

Schiff, K. J., Schiff, D. S., & Bueno, N. (2023). The Liar's Dividend: The Impact of Deepfakes and Fake News on Trust in Political Discourse. osf.io

Schroff, F., Kalenichenko, D., & Philbin, J. (2015). Facenet: A unified embedding for face recognition and clustering. *Proceedings of the IEEE conference on computer vision and pattern recognition*, 815–823. DOI: 10.1109/CVPR.2015.7298682

Schultze-Krumbholz, A. (Ed.). (2022). Special Issue "Bullying and Cyberbullying: Challenges toward a Sustainable Campus." *Sustainability*. MDPI. URL: https://www.mdpi.com/journal/sustainability/special_issues/BCCSC

Schwartz, O. (2020). You thought deepfakes were scary? Think again. *Harvard Business Review*.

Schwarz, S. (2023, August 16). *Deepfakes in marketing – from a legal perspective*. DMEXCO. https://dmexco.com/stories/deepfakes-uses-and-legal-implications/

Schwarz, O. (2020). Deepfakes and the social theory of digital falsehood. *Journal of Cultural Analysis and Social Change*, 5(1), 12–23.

Shahzad, H. F., Rustam, F., Flores, E. S., Luis Vidal Mazon, J., de la Torre Diez, I., & Ashraf, I. (2022). A review of image processing techniques for deepfakes. *Sensors (Basel)*, 22(12), 4556. DOI: 10.3390/s22124556 PMID: 35746333

Shaji George, D. A. (2023, October 25). Evolving with the Times: Renaming the IT Department to Attract Top Talent | Partners Universal International Innovation Journal. Evolving With the Times: Renaming the IT Department to Attract Top Talent | Partners Universal International. *The Innovation Journal*. Advance online publication. DOI: 10.5281/zenodo.8436646

Shaji George, D. A. (2023, September 25). Future Economic Implications of Artificial Intelligence | Partners Universal International Research Journal. Future Economic Implications of Artificial Intelligence | Partners Universal International Research Journal. https://doi.org/DOI: 10.5281/zenodo.8347639

Shaji George, D. A., & Hovan George, A. S. (2023, October 11). The Rise of Robotic Children: Implications for Family, Caregiving, and Society | Partners Universal Innovative Research Publication. The Rise of Robotic Children: Implications for Family, Caregiving, and Society | Partners Universal Innovative Research Publication. https://doi.org/DOI: 10.5281/zenodo.10045270

Shaji George, D. A., Hovan George, A. S., Baskar, D. T., & Gabrio Martin, A. S. (2023, March 31). Human Insight AI: An Innovative Technology Bridging The Gap Between Humans And Machines For a Safe, Sustainable Future | Partners Universal International Research Journal. Human Insight AI: An Innovative Technology Bridging the Gap Between Humans and Machines for a Safe, Sustainable Future | Partners Universal International Research Journal. https://doi.org/DOI: 10.5281/zenodo.7723117

Shankar, A., & Jebarajakirthy, C. (2019). The influence of e-banking service quality on customer loyalty: A moderated mediation approach. *International Journal of Bank Marketing*, 37(5), 1119–1142. DOI: 10.1108/IJBM-03-2018-0063

Sharma, D. K., Singh, B., Agarwal, S., Garg, L., Kim, C., & Jung, K. H. (2023). A survey of detection and mitigation for fake images on social media platforms. *Applied Sciences (Basel, Switzerland)*, 13(19), 10980. DOI: 10.3390/app131910980

Sharma, L. (Ed.). (2020). *Towards smart world: homes to cities using internet of things*. CRC Press.

Sharma, M., & Kaur, M. (2022). A review of Deepfake technology: An emerging AI threat. Soft Computing for Security Applications. *Proceedings of ICSCS*, 2021, 605–619.

Shin, D. (2024). Conclusion: Misinformation and AI—How Algorithms Generate and Manipulate Misinformation. In Artificial Misinformation: Exploring Human-Algorithm Interaction Online (pp. 259-277). Cham: Springer Nature Switzerland. [HTML]

Shin, S. Y., & Lee, J. (2022). The effect of deepfake video on news credibility and corrective influence of cost-based knowledge about deepfakes. *Digital Journalism (Abingdon, England)*, 10(3), 412–432. DOI: 10.1080/21670811.2022.2026797

Shirish, A. & Komal, S. (2024). A socio-legal enquiry on deepfakes. California Western International Law Journal. hal.science

Sidere, N., Cruz, F., Coustaty, M., & Ogier, J. M. "A dataset for forgery detection and spotting in document images," in *Proc. 2017 Seventh International Conference on Emerging Security Technologies (EST)*, 2017. DOI: 10.1109/EST.2017.8090394

Singer, U., Polyak, A., Hayes, T., Yin, X., An, J., Zhang, S., Hu, Q., Yang, H., Ashual, O., Gafni, O., Parikh, D., Gupta, S., & Taigman, Y. (2022). Make-a-video: Text-to-video generation without text-video data. *ArXiv, abs/2209.14792*. https://api.semanticscholar.org/CorpusID:252595919

Singh, S., & Kumar, R. (2024). Image forgery detection: Comprehensive review of digital forensics approaches. *Journal of Computational Social Science*, 7(1), 1–39. DOI: 10.1007/s42001-024-00265-8

Sinnreich, A., & Gilbert, J. (2024). *The Secret Life of Data: Navigating Hype and Uncertainty in the Age of Algorithmic Surveillance*. MIT Press. DOI: 10.7551/ mitpress/14040.001.0001

Sippy, T., Enock, F., Bright, J., & Margetts, H. Z. (2024). Behind the Deepfake: 8% Create; 90% Concerned. Surveying public exposure to and perceptions of deepfakes in the UK. *arXiv preprint arXiv:2407.05529.*

Sivathanu, B., & Pillai, R. (2023). The effect of deepfake video advertisements on the hotel booking intention of tourists. *Journal of Hospitality and Tourism Insights*, 6(5), 1669–1687. DOI: 10.1108/JHTI-03-2022-0094

SlashNext. (2023). Listen to these recordings: Deepfake social engineering scams are scaring victims. Retrieved July 8, 2024, from https://slashnext.com/blog/deepfake -scaring-victims-into-submission/?utm_content=252103511&utm_medium=social &utm_source=linkedin&hss_channel=lcp-10572287

Smith, A. D., & Offodile, O. F. (2019). Ethical dilemmas associated with social network advertisements. In *Advances in IT Standards and Standardization Research* (pp. 337–369). IGI Global. DOI: 10.4018/978-1-5225-7214-5.ch015

Smith, P., Bauman, S., & Wong, D. (Eds.). (2019). Special Issue "Interventions to Reduce Bullying and Cyberbullying." *International Journal of Environmental Research and Public Health*. MDPI. URL: https://www.mdpi.com/journal/ijerph/ special_issues/bullying_cyberbullying

Smith, P., Varela, J., & Barlett, C. (Eds.). (2023). Special Issue "Cyberbullying from a Lifespan Perspective." *International Journal of Environmental Research and Public Health*. MDPI. URL: https://www.mdpi.com/journal/ijerph/special_issues/ Cyberbullying_sensors

Solo, A. M. G. (2011). The New Fields of Public Policy Engineering, Political Engineering, Computational Public Policy, and Computational Politics. In *Proceedings of the 2011 International Conference on e-Learning, e-Business, Enterprise Information Systems, and e-Government (EEE'11)*. CSREA. URL: http://worldcomp -proceedings.com/proc/p2011/EEE5211.pdf

Solo, A. M. G. (2019a). *Brief on Effectively Combatting Cyberbullying and Cyberlibel by Online Hate Groups for the Study on Online Hate of the Standing Committee on Justice and Human Rights for the House of Commons of Canada.* Standing Committee on Justice and Human Rights, House of Commons of Canada. URL: https://www.ourcommons.ca/Content/Committee/421/JUST/Brief/BR10520155/br -external/SoloAMG-e.pdf

Solo, A. M. G. (2019b). Combating Online Defamation and Doxing in the United States. In *Proceedings of the 2019 International Conference on Internet Computing and Internet of Things (ICOMP'19)*. CSREA.

Solo, A. M. G. (2019e). *Mémoire sur la lutte efficace contre les actes de cyberintimidation et de diffamation en ligne commis par des groupes haineux présenté au Comité permanent de la justice et des droits de la personne de la Chambre des communes du Canada dans le cadre de son étude sur la haine en ligne.* Standing Committee on Justice and Human Rights, House of Commons of Canada. URL: https://www.noscommunes.ca/Content/Committee/421/JUST/Brief/BR10520155/ br-external/SoloAMG-10061182-f.pdf

Solo, A. M. G. (2020). Fighting Online Defamation, Doxing, and Impersonation. In *Proceedings of the International Conferences: Internet Technologies & Society and Sustainability, Technology and Education 2020*. IADIS. URL: https://www.iadisportal .org/digital-library/fighting-online-defamation-doxing-and-impersonation

Solo, A. M. G. (2021). Educating the Public to Combat Online Defamation, Doxing, and Impersonation. In J. Bishop (Ed.), *Cases on Technologies in Education from Classroom 2.0 to Society 5.0* (pp. 231-242). IGI Global. URL: https://www .igi-global.com/chapter/educating-the-public-to-combat-online-defamation-doxing -and-impersonation/289193

Solo, A. M. G. (2023a). Curriculum for a New Five-Year Academic Program in Intelligent Systems Engineering and Software Engineering. In *2023 International Conference on Computational Science and Computational Intelligence (CSCI 2023)*. IEEE. DOI: 10.1109/CSCI62032.2023.00280

Solo, A. M. G., & Bishop, J. (2011). The New Field of Network Politics. In *Proceedings of the 2011 International Conference on e-Learning, e-Business, Enterprise Information Systems, and e-Government (EEE'11)*. URL: http://worldcomp -proceedings.com/proc/p2011/EEE5223.pdf

Solo, A. M. G., & Bishop, J. (2016). Network Politics and the Arab Spring. *International Journal of Civic Engagement and Social Change (IJCESC)*, *3*(1), 23-27. URL: https://www.igi-global.com/article/network-politics-and-the-arab-spring/149855

Solo, A. M. G., & Bishop, J. (2017). Conceptualizing Network Politics following the Arab Spring: An African Perspective. In J. Bishop (Ed.), *The Digital Media Reader* (pp. 205-212). Crocels.

Solo, A. M. G. (2014). The New Interdisciplinary Fields of Political Engineering and Computational Politics. In Solo, A. M. G. (Ed.), *Political Campaigning in the Information Age* (pp. 226–232). IGI Global., URL https://www.igi-global.com/chapter/the-new-interdisciplinary-fields-of-political-engineering-and-computational-politics/109123 DOI: 10.4018/978-1-4666-6062-5.ch013

Solo, A. M. G. (2017). An Overview of the New Interdisciplinary Fields of Political Engineering and Computational Politics for the Next Frontier in Politics. In *Proceedings of the 2017 International Conference on Computational Science and Computational Intelligence (CSCI'17)*. IEEE. URL https://ieeexplore.ieee.org/document/8561084 DOI: 10.1109/CSCI.2017.319

Solo, A. M. G. (2019c). Combating Online Impersonation in the United States. In *Proceedings of the 6th Annual Conference on Computational Science and Computational Intelligence (CSCI 2019)*. IEEE. URL https://ieeexplore.ieee.org/document/9071354 DOI: 10.1109/CSCI49370.2019.00292

Solo, A. M. G. (2019d). The Interdisciplinary Fields of Political Engineering, Public Policy Engineering, Computational Politics, and Computational Public Policy. In Solo, A. M. G. (Ed.), *Handbook of Research on Politics in the Computer Age*. IGI Global. URL https://www.igi-global.com/book/handbook-research-politics-computer-age/228093

Solo, A. M. G. (2023b). *Curriculum for a New Four-Year Bachelor's Degree in Intelligent Systems Engineering. In 2023 Congress in Computer Science, Computer Engineering, and Applied Computing (CSCE 2023)*. IEEE. URL https://ieeexplore.ieee.org/document/10487418

Solo, A. M. G. (2023c). Preventing Twitter from Being Used for Defamation, Doxing, Impersonation, Threats of Violence, and Intimate Images. In *Proceedings of the 2023 Congress in Computer Science, Computer Engineering, and Applied Computing (CSCE 2023)*. IEEE. URL https://ieeexplore.ieee.org/document/10487355 DOI: 10.1109/CSCE60160.2023.00369

Solo, A. M. G., & Bishop, J. (2014). Conceptualizing Network Politics following the Arab Spring. In Solo, A. M. G. (Ed.), *Handbook of Research on Political Activism in the Information Age* (pp. 231–239). IGI Global. URL https://www.igi-global.com/chapter/conceptualizing-network-politics-following-the-arab-spring/110681 DOI: 10.4018/978-1-4666-6066-3.ch014

Solove, D. J. (2024). Murky consent: an approach to the fictions of consent in privacy law. BUL Rev.. bu.edu

Solove, D. J. (2021). The myth of the privacy paradox. *The George Washington Law Review*, 89, 1–48.

Somoray, K., & Miller, D. J. (2023). Providing detection strategies to improve human detection of deepfakes: An experimental study. *Computers in Human Behavior*, 149(107917), 107917. DOI: 10.1016/j.chb.2023.107917

Sopra Banking. (n.d.). Digital banking fraud: Latest challenges faced by banks. Retrieved July 8, 2024, from https://www.soprabanking.com/insights/digital-banking-fraud-challenges-banks/

Spasova, L. (2023). The third-person effects and susceptibility to persuasion principles in advertisement. *Revista Amazonia Investiga*, 12(62), 105–114. DOI: 10.34069/AI/2023.62.02.8

Statista. (n.d.). False news in the U.S. - statistics & facts. Retrieved July 8, 2024, from https://www.statista.com/topics/3251/fake-news/

Stengel, R. (2019). *Information Wars: How We Lost the Global Battle Against Disinformation and What We Can Do About It*. Grove Press.

Sternberg, P. M. (2019). *The Guide to Internet Defamation and Website Removal*. AuthorHouse.

Sumsub (2024) Sumsub Identity Fraud Report. A comprehensive, data-driven report on identity fraud dynamics and innovative prevention methods. Retrieved July 8, 2024, from https://sumsub.com/fraud-report-2023/

Sunvy, A. S., Reza, R. B., & Al Imran, A. (2023). Media coverage of DeepFake disinformation: An analysis of three South-Asian countries. *Informasi*, 53(2), 295–308. DOI: 10.21831/informasi.v53i2.66479

Suryanto, T., & Ridwansyah, R. (2016). The Shariah financial accounting standards: How they prevent fraud in islamic banking. *European Research Studies*, 19(4), 140–157. DOI: 10.35808/ersj/587

Swartz, T. A. (1984). Relationship between source expertise and source similarity in an advertising context. *Journal of Advertising*, 13(2), 49–54. DOI: 10.1080/00913367.1984.10672887

Taeb, M., & Chi, H. (2022). Comparison of deepfake detection techniques through deep learning. *Journal of Cybersecurity and Privacy, 2*(1), 89–106. Taigman, Y., Yang, M., Ranzato, M., & Wolf, L. (2014). Deepface: Closing the gap to human-level performance in face verification. *Proceedings of the IEEE conference on computer vision and pattern recognition*, 1701–1708.DOI: 10.3390/jcp2010007

Takruri, L. (2023, July 19). What are deepfakes and how do fraudsters use them? | Onfido. Onfido. https://onfido.com/blog/what-are-deepfakes/

Tal-Or, N. (2007). Age and third-person perception in response to positive product advertisements. *Mass Communication & Society*, 10(4), 403–422. DOI: 10.1080/15205430701580557

Teneo. (2024). Deepfakes in 2024 are suddenly deeply real: An executive briefing on the threat and trends. Retrieved July 8, 2024, from https://www.teneo.com

Ternovski, J., Kalla, J., & Aronow, P. M. (2021). *Deepfake warnings for political videos increase disbelief but do not improve discernment: Evidence from two experiments.* DOI: 10.31219/osf.io/dta97

The Dangers of Manipulated Media and Video: Deepfakes and More. (2021, February)

The epistemic threat of deepfakes. (2020). *Philosophy & Technology.* https://pubmed.ncbi.nlm.nih.gov/32837868/

The Rise of AI Deepfake Technology: Transforming Media and Raising Ethical Questions. (n.d.). https://techcosmictales.com/Deepfake-Technology

The Rise of Deepfake Marketing - What Are the Cons and Pros? | Brand Vision. (n.d.). https://www.brandvm.com/post/deepfake-marketing

The Rise of Deepfake Marketing - What Are the Cons and Pros? | Brand Vision. (n.d.-b). https://www.brandvm.com/post/deepfake-marketing

The Rise of Deepfake Marketing - What Are the Cons and Pros? | Brand Vision. (n.d.-c). https://www.brandvm.com/post/deepfake-marketing

The Rise of Deepfake Marketing - What Are the Cons and Pros? | Brand Vision. (n.d.-d). https://www.brandvm.com/post/deepfake-marketing

The Times of India. November 2024, https://timesofindia.indiatimes.com/

Thies, J., Zollhofer, M., Stamminger, M., Theobalt, C., & Nießner, M. (2016). Face2face: Real-time face capture and reenactment of rgb videos. *Proceedings of the IEEE conference on computer vision and pattern recognition*, 2387–2395. DOI: 10.1145/2929464.2929475

Ting, H., Sarawak, U. M., de Run, E. C., & Sarawak, U. M. (2015). Attitude towards advertising: A young generation cohort's perspective. *Asian Journal of Business Research*. DOI: 10.14707/ajbr.150012

Tolosana, R., Vera-Rodriguez, R., Fierrez, J., Morales, A., & Ortega-Garcia, J. (2020). Deepfakes and beyond: A Survey of face manipulation and fake detection. *Information Fusion*, 64, 131–148. DOI: 10.1016/j.inffus.2020.06.014

Tsui, M. (2024, January 10). *14 best deepfake apps and websites in 2024.*

Tufekci, Z. (2018). *Twitter and Tear Gas: The Power and Fragility of Networked Protest*. Yale University Press.

Turk, M., & Pentland, A. (1991). Eigenfaces for Recognition. *Journal of Cognitive Neuroscience*, 3(1), 71–86. DOI: 10.1162/jocn.1991.3.1.71 PMID: 23964806

Turner, C. (2022). Augmented reality, augmented epistemology, and the real-world web. *Philosophy & Technology*, 35(1), 19. DOI: 10.1007/s13347-022-00496-5

Tuysuz, M. K., & Kılıç, A. (2023). Analyzing the Legal and Ethical Considerations of Deepfake Technology. [journalisslp.com]. *Interdisciplinary Studies in Society, Law, and Politics*, 2(2), 4–10. DOI: 10.61838/kman.isslp.2.2.2

U.S. Department of Defense. (2023). Contextualizing deepfake threats to organizations: Cybersecurity information sheet. Retrieved July 8, 2024, from https://media.defense.gov/2023/Sep/12/2003298925/-1/-1/0/CSI-DEEPFAKE-THREATS.PDF

Ughade, N. (2024, September 18). *5 Best Deepfake Detection Tools (2024)*. hyperverge.co. https://hyperverge.co/blog/deepfake-detection-tools/

UK Government. (2021). *Online Safety Bill*. Retrieved from UK Government Publications.

Understanding the Technology Behind Deepfake Voices. (2023, April 28). Understanding the Technology Behind Deepfake Voices. https://murf.ai/resources/deepfake-voices/

University of Bath. (2023, October 6). *Two experiments make a case for using deepfakes in training videos.*

Vaccari, C., & Chadwick, A. (2020). Deepfakes and disinformation: Exploring the impact of synthetic political video on deception, uncertainty, and trust in news. *Social Media + Society*, 6(1), 205630512090340. DOI: 10.1177/2056305120903408

Vâlsan, C., Druică, E., & Eisenstat, E. (2022). On Deep-Fake Stock Prices and Why Investor Behavior Might Not Matter. Algorithms. mdpi.com

Van Den Oord, A., Dieleman, S., Zen, H., Simonyan, K., Vinyals, O., Graves, A., Kalchbrenner, N., Senior, A., Kavukcuoglu, K., ... (2016). Wavenet: A generative model for raw audio. *arXiv preprint arXiv:1609.03499, 12*.

Van der Sloot, B., & Wagensveld, Y. (2022). Deepfakes: Regulatory challenges for the synthetic society. *Computer Law & Security Report*, 46, 105716. DOI: 10.1016/j. clsr.2022.105716

Vasist, P. N., & Krishnan, S. (2022). Deepfakes: An integrative review of the literature and an agenda for future research. *Communications of the Association for Information Systems*, 51(1), 14.

Vaswani, A. (2017). Attention is all you need. *Advances in Neural Information Processing Systems*.

Veale, M., Van Kleek, M., & Binns, R. (2018). Fairness and accountability design needs for algorithmic support in high-stakes public sector decision-making. *Proceedings of the 2018 CHI Conference on Human Factors in Computing Systems*. DOI: 10.1145/3173574.3174014

Veerasamy, N., & Pieterse, H. (2022, March). Rising above misinformation and deepfakes. In International Conference on Cyber Warfare and Security (Vol. 17, No. 1, pp. 340-348). academic-conferences.org DOI: 10.34190/iccws.17.1.25

Veerasamy, N., & Pieterse, H. (2022). Rising above misinformation and deepfakes. *International Conference on Cyber Warfare and Security*, 17(1), 340-348.

Venkat Narayana Rao, T., & Yellu, K. R. (2016). Automatic Safety Home Bell System with Message Enabled Features, International Journal of Science. *Engineering and Computer Technology*, 6, 10.

Verdoliva, L. (2020). Media forensics and deepfakes: An overview. *IEEE Journal of Selected Topics in Signal Processing*, 14(5), 910–932. DOI: 10.1109/ JSTSP.2020.3002101

Verma, N. (2023). Deepfake technology and the future of public trust in video. utexas.edu

Vese, D. (2022). Governing fake news: the regulation of social media and the right to freedom of expression in the era of emergency. European Journal of Risk Regulation. researchgate.net

Vijayagopal, P., Jain, B., & Ayinippully Viswanathan, S. (2024). Regulations and Fintech: A Comparative Study of the Developed and Developing Countries. [HTML]. *Journal of Risk and Financial Management*, 17(8), 324. DOI: 10.3390/jrfm17080324

Vincent, J. (2021). Fighting deepfakes: Is AI keeping up with AI-generated misinformation? *The Verge*. Retrieved from https://www.theverge.com

Vincent, A. T., Schiettekatte, O., Goarant, C., Neela, V. K., Bernet, E., Thibeaux, R., Ismail, N., Khalid, M. K. N. M., Amran, F., Masuzawa, T., Nakao, R., Korba, A. A., Bourhy, P., Veyrier, F. J., & Picardeau, M. (2019). Revisiting the taxonomy and evolution of pathogenicity of the genus Leptospira through the prism of genomics. *PLoS Neglected Tropical Diseases*, 13(5), e0007270. Advance online publication. DOI: 10.1371/journal.pntd.0007270 PMID: 31120895

Volkova, S. S. (2023). A method for deepfake detection using convolutional neural networks. *Scientific and Technical Information Processing*, 50(5), 475–485. DOI: 10.3103/S0147688223050143

Vosoughi, S., Roy, D., & Aral, S. (2018). The spread of true and false news online. *Science*, 359(6380), 1146–1151. https://science.sciencemag.org/content/359/6380/1146. DOI: 10.1126/science.aap9559 PMID: 29590045

Vyas, K. (2019, August 12). Generative Adversarial Networks: The Tech Behind DeepFake and FaceApp. *Interesting Engineering*. https://interestingengineering.com/innovation/generative-adversarial-networks-the-tech-behind-deepfake-and-faceapp

Wagner, T., & Blewer, A. (2019). "the word real is no longer real": Deepfakes, gender, and the challenges of ai-altered video. *Open Information Science*, 3(1), 32–46. DOI: 10.1515/opis-2019-0003

Walker, C. P., Schiff, D. S., & Schiff, K. J. (2024). Merging AI incidents research with political misinformation research: Introducing the political deepfakes incidents database. *Proceedings of the AAAI Conference on Artificial Intelligence*, 38(21), 23053–23058. DOI: 10.1609/aaai.v38i21.30349

Wang, S., & Kim, S. (2022). How do people feel about deepfake videos of K-pop idols?. , 47(2), 375-386.

Wang, X., Wu, Y. C., Zhou, M., & Fu, H. (2024). Beyond surveillance: privacy, ethics, and regulations in face recognition technology. Frontiers in big data. frontiersin.org

Wang, S., & Kim, S. (2022). Users' emotional and behavioral responses to deepfake videos of K-pop idols. *Computers in Human Behavior*, 134, 107305. DOI: 10.1016/j.chb.2022.107305

Waseem, S., Abu, S. A. R. B. S., & Ahmed, B. A. (2024, September). Attention-Guided Supervised Contrastive Learning for Deepfake Detection. In 2024 IEEE 8th International Conference on Signal and Image Processing Applications (ICSIPA) (pp. 1-6). IEEE.

Watts, C. (2018). *Messing with the Enemy: Surviving in a Social Media World of Hackers, Terrorists, Russians, and Fake News*. Harper.

Webster, G. (2023, July 6). *6 best ad campaigns that use deep fakes*. Big Ideas That Work. https://blog.bigideasthatwork.com/creative-campaigns-that-use-deep-fake-technology/

Week, A. (2024, July 15). *Why the Evolution of Deepfakes Is a Wake-up Call for Brands*. https://advertisingweek.com/why-the-evolution-of-deepfakes-is-a-wake-up-call-for-brands/

Weikmann, T., Greber, H., & Nikolaou, A. (2024). After deception: How falling for a deepfake affects the way we see, hear, and experience media. [The International Journal of Press]. *The International Journal of Press/Politics*, 19401612241233539. Advance online publication. DOI: 10.1177/19401612241233539

Westerlund, M. (2019). The emergence of deepfake technology: A review. *Technology Innovation Management Review*, 9(11), 39–52. DOI: 10.22215/timreview/1282

Westerlund, M. (n.d.). The Emergence of Deepfake Technology. *RE:view*.

Whittaker, L., Letheren, K., & Mulcahy, R. (2021). The rise of deepfakes: A conceptual framework and research agenda for marketing. *Australasian Marketing Journal*, 29(3), 204–214. qut.edu.au. DOI: 10.1177/1839334921999479

Whyte, C. (2020). Deepfake news: AI-enabled disinformation as a multi-level public policy challenge. *Journal of Cyber Policy*, 5(2), 199–217. DOI: 10.1080/23738871.2020.1797135

Williamson, S. M., & Prybutok, V. (2024). The Era of Artificial Intelligence Deception: Unraveling the Complexities of False Realities and Emerging Threats of Misinformation. *Information (Basel)*, 15(6), 299. DOI: 10.3390/info15060299

Wilpert, C. (2022). 7 best deepfake software apps of 2022 (50 Tools Reviewed). [Online]. Available: https://contentmavericks.com/best-deepfake-software/

Wong, R. Y., Chong, A., & Aspegren, R. C. (2023). Privacy Legislation as Business Risks: How GDPR and CCPA are Represented in Technology Companies' Investment Risk Disclosures. Proceedings of the ACM on Human-Computer Interaction, 7(CSCW1), 1-26. acm.org

Woollcott, E. (2024, March 20). The rise of deepfakes: navigating their impact on reputation and business. *Mishcon de Reya LLP*. https://www.mishcon.com/news/the-rise-of-deepfakes-navigating-their-impact-on-reputation-and-business

Wright, N. (2024, August 19). *Deepfakes and the Ethics of Generative AI | Tepperspectives.* Tepperspectives. https://tepperspectives.cmu.edu/all-articles/deepfakes-and-the-ethics-of-generative-ai/

Wright, W. (2023b, April 3). A marketer's guide to deepfakes. *The Drum.* https://www.thedrum.com/news/2023/04/03/marketer-s-guide-deepfakes

Writer, S. (2023, September 8). *Deepfake AI and Digital Marketing: Pros, Cons and Dangers.* Bold Business. https://www.boldbusiness.com/digital/deepfake-ai-digital-marketing-pros-cons-dangers/

Writer, S. L. C. (2024, November 7). *Regulators Combat Deepfakes With Anti-Fraud Rules.* https://www.darkreading.com/data-privacy/regulators-combat-deepfakes-anti-fraud-rules

Wyszomirska, M. (2023). Technological Developments as a New Challenge for Modern Legislation. Safety & Fire Technology. cyberleninka.ru

Xu, S., Wang, J., Shou, W., Ngo, T., Sadick, A. M., & Wang, X. (2021). Computer vision techniques in construction: A critical review. [HTML]. *Archives of Computational Methods in Engineering*, 28(5), 3383–3397. DOI: 10.1007/s11831-020-09504-3

Y. (2023, May 17). The Rise of Deepfakes: Navigating Legal Challenges in Synthetic Media. CBA's @theBar.

Yeom, S. (2021). Teaching and assessing data literacy for adolescent learners. In *Deep Fakes, Fake News, and Misinformation in Online Teaching and Learning Technologies* (pp. 93–123). IGI Global. DOI: 10.4018/978-1-7998-6474-5.ch005

Youn, S., & Kim, S. (2019). Newsfeed native advertising on Facebook: Young millennials' knowledge, pet peeves, reactance and ad avoidance. *International Journal of Advertising*, 38(5), 651–683. DOI: 10.1080/02650487.2019.1575109

YouTube. (n.d.-a). Community guidelines. Retrieved July 8, 2024, from https://www.youtube.com/intl/ALL_in/howyoutubeworks/policies/community-guidelines/

YouTube. (n.d.-b). Fighting misinformation. Retrieved July 8, 2024, from https://www.youtube.com/howyoutubeworks/our-commitments/fighting-misinformation/

Yu, M., Liu, F., Lee, J., & Soutar, G. (2018). The influence of negative publicity on brand equity: Attribution, image, attitude and purchase intention. *Journal of Product and Brand Management*, 27(4), 440–451. DOI: 10.1108/JPBM-01-2017-1396

Zhang, M. (2021). 'Deep Nostalgia' brings people in old photos back to life. [Online]. Available: https://petapixel.com/2021/03/01/deep-nostalgia-brings-people-in-old -photos-back-to-life-with-movement/

Zhu, J.-Y., Park, T., Isola, P., & Efros, A. A. (2017). Unpaired image-to-image translation using cycle-consistent adversarial networks. *Proceedings of the IEEE international conference on computer vision*, 2223–2232. DOI: 10.1109/ICCV.2017.244

About the Contributors

Gaurav Gupta has earned a doctorate in the area of Marketing from Punjabi University, Patiala. He has also studied marketing at the prestigious Wilkes University, Pennsylvania, USA. He has got an opportunity to learn about teaching methodologies at IIM-Kozhikode. Prof.Gaurav Gupta has presented his research paper at IIM-Ahmedabad, IIM-Indore, IIM-Bangalore and had been included in paper review panel of many Scopus Indexed Journals. His papers have been published in ABDC listed/Scopus Indexed Journal(s). He is also acting as an Editor with Taylor and Francis Group. He has also presented his research work at University of Ljubljana, Slovenia and Wolkite University, Ethiopia. He is a recipient of various fellowships, those are being awarded by European union and IIM-Bangalore. He got an offer of a doctoral fellowship from ICSSR (Ministry of HRD, India). He has been appointed as a member of Advisory Board for Cleveland Professional University, USA. Presently he is associated with Amity University, Noida. and has worked with Christ University previously. His teaching, training, researching and consulting interests include Brand Management, Marketing Research, Mythology and management, Case writing Also, he has published about half-a-dozen research papers in leading journals and has made presentations at several international/ national seminars and conferences.

Sailaja Bohara possesses a well-rounded profile characterized by a blend of teaching and research experiences. With two years of teaching experience and four years dedicated to research, she has demonstrated a commitment to both academia and scholarly inquiry. Her contributions extend beyond the confines of the classroom, as evidenced by her published research papers in numerous prestigious international journals indexed in Scopus, Web of Science (WOS), and other peer-reviewed platforms. Specializing in marketing and human resource management, she brings a depth of expertise to her work in these domains. Her research output is notable, with seven published papers serving as a testament to her scholarly rigor and dedication to advancing knowledge in her areas of specialization. Additionally, her active participation in academic conferences showcases her engagement with the broader scholarly community. She has published 7 research papers and has attended and presented at various conferences and is currently working in Amity University as assistant professor.

Raj K Kovid is a Professor and Head-Research at School of Business at School of Business, UPES, Dehradun. He has working experience of over 27 years in academics, research and industry. His teaching and research area includes Corporate Strategy, M&A, Entrepreneurship & Innovation, Technology Adoption, Corporate Governance & CSR. He has published research papers and book chapters in Scopus/ ABDC indexed journals such as Management Decision, and edited books published by international publishers such as IGI, USA. He is involved with some journals in capacity of guest editor, board member and reviewer. His cases are available at Harvard Business School Publishing portal, Emerald Publications and he has also conducted case method workshops. He has consulted firms with respect to their growth strategies.

Kapil Pandla is a Director, PML SD Business School, Chandigarh, India and Professor and Dean at Sharda School of Business Studies, Sharda University, Greater Noida. He is passionate teacher, able administrator and a keen researcher. Prior to joining Sharda University he was Professor and Dean at ISBF (Affiliate Centre of UoL under academic direction of LSE), before that he served IMI Bhubaneswar as Dean, Business Development, NIIT University as Area Director, IFIM (now JagSoM) Bangalore, Gautam Buddha University, Greater Noida, Jaipuria Institute of Management, Noida., Aravali Institute of Management Jodhpur, Management and Commerce Institute of Global Synergy, Ajmer He has conducted various Management, Officers and Faculty Development Programmes on topics such as Gender Sensitisation, Leadership and Team Building, Self-Development, Effective Communication, Effective Teaching Methods (Role Plays, Game, Case Studies etc.) for Government and private sector employees. Trained more than 5000 Managers, Officers and Faculty Members. Wrote several case studies and research papers in national and international journals. Write up of Case study titled 'Recruitment Fiasco published in Economic Times and available on "Case Centre and Case study titled "Honda Crisis: Lessons to be learnt" on industrial relations was adjudged as one of the best case by the editorial board amongst various entries from countries like France, Germany, Thailand, Malaysia, Sri Lanka etc. There is one patent in his name. Currently he is working on ICSSR Funded project as Project Director. He is also on the Board of Advisors, Confederation of Education Excellence (CEE)

***

Vishnu Achutha Menon is an independent journalist, writer, researcher, and an Indian percussionist. He is a recipient of the Junior Scholarship the Ministry of Culture awarded. His research interests are film studies, verbal & nonverbal communication, south Asian performances, Natyasastra, media studies, media analysis techniques, Laban Movement Analysis, and Ethnomusicology.

Robin Chataut (Senior Member, IEEE) received his Ph.D. degree in computer science and engineering from the University of North Texas. He is currently an Assistant Professor of computer science with the College of Science and Engineering, Texas Christian University. His research interests include a wide spectrum of topics, with a primary focus on cybersecurity, network security, wireless communication and networks, and emerging technologies, such as 5G, 6G, and beyond networks. In addition to these areas, he is deeply passionate about the application of machine learning (ML) and artificial intelligence (AI) techniques in cybersecurity and network optimization.

Iris-Panagiota Efthymiou is a Lecturer at the Greenwich University, University of East London, an Executive, results-driven, and multi-talented enterprise, and institutional director, author, and keynote speaker with over 20 years of experience in entrepreneurship, international affairs, and executive leadership roles. Possesses a solid foundation in research, management, consultancy, and strategic development. Iris has worked as a college director and created her own Public Affairs consultancy. She worked with politicians, Diplomats, entrepreneurs, academics, and journalists, and spoke at the UN Headquarters in Geneva. She is a Board Member of HAPSc, and a Scientific Associate of the LabHEM, of the University of Piraeus. She published over 17 books, 20 articles, and Book chapters in peer-reviewed journals, and she is the Chief Editor of the Journal of Politics and Ethics in New Technologies and AI. She believes in equal opportunities, uniqueness, and the normality of imperfection! Iris has a Ph.D. in Behavioural Economics, a Master's in Health Economics and Management, and Bachelor's in Economics

Harry Efthymiou-Egleton holds a Bachelor of Science in International Relations and Affairs from the London School of Economics and Political Science (LSE), where he received an Academic Scholarship. He is the founder and CEO of Socialiti, a social enterprise dedicated to supporting young individuals facing gambling-related issues. In addition to his academic pursuits, Harry serves as the president of the LSESU Hellenic Society and vice president of the Hellenic Association of Political Scientists Abroad. He has presented speeches at global conferences and has contributed to scientific journals and three books on topics such as Smart Cities, AI and Christianity, and the future of food and its societal impact. His expertise in methods engineering, artificial intelligence, and corporate social responsibility informs his research and professional endeavours.

Vikas Garg, is the Assistant Director Executive Programs Management Domain at Amity University Uttar Pradesh, India. He has an almost 20+ years of experience with more than 10 Ph.D. scholars under his mentoring. He has published numerous research papers in various Scopus and ABDC indexed international and national journals. He is acting as the Associate Editor of Journal of Sustainable Finance and Investment, JSFI indexed in the WoS and Scopus and He is acting as the Book Series Editor for Taylor's and Francis Group for three series titled "Technology Innovations: Strategies for Business Sustainability and Growth", "Emerging Trends in Technology in Management and Commerce". and "Electronic Commerce Management for Business". He has been working with new innovative ideas in the field of Patents and Copyrights. He has been the lead organizer in conducting various International Conferences, Workshops, Case study Competitions including IEEE. He has been conferred upon many National & International Awards for Being the Best Academician, Researcher & Employee.

Nilesh Kate is an Associate Professor of Marketing Analytics, Marketing Research and Operations Research, teaching and research interests include Business Research Methods, Marketing Research, Operations Research, Marketing Analytics, Operations and Supply Chain Management. He has published cases in Harvard Business Review, Case Centre etc.

Early Ridho Kismawadi, S.E.I, MA is a lecturer at the Department of Islamic Banking, Faculty of Islamic Economics and Business IAIN Langsa, Aceh, Indonesia, he has been a lecturer since 2013, he has completed a doctoral program in 2018 majoring in Sharia economics at the State Islamic University of North Sumatra. He was appointed head of the Islamic economics Law study program (2023) Islamic banking study program (2020) and Islamic financial management study program (2019) at Langsa State Islamic Institute (IAIN Langsa), Aceh, Indonesia. His research interests include financial economics, applied econometrics, Islamic economics, banking, and finance. He has published articles in national and international journals. In addition, he is also a reviewer of several reputable international journals such as Finance Research Letters, Financial Innovation, Cogent Business &; Management, Journal of Islamic Accounting and Business Research. He has also presented his papers at various local and international seminars. Dr. Early Ridho Kismawadi, S.E.I, MA, can be contacted at kismawadi@iainlangsa.ac.id.

Shatabdi Nannaware is a distinguished academic specializing in digital media marketing. With a robust background in brand communication, she earned her MBA in this field, laying the foundation for her expertise. Professor Nannaware has made significant contributions to the field, including the publication of a book on social media, which has been well-received in academic and professional circles. Her research is centered on the evolving landscape of digital media and its impact on marketing strategies, making her a respected voice in the discipline.

Mandakini Paruthi ICFAI Business School: Hyderabad. She earned her Doctorate and Masters in Business Administration degree with a specialization in Marketing from Guru Nanak Dev University, Amritsar, Punjab, and Lovely Professional University, Punjab respectively. She is a recipient of Junior Research Fellowship grant from University Grants Commission and has also cleared National Eligibility Test (NET).

Rajasshrie Pillai is a prominent academic leader with a deep interest in Human Resource Management (HRM), Artificial Intelligence (AI), and the Metaverse. She serves as the Dean of Research and the Director of MBA Global, where she guides cutting-edge research and oversees advanced business education programs. Dr. Pillai's work bridges the gap between traditional HR practices and emerging technologies, exploring how AI and the Metaverse are transforming the future of work. Her leadership and innovative approach make her a key figure in the integration of technology and management education

Sonam Rani is a dedicated Assistant Professor with 10 years of experience in academia. She holds an MBA, M.Com, and LL.B and is currently pursuing her Ph.D., showcasing her commitment to lifelong learning and professional growth. Her expertise spans business management, commerce, and law, enabling her to contribute to interdisciplinary academic pursuits. She has authored several research papers published in Scopus-indexed journals, reflecting her strong research acumen and dedication to advancing knowledge. Additionally, she holds copyrights and patents, highlighting her innovative contributions to intellectual property and applied research. A passionate educator and researcher, Sonam excels in creating impactful learning experiences while fostering a culture of inquiry and innovation. Through her ongoing doctoral research and her dedication to academic excellence, she continues to make meaningful contributions to the academic community, empowering students and colleagues alike to achieve their potential.

Shiv Ranjan is the Director of the Executive Program for the Management domain and serves as the Program Leader for the same. With over 20 years of extensive experience in academia and industry, he is currently pursuing a Ph.D., furthering his expertise in management education. Shiv specializes in teaching marketing, operations, and business statistics, combining theoretical insights with practical applications. He has an impressive portfolio of research, including papers published in Scopus and ABDC-indexed journals, showcasing his scholarly contributions. Additionally, he holds copyrights and patents, reflecting his commitment to innovation and intellectual property development. A seasoned educator and program leader, Shiv Ranjan continues to inspire students and professionals, blending academic rigor with real-world relevance in management studies.

Prashant Kumar Siddhey is Doctorate and Master's in Management from Devi Ahilya University, Indore. He has over 16 years of experience blended with industrial and academics both. 24 publications to his credit, including Book, Research Papers, Book Chapter, Case Studies. Presently, he is working as a Professor, Chandigarh University. He has worked as with institutes and universities of repute and handled various responsibilities successfully as HoD- School of Management, Coordinator-MBA, BoS, Examinations, Training and Placements, Industrial Relations, National and International Conferences etc. He worked to transform institute to University and to establish school of management for newly established university. He is active life member of Indian Society for Training and Development. His area of interest is General Management and Human Resource Management.

Ashu M. G. Solo is an interdisciplinary and multidisciplinary researcher and developer, electrical engineering researcher and developer, computer engineering researcher and developer, intelligent systems engineering researcher and developer, political and public policy engineering researcher, mathematics researcher and developer, politics and public policy researcher, education researcher, political writer, entrepreneur, former political operative, progressive activist (including civil rights activist, activist against genocide, anti-corruption activist, justice reform activist, anti-monarchy activist, children's rights activist, anti-assault activist, secularism activist, activist against government waste and for government accountability, educational reform activist, and COVID-19 activist), environmental protection technology developer, and former infantry officer. Solo has over 1000 reviewed publications (not counting reprints) including research publications as well as political and public policy commentaries. Solo is the originator of public policy engineering, computational public policy, political engineering, computational politics, and misinformation identification engineering in reviewed and published research papers.

Aadesh Upadhyay is Graduate Research Assistant pursuing a Master of Science in Computer Science at the University of North Texas, Texas, USA. He earned his Bachelor of Engineering in Electrical and Electronics Engineering from Sri Krishna College of Engineering and Technology, Coimbatore, India. His research interests lie in leveraging Machine Learning and Large Language Models for cybersecurity applications, particularly in developing detection mechanisms for cybercrimes like phishing and spam. Additionally, he is actively engaged in exploring the potential of Generative AI models for proactive defense strategies against emerging cyber threats.

Svetlana Volkova is a Ph.D. and an Associate Professor at the Vologda State University. Her research interests primarily focus on machine learning and computer vision, including object recognition, image classification, and the development of robust algorithms for analyzing visual data. Dr. Volkova is actively engaged in academic research, while also mentoring students and fostering an environment that bridges theoretical knowledge with practical applications in artificial intelligence and related disciplines.

Index

A

AI deepfakes 77, 84, 85, 286
artificial intelligence 2, 4, 5, 21, 25, 31, 34, 40, 42, 43, 44, 45, 46, 47, 51, 52, 71, 72, 73, 78, 79, 84, 91, 95, 96, 100, 102, 104, 105, 106, 110, 111, 115, 116, 118, 120, 127, 128, 129, 133, 134, 143, 146, 149, 152, 167, 170, 173, 174, 175, 176, 177, 178, 181, 185, 186, 188, 189, 191, 193, 195, 197, 201, 205, 219, 220, 223, 224, 227, 229, 232, 237, 239, 240, 241, 244, 245, 249, 251, 254, 260, 264, 265, 295, 296, 314, 316

B

Blackmail 23, 128, 198, 221, 222, 233, 234, 235, 238, 301, 302

C

cognitive response 61
Collective Action 143, 144, 148, 155, 163, 165, 166
consumer behavior 19, 51, 52, 88, 95
corporate reputation 140
Cross-Sector Partnerships 143, 144, 169
Cyberbullying 11, 60, 92, 263, 268, 276, 277, 278, 279, 280, 282
Cyberlibel 280, 282

D

deception 17, 52, 53, 54, 60, 66, 70, 89, 101, 124, 130, 144, 162, 172, 192, 198, 199, 200, 201, 203, 204, 205, 206, 208, 209, 213, 214, 215, 216, 220, 240, 276, 277, 278, 281, 295, 300, 301, 302, 308
Deep fake 15, 16, 72, 73, 75, 77, 78, 79, 80, 81, 84, 85, 87, 88, 89, 91, 93, 94, 108, 173, 197, 243, 245, 247, 248, 251, 252, 254, 255, 258, 259, 260, 261, 262, 306, 308
Deepfake advertisements 51, 52, 56, 58, 59, 61, 64, 65
Deepfake regulation 157
Detection Technology 102, 105, 109, 114, 152, 153, 155, 160, 162, 164, 165, 166, 192, 207, 308
digital content 13, 28, 51, 52, 64, 65, 81, 89, 90, 91, 103, 111, 112, 113, 114, 123, 130, 153, 168, 170, 190, 294
digital ethics 171, 288
Digital Literacy 52, 67, 143, 150, 151, 156, 160, 161, 162, 168, 170, 172, 192, 236, 237, 251, 254
Disinformation 10, 13, 14, 17, 20, 24, 28, 34, 37, 44, 45, 46, 54, 55, 67, 70, 86, 90, 95, 97, 107, 113, 128, 129, 131, 134, 138, 140, 146, 148, 150, 151, 171, 172, 194, 205, 220, 227, 240, 267, 269, 271, 272, 275, 276, 281, 282, 283, 288, 289, 291, 292, 295, 296, 299, 308, 309, 310, 311, 314

E

economic impact 87
economic stability 19
Extortion 27, 133, 139, 197, 204, 221, 222, 233, 234, 235, 238, 303

F

Financial frauds 174, 182, 183, 186, 187, 303
financial markets 11, 19, 22, 26, 29, 103, 171, 177, 180, 183, 187, 204, 312
Fraud 11, 21, 23, 26, 27, 28, 36, 72, 80, 87, 93, 94, 95, 100, 103, 105, 106, 107, 109, 112, 113, 114, 115, 116, 118, 121, 128, 130, 131, 142, 150, 154, 156, 173, 174, 175, 176, 177, 178, 180, 182, 183, 185, 188, 189, 190, 191, 192, 193, 194, 195, 196, 198, 199, 201, 204, 207, 208, 210, 221, 222, 223, 224, 225, 234, 240,

241, 250, 253, 286, 288, 293, 304, 307

G

Generative Adversarial Networks (GANs)
1, 4, 5, 6, 16, 22, 52, 74, 84, 87, 126,
128, 141, 143, 146, 152, 164, 174,
176, 178, 181, 185, 194, 232, 245,
246, 300, 313

H

human cognition 53
human rights 46, 280

I

Indian market 51

M

machine learning 2, 5, 15, 16, 20, 29, 31,
51, 52, 72, 73, 79, 80, 87, 91, 109,
111, 112, 120, 125, 127, 130, 149,
152, 154, 155, 168, 170, 174, 176,
178, 179, 181, 183, 185, 186, 191,
198, 236, 237, 243, 244, 245, 260,
262, 266, 286, 293
Manipulation 2, 3, 4, 5, 11, 21, 24, 25, 26,
27, 31, 32, 38, 39, 42, 43, 44, 52, 54,
55, 64, 66, 75, 81, 84, 92, 93, 100,
102, 103, 104, 105, 109, 110, 112,
115, 116, 121, 124, 125, 127, 144,
145, 147, 148, 149, 153, 154, 155,
156, 164, 170, 172, 173, 175, 176,
177, 180, 182, 191, 192, 194, 197,
198, 201, 219, 220, 221, 226, 227,
228, 232, 234, 238, 241, 250, 252,
253, 260, 261, 276, 277, 287, 288,
293, 294, 295, 299, 301, 305, 306,
307, 308, 309, 311
market manipulation 11, 26, 43, 194, 197,
201, 287, 311
Misinformation 1, 10, 11, 26, 34, 39, 40,
44, 45, 46, 47, 48, 52, 53, 54, 55, 56,
58, 59, 60, 64, 65, 70, 72, 73, 77, 81,
83, 86, 87, 89, 90, 92, 94, 96, 100,
125, 126, 128, 129, 131, 133, 134,
136, 144, 146, 147, 154, 156, 158,
159, 160, 161, 162, 168, 170, 171,
172, 191, 206, 214, 218, 220, 228,
229, 238, 241, 243, 252, 259, 263,
267, 275, 276, 277, 278, 281, 282,
283, 286, 291, 293, 294, 300, 305, 307
Misinformation Identification Engineering
267, 275, 283

O

opportunities 19, 23, 26, 37, 40, 42, 46,
47, 59, 74, 79, 83, 92, 96, 103, 124,
125, 132, 158, 162, 178, 199, 203,
209, 211, 215, 217, 220, 255, 256, 265

P

perception 39, 52, 53, 54, 55, 56, 59, 64,
66, 69, 80, 106, 108, 123, 125, 144,
187, 200, 213, 214, 228, 285, 290,
302, 310
persuasiveness 51, 52, 60, 61, 62, 63, 64,
65, 67
Political Manipulation 81, 92, 156, 174,
177, 238, 288, 299
Public Trust 10, 47, 48, 55, 60, 77, 79, 80,
144, 145, 147, 152, 156, 158, 159, 163,
169, 170, 229, 231, 237, 301, 302, 312

R

regulatory frameworks 19, 34, 51, 65,
82, 92, 129, 130, 157, 158, 189, 222,
237, 261

S

Security Systems 41, 111, 133, 176, 180,
194, 231, 233, 238

T

technological countermeasures 19